TOXIC CAPITALISM:
CORPORATE CRIME AND THE CHEMICAL INDUSTRY

This book is dedicated to Doreen and Ted Tombs
and to Rory and Blake Stavro-Pearce.

Toxic Capitalism:
Corporate Crime
and the Chemical Industry

FRANK PEARCE and STEVE TOMBS

Ashgate
DARTMOUTH
Aldershot • Brookfield USA • Singapore • Sydney

Published by
Dartmouth Publishing Company Limited
Ashgate Publishing Limited
Gower House
Croft Road
Aldershot
Hants GU11 3HR
England

Ashgate Publishing Company
Old Post Road
Brookfield
Vermont 05036
USA

British Library Cataloguing in Publication Data
Pearce, Frank
    Toxic capitalism : corporate crime and the chemical
    industry. - (Socio-legal studies)
    1.Offences against the environment 2.Chemical industry -
    Accidents 3.Chemical industry - Law and legislation
    I.Title II.Tombs, Steve
    363.7'384

Library of Congress Cataloging-in-Publication Data
Pearce, Frank.
    Toxic capitalism : corporate crime and the chemical industry /
Frank Pearce and Steve Tombs.
        p.   cm.
    "Socio-legal series."
    Includes bibliographical references and index.
    ISBN 1-85521-950-6 (hardbound)
    1. Commercial industry–Corrupt practices. 4. Hazardous substances.
5. Toxic torts. I. Tombs, Steve. II. Title.
    HV6768.P43   1998
    364.16'8–dc21   97-38537
                                                                                      CIP

ISBN 1 85521 950 6

Printed and bound in Great Britain by
Creative Print and Design Wales, Ebbw Vale

Contents

PART III: HAZARDS, REGULATION AND CLASS

Preface

If the chemical industry has provided enormous material benefits, equally the costs have been enormous, even catastrophic. Moreover, both costs and benefits are distributed in an unequal manner. Of particular concern to us in this text is the development of an adequate understanding of how both the positive and negative effects of the industry are produced and also what determines how the benefits and costs are distributed. Currently, the destructive nature of the industry — the death, injury, ill-health, and environmental devastation which it causes — remains particularly poorly recognised and challenged.

This is a problem of 'law and order'. Yet, today, this problem still continues to be defined largely in terms of the crimes of 'street' offenders; by contrast, corporate abuses of power, the victimisation of employees, local publics and consumers, and the crimes of the powerful more generally, remain relatively free of critical state, public and academic scrutiny. True, in recent years we have witnessed, within and beyond criminology, some increased attention to corporate crimes, but this has tended to focus upon various forms of financial crimes, rather than upon the features of toxic capitalism that are the subject of this text. Moreover, such work has not tended to conceptualise corporate crime in terms of crimes emerging from a particular organisational form, namely, the capitalist corporation. The criminogenic features of toxic capitalism — which are no mere side effects — form the subject matter of this text.

Perhaps one reason for the relative reluctance of criminologists in particular to enter the spheres of health, safety and environmental crimes is that these cannot be understood within the narrowly defined parameters of criminology itself (as, indeed, Sutherland recognised). Further, as we argue here, any understanding of the nature of these types of corporate crimes, and thus any recognition of the potential for their more effective regulation, requires an analysis that is grounded in political economy. For this reason, we emphasise the need to understand the nature of contemporary and emergent forms of corporate organisation, of their place in contemporary economies, and of the relationships between these forms and state formations.

Thus we begin, in Part I, by examining both the nature of contemporary capitalism(s) and the corporate form, and the ways in which corporations produce crimes within our societies. In Chapter 1, we provide an overview of the key elements of a dominant contemporary discourse, neoliberalism, and specifically its representations of state, economy and society. This discourse is then subjected to critique in the following chapter (2), where we argue for the need to understand neoliberalism in terms of a struggle for hegemony. Here, we ground our understanding of the social world in Gramsci's concept of hegemony. In Chapter 3, we examine the nature of corporate crime, and address in particular the emergence of debates regarding white-collar and corporate crime, and the nature and effects of hegemonic definitions of crime.

In Part II, we turn to an examination of the ways in which particular forms of corporate crimes are produced within the chemical industry. It is this industry which sits at the centre of most contemporary concerns regarding environmental degradation and human health and safety. In Chapter 4, we begin by examining the ways in which the causes of threats posed by the chemicals industries to health, safety and the environment are represented. This entails an examination of ideological representations of the corporate production of such risks, coupled with discussions of alternative explanations of their incidence, drawing upon a range of empirical and theoretical evidence. In Chapter 5, we develop our argument relating to the corporate production of risk through particular attention to corporate structures, the *modus operandi* of corporations, and changes within each of these. Finally, in Chapter 6, the disaster at Bhopal is interrogated as an instance of a series of actions/inactions on the part of a large, multinational actor in the chemical economy, including the problems that such a disaster poses in terms of assessing liability and criminality. The Bhopal disaster also serves as testimony to the class and social power of the largest multinational actors within the chemicals industry.

In the final three chapters of the text, which comprise Part III, we consider the regulation of corporate crime in general, and safety, health, and environmental crimes in particular. In Chapter 7, we review and provide a critique of current academic and political debates concerning the most appropriate form of external regulation of corporate activity, in order to prevent, as well as more successfully prosecute, corporate crime. Particular attention is paid to two dominant sets of arguments in this sphere, namely those grounded in neoliberal and social liberal discourses. We argue that, in different ways, both these schools of thought, and the practices which they inform, conflate current predominant forms of regulation with 'feasible' forms of regulation. Chapter 8 considers in detail some of the key aspects of the regulation of chemicals and the chemical industry in the US. The changing forms of regulation are interpreted as aspects of different modes of governance, which themselves are located in relation to Gramsci's concept of hegemony in general, and his claims regarding passive revolution in particular. In this chapter we begin to detail aspects of progressive regulatory reform, a task continued in Chapter 9. Here, we set out what a more punitive mode of regulatory enforcement might look like, and consider the role that it might play in a reformed model of regulation. We document the crucial role in progress towards such reforms that has been played by, and must continue to be played by, a range of popular pro-regulatory forces engaged in activities of resistance, which take law as one, but not their only focus. We argue for an overall regulatory strategy which is based upon the principles of deterrence and rehabilitation, while developing an understanding of regulation that is both facilitative and positive rather than merely limiting and negative. We note the challenges that the logic of such forms of regulation might pose in terms of the ownership and control of the capitalist corporation: we are committed to a socialist transformation, not merely the reform and humanisation of capitalism.

This text is the result of more than ten years of academic activity. In many respects, what follows was prompted by outrage over the all too avoidable carnage at Bhopal. Thus the book is explicitly located within a class politics, a politics often focused upon issues of safety, health and environmental degradation, a politics with which we have both engaged, but to which many men and women have given far more of themselves; many have given their lives. In terms of the substance of the text, much is based upon more or less readily available empirical material. We also draw upon empirical material which we have each generated. Our focus here is primarily upon North American and British capitalism. The text is also very clearly defined by particular readings of the theoretical. In the latter context, it clearly owes a greater debt to our training as social theorists than to our involvement in the area of criminology.

One final contextual note. In writing this book, we have generally resisted the temptation to engage directly with, or to locate this work within much of the burgeoning literature on risk — work which emanates from both social theory and criminology. This was a conscious decision. There is no doubt that some of the concerns of this text are similar to the concerns of many of those working within these areas, so that there is a tendency to wish to speak directly to their work, within its own language, concepts, arguments, problematics. Nevertheless, for us there is a sense in which the term 'risk' has been appropriated, postmodernised and stripped of reference to class, exploitation and the corporate form. An awareness of the corporate production of risk — often in a criminal fashion — pervades this text, so that risk is understood concretely, in relation to corporate capitalism, rather than in relation to any abstract 'risk society'.

Acknowledgements

We both wish to thank June Pilfold and Jayne Hinchey for their secretarial assistance. We are also particularly grateful to Danica Dupont for the key role she has played both in carefully proof-reading the manuscript and in producing the camera ready copy of the text.

The writing of this text has been a truly mutual and enjoyable endeavour. For this, and for the many other projects on which we have collaborated over the years, we would like to thank each other: there are, hopefully, many more to come.

Steve also thanks the following. For critical comment and advice, in various ways, at different times, and from disparate locations: Moya Lloyd, Denis Smith, Dave Whyte, Joe Sim, Jo McCloskey, Alan Dawe, Gary Slapper, Eric Tucker, Dave Goss, Alan Dalton, Paul Shrivastava, David Bergman, Alan Irwin, Marci Green, Sol Picciotto, Rory O'Neill, and Vincente Navarro. The usual disclaimers of course apply. For her support, for the ever-critical eye of an employee in the chemical industry, and for her love, I express my deepest gratitude to Pamela, and to Patrick, the most beautiful inspiration to get this work finished.

Frank also thanks the following. For their advice, help and support: Anita Harrington, Susan Egert, Kelly Davies, Taz Pirmohammed, Frances Newman, Peter Fitting, Michal Bodemann, Brian Papizzo O'Shea, Bill Stratton, Bob Shenton, Gavin Smith, Elaine Stavro, Ivan Varga, Vincent Sacco, Margaret Beare, Frank Cunningham, James Dickinson, Michael Woodiwiss, Paul Q. Hirst, David Campbell, Steven Gill, Harry Glasbeek, and Laureen Snider. I am particularly grateful to Anthony Woodiwiss, for his friendship and for the opportunity to know at first hand the benefits of an agonistic intellectual relationship. Finally, I am grateful to my sons, Rory and Blake, for being themselves.

PART I
CAPITALISM, CORPORATIONS AND CRIME

1 Dreams of Capitalism: Neoliberalism and Contemporary Economies

Introduction: Capitalist Success Stories

Compared to most citizens in most other countries, and compared to their own previous standard of living, average citizens now living in the 24 OECD (Organization for Economic Cooperation and Development) countries have a dramatically better standard of living. On average: they work fewer hours, live longer, are healthier and better housed, have access to a greater volume and range of goods and services; they are more mobile and, through their easy access to a range of mass media, are exposed to a greater wealth of information; they have a better education and better medical care, and, through unemployment benefit, welfare, worker compensation and pensions, they have greater security. Changes in the Gross Domestic Product (GDP) per capita within OECD countries over time and the differences between their current GDP per capita and that of other countries provide telling evidence of their relative prosperity.

Capitalism as Market Economy

In all the OECD national states the dominant form of economic organisation is capitalistic; that is, according to neoclassical economic theory, they are competitive enterprise economies in which economic agents make contracts which involve the buying and selling of goods and services. These marketed goods and services are produced by 'economic organizations' which are 'social (and rarely, individual) arrangements to deal with the production and distribution of [scarce] goods and services' (Stigler 1952: 1-2). In such economies the key figure is the entrepreneur, a rational risk taker, who buys services and resources from owners of productive resources to produce goods which are then sold in the market for money to consumers. The product is

3

distributed by money incomes which are dependent upon the ownership of resources and the market price for their use. According to neoliberal theorists, the reciprocity of transactions in markets creates 'unanimity without conformity' (Friedman 1962: 23). Equilibrium, harmony and efficiency, liberty and freedom of choice are all characteristic of free market economies.

At this point it is worth summarising what, in neoclassical discourse, is understood by the term 'competitive market system':

[T]he market is a mechanism which produces prices. The function of market prices is to regulate the supply of goods in relation to the demand, and to channel the demand for goods in relation to the available supply. Hence the market may be called a supply-demand-price mechanism ...

Prices regulate the movement of goods into the market ...

[P]rices regulate the movements of goods out of the market ...

The *mechanism* of the market refers to the systematic reactions of all prices and quantities to changes in any one of them ... That is, relative prices are constantly moving toward the combination at which the quantity of each good which suppliers will sell at the market price is easily matched by the quantity which buyers will purchase at that price, thus 'clearing the market' ...

Each change in demand or supply conditions reacts through the whole system until each and every market has achieved a new equilibrium, where suppliers bring forward exactly the amount which buyers will take at the existing price, with no further pressures on either side to change the price.

(Neale 1971: 96)

How did contemporary economies emerge? According to Milton Friedman, at one time every household had the choice of either producing for its own needs or producing for the market. Households tended to produce for the market because it was advantageous, i.e., because the increased productivity from specialisation created more goods for everyone. There were strong rational reasons why individuals should prefer an economy based on markets. Under capitalism we have a similar freedom of choice since no worker has to work for any particular boss. If he or she does not like his or her current one then it is possible to go elsewhere (Friedman 1962: 14).

Nevertheless, there remains the question, why, given the centrality of the market in this analysis, does all production not take place through ad hoc and temporary contractual relationships? Why are there firms and employees? The general answer is that it is difficult and expensive for the parties to contracts to monitor those contracts effectively. People tend to lie, cheat and steal and all of us suffer from a lack of information and a limited understanding of the contexts in which we operate. There may be fewer transaction costs ('search and information costs, bargaining and decision costs, policing and enforcement costs' [Dahlman 1979]) for entrepreneurs to develop permanent, centralised, authoritative organisations (firms) than to continuously renegotiate and monitor contracts with independent agents. Firms, then arise, survive and grow when they are the most efficient way of organising production (Coase 1937). Furthermore, it may be advantageous to them as well as socially efficient to develop very large organisations indeed.

Why such large scale organizations have emerged is clarified in the elaborated version of the theory which examines the importance of uncertainty (changes can occur in the environment that an owner cannot foresee or control), small numbers bargaining (only a small number of firms or workers are available to meet the owner's needs), bounded rationality (imperfect information), and opportunism. Bounded rationality and opportunism are ever present but will only give rise to large firms where there is uncertainty and small-numbers bargaining, or when overall there has been a *market failure*. Under these circumstances:

> you can buy out the person you sell to (or set up your own organization in competition with your customer), called 'integrating forward'; or you can buy out your supplier (or build your own source of supply), called 'integrating backward' … This way you reduce the costs of transacting business …

> Thus hierarchy replaces markets when there are long-term contracts in an uncertain environment and the barriers to entry are reasonably high, because the costs of opportunism are reduced by substituting an authority relationship ('You now work for me') for a contractual one.
>
> (Perrow 1986a: 236-239)

This approach helps explain current trends to concentration in many areas of advanced industrialised economies. These can be seen as indicating efficiencies due to engineering and production developments, new distribution techniques, or new control and management techniques (Bork 1978: 205-206; Williamson 1975: 101, 102, 104). Firms often grow through mergers because economies of scale can be exploited sooner than through internal expansion and because they place assets in the hands of superior managers and penalize inefficient or corrupt managers through displacement (cf. Posner 1976: 96). Horizontal and vertical integration may increase efficiency for the firm and for the society as a whole. In North America 'efficiency is the main and only

systematic factor responsible for the organizational changes that have occurred'
(Williamson 1983; see also Chandler 1969, 1977, 1990).

In recent years we have seen trends which some equate with a process of
economic globalisation (see following chapter), as a consequence of which
national economies are increasingly being subsumed and rearticulated into the
global economic system by international pressures and transactions.
Multinational Corporations (MNCs) are similarly being transformed into
Transnational Corporations (TNCs) which are everywhere abroad and nowhere
at home (Jones 1984). These have no specific national identifications, are run
by internationalized managements, and service global markets through global
operations (Ohmae 1989). Instead of sustaining core production and Research
and Development in their home countries and building branch plants elsewhere,
these TNCs directly invest in other countries, engaging in production there in
order to meet the varying demands of distinct localized groups of consumers.
The growth of international competition means that the fact that competitors
can *potentially* enter into a market effectively disciplines behaviour almost as
well as would actual competition *within* the market even in highly concentrated
industries (Bailey 1981; Baumol 1982). Hence large scale organizations with
significant market share within particular nation states do not necessarily create
a problem for the maintenance of market competition because a perfectly
contestable market characterized by optimal behaviour can exist within a full
range of industry structures, including even oligopoly. This analysis vastly
extends the domain of the invisible hand.

Firms, then, arise, survive and grow when they are the most efficient way
of organising production. Equally, they may decline or be restructured under
other circumstances. In recent years, corporate forms have been changing
towards greater fragmentation or decentralisation, making them less
bureaucratic, more flexible, and more responsive to markets (Tombs 1995a). In
other words, this theory also provides an explanation of radical changes in the
corporate form.

There still remains, however, the question of why we find a world of
capitalist firms rather than a world of worker's cooperatives. One answer is that
cooperative effort or teamwork functions poorly because it is often difficult to
determine each individual's contribution to the joint effort. Under these
circumstances, the group members hire another person, a monitor, to determine
the input of each worker and relatedly the rewards they deserve. To be
effective, this monitor must have the authority to replace shirkers or
incompetent workers and to settle any disputes about relative efforts. The
monitor's salary comes out of the profit and the return of each worker is
reduced in order to pay this salary. And to be sufficiently motivated to do an

accurate monitoring job, the monitor should be able to also get any profits left over after the others have received returns equal to their estimated contributions. If the monitor decides it would be profitable to expand the business, it will be possible to borrow from people with excess money to invest. The investors will together select some of their members who will ensure the money is used so that the return to them as stockholders is maximized. The monitor is now agent of new principals, the chief executive officer, or CEO. The new monitors constitute the board of directors, watching over their investments and those of other stockholders. Thus, there is now a fully fledged contemporary capitalist firm (Alchian and Demsetz 1972; Perrow 1986a: 225-226).

The Organization of Contemporary Business Firms

Capital used by entrepreneurs may be raised in a whole series of different ways, legally creating a series of different rights for lenders and different obligations for the entrepreneurs. Since any individual or group has a right to register as a trading company in private enterprise economies, both small and large companies are sometimes owned by a single individual, although more often they are group enterprises. Typically individuals or groups incorporate themselves as, by becoming shareholders in, a limited liability corporation. This is now the main legal mechanism through which capital is brought together and interacts in the various market-places. Through it the earnings saved by consumers can be put at the disposal of entrepreneurs (directly or through financial institutions), so that in exchange for the payment of some kind of dividend production the market can be expanded and the general level of wealth increased. It makes possible both an accumulation of capital and dispersed individual shareholding, which, along with significant institutional shareholding, is believed to invalidate simple class polarisations. This system will be efficient insofar as 'resources are used where they obtain highest rates of remuneration, if they are employed efficiently in these industries, and if they produce the commodities that consumers most desire, [and] output is as large as possible' (Stigler 1952: 9). Overall, neoliberals would take at face value the statement made by its board of directors that 'The objective of the 3M Company is to produce quality goods and services that are useful and needed by the public, acceptable to the public, and in the best interests of the global economy — and thereby to earn a profit which is essential to the perpetuation of the useful role of the company' (cited in Benjamin and Bronstein 1987). In actual business practice there is an additional criterion of efficiency, that defined by alternative cost theory. According to this theory:

> Optimum efficiency ... is achieved when the value of the marginal product of each productive service equals its alternative cost ... A difference between alternative cost and the value of the marginal product in any firm or industry is proof of inefficiency and the magnitude of the difference is clue to the extent of the inefficiency.
>
> (Stigler 1952: 102)

The free market will ensure, then, that resources are used with optimum efficiency.

Legally, the body corporate is made up of four elements. First, there is the corporation itself. For legal purposes (more rarely substantively) the corporation is construed as a separate entity with its own 'legal' personality. Second, there are its shareholders who have bought (and can sell) a stake in the company and are entitled to a dividend but who have limited liability. Third, there are its directors who are legally responsible for setting its policy goals, determining its organisation and defining the kind of business it does. Fourth, there are its managers who range from its chief executive to those responsible for the day to day money-making activities. Fifth, for some issues of liability there are its lower level employees.

Company profits are subject to claims from a number of different agents.

> Stocks ... are loans, to ... companies, which earn the lender a fixed sum of interest. Someone buying debenture stock is merely making a loan to a company. Its possession gives no say in how a company should be run. And the income, a fixed interest payment, does not automatically increase with the firm's profits. But the return on debentures is relatively certain, because the firm has to meet its fixed-interest obligations before any other claims.

> Next call on a company's profits comes from preference shareholders. 'Preference shares' carry only limited rights of participation in the running of the firm (voting rights when dividends are in arrears, for example) and they yield only a fixed or limited dividend; but cumulative preference shares imply that if the company is able to meet its obligations in any year, the arrears of dividend become payable in the following year. [Some] part of the remaining profits may be ploughed back into the business. The leftovers, if there are any, are distributed as dividends to the 'ordinary' (or 'equity') shareholders. But although the

ordinary shareholders are thus last in the queue, they are the owners of the company and, in theory at least, elect a board of directors to carry out their policy in running the firm.

(Donaldson and Farquar 1988: 217-218)

While the legal form of the corporation helps it to make sufficient profits to satisfy its shareholders, to survive and to grow, there remain ambiguities with how it should be organized, what its functions and rights should be, and how it, its different groups of shareholders, its directors and chief executives relate to each other and to their various legal environments. These are the issues addressed in the subspecialism of corporate law (Simon 1990; Glasbeek 1995). In the US, since the Second World War, mainstream contract doctrine assumes that:

the distinctive feature of corporate organization is that it involves large numbers of people engaged in a relatively long-term collaboration. Since basic contract rhetoric tends to presuppose small numbers of individuals, arm's length bargaining, and short-term relations, adjustments seem needed in the corporate field. Corporation doctrine is focused primarily on two sets of adjustments. One has to do with the extent to which the various actors associated with a corporation should be treated as a unity. The other has to do with constraining the ability of corporate actors to abuse their discretion to take advantage of one another.

(Simon 1990: 388-389)

The first of these, 'personification', has been dealt with pragmatically. It is reasonable sometimes 'to treat the corporation as a unitary entity or fictional person' without thereby reading 'substantive significance into this practice' (Simon 1990: 390). True, corporations have had extended to them the protection of aspects of the amendments to the US constitution but this has been quite rational, for example, giving a corporation a right to privacy is justified by the need to protect trade secrets (Posner 1981: 224).

In practice, most scholars conceive of the corporation as a 'nexus of contracts' and see the central problem as

constraining the abuse of the discretion that results when direct bargaining and contractual specification are not feasible. Abuse here means the failure to maximize the value of the firm to managers, shareholders, and creditors or the expropriation by some of these participants of returns due to others.

(Simon 1990: 394; on the latter point see Latham 1961: 226)

'Agency theorists' such as Jensen, Meckling and Fama have analysed the relationship between managers, and creditors and shareholders and argue that the existence of equity markets reduces management inefficiencies (and opportunism) because their performance is adequately reflected and hence monitored by stock market evaluations (Jensen and Meckling 1976, 1979; Fama and Jensen 1983). It is therefore not surprising that when another agency theorist, Macey, turned his attention to corporate crime, he claimed that the risk aversion attributed by the theory to corporate managers meant that 'we should expect that corporate officers and directors will engage in corporate crime only rarely' and he claimed that managerial illegalities were usually to 'further their own interests rather than those of their shareholders' (Macey 1991: 339).[1]

It is also argued that the capital market may be a less efficacious surveillance and correction mechanism than the conglomerate form of corporate organization. Companies which have operations in many and diverse usually unconnected markets are 'capitalism's creative response' to the limit of the capital market in relation to the firm. The conglomerate form provides an internal rather than an external control mechanism, with the constitutional authority and expertise to make detailed evaluations of the performance of each of its operating parts; it can fine-tune as well as make discrete adjustments; the costs of intervention by the conglomerate's central office are relatively low (Williamson 1975: 159). The elite staff at the conglomerate's general office and its superior informational base allow it to best evaluate divisional performance, and to assign rewards and penalties to divisions (Williamson 1985: 284). Furthermore, they can readily make available to the component subdivisions relatively cheap capital for expansion. This may have been generated internally, or the very size and creditworthiness of the whole conglomerate may make banks willing to lend money at favourable rates.

Overall, the correspondence of affluence with trade within and between dominant industrialised countries and large corporations is seen as a vindication of the corporate capitalist market system and a demonstration that there is a generalised benefit from trading between different economic units with varied forms of comparative advantages (Dunning 1979; World Bank 1989).

Politics, Markets and Regulation

The market, then, is the most just and effective regulator of economic conduct. Everybody's lawful pursuit of self interest in the free market produces an efficient allocation of resources, maximises production, enhances individual self-satisfaction, and promotes liberty and freedom of choice. This includes, of course, corporate actors, for as Carl Gerstacker, a former chairman of Exxon, stated, 'the large enterprise has the means, capabilities, and experience to perform large-scale economic tasks in a socially responsible manner when given the opportunity and flexibility to do so' (cited in Barnet and Mueller 1974: 370).

This leaves unanswered questions concerning the appropriate role of government, its scope and who or what constitutes it. The issue was addressed in the 1930s and 1940s by both Hayek and Schumpeter in their 'catallactic' approach to politics. For Hayek, the most important issue was not whether governments were democratic or not but whether or not they would guarantee the freedom of individuals to partake in a capitalist 'competitive system based on a free disposal of private property' (Hayek 1972: 70). However, while democracy was only one among several means to this end — it was at best 'a utilitarian device for safeguarding internal peace and individual freedom' — only within capitalism 'was democracy possible' (ibid.). Democracy, for Schumpeter, was 'an institutional arrangement for arriving at political decisions in which individuals acquire the power to decide by means of a competitive struggle for the people's vote' (Schumpeter 1950: 269). This definition was adapted, but significantly modified, by Gary Becker who stressed the gap between the ideal model and the likely reality. While the model assumes that individuals would 'endeavor to acquire political office through perfectly free competition for the vote of a broadly based electorate', in practice, these individuals are expensive to reach and hence '[p]olitical competition is reduced by the large scale required for political organizations' and, since minorities receive no representation (as compared to economic market systems where minority tastes are catered for), there is little incentive for many people 'to be well-informed and thoughtful on political issues, or even to vote' (Becker 1958: 105-108). Because of these pressures towards monopoly in the political system and since, Becker concludes, these and other 'imperfections of government behavior' are 'greater than those in the market', government activity should be severely circumscribed — it should not intervene in economic life, for example through nationalisation, because it 'may be preferable not to regulate economic monopolies and to suffer their bad effects, rather than to regulate them and suffer the effects of political imperfections' (Becker 1958: 109).

Perhaps the most elaborated version of these ideas is to be found in the work of Anthony Downs who argues that 'parties in a democratic polity are analogous to entrepreneurs in a profit seeking economy' (Downs 1957a: 295).

[P]olitical parties in a democracy formulate policy strictly as a means of gaining votes. They do not seek office in order to carry out certain preconceived policies or to serve any particular interest groups: rather they formulate policies and serve interest groups in order to gain office.

(Downs 1957b: 137)

Therefore when a party espouses a distinctive political principle, or 'ideology', it is only for the advertising purpose of persuading voters that its ability to form a government is superior to that of competing parties (Downs 1957a: 96ff). These parties are appealing to citizens who are solely motivated by (short-term) self-interest, calculating anticipated balances of costs and benefits from casting votes (Downs 1957b: 138).

Since a lack 'of complete information' is 'basic to human life' this affects both political parties who need to know what policies voters want and citizens who may need to know what a political party 'has done, is doing or should be doing to serve their interests' and this lack is always costly to remedy (Downs 1957b: 139). Downs echoes Becker's views when he argues that because most voters have so little influence and it is expensive to acquire accurate information 'it is irrational for most citizens to acquire political information for the purposes of voting' (Downs 1957b: 147). Nevertheless, information may still be conveyed to the voters to help them decide how to vote by 'persuaders' who control information flows. These persuaders may demand and indeed get favours from parties for whom they have attracted undecided voters. Favours may also be sold to those who can make large campaign contributions or who engage in lobbying. The effectiveness of lobbying activities depends on the resources that individuals can use for these purposes and since the interests of individuals as income earners are much more focused than as consumers they 'are more likely to exert direct influence on government policy formation in their role as producers than in their roles as consumers' (Downs 1957b: 149; see also Popper 1961: 62).

Thus the role of the state should be restricted. It should be a 'nightwatchman', providing nothing except security from enemies without and within, the protection of individuals from force and fraud, and the provision of legal frameworks to resolve disputes about property rights. State activity should aim to achieve stable prices, to restrict the money supply, and to remove barriers to competition in labour, product and financial markets, hence encouraging innovation (cf. Clarke 1988: 60).

Law can be used to facilitate these 'natural' activities of economically rational agents and helps provide, through the courts, an objective price constraint that tells these actors what it will cost them to obtain a certain good.

Generally speaking, the courts in common law countries can be relied upon, when confronted with new or controversial dilemmas, to make decisions which contribute to economic efficiency. If and when inefficient decisions are made, then they are either evaded by private actors who write efficient contrary arrangements into their agreements or they are legislatively preempted by political pressure from interest groups acting in a generally economically rational manner (Posner 1977: 289-291; and, with some qualification, Coase 1988). Thus, the functioning of the different markets involving such legal persons as shareholders, employees and customers, and the corporate entity in combination with the right of such persons to challenge violations of their rights in the civil courts will constitute an adequate and socially efficient mechanism for producing self-interested but socially responsible behaviour. In this view, then, insofar as law is concerned, the *modus operandi* of civil law, is, or should be paradigmatic, even if, on occasion, the criminal law may be used (Posner 1980: 416-417; Kelman 1987: 120). The criminal law (and imprisonment), however, may be the appropriate mechanism to stop some (impecunious) 'predators' (and/or irrational 'ideologically motivated' extremists) from destroying the possibility of community and of 'constructive' economic activity. An economic and social system based upon markets and the civil law, and protected by the police power of the state, will be rational, efficient and just (Kelman 1987: 121-122).

In general, state intervention in the economy poses tremendous dangers to the working of market rationality. For, although state activities are usually justified as being necessary to correct allocative problems due to *market failure*, in fact, they primarily function to redistribute resources in a socially inefficient way. For example, we can earn what we are worth and what we are worth, in turn, depends upon how much we have invested in resources including ourselves (Becker 1975). The poor are poor because they have decided not to invest wisely and the well off are well off because they have invested wisely. Therefore, even the existence of unequal distributions of wealth in market economies shows how these economies make it possible for interests to be mutually harmonious. Universal welfare provision, then, is counterproductive. It discourages labour market participation and artificially inflates the wages bill for all areas of economic activity. It is also quite unnecessary if people took responsibly for their actions. These and other related state activities generate inflation, increase uncertainty and discourage productive investment.

Then, under some conditions of market failure — a high initial fixed cost capital investment, limited markets, and economies of scale only available to high volume producers — monopoly may be economically rational, but, as Becker argues, this should not be a state monopoly. State monopolies have primarily benefitted their underworked, overpaid, inefficient managers and unionised employees, not consumers (Brittan 1988: 164); moreover, they may inhibit technological progress (Foreman-Peck 1989: 146). With new technologies, conditions of natural monopoly, always rare, are becoming ever rarer. No wonder, then, that the 'communist' economies collapsed and that neoliberal economists have been prominent as advisers in Eastern Europe and in the general privatisation movement that has swept the world in the last decade.

By 1991 more than 88 countries had privatised public assets. In mixed economies the privatisation wave, initiated by Pinochet in Chile after the overthrow of the Allende regime, was an integral element of the Chilean 'miracle'. Britain followed, with estimated sales of £87 billion between 1979 and 1992 (Whitfield 1992: 141), in its attempt to establish a dynamic 'people's capitalism'. By 1991, over half of what had been the public sector had been transferred to the private sector (Jackson and Price 1994: 15), and between 1979 and 1995 members employed by nationalised industries had fallen by four-fifths (Atkinson and Laurance 1997). Between 1984 and 1988 Canada sold off all or part of 40 governmental organisations, for $4.6 billion (Mosco 1989: 208-209). This international trend has been due both to the coming to power of governments influenced by these economists (who argued that selling off assets allowed for the most efficient way of engaging in economic production and facilitated a necessary decrease in government debt)[2], and because of pressure by the World Bank and the International Monetary Fund (IMF) (Price 1994). This process of privatisation has of course provided new market opportunities for many different firms, particularly in the financial, manufacturing and service sectors.

Another way to deal with market failure is to use regulatory agencies. But in the case of both economic and social regulation, consumers end up paying higher prices than is necessary for the benefit of small groups of highly motivated and well organized actors. In the former case these are established (and inefficient) firms, full-time regulators and pork barrel politicians (cf. Stigler 1971; Peltzman 1976) and in the latter case 'politically motivated' and fiscally irresponsible moral entrepreneurs such as environmentalists, and compliant regulators and opportunistic politicians (Weaver 1978). Moreover, these individuals are often motivated by a dangerously irrational ideal, a risk free society (Aharoni 1981). It is irrational because it is unachievable and because it presents risks in an entirely negative light as opposed to recognising that progress requires a willingness to take risks, such as providing entrepreneurs at the leading edge of technology with venture capital (Douglas 1993). It is dangerous because it obscures the opportunity costs and transaction costs of regulation — excessive regulation leads to the inefficient use of resources and inhibits constructive innovations. Furthermore, since overall the wealthier a society the healthier its members — anything that inhibits wealth creation is socially regressive (Douglas and Wildavsky 1982). To avoid these consequences, regulation is best achieved by a combination of property rights, market forces and private litigation.

In recent years many of these arguments have been particularly influential in the moves to deregulate the British and American economies and in the development of such free trade zones as the maquilederos. Thus, since, increasingly, the only way of producing and distributing goods and services is by capitalist enterprises in a global market economy, with increasingly limited state interference, the world now looks like a more 'rational' place.

Externalities and the 'Tragedy of the Commons'

Let us look at some elaborations of the positions that we have been discussing. The best way to deal with environmental pollution and the degradation or exhaustion of natural resources is by creating markets and clear and extensive property rights in nature. For, if an aggregate of individuals has access to some asset in common without any system of private property rights to structure that access, then each individual will tend to use an excessive amount of that asset, thereby depleting it. The 'tragedy of the commons' will be avoided if some individual or institution comes to own the asset because he or she then has an incentive to take care of it properly (Hardin 1968; Stone 1993). An individual who privately owns something has a rational self-interest in the preservation of that thing. Whether we are talking about a piece of land, a body of water, the earth's atmosphere, or a plant or animal species, if something is used in common, then no individual has a motivation to preserve the thing in question. Private property rights to land, water, the atmosphere, species, and so on, ought to be created wherever possible. This control over the asset will also allow owners to make other potential beneficiaries pay in order to gain access, thus allowing the owner to offset the cost of any damage and the possibility of profit will provide them with an incentive to invest in improving it (Anderson and Leal 1991: 108-109). Lack of individual property rights, then, leads to a result that is collectively irrational, namely, the rapid depletion of the common asset.

Public ownership, incidentally, is believed to provide no answer because bureaucrats will either try to enhance their status by favouring big budget projects which are often environmentally unsound or by forming alliances with special interest groups. These latter may require market distorting subsidies (irrigation projects encouraging overproduction by Western US farmers) or block environmentally sound economic activity (new drilling technologies make oil drilling possible even on land where there are endangered species).

If the possible long term negative effects of positive externalities are best dealt with through the assertion of private property rights, negative externalities are best dealt with similarly while at the same time providing legal mechanisms by which businesses can be forced to internalise such costs to others. Competition forces firms to search constantly for ways to lower their costs, and they may do so by externalising some of these costs onto society as a whole; and if the costs of environmental harm are dispersed throughout society, there is no incentive to minimize these costs. Competition also makes it irrational for a firm to install costly pollution control equipment if other firms are not doing the same. The extension of property rights, and the development of strong liability laws will allow property owners to sue effectively and thus force polluters to internalise the cost of pollution (Anderson and Leal 1991: 87, 139). Then, markets in permits to pollute can be organized, thus allowing companies themselves to develop the most efficient way of reducing pollution. For example, Unocal spent $5.8 million on buying 8,300 old automobiles to avoid spending $60 billion to clean up its refinery emissions.

Again, occupational safety and health can be viewed as a good, bought and sold as part of the wage bargain (Dickens 1984). Some workers who 'do not value additional safety very highly relative to additional income — whether because they are poor, have high pain thresholds, or just do not care' (Smith 1982: 213), knowingly select hazardous jobs because they receive substantially better compensation than they would in safer ones (Viscusi 1979, 1983). Thus optimum realisable health and safety standards are reached in the equilibrium situations where the worker's total compensation (wages plus the marginal cost of safety per worker) will be equal to the value of the worker's marginal product. At that point, the supply of safety will reflect workers' demands for protection and the resource costs of reducing risk (Chelius 1977). These resource costs include the costs of workmen's compensation and other insurance and the costs of investing in safe technology and work practices and of litigation. The most that regulatory agencies can realistically do is to set performance hazard standards or develop injury taxes (Oi 1977).

Neoliberalism: Some Critiques

The Organization of the Economy

> Orthodox theory is a theory of markets and market interdependence. It is a theory of general equilibrium in *exchange*, extended almost as an afterthought, to cover production and distribution. It is not a theory of a social system, still less of economic power and social class. Households and firms are considered only as market agents, never as parts of a social structure. Their initial endowments, wealth, skills, and property, are taken as *given*. Moreover, the object of the theory is to demonstrate the tendency towards equilibrium; class and sectoral conflict is therefore ruled out almost by assumption.
>
> (Nell 1973: 77-78)

There is a massive critical literature devoted to neoliberalism as a whole and to each of the separate components of the arguments that we have systematised.[3] Since we cannot possibly develop all of these arguments here we will only be able to touch upon aspects of these critiques. It seems constructive to start our discussion by considering criticisms from economists who share many assumptions with the neoliberals. Adams and Brock, for example, while accepting the existence of economic egoism and valuing some of its effects, still recognise that it may need to be circumscribed by coercive state action. They thereby develop many telling criticisms of the neoliberal 'sunshine' boys, to borrow Dusky Lee Smith's (1964 and 1970) evocative phrase. We will use some of their arguments to reformulate aspects of the neoliberal account of politics and regulation but will draw some different conclusions than do Adams and Brock. This interrogation allow us to characterise and understand contemporary economies in radically different ways from neoliberalism.

One of the major concerns of Adams and Brock is the effect that current monopolies and oligopolies are likely to have on how business will come to be conducted in markets. They have provided a number of detailed empirical analyses of antitrust, and of some of the reasons, other than efficiency, that will allow some firms to succeed better than others. First, the authors make some general points about the consequences for social efficiency of an oligopolistic organisation of capitalistic markets. In an oligopolistic situation companies know if they drop or raise prices their competitors will follow suit, therefore they neither gain nor lose market share. Thus they have no incentive to decrease prices but little worry about increasing them. They also have an interest in restricting the range of products in their market to those which will provide the highest return — big gas-guzzling cars rather than fuel efficient ones, for example. If they compete, they will do so in ways in which they can be sure that they will recoup costs, through advertising, styling, accessories etc.

One way in which competition is reduced is by horizontal mergers between competitors. Such horizontal integration automatically reduces the number of competitors (Adams and Brock 1989: 161-163). This means that technology may be frozen at the level of the then best competitor and future innovation may be stifled. Horizontal integration makes it relatively easy to engage in 'predation'. This is a form of aggression against rivals designed not to increase immediate profits, but in the expectation that rivals will be driven from a particular market or be sufficiently chastened to forsake competitive behaviour, leaving the predator with a market share sufficient to command monopoly profits. In particular, the horizontally integrated predator can narrowly tailor its price cuts to the particular regions and locales where an upstart threatens to compete, while leaving its prices unaltered in the remainder of its markets. There are well documented recent examples of such predation in the airline, cable television, beer, and trash hauling industries (Adams and Brock 1991: 32-35; Pevsner 1992).

Vertically integrated companies which control more than one stage in the production process can thereby achieve secure access to resources or markets. For efficiency reasons it also forces other companies to do the same thus increasing the size of firms for market entry and making them concerned about their access to supplies. Vertical integration combined with oligopoly at crucial stages creates the possibility of making suppliers, competitors or customers follow the dictates of the large firms. Recent examples can be found in the aircraft industry (reservation systems) and the gas retail industry. It also allows for a vertical price squeeze when a manufacturer acquires a retailer and imposes losses on other retailers by raising wholesale prices, by lowering retail prices, or by doing both simultaneously. Recent examples are to be found in cable networks, airlines and their control over airport gates, and the oil, steel, cigarette and telephone industries (Adams and Brock 1991: 72-74). A vertically integrated manufacturer may 'foreclose' other manufacturers from distributing through its retailing subsidiary as has happened in the relation between motion picture producers, petroleum industry and independents, and cable television (ibid.: 76-78).

Then, in oligopolistic markets, it is possible for a small group of companies to engage in privately enforced social planning. For example, in the US in 1932, GM president, Alfred Sloan, organized the National Highway Users Conference (NHUC), which combined representatives of the Nation's auto, oil, and tire industries. In a common front against competing transportation interests it successfully ensured that gasoline taxes were devoted solely to highway purposes and that there would be a continuing program of highway construction. In effect, NHUC became a perpetual motion machine to promote automobiles. Another related and well documented example was revealed in 1951 when a Federal Court sustained a criminal conviction for criminal conspiracy to violate US antitrust laws. It found that, through its National City Lines subsidiary, General Motors and its co-conspirators (a tire producer and an oil company) had gained control of and engineered the demise of forty-six low pollution electric mass transit systems in forty-five cities in sixteen states' and replaced them with fleets of smog generating GM buses (Adams and Brock 1987).

With a small number of large companies dominating markets it is relatively easy for them make *quid pro quo* arrangements which may inhibit product proliferation. For example Standard Oil (now Exxon) and I.G. Farben struck a deal by which I.G. Farben sold their process for producing oil from coal in exchange for the latter staying out of the oil industry (Borkin 1978: 51). Today, because of their many joint ventures, the world's largest petroleum firms necessarily reveal to one another their long-term plans for expansion, for contraction, and for sales and marketing. At home and abroad, they are intertwined and interlocked:

> through joint exploration, joint bidding, joint production, and joint pipeline agreements … In jointly constructing and operating pipelines the major oil companies effectively allocate market shares among themselves in the course of allocating pipeline shipments.
>
> (Adams and Brock 1991: 59-60)

That large corporations in the US have long had a cynical attitude towards such institutions as the free market is well documented (cf. Kolko 1976; Pearce 1976; and see Chapter 3). For example, at the same time as the US government and big business were demanding free trade between Canada and the US, and challenging Canadian subsidies, ownership restrictions and nationalisation plans (i.e. national economic planning) (Orchard 1993), those same companies were exacting monies from communities as the cost, so to speak, of locating production in their area, such as the $100 million in incentives received by GM to engage in production in Tarrytown, New York (yet it still closed its plant in 1992) (*New York Times*, Sunday, 8 March 1992: 16E). A further example is illustrated by the stoppage of cheap oil imports in the 1960s by the large US oil companies, which had the effect of using up scarce US oil. To what extent is social efficiency achieved by this arrangement? (Adams and Brock 1986: 76-78).

Given these considerations it is not surprising that Adams and Brock are concerned that the 'largest 0.1 per cent of US manufacturing firms collectively control approximately two-thirds of total domestic assets devoted to manufacturing, while the largest 0.2 per cent control three-fourths' (cited in Adams and Brock 1986: 66). Further, while the 100 largest manufacturing firms had 22 per cent of net output in the US in 1909, by the end of the 1970s this share had stabilised at 33 per cent (Green and Sutcliffe 1987). In the 1980s the top five hundred US corporations were responsible for over 75 per cent of all sales, received as much as 85 per cent of profits and owned nearly 90 per cent of all assets (Cherry et al. 1987: 311). There is little evidence that this degree of concentration has changed in recent years although the number of people employed by these core corporations may have dropped somewhat during this time (Harrison 1994). The UK economy is also very concentrated. Focusing upon the UK manufacturing sector at the end of the 1980s, Hughes noted that the 575 enterprises which employed over 1,000 employees represented just 0.4 per cent of all firms in the sector, yet accounted for 52.1 per cent of employment and 59.9 per cent of output (Hughes 1992: 306).

The high degree of concentration in the US is, in part, the effect of four merger movements since the end of the last century — 1898-1902; 1925-29; 1955-69; 1980-1988 — none of which are adequately accounted for in terms of the greater efficiency of those companies who benefitted from it the most.

(i) The first merger movement was, conventionally caused by the business failures of the 1890s together with the proliferation of railways, telegraph and telephone leading to the establishment of the first truly national markets. The dominant types of monopoly organization were trusts, mergers, and combinations which in many industries embraced all existing capacity, that is more than 90 per cent … [T]he basic corporations were established prior to merger mania.

(ii) The second movement was governed largely by the parallel responses of separate organizations. The 1929 peak extended the domain of big business to new industries and created numerous vertically integrated enterprises, that is the consolidation of monopoly capital. The conventional cause was the shift to autos and trucks with the consequent enlargement of markets and the destruction of local monopolies.

(iii) The third movement was more of an extended trend starting in the 1950s and peaking in 1968. The process produced the giant conglomerate form signalling in part the reintegration of economic ownership and possession with the coincident elevation of the problem of multi-national companies to the political agenda. Of course effective control still extended beyond possession.

(Jones 1982: 17)

As Jones has argued, these three movements corresponded

to three definite moments within the formation of monopoly capital, namely: (a) the phase of relative transition to relations of production characterized by the preeminence of monopoly capital; (b) the phase of consolidation of the conditions of existence of monopoly capital; (c) the phase representing the partial reintegration of economic ownership and possession signalling a new conjuncture of increased political conflict.

(Jones 1982: 9)

The fourth, and most recent, of these merger improvements (between 1980-1988) was generated, on the one hand, by deregulation and the opportunities it offered the large corporations for consolidation of their control over the national economy and the possibility for corporate raiders and others to maximise the current value of assets. It was also stimulated, on the other hand, by a concern with international competition, with indigenous capital concerned with its own competitiveness and overseas capital concerned with securing access to US markets. This last merger movement is the most significant in terms of the sheer number of mergers and the dollar amounts involved. The movement peaked at just under forty five hundred mergers per year, with an eight year total of 26,671 mergers and acquisitions involving assets worth $1,083.4 billion. Corporate takeovers and reorganisations are also expensive — the bankers and lawyers involved in the RJR Nabisco leverage buyout made between $500 million and $1 billion in fees (Reich 1989; Adams and Brock 1991: 100) — and involve an extremely high opportunity cost in terms of a poor use of money which could have been used for investment in new plant and technology.

In 1988, total Japanese capital investment exceeded that of American firms by an estimated $250 billion — despite the fact that the American economy is some 40 percent larger than that of Japan. On a per capita basis, Japanese firms have been outinvesting American firms by a two-to-one margin. And over the 1985-88 period, Japanese firms increased their combined expenditures for factories, equipment and research and development by an estimated 150 percent, compared to an increase of only 23 percent by American firms over the same period ... American firms spent approximately $204 billion on mergers and acquisitions in 1986, while Japanese firms are estimated to have spent only $3 billion on corporate deals over the same year.

(Adams and Brock 1991: 108-109)

The UK, too, witnessed an unprecedented wave of mergers in the latter half of the 1980s. As Hughes writes, this movement 'generated a level of takeover activity which in terms of both values and numbers of companies acquired outstripped the previous UK post-war peak of 1969-1973' (Hughes, 1992: 309). Thus while the average annual number of acquisitions and mergers during the latter period was just over 1,000, there were almost 2,000 in both 1988 and 1989 (ibid.: 309-310; see also Sawyer 1992: 252-255).

Similar tendencies to merger and oligopoly are occurring on a global scale. Indeed, of the 100 largest economies in the world in 1989, 47 were corporations, not countries. In 1992 Exxon, General Motors, Itochu and Sumitomo all had sales revenue in excess of $100 billion a year, larger than the gross domestic product of Denmark, Finland and Norway. Many Japanese, American and French banks own assets worth as much if not more (*Forbes*, 19 July 1993: 142; Green & Sutcliffe 1987: 21). The United Nations Centre on Transnational Corporations has identified a 'billion dollar club' — a core of 600 TNCs with annual sales exceeding $1 billion. — which creates over one-fifth of the total industrial and agricultural production in the world's market economies; of these, 74 account for over 50 per cent of total sales (Dicken, 1992: 49). A recent United Nations Conference on Trade and Development (UNCTAD) report identifies a 'global network' of 37,000 firms controlling 200,000 foreign affiliates (and see United Nations 1993); two-thirds of the parent firms are from just 14 countries, a dramatic increase in concentration since the 1960s. Within this 'elite' group there is even greater concentration:

The 100 largest multinationals held $3,400 billion in assets by the end of 1992, of which about 40 per cent were assets located outside of their home countries. In addition, the top 100 ... control about one-third of the world stock of foreign direct investment.

(*Guardian*, 31 August 1994; and see Hirst and Thompson 1996: 53)

Thus, within the global economy as a whole and within the advanced national economies in particular, very large corporations are now the major economic actors (U.N. Centre of Transnational Corporations 1984; Knox and Agnew 1989: 192; Hirst and Thompson 1996: 53).

These indications of the nature and effects of the class and social power of capital point to a profound problem with the assumption that business enterprises ever willingly subordinate themselves to competitive free market rules unless they perceive these as of benefit to themselves. It is no irrelevance that, in different ways, Marx and Engels on the one hand, and Adam Smith on the other, were highly perceptive regarding the moral underpinnings of late capitalism. Marx and Engels acknowledged that in the early phase of capitalism, in its struggle to create a new order, the bourgeoisie had sometimes been inspired by a moral and universalising vision, but once their regime was securely established: 'The dissolute bourgeois evades marriage and secretly commits adultery; the merchant evades the institution of property by depriving others of property by speculation, bankruptcy, etc.; the young bourgeois makes himself independent of his own family, if he can by, in fact, abolishing the family as far as he is concerned' (Marx and Engels [1845] 1976: 180). With similar moral overtones Adam Smith warned that 'People of the same trade seldom meet together even for merriment and diversion, but the conversation ends in a conspiracy against the public or some contrivance to raise prices', and he criticised 'merchants and manufacturers' for 'extorting from the legislature ... support of their ... oppressive monopolies' (Smith [1776] 1937: 128). These seem far more apposite characterisations of the moral character of late capitalism than those of Hayek. He acknowledged that the freedom which is the market 'has never worked without deeply ingrained moral beliefs ... [and that] coercion can only be reduced to a minimum only where individuals can be expected as a rule to conform voluntarily to certain principles' (Hayek 1960: 62 cited in Hindess 1987: 130). Yet, at the same time, he still advocated the untrammelled freedom of large economic actors, thereby displaying a naive faith in the morality of large economic actors and their owners and controllers. Indeed, the fact that business leaders in the US and other leading capitalist economies have a cynical attitude towards such institutions as the free market and the law and, of course, the ability to act upon such cynicism 'successfully' — that is, in a self-interested and calculative fashion — is furthered by the degrees of concentration in many sectors and economies, and the sheer size and economic and political power of many leading corporate players, the transnational corporations, in their spheres of interest. Bearing all of these points in mind, we shall below return to the neoliberal accounts of regulation and politics. First, let us spell out some of the implications of the previous analysis.

Neoliberal theory ultimately presupposes that individuals and organizations as autonomous entities are free to make contracts or to not make contracts and hence any contracts that are made are consensually produced.

However, we have seen in the previous pages how monopoly power allows large corporations to dictate the conditions under which contracts are made. It is worth recalling here Friedman's explanation of why market economies emerged and why they are desirable. Although at one time every household could either produce for its own needs or produce goods that it exchanged in the market, it did the latter because the increased productivity from specialisation created more goods for everyone. Capitalism provides a similar freedom of choice since no worker has to work for one particular employer because there are always other potential employers, and therefore the labor contract illustrates the general principle 'that individuals are free to enter or not enter any particular exchange so that every transaction is strictly voluntary' (Friedman 1962: 14). As C.B. Macpherson rightly, and elegantly, has pointed out (Macpherson 1968), there is a great difference between the two situations. In so far as one owns one's own means of subsistence one can decide whether to engage in market relations or not but, for capitalism to function *qua capitalism*, workers do not and cannot normally own their own means of subsistence, and only a minority of the population is able to own and control the means of production. Thus, the worker who needs to work — and what worker does not need to work? — has no real choice but to work for some employer. Freedom of contract means both the freedom to make a contract and the freedom to refuse to make a contract, and in the asymmetrical relation between capitalists and workers it is the former who dictate the conditions under which contracts are made. After all, 'the free labourer' is 'free in the double sense, that as a free man he can dispose of his labour-power as his own commodity, and that on the other hand he has no other commodity for sale, is short of everything necessary for the realisation of his labour-power' (Marx 1965: 169). *The inequalities of condition between workers and capitalists create relations of unequal exchange which work to the benefit of capital.* Moreover, these unequal conditions allow for capital to secure, reproduce and expand its control over wealth and wealth producing social labour, and hence determine the purposes for which society's productive capacities are deployed (Wolf 1982: 73-79).

This leads into the problems with the explanation offered as to why capitalist firms rather than worker's cooperatives emerge and survive. It is unlikely to be because a group of workers cannot work out a way of monitoring each other. The principals, for example, could take turns monitoring each other or they could pay some monitor a lower wage for doing easier work. But this would not happen in real capitalist enterprises because the principal-agent relationships is really an authority relationship not a contractual one. The authority is based upon a *pre-existing* control of the enterprise by a capitalist who then either exercises that control or employs a manager to exercise it over workers.

[T]he boss can dismiss any or all of the workers, while they cannot dismiss her, so the relationship is not the symmetrical relationship of contracts but an asymmetrical one.

[The theory] almost exclusively emphasizes shirking by subordinates (agents) as the only form of egoistic, self-interested behavior that must be guarded against. The possibility that the capitalist, (principal) might lie to the workers about profit levels or threats of lost business, falsify the records of their outputs, endanger agents' health, all to extract more profit, or simply shirk her responsibilities is ignored or swept aside by mentioning that a firm will protect its reputation ... [T]he possibility of organized action by workers, who presumably fear exploitation from management more than shirking by fellow workers, is rarely considered.

(Perrow 1986a: 226-228)[4]

Politics

As we indicated above, in the neoliberal view regulatory agencies are easily captured by small groups of strongly motivated, (usually well ensconced) and highly organized actors to form iron triangles, and function counter-productively to skew the workings of the market. However, there seems no justification for only focusing on these kinds of interference in the workings of free markets, since, as we have seen, traditional economic oligopolies are equally subversive of free markets and allow for the exercise of all sorts of coercive power.

Similarly, if we turn to politics, we find that while some of the effects of 'market imperfections' are acknowledged the discussion is overly truncated. Politics is seen to be about political entrepreneurs seeking power and the spoils of office through choosing and pursuing those policies most likely to appeal to relatively poorly informed and self-interested voters. Politicians do this by making alliances with 'persuaders', those capable of shaping public opinion by their ownership and control of information flows, and also with those who are able to provide the material and other resources necessary for running effective campaigns. Producer groups are the most likely to directly influence government policy formation.

Interestingly, at one point Downs explicitly draws the obvious conclusions from these considerations:

[P]ersuaders are not interested per se in helping people who are uncertain become less so: they want to produce a decision that aids their cause. Therefore, they provide only those facts which are favorable to whatever group that they are supporting. Thus, even if we assume that no erroneous or false data exist, some men are able to influence others by presenting them with a biased selection of facts ...

[I]nequality of political influence is a necessary result of imperfect information, given an unequal distribution of wealth and income in society.

(Downs 1957b: 139-141)

What we might have expected from neoliberals deploying their own categories would be an argument that the media, the government, regulatory agencies and the legal process would all function in the interests of the best funded and best organised minorities within society. Thus, although the issue of the incompatibility between inequality and democracy is sometimes posed within the work of these writers, it is also continually obscured. Despite Downs' comment above, this argument rarely surfaces.

Interestingly, Downs indicates a process, the circulation of a stream of 'free information', which could provide a way around the problem that the lack and costs of information pose for democracy. 'Free' information is produced through informal social contact in public and private spaces and through 'reading the newspaper in a barber shop, and listening to the radio while driving to work' (Downs 1957b: 146). A mass media system, independent of commercial interests and uncontaminated by advertising, financed from general taxation and licence fees, and with maximal public access, would maximise the amount of free (or at least, socialised, low cost) information available to all citizens and hence increase the rationality of the political process. Thus, even if we accept elements of the catallactic perspective, it is not necessary to accept their judgment that — what Cunningham (1995) has described as — 'democratic defects' are intrinsic to all market societies. True, in highly unequal and totally marketised societies these effects may be inescapable but it is possible to achieve economic efficiency and political democracy while giving less of a role to markets, and in both economics and politics to recognise the key role of collective institutions, including but not restricted to the state (Hirst 1994).

However, if drawing upon the (well documented) research of some of the more instrumentalist Marxists, Tushnet (1981), for example, we add three further points, we will see why this solution in our societies is a less than likely one.

First, since capitalists are fewer in number and control a much larger amount of resources (of all kinds) than do employees, and, crucially, they are much more united in their interests vis-à-vis employees than are the latter — differentiated by status, ethnicity and gender — vis-à-vis employers, they are likely to be the most effective producer group.

Second, if the degree of control by the world's largest corporations over economic activity is startling, equally startling is the control over these corporations exercised by leading financial institutions and the wealthiest families. So, for example, in the US in 1983, the richest 1 per cent of families owned 'a fifth of all real estate (and over twice that much of the commercial real estate), three-fifths of the corporate stock, and over four-fifths of all the trust assets owned by all of us' (Zeitlin 1989: 145). These stock holdings, like those of a minority of commercial banks, tend to be in the largest corporations, corporations which also receive investment funds from the same minority of banks and insurance companies, and from other major institutional investors, which are effectively controlled by a minority of wealthy shareholders, large corporations and other institutional investors (Zeitlin 1989: 30-36, 66).

These kinds of relationships enrich and empower those who have controlling interests, majority or minority, in companies and other institutions:

> [These] control not only the capital represented by the small shareholder and the institutional investor, but also that represented by debt obligations (bonds, mortgages, short term loans) and internally generated funds (undistributed profits and depreciation and depletion allowances). Together these have accounted for approximately 90 per cent or more of all sources of corporate financing in North America and Britain since the 1960s.
>
> (Phillips 1992: 73)

This concentration of ownership, wealth, and control is graphically represented in the ownership and control of pension funds. Global pension fund assets stood at approximately $10,000 billion in 1994, or the equivalent of the market value of all the companies listed on the world's three leading stock exchanges (Minns 1996: 48, 43; and see Atkinson 1996). The vast majority of these are held in US and UK funds (ibid.). Further, 'about 80 per cent of this money is controlled, or "managed" in the parlance by a small group of US, UK and Swiss banks and insurance companies' (Minns 1996: 48).

Five US companies and five UK financial houses dominate. In the UK, the top five investment managers controlled nearly two-thirds of all pension fund assets in 1995 (ibid.: 43). Thus there are ten financial houses in the US and UK, within which there are a relatively small group of fund managers, or rather 'professional fund managers' who:

> have virtually total discretion over what happens to the money. This makes them arbiters of company takeovers, privatisation flotations, corporate policies, as well as, internationally, the purchase of government debt with knock-on effects for national exchange rate and interest rate polices.
>
> (Minns 1996: 48)

In so far as wealthy and powerful individuals and corporations do not obey free market rules one would also expect them to increasingly structure the social world for their profit and not necessarily for maximum social efficiency (Atkinson 1996).

Third, the more that the control of the media is exclusively in the hands of private business corporations and the greater the degree of concentration of media ownership, the easier it will be for a small select group of persuaders to dictate the agenda for public debate and political action (on current media ownership, see Bagdakian 1997; Dizard Jr. 1997; Lorimer 1994; McChesney 1997). It is not surprising to find that public broadcasting systems have been a major target of corporate capital and right wing groups. This is of particular importance because there is no reason to accept Downs' claims, that people's estimation of the value of government policies is restricted to their own short term gains or losses, and that they necessarily ignore long term outcomes and altruistic concerns (Downs 1957b: 140).

Not unrelatedly, given how few political options are discussed in the media, large corporations can often dictate to governments the conditions under which they will invest, or continue to invest in particular areas. In the context of such 'Job Blackmail' (Kazis and Grossman 1982) de-unionisation, environmental deregulation, and financial incentives are all demanded from, and offered by, desperate countries, states and communities. On Sunday, 13 October 1991, the *New York Times* (on page 10F) published the results of an EPA survey of the more polluted states in the US, and the following day the *Financial Times of Canada* ran a feature on which US states provided good incentives for Canadian companies to invest there. The list of the *Financial Times of Canada*, 14 October 1991 comprised Ohio, Tennessee, Illinois, Georgia, Florida, Michigan and North Carolina. Presumably, incentives included tax concessions, subsidies, low wages, weak 'social' regulation and anti-union laws. The *New York Times*' list showed that Ohio and Tennessee were among the most polluted states for both air and water; Illinois was among the most polluted states for air and measurably worse than average for water;

Georgia and Florida were measurably worse than average for both air and water; Michigan and North Carolina were measurably worse than average for water (see also Natural Resources Defense Council 1991).

Drawing upon our modified neoliberalism we would expect state taxation policy (and its distributive policies) to favour the smaller, better organised and wealthiest minority, taxing them relatively lightly and providing them with state subsidies, while disadvantaging the larger, less well-organised and poorer groups, taxing them proportionately more and subsidising them proportionately less. Corporate taxes have never been high, but their contribution to federal tax receipts has progressively dropped from 32.1 per cent in 1952 to 6.2 per cent in 1983 (Phillips 1992: 78), and to even less since then with many corporations avoiding taxation completely (Vanick 1978: 106). Similarly, whereas the nominal top personal tax rate was as high as 91 per cent from the Second World War through to 1964, it then dropped to 70 per cent and subsequently in the 1980s to 28 per cent. Again avoidance and evasion have always been widespread (Kolko 1962; Lampman 1970) and, indeed, many of the wealthiest individuals pay no taxes — at least 595 in 1987 (*New York Times National*, Sunday, 22 October 1989: 29; and see Lundberg 1968: 404). Further, studies of transfer payments routinely show that either through direct subsidies, indirect subsidies by cost-plus military contracts, and collusion in illegal subsidies by misreporting of costs, that capital is the major beneficiary of transfer payments from the state (Wachtel and Sawyers 1973).

This is a useful point to return to Hardin's argument that the cure to 'the tragedy of the commons' is to extend private property rights and markets, for an individual who privately owns something has a rational self-interest in its preservation. However, small producers have no control over market conditions, hence farmers who may wish to engage in careful husbandry, may, because of a drop in the price of their commodities, have to produce crops in an ecologically unsound way. Similarly, a demand for high returns by investors or banks may pressure farmers to produce short term profits rather than invest for longer term returns. The same general point applies to investment in all technologies including pollution technologies (Smith 1995). Similarly, the idea that the way to force polluters to internalise the cost of pollution is to allow the owners of property damaged by polluters to sue for damages is flawed. This does not diffuse conflict but actually displaces it to the judicial apparatus and similar questions of access are raised (Barnett 1992; 1994; 1995). In a situation where there is a market in legal skills, the best representation will generally go to those with the most assets. Race and class, then, will effect outcomes. Then, litigation may — through transaction costs — benefit lawyers more than any of the litigants — in the Johns Manville Asbestos cases (some of the) claimants expected to receive $59 million, their lawyers $34 million and the Johns Manville lawyers $76.4 million. Then, of the $470 million paid out in Superfund related cases by insurance companies in 1989, $410 million went to the legal costs of defending their policyholders and disputing whether their policies covered the cleanup (Acton and Dixon 1992). As a result of this, corporations, and indeed some who generally support the free market model, argue that since hazardous wastes are a side effect of general economic progress from which allegedly everybody benefitted, the costs of coping with them should be socialized through general taxation. This makes the highly contestable assumption that costs and benefits are widely and equally distributed, whereas there is strong evidence that those of higher social status receive many more of the benefits and those of lower social status suffer many more of the costs (cf. Hofrichter 1993; Barnett 1994; and for a contrary view see Hird 1994). Pollution permits are a problem because the setting of appropriate pollution levels is inevitably a political and not merely a technical decision. It is only if there is a steady and significant decrease in levels that it will lead to a reduction in pollution. Pollution may be concentrated in more vulnerable communities and in areas bordering on other less powerful countries such as the US — Canadian border. Accurate measurement of actual pollution levels cannot be entrusted to the companies themselves since they have an interest in underestimating these levels (Pearce 1990).

Neoliberals believe that common law judges tend to make decisions that contribute to economic efficiency (Posner 1977: 289-291) and that irrational decisions by them will be legislatively preempted by political pressure from rationally acting interest groups, or, alternatively, private actors will simply work around them. A British version of this argument has been developed by Bartrip and Fenn (1980) in their 'Re-assessment' of Kit Carson's (1979) article on 'The Conventionalization of Early Factory Crime'. Carson's article explored the contradictory forces and ideologies which produced as a largely unintended but — given the nature of these forces and ideologies and their more general structural context — predictable consequence, a relatively non-punitive response to the criminal acts of employers, as employers. Bartrip and Fenn argued, however, that as opposed to Carson's tendency to see 'social policy as an extension of the class struggle' (1980: 175), we should recognise that the legislative and enforcement outcomes involved the development of 'efficient legislation' by which the 'community', having compared its gain 'from reducing the number of hours worked with the costs of so doing, where these costs are not only the cost of enforcement, but also the costs of any lost production', decided on an appropriate mode and level of enforcement (ibid.: 178). 'Who on earth', responded Carson, with understandable exasperation, 'or more precisely, who in mid-nineteenth century Britain, comprised this "community"?' As he points out, Bartrip and Fenn's view depends upon the highly metaphysical assumption that 'somehow or other' the factory inspectorate 'encapsulated the transcendental rationality of the collective mind' (Carson 1980: 190). This is a particularly absurd view in light of the limited nature of the franchise at the time. Such arguments share all the flaws of the discredited evolutionary (and 'objective idealist') functionalism found in much early anthropology and sociology where it has long been successfully challenged (see, for example, the discussions in Swingewood 1984; Lockwood 1956, 1964) and in law it has been named and dissected most recently by the members of the Critical Legal Studies movement (Gordon 1984; Kelman 1987).

Of course, our reconstructed law and economics discourse is not unlike Marxist instrumentalism and shares many of its problems (Barnett 1992). Ultimately more satisfying, in our view, are some of the recent interpretations of the legal system and forms of regulation found in the work of Horwitz (1986, 1989), Fraser (1983, 1990) and Woodiwiss (1990a, 1993b). What all three share is the view that the historical outcome of the disputes about legal meaning were non-necessary, and were neither the unfolding of some immanent logic nor the vision of some group. At the same time, all view the actual outcomes as the result of struggles between different groups, with unequal resources at their disposal, with different discursively defined interests, and all constrained by, but at the same time drawing upon, pre-existing but potentially transformable legal discourses. If Fraser tends to overly stress the discursive and Horwitz the (preconstituted) group existence of capital, Woodiwiss rightly stresses both the relational nature of capitalism and the constitutive role of these social relations.

A Politics and Sociology of Economic Solutions

If oligopoly produces forced planning, then to counteract this a solution is to use antitrust laws to produce and sustain competitive markets. In certain situations this solution has some merit, although many of the arguments in favour of it are also quite compatible with some arguments for flexibly specialised industrial districts and some versions of market socialism. Competitive markets and/or industrial districts are seen as economically efficient and, hence, viable alternatives to large scale corporate capital. We have some sympathy with this view but we would like to make two major points. First, there are intrinsic to the economic process certain pressures towards monopoly. If there are high sunk costs involved in entering and operating within a market, and if the consumer demand in the market is relatively restricted vis-à-vis these costs, and/or if it is subject to extreme periodic fluctuations (these fit many of the markets in energy), then it may be difficult and, indeed, economically irrational to sustain competition. It is worth noting, for example, that the recently privatised British bus and rail systems are increasingly coming under the control of one private operator, and that, in the US the commercialised and privatised garbage industry after periods of fierce competition is now divided up nationally between three or four companies (Crooks 1993). This may show either that oligopolistic arrangements, even under current 'globalised' circumstances, have very specific identifiable effects which undermine 'market efficiency' or that it is difficult to organise the provision of some goods and services through competitive markets. As Bennett Harrison (1994) has argued recently, the continued domination of the global economy by large companies is an effect of both their ability to use their vast resources to continually innovate and achieve economies of scale, and *also* their ability to use their economic and political power to secure for themselves favourable operating conditions. More generally, the development of competitive markets in all areas of economic activity may undermine the ability of the economic system as a whole to function efficiently. It is better to accept that some areas of economic activity are 'natural monopolies' and/or that, in order to avoid the error of composition, our criteria of efficiency must include holistic categories. In other words, there are real choices to be made about the best way to organise both the provision of specific goods and services and the economy as whole. Neoliberal forms of describing and theorising about economies and states deny the existence of these choices. But they can never do so successfully, due in part to the internal contradictions within these representations, and, more generally, due to the fact that these representations themselves form part of a constant struggle to secure and maintain hegemony.

Notes

1.   We should, perhaps, note that he based his argument on Cohen's (1989) study which found a low number of *convictions* for corporate illegalities (but he did not use the studies of Clinard and Yeager 1980) which found a higher number of convictions and also examined *nolo contendere* pleas. Further, Mann has shown how the prosecution *process* itself in such cases gets to be pre-empted (Mann 1985; see also generally Fisse and Braithwaite 1993), and one must add that there is a difficulty of even detecting some forms of corporate crime.

2. In Britain, privatisation sales were used to lower the Public Spending Borrowing Requirement — Whitfield (1992: 141-151). However, by 1993 this had soared again. A similar argument, the need to slash the national debt, was used to justify the sale of 21 state companies in France including Banque Nationale de Paris, insurance company Assurances Generales de France and drugs group Rhone-Poulenc and the Elf-Aquitaine oil group (*Globe and Mail*, Thursday, 27 May 1993: B4). In fact, pre-privatisation France was in better shape than privatising Britain in terms of its government debt (in 1991), current account deficit (1992), although worse off in terms of interest payments as a percentage of revenue (*Globe and Mail*, Saturday, 24 April 1992: B4).

3. Given the volume of, and variety in, these bodies of literature, only indicative references can be noted here. However, each of the following texts contains contemporary critiques of aspects of neoliberal arguments, as useful bibliographies pertaining to these critiques. For a critique of mainstream versions of the 'science' of economics, see Lawson (1997); for an excellent overview of the relationships between economics on the one hand, and sociology and politics on the other, (and of the origins and natures of organisational economics), see Rowlinson (1997). On 'Capitalism as Market Economy', see Hutton (1995), Sayer (1995); on describing, theorising about, and understanding the 'Organisation of Contemporary Business Firms', see Clegg (1990), Hassard and Parker (1993), Reed (1992), Reed and Hughes (1992); on 'Politics, Markets and Regulation', see Hutton (1995), Jessop (1982, 1990b), Kelly et al. (1997), Sayer (1995). And on the question of externalities, see O'Riordan (1997), Ekins and Max-Neef (1992).

4. Furthermore, current legal and financial arrangements give capitalist enterprises many advantages over workers' cooperatives. For a useful discussion of current arrangements and suggestions of alternatives that could benefit cooperatives see Doucialogos (1990).

2 Constructing and Conceptualising Capitalisms: Beyond Neoliberalism

Introduction

Any study purporting to deal with corporate crime and regulation in the last decade of the twentieth century must address questions about the nature of states and economies within which corporations operate. More specifically, and pointedly, a key contemporary issue concerns the continuing viability of the nation-state. Legislation originating in national (federal) or provincial (state) levels has been the main vehicle for controlling the offences of corporations in Western democracies. However partial and inadequate regulation has been, there is no comparable countervailing body with the motivation or ability to oversee the vast agglomerations of privilege and power known as corporations. Recently, moreover, the nation-state has been undermined both externally and internally. Internally, ethnic tensions, the rise of interest group politics, increasing unemployment and lower standards of living have led to unprecedented levels of cynicism and discontent with politicians and politics in major Western democracies. Externally, the power of transnational corporate bodies has grown exponentially, fuelled by technological advances freeing capital from national or temporal boundaries, the corporate take-over frenzy of the 1980s, and the proliferation of free trading zones. These new mega-corporations are not responsible to any nation-state, as they do not need a geographic centre or headquarters in the traditional sense, and operate around the world moving capital and resources with lightening speed. The ability of the weakened nation-state to handle the reinforced power of private capital, and the viability of the nation-state in an era of free trading zones are critically important issues to address.

In this chapter we develop a critique of neoliberal arguments about state, economy and society, building upon the elements set out in the previous chapter. We argue that the interpretations of state, economy and society developed by neoliberalism actually obscure more than they reveal. Yet they need to be addressed not simply in terms of their empirical and theoretical adequacy, but also in the context of a more general, and partially successful, attempt to construct a new capitalist hegemony, a hegemony in which the structural power of capital (particularly in its transnational manifestations) is augmented. In examining the extent to which this hegemony is only partially successful, we also provide alternative interpretations of state, economy, society. These alternative interpretations, which draw upon structural Marxism, and particular readings of the work of Gramsci, Foucault, and some contemporary regulation theorists, will be further developed through the course of the text, as we turn to focus specifically upon corporate crime and the chemical industry.

States, Capitals and Hegemony

Central to the theoretical position that we develop in this text is the notion of hegemony, and a particular reading of the work of the Italian Marxist, Antonio Gramsci. However, both the work of Gramsci in general, and the concept of hegemony in particular, have been so widely and variously appropriated (and in places distorted) that it is necessary to begin by stating explicitly how we use, and understand, the concept of hegemony.

The reading of Gramsci from which our concept of hegemony is drawn is a materialist one, in some ways closer to the development of his work presented in Anderson (1977), Jessop et al. (1988), Morera (1990) and Sears and Mooers (1994), than to that found in Laclau and Mouffe (1985) and Hall (1984). In this materialist reading, the logically primary concept in Gramsci's work is that of the historical block. This has two major meanings. First, '[s]tructures and superstructures form an "historical block" ... the complex, contradictory and discordant ensemble of the social relations of production' (Gramsci 1971: 366). This is no simple reproduction of Marx's mechanical model since, for Gramsci, there is a 'necessary reciprocity between structure and superstructure reciprocity which is precisely the real dialectical process' (Gramsci 1975: 2:1052, cited in Morera 1990: 140). Thus, for Gramsci, the historical block will play a key role in structuring other relations in any social formation but its very functioning will also produce contradictions and conflicts. The historical block is a relatively permanent 'organic' or deep structure, which, of course, changes and develops, but must be distinguished from more superficial, transitory or 'conjunctural' relations (Gramsci 1971: 177). The term 'historical block' also refers to an historical grouping of social actors who have been organised and led by a fraction of the class who play a key role in the extraction of the surplus in 'the decisive nucleus of the economy' (Gramsci 1975: 3:1591, cited in Morera 1990: 168). This fraction needs to have persuaded other members of its class, other dominating classes and other professional groupings to accept its moral and political leadership and to both accept and contribute to its mode of governance. It will need to organise the key social relations in a way that is compatible with its rule and to shape institutions so that the everyday life of the members of society will not frustrate its goals. This grouping, while not as enduring as 'the ensemble of the social relations of production', is also likely to persist over a significant period of time — particularly in contemporary societies, when it is constituted in and through the state — and it may rule in a number of different ways. Its leadership may simply involve the management of society and the coercive domination of subaltern groups. It may also involve 'ethical-political' leadership or hegemony. Under these conditions the members of an historical block expect their ideas, their understanding of the world, and their specification of historical possibilities to become the general common sense so that subordinate classes will, to a considerable extent, formulate their interests within the categories of the dominant ideology (Gramsci 1971: 180-195). The ability of the members of the historical block to set this agenda will depend upon their degree of dominance over mainstream social institutions, including those involving education, communication, mental and physical health, political organisation, the means of production (all involving disciplinary practices by which subjects are socially constituted, distributed to different tasks, and empowered to fulfill these in an appropriate manner) and apparatuses of repression. Hegemony involves:

> the entire complex of practical and theoretical activities within which the ruling class not only justifies and maintains its dominance, but manages to win the active consent of those over whom it rules.
>
> (Gramsci 1971: 244)

Hegemony is only one form of rule, and, although Gramsci himself tends to work with bipolar oppositions (Anderson 1977), it not useful to construe it as simply the opposite of coercion. Moreover, it is quite possible for a society to oscillate between periods where hegemony exists — when there exists a 'national-popular collective will' (Gramsci 1971: 130) — and periods where the historical block works primarily through domination. Indeed, 'true' hegemony could only be achieved in a democratic classless society when the material roots of contradictions and conflicts are eliminated and where differences between groups are relatively inconsequential.

In a hegemonised class society a wide range of disparate activities and disparate social groups are articulated together under a misleading unifying (national) ideology which more or less successfully represents them as all partaking of the same (national) essence (Laclau 1977). This, however, is a very delicate operation. In Foucault's terms:

It would not be possible for power relations to exist without points of insubordination which, by definition, are means of escape. Accordingly, every intensification, every extension of power relations to make the insubordinate submit can only result in the limits of power. The latter reaches its final term either in a type of action which reduces the other to total impotence ... or by a confrontation with those whom one governs and their transformation into their adversaries.

(Foucault 1982: 225)

Institutions do not merely express the interests and ideas of the historical block: they have their own histories and their own truths, adaptable to more than one purpose, and are themselves sites of struggle.

Now, in the United States, for example, there has emerged an historical block that includes corporate capital, a professional and technocratic elite, and those state functionaries associated with economic policy and/or the security state (Weinstein 1968; Greenberg 1971; Wilson 1976; Lustig 1982; Sklar 1988). More generally, each of these social groups comprising this elite work according to their own social logic but are unified by their dependency upon each other and also through shared practices, programmes, utopias and rhetorics. All subscribe to, develop, and promote an abstract and manipulative mode of thinking about nature and the social world. To some extent, these are viewed as homogeneous fields apprehendable through prices, physical measurement and quantification, and through the specification of population attributes. Knowledge of these is seen as an aid to the control and remaking of society and nature.

However, even in the United States, the archetypical liberal society, the historical block has always had to deal with the threat of counter-hegemonic movements, thus the tendency for struggle and conflict is always present. Since subordinate groups are never completely powerless one would expect 'the block' to work at fragmenting them, through repression, by creating divisions through limited reform with the selective incorporation of some personnel into the hegemonic block and some cultural symbols into its ideology. Hegemony always involves the fragmentation of counter-hegemonic groupings. In addition, attempts may be made at achieving a 'passive revolution' (Gramsci 1971: 119-20; Sassoon 1987: 204-217) in which some of the demands of subordinate groups are acknowledged but deradicalised through procedures and through discourses that modify marginally, but crucially sustain, both the overall conception of group and societal interests held by the groups comprising the historical block and, relatedly, the preexisting modes of hegemonic dominance. This, however, is a perilous path because, as Pat O'Malley has argued, if we examine relations of ruling we find 'the imbrication of resistance and rule, the contradictions and tensions that this melding generates, and the subterranean practices of government, consequently required to stabilise rule' (O'Malley 1996: 311). This means not only that government may have an 'incorporative relationship with resistance' but that 'processes of resistance [may be] carried into the subjugating programme of rule along with the appropriated forms' (O'Malley 1996: 323).

Now, although it is true that Marxism often assigned too great a role to the sovereign state and to juridico-discursive power, it is important not to discount these completely, substituting for them disciplinarity and governance, but rather to analyse specific articulations of the 'triangle sovereignty-discipline-government' (Foucault 1979c: 19; and see also Foucault 1982: 222). After all, *contra* the tendency of Gramsci and some of his more recent followers to overemphasise the 'war of position' at the expense of 'wars of manoeuvre' (Gramsci 1971: 170, 246; Hall 1984: 168-169), we would argue that it is better to conceive of hegemony as always entailing both wars of manoeuvre and wars of position (Anderson 1977; Jessop et al. 1988; Sears and Mooers 1994) which occur on 'ready made' social terrains that all social groups find to some extent intractable. No social group, no class, has ever made society in its image, nor controlled it. Although members of a power block can realise their will better than most of us can, and often at our expense, the goal of social fabrication according to some detailed blueprint is, of course, a modernist phantasy.

Within the theoretical perspective being utilised and developed in this text, we argue that social relations are irreducible to subjectivities or interpersonal relations alone. At the same time, social relations are dependent upon, and sometimes transformed by, the forms of understandings that we develop to describe them, and by our capacity to have a reflexive relation to these understandings (Pearce 1989a). However, the inflection given to mentalities and techniques or discourses (and, hence, development of these) will not depend upon an internal logic alone but also on the nature and development of the other social relations with which they are imbricated (see Chapter 5). After all, discursive formations include both discourses and their various conditions of existence, and, as Foucault argued consistently throughout his work, the latter are only ever partially understood by individual actors. This refusal to ontologically privilege the human subject does not entail its replacement with some self-perpetuating structure or some totality wherein the economic is dominant in the first or last instance. Relations of production are always articulated with different legal and organisational forms, and are affected by different ideologies and practices and, hence, reference to these must play a role in any adequate explanation.[1] The best that even a dominant block can do is to modify a pre-existing social order in such a way that it can maintain or increase its comparative advantage over other groups. For example, as we discuss below, currently predominant forms of economic, social and political organising — monetarism, privatisation, and the development of the workfare state — may have increased 'the structural power of capital' (Gill and Law 1993), but these forms of organizing can never give dominant blocks complete control of our societies.

Thus, although new modes of governance always help 'constitute new sectors of reality and make new fields of existence practicable' (Miller and Rose 1990: 7), it is never simply a matter of realizing some 'programmer's dream'. The 'real' always resists programming, hence, of necessity, 'the programmer's world is one of constant experiment, invention, failure, critique and adjustment' (Miller and Rose 1990: 14). In the US, the power block has been confronted with a number of crises and evidence of its own hubris, not least in the immediate and chronic effects of nuclear and chemical production. These have involved problems for the social logics of corporate capital, science/technology, and the security state. Thus legitimation crises may be precipitated by an inability to contain tensions that are generated in a wide range of contexts. Hegemony refers to far more than class relations and the phenomena directly associated with their reproduction. There may be conflict over class relations, in the sphere of reproduction of the social or technical division of labour, over morality, over what interests should be secured by state activity, over whether the quality of life being made available to individuals is of such value that any sacrifices are justified by the related rewards, and so on. Such conflicts or tensions have, at times, engendered a more general questioning as to whether corporate capitalism can deliver what it promises, whether the American state can act in the interests of all citizens as it claims, and whether developments in science-technology necessarily entail the progress for humanity which is represented as its very rationale. The power block has responded to these (real or potential) conflicts with important changes in the way some aspects of economic life are regulated and in the content of some collective representations.

In general, the kinds of relatively autonomous spaces that must be governed at a distance determine the outer limits of the 'art of the possible'. There is a need for 'a mutuality between what is desirable and what can be made possible through the calculated activities of political forces' (Rose and Miller 1992: 182). What is at stake, but remains under-theorised in the governmentality literature, is the nature and fate of such forces.

Although such forces will be, in part, an effect of extant modes of governance, these will not be adequately understood through the concepts of rights and personhood to be found in the language of liberal political economy. For, while eighteenth and nineteenth century rulers may have been confronted 'with subjects equipped with rights and interests that must not be interdicted by politics' (Rose 1993: 289), only some rights were, or ever are, acknowledged, as any analysis of the struggles of workers to unionise makes clear. Equally important is the need to develop the concept of rights by deploying the Hohfeldian distinctions between right-duty, liberty-'no-right', power-liability, and immunity-disability (Hohfeld 1913; and see Woodiwiss 1998).

For example, if we wish to analyse the social forces at work within the US economy, it is important to recognise the significance of the fact that most enterprises within it are (legally privileged) limited liability corporations, and that the conduct of employees, both individually and collectively, are legally severely circumscribed. As we have briefly indicated in the previous chapter, the corporation is made up of four or five elements. The corporation itself is a trading company, the general purposes of which are set out in its initial (and often rather general) memorandum of association. For legal purposes it is construed as having its own legal personality, so that: it has an existence independent of its members and it continues to exist until steps are taken explicitly to terminate it; it can sue and be sued in its own name with respect to contracts, torts, breaches of trust, and crimes; it can sue or be sued by its own members; it can own property (Perrott 1981: 83-4). Its shareholders can buy or sell stakes in it or other companies and are entitled to shares of profits, but, other than the monies that they have invested in a particular company, are personally immune from the consequences of its actions or its debts. Its managers are responsible for the day to day activities of a corporation's factories, chemical plants, supermarket stores, and so on, and have the freedom and power to organise these, as well as a duty to ensure consistency with lawful company goals (including appropriate instructions to workers regarding their duties). Its directors are legally responsible for determining its policy goals, organisation and the kind of business it does, and thus have the power and the liberty, subject to their duties to their shareholders, to use assets appropriately. They may do so by buying a factory or another company, or by selling any such assets and by reinvesting them, for example, in speculative currency markets. They (and, in the US, dominant shareholders) owe fiduciary duties to the company and its shareholders and may also be liable for some claims by some of the company's creditors (Sugarman 1990: 23). Finally, there are the corporations' lower level employees. Insofar as their actions can create vicarious liability for the corporation they are part of it. However, they cannot commit the corporation to new lines of action and, hence, are its hands rather than its brains (Leigh 1969).

The corporation and its officers have the liberty and power to hire and fire workers and to instruct them to perform lawful tasks and to say when workers can have access to the factory (hence the lawfulness of lockouts). On the other hand, workers have no right, individually or collectively, to be hired, to use company property, nor to refuse lawful managerial commands. Whereas capital has the liberty and power to dispose of its means of production, workers have no right to challenge such a decision even though they are personally 'liable' to become unemployed. Furthermore, they have a duty not to interfere with a company's lawful activities and the company has a right to sue them for the consequences of any such interference. Any particular regulatory regime, then, will facilitate some, while inhibiting other forms of social arrangements, not least those involving class relations.

Obviously the state plays a key role in these and other social arrangements (Jessop 1982, 1990a). State activities are preconditions for the risk-taking activities of entrepreneurs (Lowi 1993: 20-2). The state helps to constitute capital, commodity, commercial and residential property markets. It produces different kinds of human capital and constitutes labour markets; it also regulates the employment contract. Further, it plays a role in constituting economic enterprises through specifying rules of liability and possibly specifying rules of incorporation. These are put in place by regulatory instances which include, but are not exhausted by, regulatory agencies.

Such regulatory agencies develop decision procedures, regulatory knowledges, policy objectives, systems of rewards and sanctions. These, in turn, are affected by an agency's formal organisational structure, modes of training and discipline, approved techniques of calculation, and by its segmented practices and local collective representations, but also by the ways that people speak to themselves and to each other about their work and its parameters. Personnel will also have a relation to other professional, political, and ethical practices. This creates contexts where, as human actors, they can act in innovative ways which may or may not be defined by their superiors as diverging from the organisation's basic assumptions. They may well be sanctioned for doing so. Both agencies and regulatory agents have some relative autonomy but both, like the more general 'populations', are subject to Foucault's triangle of 'sovereignty-discipline-government'.

This relative autonomy of regulatory agencies is usefully expressed by Mahon, who has argued that such regulatory agencies may often:

> constitute a 'special case' of (the) unequal structure of representation through which class hegemony is produced. Like other parts of the state apparatus, these institutions represent the interests of a particular fraction — but in a particular way, as they are effectively combined with the long-term interests of the hegemonic fraction. That is, they simultaneously represent and regulate. Such agencies derive their special status from their origins in an issue that contains a particular kind of threat to the fundamental relations of a capitalist formation.
>
> (Mahon 1979: 154)

Marx's discussion of the transition to factory production, based upon a shift from the extraction of absolute to relative surplus value in late eighteenth and nineteenth century England, is illustrative here. In his discussions of struggles around the introduction of early Factory Acts in England, Marx documents the efforts of domestic social reformers and the relationships of these efforts to upheavals in continental Europe, widespread employer opposition to the introduction of factory regulation, and clear conflicts amongst different groups of employers. He also shows that, in the very attempts to impose minimal conditions for workers, the state played a crucial role in forcing the qualitative leaps in the nature of capital investment and concentration of production that were crucial to the development of the factory system — this effecting the real rather than the formal subsumption of labour. Yet, 'for all that, capital never becomes reconciled to such changes — and this is admitted over and over again by its own representatives — except "under the pressure of a general Act of Parliament"' (Marx [1867] 1976: 610).

In imposing upon capital conditions of production that were required for what, in retrospect, was a crucial shift in the development of capitalism, the state helped to establish the conditions of existence and further development of capitalism while apparently acting against the interests of individual employers. It is no casual turn of phrase, then, when Marx refers to this period of early factory regulation (1846-1867) as both 'epoch-making' and constituting the arrival of 'the millennium' (Marx [1867] 1976: 395).

Regulation, then, is often the outcome of conflict, negotiation and (class) compromise, an outcome which represents an attempt to manage, alter, and neutralise conflict, though these ends are never achieved in a once-and-for-all fashion (Mahon 1979: 160). Thus, regulation is best viewed as a process within which 'agency, struggle and resistance' are intrinsic (Snider 1991).[2] Moreover, understanding regulatory agencies as part of an unequal structure of representation allows us to avoid the inadequacies of capture theses of regulation, in either their liberal or instrumental Marxist versions. Regulation, and regulatory agencies, are crucial apparatuses within 'the dynamic equilibrium of compromise that organises the interests of various social forces around the core [i.e., long term economic and political] interests of the hegemonic fraction' (Mahon 1979: 165-6). Of course, the *modus operandi* of any particular agency is affected by the nature of its mandate and by the resources available to it. These in turn are affected by the current constellation of political forces, by the state's potentially contradictory tasks, by the agency's relationship to other state apparatuses, particularly the apparatus used to monitor its performance, and by the agency's relationship to its object of regulation.

These complex relationships between states and capital, and the functions of regulatory agencies in terms of both representation and regulation, are partly illustrated in the context of the chemical industry, certainly as it has developed within the UK, US, and other advanced industrialised states. The chemical industry is at once both integral to national economies, but a focus for oppositional movements within national polities, and thus in the latter respect a source of potential legitimation crises which require (always precarious) management by states and regulatory agencies.

Perhaps most obviously, and an enduring theme of this text, is that the chemical industry is inextricably associated with risks to safety, health and the environment. Such risks span the history of the industry, from the scrotal cancers which resulted from early attempts to separate oils in shale works, the bladder cancers associated with the first industrial chemistry of dye-working, the carcinogenic effects of exposures to benzene and asbestos, not to mention numerous other carcinogenic substances related to chemicals production (Lappe 1991), through to the recent acknowledgements of the environmental effects of CFCs (in the Montreal Protcol) and of possible hazards in the development of biotechnologies (Goodman and Redclift 1991). In technological terms, a certain level of risk is inherent in the very products and processes which are integral to the operation of chemicals companies, yet such risks have been magnified and augmented through the particular ways in which these operations have been, and are, organised. Further, the significance of such risks relates as much to the industrial pervasiveness and the international scale of the activities of the industry. It is hardly surprising that the chemical industry has been, and remains, at the centre of environmental, safety and health concerns, in both acute and chronic forms, and that a wide range of its activities have been associated consistently with public concerns, and have been the object of activism around human and environmental health and safety. Such activism has pressured states into the development and enforcement of regulation. There is no doubt that regulation by nation-states has attenuated some of the most injurious aspects of the activities of this industry; there is also little doubt, as we shall see, that these forms of regulation are inadequate, and, indeed, regulation has not become, over time, progressively more effective in any linear sense.

At the same time, chemicals industries are integral to national economies. They are 'closely interlocked with every other industrial sector' (Pettigrew 1985: 59; Chenier 1986: 8; see also Hays 1973: 6-7). About 60 per cent of the industry's products are further modified (Chenier 1986: 5), so that the industry has been referred to as 'the handmaiden of other sectors', and as 'industry's industry' (Ilgen 1983: 650). Chemicals industries are, therefore, critical to, and pervasive within, complex industrialised economies (Lever 1986; Stopford and Dunning 1983: 99; Wei et al 1979: 298; Witcoff and Reuben 1980: 14). And given this pivotal role in national economies, it is unsurprising that national states have played crucial roles in the development of chemicals industries (Ilgen 1983: 655; see also Grant et al. 1988). This role has been discussed in various works — mainly historical — on the international and national chemical industries. Of particular interest to scholars has been the relationship between IG Farben and the Nazi leadership in the Third Reich (for example, Borkin 1978; Hayes 1989), and the role of chemicals companies in the development of agents of chemical and biological warfare. While some wish to dismiss these activities without any reference to the role of particular companies nor benefits to companies or industry (Crone 1986), or simply to explain them in terms of external, state compulsion (Aftalion 1991), they much more usefully indicate particular manifestations of enduring and, from the industry's point of view, crucial historical relationships. Certainly, the particular form of the state-industry relationship in the context of chemicals clearly raises contemporary issues, such as how we conceive of regulation, and how effective state regulation can be (see Chapters 7, 8, and 9). In this respect, it is important to understand the intimate role that nation-states have played in the development of the sector, through securing and maintaining the conditions of chemicals production and use.[3]

It is also worth noting that the state may play a crucial role in the development of the industry, even where it appears to be acting against the interest of particular corporations within that sector. The development of more progressive forms of regulation around safety, health and environmental protection is a case in point.

The past two decades have seen numerous instances of international restructuring of productive activity on the part of the genuinely transnational corporations which dominate most of the constituent businesses of the chemicals industries.[4] Thus, most commentators agree that it is now possible to speak of an emerging 'new international division of labour', with high value-added speciality chemicals increasingly being produced in the home, Western states, whilst the production of bulk chemicals has been consistently shifted towards 'eastern Europe, the Middle East, and Third World countries such as Mexico, Brazil, and South Korea' (Ilgen 1983: 659; see also GMB 1983: 20; Grant et al. 1988: 46; Heaton 1996; McCloskey 1996; Pettigrew 1985: 61). Speciality production tends to be environmentally cleaner, less resource intensive, and requiring less, but more highly skilled, labour. In general, bulk production has almost the opposite characteristics.

Now there seem to have been two key sources of impetus for these generalised changes in the international structure of production. First, the oil shocks of 1973 and 1979, which forced many chemical industries to engage in massive restructuring in the face of both raised costs of production and a crisis of over-capacity due to worldwide recessions amongst the industries that are its key customers (GMB 1983; Grant et al. 1988; Molle 1988; Spitz 1988). Thus, many companies began to develop their speciality businesses at the expense of their bulk, oil-based forms of production. A second impetus providing a rationale for relocating declining, and increasingly less significant, bulk production away from advanced industrialised economies was the development of more protective forms of safety, health and environmental regulation. While we would not wish to overstate the significance of the 'export of hazard', as this phenomenon has been labelled, it is clearly one factor in explaining the shift of more hazardous forms of production. Moreover, any relocation that has occurred has been facilitated by the global emergence of the key legal (infrastructural) supports of capitalist production, a trend for which there is more general evidence, as outlined below.

Now, this shift from bulk towards speciality production in 'home' economies is significant, because the latter are the high value-added areas of economic activity, that is, the areas through which profitability will be maintained and developed. If the development of regulation by the state was one factor in influencing the development of such production, as it clearly has been, then this is an interesting case of regulation working against the immediate interests of particular corporations, but for the long term interests of those companies, and indeed the sector as a whole. It is a clear illustration of regulation operating in an hegemonic fashion.

One further consequence of this shift in production should be noted. The chemical industry is characterised by higher than average levels of research and development expenditures (Witcoff and Reuben 1980: 21; and see Chenier 1986: 21-2). One calculation claims that over 20 per cent of 'scientists and engineers' working in manufacturing industries across OECD countries are employed in chemicals (Pettigrew 1985: 57); and the world's largest chemical industry accounts for 10 per cent of all research and development expenditures in the US (Chenier 1986: 21). In this respect, it is a paradigmatic science-technological sector. And within this sector, perhaps more than any other save the nuclear industry (itself even more implicated within the warfare/security state), the technocratic scientism which is central to technocratic elites is exemplified. Within this technocratic scientism, scientific discourse becomes articulated onto, or gets transposed into, metanarratives of progress (Lyotard 1984). Not infrequently, we find more restricted claims of scientific expertise (Killingsworth and Palmer 1992) extended beyond their legitimate purview (Pearce and Tombs 1989).

Moreover, these research and development expenditures — and thus the role of scientific expertise — will remain significant as companies in traditional chemicals-producing states shift their focus of activities and attention away from bulk chemicals and towards speciality chemicals (Bertin and Wyatt 1988: 102). At the same time it is also worth noting that, in the key speciality areas of agrochemicals and pharmaceuticals, pre-marketing testing requirements (emerging from safety, health and environmental regulatory concerns) have increased the statutory level of research and development expenditures for new products; and, indeed, such testing requirements are increasingly being extended to substances and products in use (on pharmaceuticals, see de Wolf 1988: 223; Grant et al 1987: 48-9, 1988: 272-306; Thornber 1986: 220; and on agrochemicals, see Heaton 1986: 237-8; Ilgen 1983: 652; Watterson 1988b: 17). As in the case of the pharmaceutical industry (Braithwaite 1984), there are clearly good reasons for suggesting that high research and development expenditures produce motivations for corporate crime as corporations seek to recover significant 'up front' costs.

Returning to our more general level of analysis, we argue that regulation is always productive and implicitly moral (Hunt 1993), even in the case of regulatory instances which rely strongly upon the power of markets and the coercive effect of civil courts through actions initiated by private legal subjects, and where regulatory agencies are reduced to an advisory role. Thus, the recent deregulation associated with the 'discourses of enterprise' has not meant that problematic areas of economic and social life were 'rectified' merely by removing extant forms of intervention, but that these have given rise 'to all manners of programmes for reforming economic activity in order to construct such a virtuous system, and to a plethora of new regulatory technologies that have sought to give effect to them' (Miller and Rose 1990: 25). In other words, as well as deregulation there has been re-regulation. Indeed, the property rights to be found within all such market systems depend upon custom and tradition, the action of state bureaucracies, and of the legal system (Hazard 1993: 238; Pashukhanis 1978). The latter is not merely enabling but is also constitutive and depends on the 'myths' of sovereignty and consistency (Hirst 1979), and the reality of coercion (Pearce 1989a). Furthermore, some form of displacement of free markets as both an organising and regulative principle, is, in fact, the historical norm. It is modified through oligopolisation (viewed negatively as in Adams and Brock 1986) or as a condition of viability (as in Crooks 1993), state regulation (Kolko 1962), nationalisation (Fine 1990b) or through networks (Powell 1990). As Sayer has recently demonstrated, not only has there never existed, but there cannot exist, any economy which is adequately characterised by the term 'free market'. While 'the ideological notion of latent or implicit markets which only need freeing figures strongly in neoliberal rhetoric' (Sayer 1995: 104), this contrasts with the overwhelming empirical and theoretical evidence attesting to markets as social constructions. The creation, maintenance and development of 'markets' requires coordinated, extensive and ongoing involvement of the state and other institutions (Sayer 1995).

The nation-state, then, is a set of apparatuses through which a power block constantly seeks to secure, maintain and extend its dominance over an economy, polity and society. Moreover, regulatory agencies also function as hegemonic apparatuses. Yet the struggle for dominance is never finally achieved; conflict and struggle are constant, if at times more or less present threats. Any real economy, polity and society has dynamics which are independent of, or not subject to the rational ordering of, the dominant power block. In this respect, we need to turn to arguments regarding a recent series of significant changes in the nature of industrial societies, changes which are said by many to mark a new phase of capitalist development (even, for some, a stage of post-capitalism), changes which render the efforts of states, regulatory agencies and oppositional social forces increasingly redundant. This 'new orthodoxy', or 'common sense' (Harman 1996), now widespread in political, cultural, popular and academic contexts (Hirst and Thompson 1996: 1, 4), proclaims, in its strongest variants, the emergence of a new, globalised economic order. And this is an economic order which bears a striking affinity with many of the prescriptions of neoliberalism regarding the primacy of markets, capitalist production, and the minimised role of nation-states.

Globalisation, Capital and Nation-States

What we want to suggest here, is that the emergence of arguments and claims around globalisation themselves represent part of a project of hegemonic reconstruction. While many of these arguments and claims seem to us to be either misinterpretations, exaggerations, or ideological claims about the creation of something new, when what is being described is actually the old in different forms, certain aspects of globalisation rhetoric seem incontrovertible. While this is not the place to enter into a detailed critique of large and rapidly growing bodies of literature around various aspects of globalisation, there are several observations we need to make.

First, there is no doubt that even without accepting some of the more exaggerated claims around globalisation, enormous class and social power accrues to transnational corporations in particular, and to capital in general, and to the extent that arguments for globalisation reflect real trends, then this class and social power is likely to be augmented. This observation is particularly the case in the chemical industry, given the historical and continuing dominance of this area of activity by large, multinational corporations, operating oligopolistically, within a highly strategic sector.

Thus, it is important to emphasise, that even without any reference to globalisation, and the implications of any such trend(s) for the relative power of transnational corporations and national-states, that the chemical industry is one historically dominated by large, genuinely multinational operations (Wooding et al. 1997: 126-7, 137). Thus, despite the chemicals industries consisting of a large number of companies (Chenier 1986: 5; Ilgen 1983: 652; Lever 1986; *Chemistry in Europe*, November 1996: 1), there is a significant presence of enormous, transnational actors. True, the degree of concentration varies greatly across sectors within the industry (Thornber 1986: 172-3; Weir 1986: 7, 111), so that some claim 'producer dominance' cannot be assumed and is notoriously difficult to quantify (Comanor 1986; de Jong 1988), but it is clear that enormous economic and social power accrues to the world's largest chemicals producers. And this is a power which partly reproduces itself through the maintenance of costs of market entry which are so high that 'only governments, oil companies, and other giant enterprises can find the necessary capital' (Witcoff and Reuben 1980: 28; Tandy 1987: 148-9). Other socially organised barriers to entry are control over access to resource supply, scientific and technical expertise, exclusion by contract, systems of government franchise, and exclusion by patent protection (Wei et al. 1979: 48; see also Bertin and Wyatt 1988: 123-126).

Certainly it is the case that, with the possible exception of Japan, 'a limited number of giant multinational chemical companies play a key role throughout the world' (Heaton 1996: 92). Moreover, as Grant and his colleagues have noted, despite this being an industry of 'giant companies ... trading on an international scale', the 'number of key decision makers in the industry, even on a global level, is relatively small', so that these meet and engage in debate frequently. Thus, one has an 'international industry which is able to function as a "global village" in which it is possible to develop effective policy networks' (Grant et al. 1988: 7; see also Boons 1992). Thus,

> it is becoming more and more necessary to ask whether the concept of the firm or company should not be replaced by that of the group, that is, a set of distinct legal entities controlled by a central economic unit calculating on an overall basis ... By means of (minority) shareholdings, interlocking directorships and personal ties, groups are able to control larger amounts of human and financial resources than concentration measures would suggest.
>
> (de Jong 1988: 10)

On more recent changes in the industry, then, the general wave of mergers in the US and UK (which we noted in the previous chapter) was also reflected in the chemicals industries, so that in the mid-1980s, and then again at the end of the eighties and beginning of the 1990s, there occurred two massive waves of mergers and acquisitions throughout the industry (de Jong 1988: 6; *Chemistry & Industry* 18 March 1991: 188; Heaton 1996: 92-3). During this latter period in particular there also occurred a proliferation of joint ventures and strategic alliances across the industry through which larger companies have sought to regain market power while spreading risk and profits. That is, so called 'new' organisational forms have been more significant in this sector than in most others (Tombs 1995a). It is of further interest that much of the more recent wave of merger, acquisition and alliance activity has occurred amongst the largest transnational actors within speciality, high-value added businesses (see for example, *Chemistry & Industry*, 4 March 1996: 173; 2 December 1996: 921; McCloskey 1996: 96).

Given many of the characteristic features of the industry — the sheer size and scale of many chemicals companies, their dominance in home markets and the role of many chemicals companies as national champions, the restricted nature of entry to oligopolistic, science-technological markets, particular forms of state-industry relationships, the interrelationships between key actors within the largest companies on an international scale, the vulnerability of companies to recessions and in particular to oil prices — it is hardly surprising that the chemicals industries have a long history of activity bordering upon the illegal. This includes documented histories of: illegally unsafe products, from household cleaners (Birkin and Price 1989) to food additives (Lang and Clutterbuck 1991), causing acute and chronic ill-health on the part of consumers; financial illegalities, including price-fixing and tax offences (Ross 1980); involvement in the perjury leading to the resignation and prosecution of senior EPA administrators (the so-called 'Sewergate' affair, see Barnett 1994; Szasz 1986b); and, of course, those activities which are the focus of, and considered throughout, this text — namely, death, injury and ill-health caused to workers and populations through occupational and environmental health and safety practices and offences.

Moreover, other sectors with which the chemical industry is most intimately related, within which some of the largest chemicals companies operate, and from which major corporate actors also have significant chemicals industry interests, namely the oil and pharmaceuticals industries, are also amongst the most criminogenic (Braithwaite 1984, 1993; Carson 1982; Finlay 1996; Peppin 1995; Woolfson et al. 1996); indeed, oil and pharmaceuticals were two of the three most significantly represented industries in Clinard and Yeager's study of recorded violations (Clinard and Yeager 1980).

As we discuss any changes associated with globalisation, then, it is important to bear in mind that some industries have for some time operated on a genuinely international, even global basis; and that this has partly been a consequence of, and partly reinforced, the structural power of the industry. Thus, some of the features associated with globalisation are hardly new. Yet there is a sense in which some of the power of Transnational and Multinational Corporations derives from the proliferation of globalisation rhetoric itself. Thus, our second general observation on globalisation arguments is that they form part of a more general struggle for hegemony, within which they exert power. That is, the idea of globalisation has become a very powerful one, not in any 'free-floating' sense, but as it is propagated in forms that are linked to certain agents, institutions and practices. If we view globalisation as 'hyper-liberalism' (Cox 1993: 272), it is possible to link this idea to the claim by some that there has occurred a conscious process of hegemony (re)construction, key agents of which have been large multinational companies, right wing governments and politicians, particularly from the US and Britain, and right wing academics (Gill 1990; Cox 1993). As Cox has pointed out, their ideas have developed within such unofficial bodies as:

> the Trilateral Commission, the Bilderburg conferences, the Club of Rome, the more esoteric Mont Pelerin Society among others — and then endorsed through

official consensus making agencies like the OECD. A new doctrine defined the tasks of states in relaunching capitalist development out of the depression of the 1970s. There was, in the words of a blue-ribbon OECD committee, a 'narrow path of growth' bounded on one side by the need to encourage private investment by increasing profit margins, and bounded on the other by the need to avoid kindling inflation.

The government-business alliance formed to advance along this narrow path ruled out corporative-type solutions like negotiated wage and price policies and also the expansion of public investment. It placed primary emphasis on restoring the confidence of business in government and in practice acknowledged that welfare and employment commitments made in the framework of the post-war social contact would have to take second place.

(Cox 1993: 266)

By the early 1980s, there had emerged a consensus:

about the needs of the world economy and appropriate economic policies for developing countries. Reflecting the demise of Keynesianism and the ascendancy of supply-side economics in the US and some parts of Europe, the consensus ... was based on the twin ideas of the state as the provider of a regulatory framework for private sector exchanges (but not as a *director* of those exchanges), and of the world economy as open to movements of goods, services, and capital, if not labour.

(Wade 1996: 5)

Thus globalisation tendencies are symbiotically linked to deflationary macro-economic policies (Elliott 1996). Of course, such policies, in the name of 'adjustment', have been rigorously pursued within many national states under pressure from the IMF, the World Bank, the G-7, the OECD, the Bank for International Resettlement, the European Bank for Reconstruction and Development, and even, so it has recently been claimed, from Unctad (Cox 1994; Gill 1994, 1995; Gowan 1995; Jackson and Price 1994; Nelson 1996; Petras and Morley 1990; Pacific Asia Resource Center 1994; Price 1994; Tran 1996; Wade 1996; Whitfield 1992; World Bank 1994). Moreover, the role of such institutions embraces normative as well as material elements (Pauly 1994; Price 1994; Young 1995). Thus, more generally, Gill and Law argue that 'during the 1970s and the 1980s, the emphasis, certainly with regard to economic policy, has shifted towards *a definition of questions and concepts which is more congruent with the interests of large-scale, transnational capital*' (Gill and Law 1993: 104, emphasis added; Strange 1994: 215).

Consistent with our reading of the Gramscian notion of hegemony, we would argue that the construction of this new hegemony relies not just on material power (the ability of capital and national states to distribute benefits and disadvantages), but also on a moral and intellectual leadership, so that the ideas associated with globalisation become predominant to the extent that they seep into popular consciousness, ruling out alternatives, and integrating into the ranks of the (relatively) advantaged some 'subordinate' groups whilst (often safely) consigning to economic and social marginalisation and exclusion whole segments of populations (Pearce and Tombs 1996).

Thus, the utilisation and development of the idea of globalisation has involved the creation of a new set of economic and political realities; realities which constrain the possible, the desirable, the feasible within and beyond national states. This has profound implications for those who would seek to improve protective regulation, and places constraints upon the operation of capital. In this sense of the creation of new discursive terrains, terrains which set these limits, then it makes sense to speak of an increase in the structural power of capital.

A third general observation is that to the extent that globalising trends — and representations of these — become more significant, then this does have consequences for the nation-state, consequences which are generally constraining of any national-state autonomy. It makes democratic demands less articulable, less realisable and hence, if they are designed to constrain capital, much less effective. Employers in both public and private sectors are convinced that it is too expensive to regulate or pay 'decent' wages or benefits, and that the requirement of competing in a global marketplace *demands* 'roll backs' and benefit reductions. They are also convinced (despite the evidence, as we shall see), that government regulatory structures are inefficient and essentially produce counter-productive effects. Bargaining takes place in a world where reducing the deficit has become the number one economic priority (even if the deficit is due to borrowing for productive investment), an article of faith now with governments of every political stripe.[5] These ideological changes mean progressive forces have lost legitimacy and the indirect leverage this provides, and have lost bargaining power as well because of structural changes in the nature of capital, and allied reductions in the percentage of work forces in unions.

The apparent reduction in the role of the state has other effects as well. In the different settings where capital and other groups — workers, consumers, communities and nation states — are players, capital, particularly that mobilised through the massive, relatively geographically mobile multinationals, has a tremendous relative (but not absolute) advantage. If the state does not provide goods and services, governments have to persuade capital to provide them, and they do so in a world where capital increasingly holds the best cards.

Yet we need to be clear that these trends, and their promotion through the arguments and agendas of the neo-monetarists and neoliberals, are by no means unidirectional, and certainly not inevitable; they are 'at best' a set of emerging institutional arrangements, more a hegemonic project than a hegemonic reality. Indeed, we also need to be clear, fourthly, that the national-state remains crucial within any development of a globalising economic order (Cerny 1997). Capital is hardly operating in an autonomous, 'footloose' fashion — if globalisation is a nascent trend, then it is a trend that is dependent upon legal, regulatory and institutional arrangements in which state forms play a key facilitating and organising function. Thus as Hirst and Thompson (1992) have recently argued, we should not become too carried away with the concept of a global economy since activities by nation states, regional organisations like the European community, and international bodies (not to mention military alliances) all play key and often opposing roles in the organisation of economic activity. That is, to the extent that activities by national and international bodies other than nation states are becoming more significant (Nelson 1996), this does not necessarily entail any reduction in the power or autonomy of any particular national state (Picciotto 1997).[6]

Of particular relevance for this text, and for more general considerations of the nature and possibility of more effective forms of regulating capital, are those claims which relate to the mobility of capital, particularly transnational capital. In their constructed ideal typical globalised economy, Hirst and Thompson provide a vivid statement of the supposed new realities engendered by the emergence of TNCs as 'the major players in the world economy' (Hirst and Thompson 1992: 362). Thus, 'The TNC would be genuine footloose capital ... the main manifestation of a truly globalised economy' (ibid.).

Now, it is certainly the case that national-states are, as they always have been, engaged in a constant, 'competitive process of attraction-and-immobilisation' (Holloway 1994: 38) of capital, one element of which is to provide the most 'favourable conditions for the reproduction of capital within its boundaries' (ibid. 1994: 34-5). In the 1980s, many would agree that this process had taken the form of competitive deregulation or, perhaps more accurately, competitive re-regulation, with many national states attempting to 'redefine market rules under new conditions' (Gill and Law 1993: 98).

Within the political, and certainly neoliberal, rhetoric of globalisation, the idea of globalisation is often presented as an argument against the development of protective regulation, or in favour of complete 'liberalisation'. The assumption upon which such arguments are based is that the development and enforcement of 'social' regulation will prompt capital to seek out less regulated contexts in which to locate. As Hirst and Thompson have written of 'the political rhetoric of globalisation':

> National policies and political choices have been sidelined by world market forces which are stronger than even the most powerful states. Capital is mobile ... it will locate wherever economic advantage dictates, but labour is both nationally located and relatively static, and it must adjust its political expectations to meet the new pressures of international competitiveness. Distinct national regimes of extensive labour rights and social protection are thus obsolete.
>
> (Hirst and Thompson 1996: 175-6)

Now there is little doubt, as some studies of environmental, safety and health regulation indicate, that such arguments point to real phenomena (Castleman 1979; Ives 1985); yet at the same time it is important that some caveats are entered here. We should not ascribe to capital an excessive capability (Pearce and Tombs 1997). Nor should we exaggerate the extent to which capital places a primary emphasis upon levels of social protection, the social wage and the cost of labour in location decisions.

As Thompson and Hirst note elsewhere, even 'truly footloose capital' can only at best be 'potentially willing' to locate or relocate anywhere in the world. And if we examine the question of social regulation in particular, and the strength of labour in general, these factors are only likely to become *determinant* factors when other criteria are 'equal'. But, of course, very often other things are not equal. Factors that need to be taken into account in the establishment of new production sites include proximity of markets, the nature of local labour markets (particularly the availability of specific skills), the nature of local and national infrastructures, access to feedstocks and other raw and intermediate materials, considerations of social, economic and political stability, and so on (Pearce and Snider 1995; Dicken 1992: 131-7). Even *within* considerations of the supply of labour, the cost of labour, and the nature of statutory employment rights are just two of several considerations (Marginson 1994; Wagstyl 1996). And if these factors are relevant to the possible location of new plant and processes, they are clearly even more significant in the issue of the relocation of existing plant or processes.

In these latter contexts, it should be noted that while there is evidence of the globalisation of capitalist economic activity, it nevertheless remains the case that productive activity, foreign direct investment and trade are all relatively concentrated within advanced industrialised economies.

These particularly prosperous countries are pivotal in international trade: in 1988 over 80 per cent of international trade occurred between OECD countries (U.N. Centre of Transnational Corporations 1984; Knox and Agnew 1989). Further, they are the core of the three emerging trade blocs — those based in Europe, the Americas and the Pacific Rim — which, in turn, incorporate virtually all of the other dynamic national economies including, the Southern European countries, Mexico and Chile, China, and the four Asian tigers, namely Hong Kong, Singapore, Taiwan and South Korea (Dicken 1992: 45; *Guardian,* 21 July 1994: 12-13). These three regions dominate global production and trade:

> Seventy-five per cent of world exports are generated by them; 62 per cent of world manufacturing output is produced within them. They are the 'megamarkets' of today's global economy ... they are also the dominant generators and recipients of international investment.
>
> (Dicken 1992: 45)

The same three regions dominate foreign direct investment: North America, Western Europe and Japan accounted for three-quarters of world overseas investment in the early 1990s (Harman 1996: 7; Hirst and Thompson 1996: 63). Moreover, these general points hold as true in the case of services as they do for manufacturing, even if the latter activity is that upon which commentators of economic activity have traditionally focused. This is hardly surprising, of course, when one views the range of commercial, financial and business activities that constitute services as *'circulation activities'* (Dicken 1992: 18). Thus 'league tables' of manufacturing trade, manufacturing production, and trade in services are extremely similar, both in terms of those states appearing and in terms of their relative rankings (ibid.: 22, 30, 43).

Moreover, with few exceptions, it is grossly inaccurate to talk of the 'stateless corporation'. Even within the chemical industry, which has long been one of the most internationalised sectors of economic activity, it is clear that while globalisation may have been an aspiration for the largest chemicals companies for at least a decade, data on the direction and sourcing of sales, and on the distribution of operating income, assets, capital expenditures and research and development expenditures indicates that all remain concentrated within 'home' economies and long-standing markets. Thus, 'For most of the major chemicals companies, globalisation is in its early days' (*Chemistry & Industry*, 3 March 1997: 160).

None of this is to deny that various companies and capitals have used — successfully — the 'reality' of globalisation to threaten particular location/

relocation decisions, thereby influencing the conditions in which they operate; equally, national states have used such threats in order to legitimate certain policies or practices (Strange 1994: 215).

If there is an emerging global/international economy, then its existence and emergence depends, in part, upon relatively successful attempts to universalize certain legal categories — the corporate form and patent and intellectual copyright laws, for example. These social relations are not merely regulated by legal systems, they are partially constituted by them. National or transnational institutions are therefore intrinsic to the operation of the global/international economy. For Hirst and Thompson, indeed, however much corporations describe themselves as transnational, they remain heavily involved with and strongly dependent upon specific nation states (Hirst and Thompson 1992, 1996). While agreeing with much of their argument, we would, however, stress that since the corporate form has become very general, investors, including already constituted corporations, do have a greater objective freedom, all other things being equal, to make decisions to create and register new corporations. Certainly this *does* increase the *potential* for capital to consider location in global terms, and make possible truly global trade-flows (Picciotto 1997: 260-1; Pearce and Snider 1995: 30). Such corporations, then, have become relatively more independent of the good will of any *particular* nation state. Arguably, this is a similar process to the original spread of the limited liability corporate form in the nineteenth century. In the Americas in the 1840s it became relatively easy to register as a limited liability company, and then in the 1850s those seeking easy access to limited liability in Britain argued that if it was established in Britain it would stop capital haemorrhaging to Pennsylvania, Mississippi and wherever else limited liability was already established (Hunt 1936: 138). In 1862, five years after the limited liability company form became easily available in England, the French introduced their equivalent, the *société anonyme* (Saville 1955).

Yet, as we have noted, nation-states and forms of regulation remain crucial, both institutionally and in terms of legitimation (Cerny 1997). For example, whilst in the 1980s financial markets in London and New York were significantly internationalised and deregulated, scandals such as the (UK) Polly Peck (Levi 1995) and the (US) savings and loans crisis (Calavita and Pontell 1995) have prompted the development of new national modes of regulation. The changing fortunes of environmental regulation and deregulation (Yeager 1991), the cleanup of toxic waste in the US, and the regulation of occupational safety and health provide examples of situations too complex to sum up in a simplistic anti- or pro- regulatory formula, or a regulation/deregulation dichotomy (Barnett 1995; Block 1993; Tombs 1995b).

Effective global economic institutions to supplement if not replace the nation-state remain underdeveloped, and the diffuse markets in currency, capital, commodities and services remain unintegrated but nevertheless interdependent. At the level of the global economy there are no mechanisms to determine the relationship between what is produced *for* the different markets (and by whom), and the scale and nature of these markets. If too much money goes into investment compared to wages, then one result may be an unrealistic inflation in the value of stocks and shares and property. In other words, as Black Monday (October, 1987) suggested, global stock market crashes remain a threat; or, to the extent that pressures to decrease wages limits or reduces effective demand, then crises of overcapacity retain a constant potential (Lipietz 1992; Hirst and Thompson 1996). It is difficult to conceive of an international or national economic order without key interventionist roles for state forms.

Indeed, to further emphasise the role of regulatory agencies as hegemonic apparatuses, it is worth noting that just as 'unbridled' capitalism in the nineteenth century was only made viable by the development of national forms of regulation, usually initiated (if not finally controlled) by oppositional social movements, then the same is probably true of any emerging new global economy (Cox 1993). The issue therefore raised for us is not whether or not states — both at a national and international level — will exert and develop forms of control, but the extent to which these can be subject to democratic control (Paehlke 1995; Snider and Pearce 1995). The achievement of democratisation remains a key political goal, the potential of which is obscured by the rhetoric of neoliberals, and others, around globalisation.

National and International Capitalisms

There are good reasons for thinking, then, that the claims of neoliberalism relate more to a desired than to an actually existing national or global capitalist order, and that they obscure as much as they reveal in their arguments regarding state, economy and society (and see Smith, P. 1997). Indeed, one of the key aspects of contemporary capitalism that neoliberal arguments obscure is the variety of ways in which capitalist social relations can be organised. That is, while there are features intrinsic to capitalism, different national-states both can and do organise and regulate capitalist production in very different ways. And these differences are significant in that they may produce more or less unequal distribution of benefits and disadvantages, including wealth, income, and threats to human and environmental health and safety. In the remainder of this chapter we consider some of these alternative ways of organising capitalist production. In so doing, it becomes clear that, *contra* Thatcher's oft-quoted dictum that 'there is no alternative', the possibilities for organising production within and beyond capitalism are much wider than neoliberalism allows.

At the most fundamental level, capitalism as an economic system is characterised by relations of antagonism between capital and labour, and between enterprise and enterprise. These antagonisms are sources of dynamism as well as instability. A capitalist enterprise cannot rest on its laurels; it must always seek through all available means to protect or increase its market share. This is true of a single enterprise, of a cartel or group of national enterprises, or, indeed, of a national capitalist economy.[7] At this point it is worth asking how capitalism, a system riven with and rendered unstable by antagonism between classes, enterprises and nation-states, has reached its present preeminence. The Chicago school of economics, as we have seen, does not address this issue. It assumes, rather, that market systems are the only 'rational' way to organize production as well as social orders, and rationality must eventually win out. The question has been addressed, however, by scholars of the 'regulation school'. Like structural Marxists, they focus on the reproduction, development and transformation of complex social entities. However, they try to go beyond the somewhat abstract and schematic general concepts of modes of production and social formations, and the somewhat functionalist concept of the state and reproduction that structuralists were prone to adopt. Their preference is to specify more closely the different forms that capitalist modes of production can take and have taken. Given that endemic antagonisms, contradictions, and crises have made continuing accumulation improbable and regularly generated major ruptures and structural shifts, what mechanisms account for the continued survival and development of the capitalist mode of production? The explanatory model developed by the regulation school is based upon the related concepts of the regime of accumulation, mode of growth, mode of regulation and model of development:

> An accumulation regime comprises a particular pattern of production and consumption considered in abstraction from the existence of national economies which can be reproduced over time despite its conflictual tendencies. A national model of growth comprises the pattern of production and consumption of a national economy considered in terms of its role in the international division of labour. Relatively stable accumulation regimes and national modes of growth involve a contingent, historically constituted, and societally reproduced correspondence between patterns of consumption and production. A mode of regulation refers to an institutional ensemble and complex of norms which can

secure capitalist reproduction *pro tempore* despite the conflictual and antagonistic character of capitalist relations. And, finally, a model of development ... refers to a pattern of development based on a) a dominant paradigm of industrialization, b) an accumulation regime, and c) a mode of regulation.

(Jessop 1990b: 174)

This approach takes the question of regulation beyond the enumeration and analysis of specific national regulatory bodies to broader, more systemic questions which include analyses of institutional ensembles, class relations and the relative strengths of different class forces. It allows one, for example, to assess strategically the significance of particular tactics undertaken by regulatory agencies. Extensive consultation and the sparing use of prosecution for health and safety offences may be found in situations when capital has been forced to be compliant and is therefore generally following strict rules demanded by organised labour, or in situations where capital has been able to effectively deregulate health and safety (Pearce and Tombs 1992; Snider 1991). For scholars attempting empirical analyses and politicians evaluating regulation, this may mean that lax, ineffective regulatory regimes will look very similar to effective, efficient institutions if *success* is measured in terms of the number of complaints investigated and sanctions deployed.

The evidence from the United States, one of the most successful capitalist economies throughout the twentieth century, indicates the utility of the regulationist model. Aglietta (1979), for example, argued that there have been two major regimes of accumulation and modes of regulation in the US — the extensive and the intensive. The first was based on competitive regulation, and the barrier to sustained accumulation was primarily the limitations on the ability of the mass of the population to consume very much.[8] This created a 'realisation problem' and a related speculative pressure which inflated the value of stocks and shares. These class-related factors, and the decline in world trade, precipitated the Great Crash of 1929.

The second was based upon the Fordist regime. The term Fordism is employed to describe that stage of capitalism characterized by the manufacture of goods through the use of large production runs over 24 hour cycles (yielding maximum economies of scale), maximum use of machinery, and correspondingly minute divisions of labour. Abundant consumer goods were thereby produced, and workers receiving high wages in the monopolistic industries that dominated key manufacturing sectors could afford to buy them. Wage increases were tied to increasing productivity and, hence, to the intensity of labour. Neo-Keynsian policies were instituted to create a social wage, administered by a bureaucratic welfare state. This created a (national) virtuous circle of rising living standards and rising productivity, rising wages and rising profits, economic stability and social harmony. It also produced inflation and worker dissatisfaction, as we shall see.

Under Fordism a continuous revolutionising of the means of production occurred, which resulted in the overaccumulation of capital in the manufacturing sectors producing goods. However, the high degree of monopolisation in this sector made it possible, at least for a time, for corporate executives to anticipate the ensuing devaluation of capital and destruction of productive capacity by an inflationary increase of prices and expansion in credit. Although the rising productivity of labour and the erosion of real wages through rising prices acted as counter-tendencies, nevertheless, they were insufficient to combat the tendency of the rate of profit to fall. Inflation and an increase in class conflict were the result. Class conflict over wages was exacerbated by dissatisfaction with working conditions associated with the autocratic Fordist production process. Machine paced and repetitive, based on piece work and undertaken in shifts by unskilled workers, this mode of production is associated with high accident rates and occupational ill-health such as gastrointestinal disturbances, sleeping problems, anxiety, depression, irritation, loss of appetite, accelerated heart rate, indeed, general morbidity (Navarro 1983: 550).

Aglietta's attempt to track the development of the American economy is partially successful, but it does not provide an accurate or complete analysis (Clarke 1988, 1990). The arguments need to be reformulated and supplemented. The vaunted success of American capitalism required two world wars to decimate the infrastructure and economic base of its major competitors. Indeed, World War II provided the definitive stimulus to the American recovery from the overwhelmingly destructive Depression of the 1930s (Dowd 1977: 105). And by the 1960s it was clear that even the mighty US could not sustain the heavy military spending required by the Vietnam War as well as the social expenditures necessitated by Lyndon Johnson's 'Great Society'. It is unlikely that there has ever been a self-sustaining Fordist regime. Indeed, the use of the generic term Fordism to describe a whole economic system, and its subsequent use as a model to which specific systems are compared, involves processes akin to abstract empiricism with all the attendant consequences and intellectual baggage.[9] A more useful analysis would aim for greater specificity and explore the presence or absence of Fordist elements in different economic systems, then examine how these relate to other elements.

Japan is a case in point. Although elements of Fordist production techniques are apparent in productive processes, they have been modified in significant ways. Moreover, the relationships between enterprises and between enterprises and the state are quite different than those in the US (Henwood 1997: 275; Wade 1996). There are two groups of *keiretsu* — those firms interconnected, in a *zaibatsu* manner, by central banks or by trading companies but in unrelated businesses; and the *kaisha*, large manufacturing companies that relate to smaller enterprises (and customers) in a sustained but more hierarchical manner (Scott 1997: 181-195). The latter focus on producing particular kinds of commodities and, hence, develop very detailed and cumulative knowledge in specific areas. These 'enterprise groups' are a crucial (and dedicated) source of long term finance for industrial investment. Other sources are the publicly regulated banking system and, more recently, internally generated profits. All three provide relatively cheap capital.

Coordination and long term planning is encouraged externally by the Ministry of International Trade and Industry (MITI), which also actively promotes a modernising small business sector (Clegg 1990). Further, relatively low dividends on invested capital facilitate long term planning (Williams et al. 1990). Contrariwise, Thurow (1984) found that the average time horizon of firms in a thirty firm conglomerate he investigated in the US was only 2.8 years, clearly inadequate for planning investments in processes with lifespans covering several product-generations. Furthermore, national accounting practices and continuous stock market evaluations in the US (and in Britain and Australia) make it 'rational' for managers — assessed on performance at their 'profit centre' — to delay 'replacement of old or worn out equipment, replacing equipment eventually with technologically dated or inferior substitutes, and skimping on maintenance, research and personnel development' (Clegg 1990: 197). This may have literally disastrous consequences (Pearce 1993; Pearce and Tombs 1989, 1993).

Long term planning, together with Japanese investment strategies, intensive working styles and relatively low dividends on invested capital (Williams et al. 1990), have given Japanese companies an advantage over their American rivals (Hutton 1995: 275). In the case of automobiles and in many areas of electronics Japanese companies have clearly outperformed those commonly recognised as American in origin: 'Between 1962 and 1982 the number [of 483 of the world's largest industrial enterprises] of US origin dwindled from 292 to 213; while that of Japanese companies rose from 29 to 79; and that of developing countries from 2 to 23' (Dunning 1988b: 82). The organisations where Japan has the advantage all focus on producing particular kinds of commodities where the development of very detailed and cumulative knowledge in specific areas is a distinct advantage.

In large firms this is facilitated by the fact that relatively small salary differentials and status divisions are the norm, as are job rotation at all levels, and seniority systems for core workers (Wokutch 1990). During the post 1973 recession the large Japanese companies laid off fewer employees than was true in the US, and, during that time, the companies accepted a concomitant lower rate of return on total assets than did US companies (Clegg 1990). Workers are organised in self-managing small groups, with each individual continuously updating his/her skills, and those of the group overall. This tends to give workers an active involvement in 'quality circle' and 'zero defect' movements (Itoh 1992: 201). Workers are flexible about the tasks they undertake and the hours they will work. Further, companies make a relatively high capital investment per worker — roughly twice that of US companies. Japanese capitalism also provides legally enforced security of employment. This is due not so much to the remnants of feudalism (Abegglen 1975), as to interwar and post war class conflict (Clegg 1990: 140), which led to attempts to legitimate these relations by offering job security to gain the loyalty of skilled workers in tight labour markets (Taira 1970; Woodiwiss 1992). Nevertheless, these conditions provide a rational basis for a much greater degree of loyalty than is true in US companies (Hutton 1995: 274).

Yet these conditions hold true only for those working directly for major Japanese corporations. These have been almost exclusively male white collar workers, who comprise less than 30 per cent of the waged workforce (Clegg 1990: 186). And these workers put in at least 13 per cent more hours than similar Americans and 31 per cent more than West Germans; their free time was 23 per cent less than Americans and 45 per cent less than West Germans in the average year (Itoh 1992: 204). Moreover, within the actual enterprise workers have few rights. Their unions are basically company unions, their union representatives are often also their supervisors (Beynon 1985), and managerial authority is absolute (Woodiwiss 1992: 141). Innovation, quality, just-in-time production, low cost and flexibility are, in part, attributable to the complex subcontracting systems whereby subcontractors employ less secure and less well paid workers. And many of these enterprises are partly owned but effectively controlled (relatively cheaply through a 20 per cent or so share) by the major automobile manufacturers themselves (Stinchcombe 1990).[10] This strategy has made it possible to achieve productivity increases at a rate twice as fast as the rise in real wages (between 1975 and 1985) (Itoh 1992: 203) and, (between 1965 and 1980), to expand nominal production by Japanese auto firms by 600 per cent while raising per capita fixed investment by only about a third as much (Cusamo 1989: 215).

This suggests that 'the Japanese miracle', characterised by long term collaboration between large firms and their primary subcontractors producing high quality products at low cost, depended on specifically Japanese social relations and by 'outsourcing to low wage areas' (Powell 1990: 321).[11]

In the case of the four Asian tigers, the state has played a key role in self-consciously specifying and developing particular industries. Strategies have included the development of state owned industries which are joint ventures between the state and private capital; the control of investment by nationalising the banks and/or by providing cheap credit or subsidies to selected industries; and the provision of protection from international competition. In Hong Kong, a low wage economy has been made significantly less harsh by the state's provision of education and medical care and low cost public housing for about 85 per cent of the working class, and by cheap food supplied by the Republic of China at below market prices. The state's ownership of all land has enabled it to combine these measures with low individual and corporate taxes since it generates revenue by leasing land to businesses. Singapore also has a highly developed welfare state. And Taiwan, according to Gini analysis, has one of the most egalitarian income distributions in the world.[12] The similarities with the Japanese model are obvious, and include active measures to marginalise trade unions (Henderson 1993; Clegg 1990). Finally, we should note that China, with its own version of a mixed economy, is the fastest growing economy in the world (Smith, R. 1997: 3-4). It is these (national) structural factors, rather than some cultural phenomenon such as 'Asian capitalism', that explain the success of these economies (Woodiwiss 1993a, 1998).

There was, in fact, a third major model of successful growth, also incorporating Fordist elements, that emerged by the late 1950s — the Swedish model. As in other nation-states, large corporations played a major role in economic development, but their relationships to each other, to smaller companies, employees, trade unions and the state were again all quite distinctive. In Sweden, the private manufacturing sector has long been dominated by a small number of large family owned firms: 'fifteen families and two corporations have majority ownership in 200 large industrial companies employing almost half of those employed in private industry' (Scott 1979: 71). These families developed close working relationships with both the state and the trade unions. The latter, intimately tied to the electorally dominant Social Democratic Party, became an extremely creative form of corporatism.

Swedish social democrats believed that (speculative) capitalism was inherently irrational and that the state and an institutionalised union countervailing power were needed to make it operate efficiently and humanely. Their aim, largely successful, was to raise the material level of working class people as a whole, and to create a situation where there was 'equal pay for equal work and reasonable and fair pay differentials', with 'work for everyone' including part-time work at a living wage (Backstrom 1988: 246-248). Through their 'active market policy', involving job retraining, generous unemployment benefits and moving costs, information on employment possibilities and public works jobs, they helped structure the labour market, and determine the composition of jobs and skill levels (Navarro 1983: 528). The implementation of these policies and many others was decided in a tripartite manner with participation from labour, capital and government. This produced a high wage, relatively skilled, highly productive economy with low unemployment and few low wage jobs (Clegg 1990: 225-230). Furthermore, whereas management's right to manage was left relatively intact until the 1970s — indeed until that time there was a somewhat consumerist, welfare state orientation — in a challenge to Fordism there developed a general concern with the quality of life, particularly at work. New kinds of team work, including a single team building a whole car, the Volvo solution, produced a kind of de-differentiation (Clegg 1990) that helped deal with some of the work-induced *anomie* (Durkheim 1984) associated with Fordist productive techniques. Moreover, having observed the rapid internationalisation of Swedish capital, the state pushed to limit the extent to which profits could be invested outside Sweden, via the Meidner plan, to socialise the ownership of the enterprises themselves (Meidner 1978; Abrahamson and Brostom 1980) and to develop workers' control of the organisation of production.

In the 1980s, the average Swedish worker was among the best paid in the world. In fact, one might argue that in the 1980s this worker was the highest paid, if one takes into account the social wage (free health care, social welfare payments, unemployment payments, child care provision, maternity and paternity leave, etc., etc.), good working conditions, short work week and long generous holidays. Furthermore, unions had won the right to representation on the boards of most companies and the right to bargain over the organisation of many aspects of the work situation. Shop stewards and safety representatives garnered increasingly greater powers and greater protection. Under the Work Environment Act of 1977, safety representatives and safety committees could play an active role in the planning of new premises, work processes and working methods, and, famously, the former had the right to unilaterally stop any dangerous process until an inspector arrived.[13]

Capital retained a significant degree of power despite the advances of social democracy. Although firms *could* avoid taxation of their profits by allowing for state and union control over investment decisions, they still retained *the right* to invest them overseas or to pay them out in dividends. Nor did capital surrender any significant control over production. In part because of the threat (and the subsequent reality) of the internationalisation of competition, the internationalisation of its own production, and a significant decline in the global economy, the truce between capital and labour broke down in the 1980s and capital gained greater independence. The SAF (the employers' federation) became increasingly vocal (Thompson and Sederblad 1994: 261), and increasingly successful in national politics, resulting in cutbacks in the welfare state and a total repudiation of the Meidner plan (Pontusson 1987: 24-31). This suggests that, by not attacking capital's fundamental power — its ownership of the means of production — Swedish social democracy left itself open to counter-attack. Whether this would have survived or not, we have here a different form of economic organisation, highly effective for employers and the state, which offered superior employment and living conditions for working class people.

Some regulation theorists (Jessop 1993; Lipietz 1987) believe that new forms of viable national and international organization and regulation may now be emerging. Some of these forms are viewed negatively, some positively — Jessop (1993), for example, sees the 'Schumpeterian workfare state' as providing no more than 'the best possible political shell for post-Fordism' (1993: 7). Others are more optimistic. Charles Leadbeater, of *Marxism Today* and *The Financial Times*, argues that, in Fordist regimes, there was an assumption that the social-democratic state would look after collective social interests and that economic decisions should and would take this into account. However, the welfare state did not work; it was overly bureaucratic, paternalistic, and inefficient; and it could produce only mass quality products for mass populations (Leadbeater 1989: 139).

When the world economy became bedevilled by stagflation and mass markets were saturated, demands by contemporary consumers for more differentiated and high quality products were initially frustrated.[14] Now, however, these demands are seen as providing a way out of the crisis. Not only do smaller production units make old-style corporate bureaucracies unnecessary, but the need to recruit individuated, skilled, flexible and autonomous workers has led to decentralised bargaining and rendered old-style unions unnecessary. These new workers define themselves in a postmodern way; their identities are fluid, their life-styles idiosyncratic and transient. This further reinforces product differentiation. Old class-based identities and oppositions, and affiliated demands for universal state services or nationalised industries, become obsolete.

Although Leadbeater and allied theorists acknowledge that the new societies will be capitalist and 'riven with inequalities in income, wealth and power' (Jacques and Hall 1989: 23), they downplay this fact and discount the social forces that could challenge it.[15] Thus, Leadbeater has advocated an incomes policy 'formed around a publicly declared minimum standard of living', and a change of ownership of the means of production that eschews state or trade union ownership of assets in favour of worker ownership through share purchase (Leadbeater 1989: 147). The state would exist only to provide public space, not necessarily public services, on the model of the public park where a range of private activities, from boating to selling ice cream to sunbathing, are possible: 'The state is vital to ensuring a space continues to exist and is developed; but beyond that its direct role depends on whether it is the most efficient provider of services' (Leadbeater 1989: 148-49).

This analysis, however, ignores the fact that those running the ice-cream vans would probably be employed by a multinational company using part-time workers on subsistence wages with no benefits. The company would soon demand the concession to run the boats on the lake and eventually push for privatisation of the park so it could charge sunbathers user-fees. They might well sell sunblock to provide protection from the depletion of the ozone layer caused by another component of the multinational's activities, then sell medical services to those who contracted skin cancer!

More sophisticated approaches to the emergence of new economic forms are found in the work of 'network analysts' (Powell 1990), particularly as this relates to flexible specialization and industrial districts (Sabel and Zeitlin 1985; Hirst and Zeitlin 1991). These theorists have challenged the assumptions of conventional economists including those of the Chicago school. They refuse to reduce viable forms of economic organization to *either* the hierarchical and authoritarian firm *or* the free market. Markets may be elements of complex social organisations, but they depend on other social forms for their very existence.[16] Many successful, 'networking', flexible and innovation-generating ways of organizing production have not been adequately investigated. Examples include the creation and reproduction of economic districts, the facilitation of cooperative relations between groups of enterprises, the promotion of viable small enterprises, and the development of independent skilled workforces who would move from firm to firm with a significant amount of infrastructural and coordinating activity undertaken by the local state.

These kinds of networks are not a hybrid form of organization, but an analytically distinct way of organizing collective behaviour, particularly economic behaviour. They make possible unified collective action, actions denied to those involved in bureaucratic firms and markets, both of which assume and generate people who act as egoistic rational calculators. The networks generate, instead, a more sustained, cooperative, trusting and less calculative attitude. Information about new processes, products, changes in tastes and modifications in reputations tends to be disseminated spontaneously. It becomes relatively easy to quickly translate new ideas into new products. For example, in the textile industry, thanks to Computer Aided Design, a new design that formerly took over three weeks to put together now takes six hours (Mytelka 1991: 122). Relations of production are transformed while efficient production is facilitated.

These have been very successful, particularly in situations where there is a high rate of innovation and a demand for quality and low batch customised production for targetted customers. Such networks can already be found, to varying degrees, in Silicon Valley, California, in Massachusetts, the Alsacean region of France, the English Midlands, Baden-Wurtenberg in Germany, and Emiglio Romagna in Italy (Sabel et al. 1989).

Although the development of these industrial districts certainly challenges the notion that large, hierarchical, impersonal, bureaucratic corporations are the only efficient form of organisation, they too have problems their advocates have thus far failed to confront. First, their success depends not just on local factors, but on the fiscal policies of the national state generated to maintain conditions of sustained demand for their products (Thompson 1989). Second, large scale capital itself has learned from the profitability of such experiments, and has appropriated elements of this model to its own ends. Kanter (1989), for example, has argued that the number of people employed by corporations has decreased, internal markets and decentralised profit centres have developed, and an openness to extra-organizational inputs and partnerships has produced organisations that are more viable, creative and flexible. Changes in market foci and *modus operandi* have already taken place in Exxon, IBM, Xerox and Kodak (in 1992 the first, third, fourteenth and sixteenth largest US corporations — *Forbes*, 19 July 1993: 182-183). Thus, such models may be co-opted, their cooperative tendencies removed or reconfigured to serve the interest of immediate increased profit levels. Fiscal control remains centralised, and the accompanying decentralisation of production may have deleterious as well as beneficial effects (Pearce 1993; Tombs 1995a).

Furthermore, we have already seen that Japan has constructed itself on a national level as an industrial district. Increasingly, international joint ventures between firms in very different markets are being forged — automobile, steel and telecommunication firms provide recent examples (Dunning 1988a; Adams and Brock 1991: 57-58). Transnational corporations can combine these new forms with their other economic advantages — including those derived from economies of scale and those derived from monopoly power — to reassert their dominant positions. Economies of scale remain important: the last twenty years have seen a diminution in the number of car producers, a growth in their size, and the maintenance if not enhancement of large production runs (Williams et al. 1987; Callinicos 1989). Furthermore, there is no evidence that demand for mass consumption goods has decreased, and the differences between these and so-called niche products are often minuscule. This is not to deny that more flexible technologies have the potential to increase the rates of change of design, to improve quality and sometimes to reduce the size at which production runs become viable. It is, however, to question the technological determinism inherent in many of these analyses. In fact, these changes, combined with the globalisation of production, mean that transnational corporations are, in some ways, creating global industrial districts. Thus, both of the schools discussed tend to underestimate the power and resourcefulness of corporate capitalism and its ability to appropriate potentially liberating technologies and subordinate their uses to its own agenda (Mosco 1989).

This is an appropriate point to return to Jessop and the prognoses of regulation theorists. He argues that recent years have seen a 'tendential shift' from the Keynesian welfare state, and a 'hollowing out' of national states in advanced capitalist countries (Jessop 1993: 7-8). Thus, states have lost power to international bodies or, conversely, to 'emerging horizontal networks of power — which bypass central states and link regions or localities' at regional or local levels (Jessop 1993: 7-8). These changes occur in a context where the internationalization of financial and product flows limits the autonomy of states while forcing them to adopt policies geared to attract new investment, particularly in knowledge-intensive industries and technologies. He is not arguing that these changes will automatically produce a viable regime of accumulation, nor that they are an inevitable outcome of current technological and economic changes. However, the power of capital has vastly increased, with the result that people and their communities have less ability to influence or block hurtful changes. It also means that changes will take place on levels other than the nation-state.

We would argue that it would be wrong to conclude from the foregoing that such transformations leave nation states helpless. Specific political decisions and programmes make nation states weaker or stronger than they might otherwise be. For example, Article 2010 of the US Canada Free Trade Agreement called Monopolies:

> states that if national or provincial programs are introduced in Canada, for example, an auto insurance scheme such as is found in British Columbia and Saskatchewan, the government would be required to give advance notice to the

United States to 'engage in consultations' if Washington asked for them, and be prepared to modify the program in order to eliminate any adverse effect or loss of business — real or potential — to American companies. This last requirement includes being prepared to compensate American corporations affected by the program's implementation. A graphic example of this reality was seen in 1991, when the Ontario government backed down on its 1990 election promise and scrapped a long-standing NDP commitment to introduce a provincial auto-insurance plan after learning that State Farm, the largest US auto insurance company, claimed that under the FTA $1.3 billion would be owed by Ontario as compensation to US auto-insurance companies.

(Orchard 1993: 169)

Although the foregoing provides an example of a nation restricting its scope through trade agreements, this outcome is not inevitable. Given sufficient pressure, agreements can be reopened, renegotiated. There is already some evidence that there is a 'post-globalisation' movement against the liberalisation of international financial activity (Cox 1993). Reasons for this include: a general fear of major international financial crises, the uncertain future of such interstate bargains including some between the countries of the European Community, and the declining benefits of liberalisation for its major early proponents, the US and the UK (Helleiner 1994). Similarly, renegotiation, even of GATT[17], could also be used to widen protection for relatively powerless groups, the environment and similar causes. Further, Gordon (1988: 58-59) has provided evidence that the most important factors determining foreign direct investment in different countries are the size of the home market, the degree of political stability, and price/exchange-rate stability. Other factors include the condition of the infrastructure and the skill-levels of the workforce, and, to a lesser extent, wage levels. Most of these criteria are compatible with a range of different state structures and economic policies even in the absence of successful struggles modifying these criteria or removing low-wage options. Then, Lipietz (1992) has argued that the post-Fordist world order does not necessarily have to be neoliberal. Instead, within countries, there could be both increased worker involvement in production decisions, and an increase in leisure time and employment by reducing the standard working week. Unemployed people or local municipalities could provide subsidized services for community groups and ecologically oriented projects, thereby allowing workers to earn a living wage.

It appears to be feasible, then, to conceptualize strategies that include state planning, state ownership of enterprises, particularly 'natural' monopolies, a welfare state based on universalistic principles (Holland 1975; Wainwright 1992), and similar advanced policies where historically and culturally appropriate. It is both possible and desirable to develop state-funded research and testing laboratories to allow the independent assessment of corporate products, and similar institutions to check corporate power and minimize corporate abuse. Indeed, it is absolutely essential for progressive scholars, as well as activists in oppositional social movements, to provide countervailing initiatives, given that traditional progressive forces in the welfare state, notably trades unions, have been subjected to such sustained (but only partially successful) attacks on both structural and ideological levels.

Conclusion: Costing Capitalist 'Success'

It should be clear from the preceding that there are enormous discrepancies between, on the one hand, actual existing capitalism — or, rather, capitalisms — and, on the other hand, the claims of neoliberalism regarding the nature and functioning of contemporary capitalism. Two final, general issues are worth considering, issues which are of general relevance throughout the following chapters, and issues which in a sense take us back to the beginnings of our considerations of capitalist economies, at the start of Chapter 1.

We have indicated in this and the previous chapter that no real capitalist economies do, or in fact could, fit the neoliberal model. Yet there is a further point to be made. For, it is far from clear that private enterprise, which is the central form of organisation within all the economies to which we have made reference, is unequivocally more viable or more efficient than public or state ownership.[18] It is perhaps testimony to the status as dominant hegemonic 'truth' of the superiority of private enterprise that this issue tends to be broached with seemingly less and less frequency (not least, and particularly unforgiveably, by 'radical' academics). Yet historically, many nationalisations took place because private enterprise failed to run key industries effectively and/or because of a need to resolve *for capital* a more general crisis of accumulation (Jessop 1990b: 157) (see Britain, Chile and Mexico, for example — Whitfield 1992: 281-282).[19] Then many public enterprises, such as SNCF and other nationalised European rail networks, have been economically efficient. Others, like the Norwegian North Sea natural gas company (Statoil Group) and the French Société Nationale Elf Aquitaine Group, Thomson CSF (*Forbes*, 19 July 1993: 134) and Renault (*Globe and Mail*, Tuesday, 7 September 1993: B11) have also been profitable. Writing from a perspective hardly sympathetic to national or social ownership, Jackson and Price concede that 'Not all state owned enterprises are inefficient' (Jackson and Price 1994: 20; and see also Martin and Parker 1997). Thus, they note that, 'The most efficient steel company in the world is the Korean Posco (Pohang Steel Company) which is state owned', before listing a series of other 'examples of high-performing public enterprises' (ibid.).

When private enterprise has been more profitable than publicly owned enterprise, this has often been because it has been able to avoid the restrictions imposed on state enterprises, for example, the freedom to enter new markets or raise funds commercially (Whitfield 1983: 37), or, indeed, the obligation to strategically subsidise other areas of the economy as the nationalised British coal industry in the 1950s subsidised the private enterprise steel industry (Jenkins 1959). Private service providers often reject the obligation to service all income levels, as opposed to providing for those with the ability to pay the price demanded, thus leaving sizable minorities without heat, electricity, or health care, and repudiate obligations to provide workers with a living wage or a reasonable pension, and evade obligations to implement employment equity.

Indeed, the move to privatise many industries has been associated with a non-contingent increase in inequality — generally, the lower the wage and benefit level the fewer the 'natural monopolies' (Fine 1990b: 124-126). This, combined with deregulation and the move away from progressive taxation policies, has led to a tremendous shift in resources and power to capital (Edsall 1984; Hudson and Williams 1989; Field 1989; Phillips 1991, 1993; Whitfield 1992; Wilson 1992; Bartlett and Steele 1992; Glyn and Miliband 1994; Jordan 1996).

Then the Pinochet dictatorship's IMF-monetarist-free market experiment of the late 1970s and early 1980s in Chile, which involved significant denationalisation, first produced a boom and then a devastating recession as industrial production plummeted. Thousands of small enterprises went bankrupt, the trade deficit worsened, and the living standard of the mass of the population deteriorated as wages declined and unemployment rose' (Petras and Morley 1990: 15-16). The economy recovered from 1984 to 1989, but the benefits were restricted to a narrow (and often expatriate) elite. The income share for the top and bottom fifths of the population went from 44.5 per cent and 7.6 per cent respectively in 1969, to 65.4 per cent and 4.4 per cent respectively in 1989 (Ornenstein 1993). During roughly the same period, the profits of the country's top two hundred companies quintupled, and 'the socioeconomic status of the Chilean masses worsened immeasurably: real wages declined by 15 per cent and minimum wage earners made 40 per cent less in 1987 than they did in the 1978-81 period' (Petras and Morley 1990: 15-16; on the effects of neoliberal 'reforms' throughout Latin America see Richards 1997).

Thus these forms of organisation reproduce and exacerbate pre-existing inequalities and limit the production of healthy, well educated working people. They waste human lives and human resources. And it is surely no accident that countries with the most 'pure', market-driven versions of capitalism also suffer the highest rates of violent, anti-social behaviours, forcing them to spend billions of dollars through the state and private sectors on social control (Christie 1992; Currie 1997). Perhaps, then, in *assessing* the impact of economic activities, it is important to go beyond the narrow confines of the rate of profit, partial productivity statistics or even consumers' satisfactions. Economics, after all, 'is concerned with the efficient use of resources, and many economic activities which may be non-commercial (i.e. non-profitable for the enterprises concerned) may prove still to be *economic* — in the sense that for the economy as a whole the total gains exceed the total costs incurred' (Donaldson and Farquar 1988: 141).[20]

Thus Lipietz explores how, on a global level, trade, deficits, debts and development could be ordered in more constructive ways, to avoid the maintenance of consumerism in the First World and the displacement of life endangering and ecologically destructive economic activities to the Third World. In fact, a per capita energy tax on all countries could provide an interesting, effective and ecologically sound way of transferring wealth — one North American uses as much commercial energy as 2 West Germans, 3 Japanese, 16 Chinese or 1072 Nepalese (Gordon and Suzuki 1990: 211). Smith gives a slightly different indication of the scale of inequality in terms of the use of resources and the sources of environmental degradation:

> Today the industrialised North, which has 25 per cent of the world's population, owns 86 per cent of the world's industry and consumes 80 per cent of world energy. Moreover, developed countries account for roughly 80 per cent of global pollution of all kinds. On a per capita basis, the discrepancy is even greater ...
> (Smith, R. 1997: 25, see also 15)

We would argue that meaningful criteria for judging efficiency should 'include an assessment of the ability to innovate in the widest sense', because 'the dynamics of entrepreneurial performance must surely be a major factor in explaining differences in the growth of total factor productivity' (Fine 1990b: 131-132). Furthermore, it is important to explore which specific kinds of activities contribute to the growth of the economy as a whole and particularly how they link into other key manufacturing activities. In the United Kingdom, for example, 'the fate of the coal, steel, and water industries are closely tied together' (Fine 1990b: 133). Moreover, state owned utility companies, under no intrinsic pressure to increase or maintain revenues and, hence, profitability, are much more likely to develop ecologically sound energy saving policies than are capitalist enterprises.[21] Such suggestions indicate the need to critically examine conventional measures of economic performance and prosperity.

This need is further indicated through brief reference to a further way in which corporations externalise legitimate costs of production. Two recent studies in the UK have attempted to quantify the costs of occupational accidents. The first, produced by the Accident Prevention Advisory Unit (APAU) of the Health and Safety Executive (HSE), concluded that costs arising from accidents involving injuries, damage, disruption and production losses represented: 37 per cent of annualised profits, 8.5 per cent of turnover, 5 per cent of operating costs, or, for example, in the case of a North Sea oil platform, the equivalent of shutting down the platform for one day a week (HSE 1993). Further, considering the costs of occupational accidents and ill-health at the level of the British economy as a whole, these costs were put at 2-3 per cent of Gross Domestic Product. More recently, a second HSE sponsored report concluded that the overall cost to British employers of ill-health and accidents at work ranged somewhere between £4-£9 billion per year; this is equivalent to 5-10 per cent of all UK trading companies' gross trading profits in 1990 (Davies and Teasdale 1994).[22] Thus, as Woolfson and Beck have recently noted, 'most of the costs of accidents do not fall upon employers. The primary costs are borne by insurance, injured employees' families, and, to a large degree, the welfare state' (Woolfson and Beck 1997: 15). In other words, much of these costs of production are being externalised. Moreover, to the extent that these costs fall upon welfare recipients, that is, upon the weakest and least protected members of capitalist societies, then the externalisation of such costs exacerbates what have been referred to as existing 'structures of vulnerability' (Nichols 1986).

This takes us back directly to our brief overview of capitalist success stories at the start of Chapter 1. While we noted there the average standard of living of people in the 24 OECD countries, as measured by their GDP per capita, has improved over time and is much better than that of non-OECD countries, it should also be clear that such a statement is at such a level of generalisation that it obscures a great deal. Most obviously, if there is any emerging global political economy, then this emergence has, with the exception of the four Asian tigers (Hong Kong, Korea, Singapore and Taiwan) and China, been accompanied by increasing disparities in wealth between developed and 'Third World' countries (Korzeniewicz and Moran 1997), with the latter group seeing their relative role in world trade declining, their debt burden increasing and balance of payments deficit continuing (Magdoff 1992: 63-70). Further, globalised economic activity, and the increasing mobility of capital, has heightened the insecurities that individuals and communities, even nations, experience about their economic future. The commodification of most productive activity and an orientation towards international markets makes all countries dangerously vulnerable to global economic fluctuations (Waring 1988).

If we turn to conditions within OECD countries, it is clear that figures relating to increasing living standards are averages, and must, therefore, be supplemented with some analysis of the distribution of income and wealth within these countries. Within all of these nations there are significant inequalities. Thus in the UK and the US, where the neo-liberal experiment emerged and has been most thoroughgoing (Cerny 1997), as well as in some parts of Europe, economic and social inequalities have been increasing since the beginning of the 1980s, even if these are often officially masked (Cashmore 1989; Currie 1990, 1997; Council of Churches for Britain and Ireland 1997; Oppenheim and Harker 1996; Phillips 1991; Wilson 1991; Zeitlin 1989).

Moreover, there are problems not simply with the organisation of production within these economies; there are problems with the ways in which production is measured in such economies; that is, their GNP and GDP are highly problematic as measures. Significantly, they are measures which do not provide an accurate indication of the distributions of inequality in terms of wealth, income, and quality of life. They measure only goods and services that are bought and sold for a price in the market or, as in the case of the services derived from owning rather than renting a house, a shadow price. They can be measured in terms of demand or the volume of production by summing the total expenditures of consumers; of the government estimated with reference to the expenditures, including salaries required for it to provide goods and services; on investment in assets, and, finally, the net relation between imports and exports. They can be measured in terms of supply or the costs of production by measuring the incomes received in corporate profits, proprietor's income, interest, rent, and employee wages and salaries (and by including a 'statistical discrepancy'). These provide reasonable accounts of the scale of output of the formal economy within a specific period of time, a reasonable indicator of how well a country fares in international economic competition and of how well it can cope with the expenditure required for military struggle (Waring 1988: 54-56). It is now acknowledged, however, that this articulation with the international economy produces many problems — for example, it produces an underestimation of what wages can buy in many low wage economies and hence underestimates both the standard of living of individuals and the productivity of their economies. This has led to significant changes in the estimate of the GNP of such countries as China. Even so, GNP and GDP do not provide measures of the complete output of a country's goods and services, nor what is occurring to its capital stock, nor the state of the welfare of its population. Furthermore, in recent years the tendency has been to use the GDP rather than the GNP as a measure of economic output. In fact, GDP figures are misleading because (as opposed to GNP figures) all income generated by activities within a country is counted as part of the GDP even if firms are owned by overseas investors and profits are sent abroad (Waring 1988).[23] This is of particular importance in Third World countries where there is significant foreign ownership.

So the method of counting makes a great deal of difference to the amount of the pie that appears to be available to be divided up. The way in which the pie is actually divided up makes a great deal of difference to the quality of life of the whole range of inhabitants.

Excluded is the 'irregular economy' involving everything from corporate crime, to the transaction costs entailed in the exchange of stolen commodities (since estate agents' fees are counted even if they are buying and selling already built houses these should be included too), to the untaxed provision of services, to forms of barter. Excluded also are the goods and services produced and consumed in the non-market social economy — domestic labour including home repairs, voluntary work, and subsistence farming. Included are any increases in measured economic activity even when this involves goods and services that replace previously unmeasured services, and even if the new services are inferior, such as fast food replacing home cooking. This is also true even if the increase involves new services repairing environmental damage treated as externalities by previous or current market oriented production (Giarini 1992: 146). Excluded, therefore, from measurement is the degradation of the environment or the depletion of environmental resources wherever these are considered to be free goods, or such 'human costs' as the decrease in leisure time caused by traffic congestion (Waring 1988: 292-293). Further, although inventory changes in stocks of raw materials or partly processed goods are measured, those due to such natural growth as spontaneous reforestation are ignored. Then, government expenditure on public goods such as the infrastructure are not counted as investment since investment must be geared to the 'production of goods and services for sale' (Waring 1988: 63). In fact, a much better way of describing and measuring capital is to relate it to the different sustainable sources of human welfare. This entails a recognition that capital includes *all* physically produced capital, and environmental capital, human capital and social/organizational capital (Ekins 1992: 147-150).

Not all of these can be measured in monetary terms, although shadow prices can be constructed in some cases (Hueting 1992). Others can be assessed using other kinds of quantitative measures, such as environmental resource accounts, for example measuring the physical volume of reserves or the potential energy contained within them (Chapman 1979; Lone 1992). This allows for the measurement of the rate of resource depletion and the level of defensive expenditures within an economy. Leipert estimated that 'defensive expenditures in the Federal Republic of Germany increased from 5.6 per cent to 10 per cent of GNP from 1970 to 1985. GNP itself only increased by 39.4 per cent during that period' (Lone 1992: 254). Taking account of these measures helps to develop an index of the Net National Product, approximating what Hicks (1946, 1948) described as sustainable income.

Thus, if we examine the estimated GDP per capita for different countries in 1991, we find the US clearly in the lead; and if we examine its GNP per capita between 1950 to 1986, we find that it has steadily increased during this whole period. However, when we use an adjusted Economist composite index, the US's position drops to eighth for GNP per capita; and if we use Daly and Cobb's Index of Sustainable Welfare, we find that the per capita sustainable welfare peaked in the US in 1976 and subsequently declined. The details of this Index are themselves revealing. The Index of Sustainable Welfare includes measures of personal consumption, weighted by distributional inequality and adjusted in various ways. First, there are adjustments downward to account for depletion of non-renewable resources, long-term environmental damage, expenditure on consumer nondurables and national advertising, defensive private expenditures on health and education, costs of commuting, urbanization, car accidents, water, air and noise pollution, and the loss of wetlands and farmland. Then there are adjustments upwards for services from household labour, consumer durables, and streets and highways, public current expenditures on health and education, net capital growth and net change in international financial position (Ekins and Max-Neef 1992: 232).[24]

At best, the measures GNP and GDP provide information only on some aspects of one element of such an index, namely, on the provision of the consumption of monetarized goods and services. Now, according to Ekins, there are four different kinds of utility, and commodified goods and services primarily relate to that associated with 'having' but have little to do with others which involve 'being', 'doing' and 'relating' (Ekins 1992: 151). Max-Neef has in turn explored how these can be defined as needs and combined them in a matrix with other 'axiological' needs 'such as Subsistence, Protection, Affection, Understanding, Participation, Creation, Leisure, Identity and Freedom'. It then becomes clear that:

To assume a direct relation between needs and economic goods has allowed us to develop a discipline of economics that presumes itself to be objective, a mechanistic discipline in which the central tenet implies that needs manifest themselves through demand which, in turn, is determined by individual preferences for the goods produced.

(Max-Neef 1992: 202)

This is even true of environmental economics. Frances Cairncross (1993), for example, while admonishing companies to reduce the materials they use that could do environmental harm, is nevertheless impressed by the radical corporate thinking of 'progressive' companies such as Du Pont, citing as an example of 'green leadership', Du Pont's promise to reduce emissions by 90 per cent by the end of the century. While any corporation's reduction in emissions and other pollutants provides obvious benefits, theorists such as Smith question whether such 'green' policies make any real difference in global terms. As Smith (1997) notes, production methods may be changing for the better, yet the final outcome of the production process — the product — remains unchanged:

What real difference does it make if H. B. Fuller shares profits with its employees and gives endowments to universities, winning it rave reviews from the Socially Responsible Investment community, when one of its main products is a shoemakers' glue laced with the neurotoxin toluene that has addicted millions of Latin American street children, causing neurological damage, kidney and liver failure, paralysis and death? What real difference does it make if Du Pont uses 'clean production' techniques to produce its Express herbicide, marketed in China, when this herbicide is classed as a human carcinogen?

Chemicals, pesticides, plastics, disposable cameras, nuclear reactors, cars, books-on-CD-ROM, 'Mortal Kombat', junk food, MTV — whole slabs of global industry are geared to produce unnecessary, unhealthy, dangerous, destructive, anti-social, redundant or superfluous junk. Much of it is designed to fall apart or become obsolete 'to be consumed and discarded at an ever-increasing rate' so the cycle can go on endlessly.

(Smith, R. 1997: 38)

Thus, such putative improvements as the greening of the production process, conflate the 'symptom' with the 'disease'. The problem resides not in the *process* of production, but rather in its very *nature*. The problem is not just that companies use particular methods of production, but rather what and how much they produce. As Paul Hawkin suggests:

Despite their dedicated good work, if we examine all or any of the businesses that deservedly earn high marks for social and environmental responsibility, we are faced with a sobering irony: If every company on the planet were to adopt the environmental and social practices of the best companies — of, say, the Body Shop, Patagonia, and Ben and Jerry's — the world would still be moving towards environmental degradation and collapse. In other words, if we analyze environmental effects and create an input-output model of resources and energy, the results do not even approximate a tolerable or sustainable future. If a tiny fraction of the world's most intelligent companies cannot model a sustainable world, then that tells us that ... what we have is a not management problem but a design problem.

(Paul Hawkin as cited in Smith, R. 1997: 38)

This means that we should use a somewhat wider definition of economics than that implied by the neoclassical model, namely that it is 'the science which studies human behaviour as a relationship between ends and scarce means which have alternative uses' (Robbins 1984: 16), where 'ends are capable of being distinguished in order of importance' (Robbins 1984: 14) and that this 'ordering takes place with a view to increasing human welfare' and, that this ought to be inter-generationally sustainable. We can then distinguish between, and hence judge independently, '*Economic Growth*, defined as an increase in (a wide range of) utility or welfare. *Material growth*, growth in the economy's throughput of matter and energy ... *Productive growth*, increase in GDP and non-monetary production leading to an increase in consumption and ... *Environmental growth*, leading both to an increase in resources for consumption (e.g. fuelwood) or for environmental services (e.g. forests)' (Ekins 1992: 154).

One concluding point needs emphasis. An economics so defined and operationalised would vastly alter our calculations as to the costs and benefits of regulation; concomitantly, it would vastly alter our understanding of the costs and benefits of various forms of production. Indeed, it is possible that, on the basis of such an economic assessment, the costs of chemicals production, that is, production which is forced to internalise many of the costs which the industry has historically managed to externalise, might be so great as to render the only feasible chemical industry one which is massively subsidised by the state. With such an explicit socialisation of the costs of chemicals production, there would emerge a strong case for the socialisation of ownership and control. Re-conceptualising the nature of production opens up and legitimates different ways of organising production.

Notes

1. Thus, for example, technocratic and racist ideologies, educational and racial inequality, as well as class ideologies and inequalities, must be invoked to explain the Bhopal disaster or the disposal of toxic waste near communities of African Americans and aboriginal Americans (Pearce and Tombs 1989; Hofrichter 1993).

2. We discuss other versions of the nature of regulation and regulatory agencies at different points in the text; see particularly Chapters 7, 8, 9.

3. Useful here as general, but informed, histories are those by Davis (1984) and Grant et al. (1988). Davis (1984) has documented the role of the State in his study of the emergence and development of West European and American chemical industries. Grant et al. (1988) explore at much length contemporary government-chemical industry relations in the UK and Germany, albeit within a historical context.

4. The chemical industry actually consists of some thirty or so distinct businesses, which range from the supply of large tonnages of commodity chemicals for use by other industries or for further chemical processing, through a wide variety of speciality chemicals mainly for industrial use, to a number of products for the consumer. Thus, there are clearly some significant differences between these. However, most commentators upon the sector refer to a number of 'well-defined characteristics' which most of these business have in common (see, for example, Chenier 1986: 20, 21-27; Gill et al. 1978: xvii-xix; and, more generally, Grant et al. 1987, 1988; Hays 1973; Heaton 1996; Ilgen 1983; Reuben and Burstall 1973; Wei et al. 1979; Witcoff and Reuben 1980).

5. This is clearly illustrated as we write given the European-wide imposition of economic austerity measures as EU members seek to trim their deficits in order to meet convergence criteria for European Monetary Union.

6. For example, British attempts to attenuate or abolish occupational safety and health and environmental regulation have been thwarted in part by EC directives occasioned by some of the political fallout of Seveso and Bhopal; however, these directives have been supported by other member states (Tombs 1995b, 1996).

7. Weber's discussion of the relationship between capitalism and the nation-state is of relevance here. See Chapter 3.

8.   The application of Taylorist techniques (Aglietta 1979: 114) and Fordist redesign of work around the possibilities of machinery (Hounshell 1984: 251-253) increased productivity and the percentage of unskilled labour dramatically (Levine 1988: 27-33). However, expensive fixed capital costs made assembly line production very dependent upon economies of scale and hence required a large standardised market. At this time, this demand was concentrated in the producer goods sectors of the economy. Incomes from profit, interest and rent rose dramatically while wages remained stagnant (Aglietta 1979: 94) and the number of unemployed — fuelled by the influx of rural labour — high (Bernstein 1966: 41-82).

9.   See Willer and Willer (1973), Althusser and Balibar (1970), Hindess and Hirst (1975). For a defence of regulation theory against such charges and a construction of it in a mode akin to a realist epistemology see Jessop (1990a). For additional critiques of the New Times version of Fordism/PostFordism, see Rustin (1989), Hirst (1989), and Hirst and Zeitlin (1991).

10.   In 1983 while Nissan only directly employed approximately 30 per cent of production workers, the Nissan group controlled approximately 78 per cent of firms involved in the production process, the Toyota (group) approximately 73 per cent, whereas in the US GM controlled about 43 per cent, Ford about 36 per cent and Chrysler 28 per cent (Cusamo 1989: 190). Toyota has as many as 30,000 tertiary, 5,000 secondary and 220 primary subcontractors. Of the latter, 80 per cent had plants within the production complex surrounding Toyota in Toyota City. As one moves from primary to tertiary subcontractors, in part because of an ability created by the micro-electronics revolution to spread factory and office automation, an increasing percentage of workers are non-unionised poorly paid housewives.

11.   Although the health of core workers are better looked after in large Japanese companies than in comparable US ones (Wokutch 1992), the majority of these are in white collar posts. Moreover, given that a great deal of money is invested in their training and that they have contracts until the age of 55, it makes sense for companies to take some care with their health. No such rationale exists for the care of the health and safety of workers employed by subcontractors. There is a practice of subcontracting more hazardous jobs to smaller companies and they generally provide much poorer working conditions and continuity of employment. Not surprisingly, we find that the injury rates for workers employed in enterprises with less than 30 workers are nearly 20 times those for workers in enterprise that employ more than 1000 workers (Reich and Frumkin 1988: 809). Most part-time, temporary and seasonal workers are women, underemployed rural labourers, Burakumin (untouchables), or of Korean descent. State regulation tends to follow a compliance model (Hawkins 1984), of the type that prevails

where capital is dominant and no real countervailing power exists (Pearce and Tombs 1990, 1991; Snider 1991). Although, formally, occupational health and safety is organised according to a corporatist tripartite model, and there is some evidence of managerial and worker involvement within the plant and a reasonably professionalised inspectorate (Wokutch 1992), in practice it is dominated by the large corporations and their narrow partisan view of the appropriate balance between costs and benefits.

12. The Gini coefficient is a measure of the degree of inequality and is based upon the degree of divergence between the actual distribution of a country's income between the ten deciles of a population and what the distribution would be if every decile received the same income (Green and Sutcliffe 1987: 150-153).

13. Occupational health services improved dramatically and were under the control of safety committees. The evidence on accident rates is less clear — they seem to have neither worsened nor improved dramatically in the last decade. Reforms do not seem to have been translated into new workplace practices. Capital and the Labour Inspectorate have focused on designing safety into new processes but have not sought a significant input from workers and their unions. Safety committees have been more involved with immediate workshop issues than in the planning of the production process, and even there they have lacked effective power — only a minority of their complaints and recommendations are acted upon (Tucker 1992a: 110-111).

14. Since the 1920s, even in the case of motor cars there has always been product differentiation — a range of models has been offered, and, thanks to the 'genius' of General Motors, there have been yearly model changes (Hounshell 1984: 13). 'Fordist' production equipment always had some flexibility and was *never* totally dedicated.

15. For a superb critique of the role that 'postmodern' scepticism plays in the equivocal tone of recent writings of Stuart Hall, see Norris (1993).

16. See Polanyi (1944), White (1981), Perrow (1991), and Clegg (1990).

17. There was some progress in arguing for workers' rights in the 1994 GATT negotiations. For an example of a developed argument on this issue see Kimon Valaskakis 'Wanted: a GATT agreement that covers workers' *Globe and Mail*, Friday, 22 April 1994: A21).

18. Nationalisation has been less part of a socialist than a nationalist capitalist strategy — relatively successfully implemented in France, never adequately so in Britain (Gamble 1990). In the latter country, when it has occurred it has often

involved compensation to the previous owners, providing an unreasonable burden of reparation payments on public industries (Jenkins 1959). With wonderful symmetry, the sale of nationalised industries and other state owned assets have only too often been at fire-sale prices (Whitfield 1992: 281-282).

19. In comparing the relative efficiency of state and private enterprises, the conclusions are at best ambiguous — see also such studies as Parris, Pestieau and Satnor (1988), and Foreman-Peck (1989), focusing on the evidence (as opposed to the authors' conclusions).

20. By these criteria, in Britain, Thatcherite policies which produced an acceleration in the rate of deindustrialisation, a decline in the quality of the housing stock and in the rate of building new houses, the overbuilding of offices (*vide* Canary Wharf), and the concomitant increase in homelessness, must be seen as extremely economically inefficient.

21. Examples include French energy policy after 1973 (Parris et al. 1988: 124-125) and municipal utility energy policy in Osage, Iowa (Gordon and Suzuki 1990: 215-217).

22. These costs are under-estimates. The methodology by which these figures were reached defined accidents as unplanned events resulting in injury or ill-health or damage to property, plant, materials or the environment, or a loss of business opportunity (HSE 1993: 2). As Cutler and James (1996) note, however, 'an accident falling within this definition was only included if it had either caused a personal injury or was an event deemed, in the view of a steering committee drawn from both management and members of the APAU, to be "economic to prevent"' (Cutler and James 1996: 757; HSE 1993: 4). Similarly, in the later HSE study, 'unpreventable accidents' were excluded (Davis and Teasdale 1994: 73). Any accident also had to exceed an agreed minimum level of loss (HSE 1993; Cutler and James 1996). Indeed, 'no information is provided [in the HSE study] on the number of accidents excluded from the study on economic grounds of the risks associated with them. It cannot, therefore, be ruled out that a proportion of these accidents had the potential to cause serious injuries, if not fatalities, or that these accidents were more likely to cause injury than those which were costed' (Cutler and James 1996: 759).

23. In the US recently the GDP has displaced the GNP as the major measure of national income (cf. US Dept of Commerce 1991, August 1991: 8)

24. To what extent that these could be measured on a single index, however, then becomes increasingly debatable (Miles 1992).

3 Corporate Crime

Introduction

David Friedrichs has (rightly) noted that in both Europe and North America, there have been long traditions within which it has been recognised that 'the powerful and the privileged commit "crimes", loosely defined, as a consequence of the character of the economic system, and their special status within it' (Friedrichs 1992: 6). It is equally the case that such traditions have, for hundreds of years, encompassed social critics who have been clear that constitutions and legal systems, regimes of rights, duties and enablement, can be used both to challenge oppressive power and also to buttress such power.

Europe

In Britain, for example, there was a long struggle against both 'benefit of clergy' and aristocratic legal privileges (Jefferey 1957; Harding 1966; Tigar and Levy 1977). Interestingly, Thomas Hobbes, supposedly an intellectual predecessor of control theorists like Hirschi and Gottfredson (Ellis 1988), believed that:

> Of the passions that most frequently are the causes of crime, one, is vain glory, or a foolish overrating of their own worth ... From whence proceedeth a presumption that the punishments ordained by the laws, and extended generally to all subjects, ought not to be inflicted on them, with the same rigour they are inflicted on poor, obscure, and simple men, comprehended under the name of the *vulgar* ...
>
> Therefore it happeneth commonly, that such as value themselves by the greatness of their wealth, adventure on crimes, upon hope of escaping punishment, by corrupting public justice, or obtaining pardon by money, or other rewards.
>
> (Hobbes [1651] 1960: 193-194)

The same was true of other countries, notably France. Whilst such antagonisms were sometimes cynically manipulated by centralising monarchs, the related sense of injustice and the demand that all should be equally subject

83

to the law was an integral part of bourgeois ideology and part of its appeal for other social classes, and played a key role in the French revolution (Tigar and Levy 1977). When capitalism was triumphant and the bourgeoisie had established itself as the dominant class, it became clear that the law was once again supportive of substantive inequalities. By proclaiming that 'property is theft', Proudhon ([1840] 1966) indicated that private ownership by a minority of the means of production exploits workers and consumers. The Fourierists developed a theoretical critique of the nature of society and the workings of the law:

> Licensed prostitution, direct material theft, housebreaking, murder, brigandage for the lower classes; while skilful spoliation, indirect, refined theft, clever exploitation of human cattle, carefully planned and brilliantly executed betrayals, transcendent pieces of sharp practice in short, all the truly elegant vices and lucrative crimes which the law is far too polite to interrupt remain the monopoly of the upper classes.
> (*La Phalange*, 1 December 1838, cited in Foucault 1979a: 324)

There was thus no criminal nature but rather a play of forces, which according to the class to which individuals belong, will lead them to power or to prison; convicts, if they had been well born 'would be presiding in the courts and dispensing justice' (ibid: 289).

Marx and Engels built upon these arguments. The law's very content meant that it disproportionately benefitted the bourgeoisie. A society based upon freedom of contract is inherently unjust when the parties to such contracts are in substantively different situations — the bourgeoisie are free to devote their wealth to productive investment and to decide who they will employ or refuse to employ, *or*, alternatively, to simply consume, but their propertyless proletarians are (at best) free to choose to work for one or other employer *or* (at worst) to starve (Marx 1965: 169). In addition, whilst proclaiming that all were subject to the law and to the common morality, individual bourgeois often cynically violate both with impunity. But Marx and Engels pointed out that there were limits to such deviations, imposed not by abstract legal or moral principles but by the needs of the capitalist mode of production (Marx and Engels [1845] 1976: 180). If these and other contradictions of the capitalist system were not successfully 'managed' (above all by the national state), then ordinary people would either benefit from a transformation of the system into a socialist one, or suffer from its collapse into barbarism.

At the beginning of this century, the Belgian criminologist, Bonger, pointed out that the normal workings of the capitalist economic system and its motivating ideologies tend to generate crime amongst the bourgeoisie. Uncontrolled economic fluctuations mean that businessmen facing bankruptcy often resort to swindling or fraud. A society which enjoins morality on such narrow self-interested bases as 'Honesty is the best policy' and which generally upholds the principle of 'Each man for himself' does not encourage its respectable members to accept misfortune. In a society where the ostentatious display of wealth is encouraged and where the wealthy ignore the social costs of accumulation, there is a relative indifference to the illegality of methods of profit maximization like the adulteration of food. However, there will not be the same indifference to the perhaps less morally reprehensible practice of manipulating stock prices and issuing worthless shares. These are classed as crimes because:

> They are harmful to the regular progress of capitalism and consequently are threatened with penalties. The punishment of the adulteration of food stuffs, on the contrary, is a consequence of the opposition of the consumers to one of the harmful effects of the system.
>
> (Bonger [1905] 1969: 142)

Max Weber also addressed the issue of the potentially destructive consequences of an unfettered search for profit. Weber was no socialist but as a German nationalist he was committed to the German State and as a Bourgeois to capitalism. He was concerned to make both strong, and German civilization of world historic importance. For Weber the nation state was a powerful, effective, and now indispensable form of social organization. Its emergence and growth had been intimately connected with the development of capitalism since both were aspects of the development of western rationalism (Weber 1961: 232-3), but also because:

> The separate states had to compete for mobile capital, which dictated to them the conditions under which it would assist them to power. Out of this alliance of the state with capital, dictated by necessity, arose the national citizen class, the bourgeoisie in the modern sense of the word.
>
> (Weber 1961: 249)

Bismarck had tried to neutralise Social Democracy by measures aimed at repressing it and by creating an authoritarian welfare state, and, at the same time, trying to balance the interests of the middle classes and the aristocracy (Dickinson 1986). For Weber, however, the danger did not lie with the masses, as is believed by people who stare as if hypnotised at the depths of society. The final content of the *socio*-political problem is not the question of the *economic* situation of the *ruled* but of the political qualifications of the *ruling* and rising classes. The aim of our socio-political activity is not world happiness but the *social unification* of the nation, which has been split apart by modern economic development, for the severer struggles of the future.

(Weber 1895, translated in 1980: 446-7)

The Junkers were no longer capable of providing such leadership, and there was reason to doubt the capacities of the Bourgeoisie. Indeed, in 1918 Weber pointed out that despite the crisis in politics, 'big business' irresponsibly pursued profit in a way that was indifferent to the national interest. Because 'the expert knowledge of private economic interest groups in the field of "business" is superior to the expert knowledge of bureaucracy' (Weber 1978: 994) they were willing to support 'as one man the retention of an unsupervised bureaucracy' (Weber 1978: 1430).

Germany needed a political system in which all the social groups necessary for social reproduction including the 'responsible' working class (Weber 1978: 1428; Weber 1980: 445-7) would, though universal suffrage, have some form of representation. This would force even 'big business', to recognize a certain level of mutual interdependence and thus to define their own interests in a broader and more long term manner.

As we have seen, for Weber, capitalism and the nation state were both aspects of the development of Western rationalism. He believed that for the profit seeking enterprise to engage in 'rational capital accounting', it requires, first 'the appropriation of all physical means of production ... as disposable property of autonomous private industrial enterprises'; second 'freedom of the market'; third 'rational technology'; fourth 'calculable law' facilitating 'calculable adjudication and administration'; fifth, 'free labor' — 'Persons who are not only legally in this position, but are also economically compelled, to see their labor on the market without restriction'; sixth, 'the commercialization of everyday life' (Weber 1961: 208-9). Furthermore, the working of the market system as a whole needs a 'promptly and predictably functioning legal system, i.e., one which is guaranteed by the strongest coercive power' (Weber 1978: 377), a coercion that complemented that which economically compelled the propertyless to work for some capitalist enterprise or find themselves or their dependents 'without any provision' (Weber 1947: 214). Capitalism required a homogenous national space subject to a classic liberal legal rational order.

Under such a system, he believed that capitalism was not only the most formally rational means of engaging in rational economic action at the level of the enterprise but it could also be substantively rational (i.e. in terms of its ability to realise desired outcomes) 'if the standard used is that of the provision of a certain minimum of subsistence for the maximum size of population' (Weber 1978: 108-9).

Weber, however, added — 'it nevertheless holds true under all circumstances that formal rationality itself does not tell us anything about real want satisfaction unless it is combined with an analysis of the distribution of income' (Weber 1978: 109). He further acknowledged that given the limitations on how many goods can actually be profitably produced — and, we would add, given the existence of what have become inherently scarce goods such as pollution free living space — an individual's 'need may fail to be satisfied not only when an individual's own demand for other goods takes precedence but also when the greater purchasing power of others for all types of goods prevails' (Weber 1978: 93). Weber, further, recognized that while abstract formal justice

> guarantees the maximum freedom for the interested parties to represent their formal legal interests ... because of the unequal distribution of economic power, which the system of formal justice legalizes, this very freedom must time and time again produce consequences which are contrary to the substantive postulates of religious ethics or political expediency ... It is precisely this abstract character which constitutes the decisive merit of formal justice to those who wield economic power at any given time and who are therefore interested in its unhampered operation.
>
> (Weber 1978: 812-3)

Thus, E. P. Thompson may well be right when, in opposition to certain ultra-leftist interpretations of law, he argues:

> If the law is evidently partial and unjust, then it will mask nothing, legitimate nothing, contribute nothing to any class's hegemony. The essential precondition for the effectiveness of law, its function as ideology, is that it shall display an independence from gross manipulation and shall seem to be just. It cannot do so without upholding its own logic and criterion of equity; indeed, on occasion, by actually being just.
>
> (Thompson 1980: 263)

And we would certainly endorse the view that law is a site of struggle and that its content and mode of social organization have varying effects. Yet,

Weber sensitises us to the ways in which formal legal rationality is inherently limited in its ability to achieve substantive social goals — and this is true even when its content is most progressive and social equality is greatest — but its limitations are particularly evident under our current situation of massive inequalities of power and wealth (McBarnet 1992). The legal system should therefore be used (with great care) as a resource by those who seek substantive goals (Pearce 1995). It is for these reasons that throughout this text we advocate reform of the law, changes in the way it is implemented *and* new institutional forms that will facilitate active democratic involvement and agenda setting by workers and local communities.

North America

If, in North America, the move to democratic politics was more dramatic than was the case in Germany, its containment was equally complex. Although there was widespread support for the Declaration of Independence there was little consensus about the nature of the new Republic (Hofstadter 1967). Whatever their democratic rhetoric, in practice, the Federalists and their supporters remained committed to a Whiggish politics. Of particular interest to us, in this text, is that this could be seen in their use of the corporate charters for both commercial corporations and municipal corporations.

By granting corporate charters to various forms of business activity, the state legislatures formally acknowledged the civil status of property devoted to the pursuit of corporate ends. Possession of a corporate charter allowed bankers, turnpike, canal and railroad operators — and even a few manufacturers — to claim that their business enterprises were infused with a substantial public interest. Any enterprise endowed with a charter was lifted above the crass pursuit of a merely private interest by the common law conception of the corporation as an association of persons vested by policy of the law with certain powers deemed necessary to the promotion of some design of general utility and public benefit (Fraser 1983: 10-19).

Commercial and professional gentry tried to use the traditional corporate form as a way of both consolidating their hold on social life and of asserting the importance of a conception of property which tied it intimately to public duties and their civil dominion. The opposition to these privileges, including the state's privilege of incorporation, came from religious, fundamentalist and democratic forces as well as those capitalist ones committed to the development of an autonomous 'economy' (Chayes 1961); and such opposition successfully challenged the state's privilege of granting incorporation so that by the 1840s the incorporation process had become very open indeed (Davis [1905] 1971).

It was this ease of incorporation and of achieving limited liability in the US that was to provide strong ammunition for the development of limited liability corporations in the 1860s in Britain, and this in turn created the same response in France.

Obviously, the American Civil War can also be construed as an attack on a highly organised and legitimated (Genovese 1967, 1969, 1971) relative privileging of some groups and the disadvantaging of others, this time on the privileging of whites and the oppression of blacks in the Southern slave states. True, the roots of civil war lay in the competition for dominance and territory between the Northern and Southern economic systems (Hindess and Hirst 1975), but the North's opposition to the mode of production based on slavery necessarily challenged the racial privilege that was sustained, organised and enforced by the Southern legal code.

Slave rebellion and resistance had always challenged this Southern system, and although its final defeat required the intervention of Northern whites, defeat depended to a significant degree upon the massive involvement of black soldiers — black people played an important role in their own emancipation (Zinn 1980: 167-191). For a short period, during Reconstruction, they even exercised some real political power in the South (Stampp 1965; Woodward 1960; Washington 1967). However, they never received the ten acres and a mule promised by Lincoln, and when the Northern merchants and industrialists and the Southern Bourbon Aristocracy made their peace, most found themselves in peonage, as sharecroppers.

Despite the general co-option of Southern poor whites into that new racist system of 'Redemption' (Woodward 1996a), as it was tellingly called, there was a period when poor blacks and poor whites made common cause. This was through the dynamic and complex populist movement which ebbed and flowed from the time of the great depression of the 1870s through until the mid 1890s, but ultimately failed to realise its more radical aspirations. It failed, however, not, as later 'evolutionary pluralists' believed, because its more rational elements were compromised by the faith of its haunted, terrified followers in 'the idea of a golden age; the concept of natural harmonies; the dualistic version of social struggle; the conspiracy theory of history; and the doctrine of the primacy of money' (Hofstadter 1955: 62). Nor is it accurate to suggest that its rational elements lived on in progressivism and the irrational in the jingoistic nationalism of the later William Jennings Bryan. Such accounts do violence to the 'people's party' and the populist movement, and have been profoundly challenged by the works of C. Vann Woodward (1938, 1966b), Norman

Pollack (1962) and to an even greater extent Lawrence Goodwyn (1976). These historians show that it was vital, critical, practical, and *contra* Jones (1982) confronted all elements of property relations.[1]

Populism was a movement which challenged the direction in which American society was moving, and which called into question its evolving mode of economic organisation, its political forms and its legal system. It denied that the increasing concentration of industry was both inevitable and progressive. The 'muckraker', Henry Demarast Lloyd, for example, not only accurately documented much of the chicanery associated with the rise to prominence of the Standard Oil Company and other trusts, but he also attacked the principle 'that strength gives the strong in the market the right to destroy his neighbour' (Lloyd [1894] 1963: 170). In Lloyd's view, big business needed to be replaced by collective ownership. Without this there were limits as to what could be achieved by state, and particularly legal, intervention in the economy: 'The possibility of regulation is a dream. As long as this control of the necessaries of life and this wealth remain private with individuals, it is they who will regulate, not we' (ibid.: 182). Not surprisingly, in its 1892 Omaha platform the populist party proposed to nationalise the railroads.

Many 'robber barons' worked to legitimate their wealth through well publicised philanthropy (Josephson 1962; Lloyd [1894] 1963: 122) and one of the most ostentatious, Andrew Carnegie, also tried to redefine the nature of society's social problems. For Carnegie there was no need to redistribute wealth. Instead, in language curiously close to some of the arguments for corporate philanthropy within contemporary 'social responsibility' and 'business ethics' movements (see, for example, the papers in Houck and Williams, eds. 1996), Carnegie claimed that 'The problem of our age is the proper administration of wealth so that the ties of brotherhood may still bind together the rich and poor in harmonious relationship' (cited in Collier and Horowitz 1976: 48).

But, as Lloyd points out, however magnificent these gifts, they do not compare with what might have been given voluntarily in a more equal society — 'Aristocratic benevolence spends a shrunked stream in comparison with democratic benevolence' (Lloyd [1894] 1963: 164-165). A somewhat similar point would be made in the wake of the 1913 massacre of forty men and two women and eleven children during the Ludlow coal mine strike led by the Union of Mine Workers against the Rockefeller owned company, The Colorado Fuel and Iron. When, John Lawson, the leader of the UMW, was asked what he thought of Rockefeller's philanthropy, he replied:

It is not their money that these lords of commercial virtue are spending but the withheld wages of the American working class ... Health for China, a refuge for birds ... pensions for New York widows, and never a thought of a dollar for the thousands who starved in Colorado.

(cited in Collier and Horowitz 1976: 121)

Moreover, such benevolence is inexpensive compared to what they would have had to pay if there was an adequate redistributive taxation system — something never realised in the US. Lloyd's crucial point was this — inequality of power and wealth were a natural result of the development of large scale capitalism, and these same inequalities helped ensure its survival and expansion.

Populism failed to achieve many of its goals and disappeared as a collective movement. Significant to its eclipse were: its inability to form effective alliances with the urban trade unions and socialist parties; its ambivalence about private property and the market economy; its involvement in the 'free silver' issue; and its unwise fusion with the Democratic Party. Then, what had become a 'shadow movement' was no match for the forces and money mobilized against it by the Republicans. Symptomatic of all of this was the passing of the Sherman Anti-Trust Act which condemned conspiracies in restraint of trade. It was used against separate and independent companies (or groups like trade unions), but already in 1889 a New Jersey law allowed one corporation to own the stock of another. If the Sherman Act failed in its goal of regulating the economy, subsequent legislation and the regulatory agencies set up during the progressive era were part of the process by which capital asserted the primacy of its long term over its short term interests and tied it to the American state. By surrendering some autonomy and by recognizing that oligopoly, not monopoly, was to become the norm, it gained legitimacy and security (Kolko 1965; Pearce 1976).

After the 'populist moment' the muckraking tradition still continued to expose the dangers, injustice and chicanery so prevalent in the emerging corporate capitalist industrial order, but it was now articulated with either socialism, on the one hand, or progressivism, on the other. The socialists, such as Upton Sinclair, viewed the evidence of capitalism's ruthlessness as symptomatic of the inherent corruption of the system, and believed that capitalism itself needed to be eliminated. Progressives were more concerned to tame the evident excesses of individual capitalists in order to re-legitimate the system as a whole and in order to make it work more efficiently *qua* system. In 1903 the editor of McLures treated as equally problematic and equally a threat to 'liberty' — the illegal and unfair business practices of Standard Oil, municipal political corruption, and illegal and illegitimate but effective practices by trade unions (cf. Hofstadter 1963: 16-17).

American Sociology, Corruption and Crime

A major and necessary mechanism for the development and transformation of capitalist economic and social relations in the US, and also therefore a site of ideological struggle, is its legal system. It is therefore of some interest, that, in 1907, when the sociologist Edward A. Ross identified the 'criminaloid', he did so within a 'progressivist' framework:

> [T]he director who speculates in the securities of his corporation, the director who lends his depositors' money to himself under divers corporate aliases, the railroad official who grants a secret rebate for his private graft, the builder who hires walking delegates to harass his rivals with causeless strikes, the labor leader who instigates a strike in order to be paid for calling it off, the publisher who bribes his textbooks into the schools.
>
> (Ross 1907, reprinted in Geis 1967: 27)

There was little further written on this issue in American sociology until 1935 when, six years after the Great Crash and one year after the Nye committee's investigation of the role played by bankers and armaments manufacturers in America's involvement in World War I (Leuchtenberg 1963: 148, 217), Albert Morris developed an extensive listing of 'criminals of the upperworld' which included those engaging in financial fraud, fraudulent jingoistic propaganda and violations of international law (Morris 1935, in Geis 1967: 34-39). Similar concerns and the Brandeisian attack on monopoly provided the context for the development of Edwin Sutherland's concept of 'white-collar crime'.

In a series of papers, articles and a book published between 1940 and 1949 Sutherland developed the concept of 'white-collar crime' — 'crime committed by a person of respectability and high social status in the course of his occupation' (Sutherland 1949: 7). He thus challenged the stereotypical view of the criminal as typically lower class since 'powerful business and professional men' also routinely commit crimes. Criminal acts are not restricted to those dealt with in criminal courts. Other agencies such as juvenile courts may deal with 'violations of the criminal law' and some offenses can be dealt with by either criminal courts or civil courts. Some individual white collar offenders avoid criminal prosecution because of the class bias of the courts — although businessmen could often be charged as accessories to such crimes as bribery, unlike politicians they usually escape prosecution — but more generally they are aided by 'the power of their class to influence the implementation and administration of the law'. Thus the crimes of the upper and lower classes 'differ principally in the implementation of the criminal laws that apply to them' (Sutherland 1940 in Geis 1968: 45-7).

In his 1945 article 'Is "White-Collar Crime" Crime?' Sutherland drew upon Jerome Hall to produce a more encompassing and abstract definition of crime. Crime requires the 'legal description of an act as socially injurious and legal provision of a penalty for the act' (Sutherland 1945 in Geis 1968: 354). Many laws which are enforced by administrative bodies through the civil courts also regulate actions which cause injuries to specific individuals or which undermine social institutions, and they also routinely impose punitive sanctions. Moreover, *contra* the view that such acts are merely 'technical violations and involve no moral culpability', in fact they are 'distributed along a continuum in which the *mala in se* are at one extreme and the *mala prohibita* at the other' (ibid.: 363). The content of laws and such legal distinctions (a more contemporary one is that between felonies and misdemeanours) are themselves social products (ibid: 363; and see also Palmer 1976).

If one used these definitions, one found: first, that the common image of typical crimes and typical criminality was inaccurate, crime is widespread throughout society; second, that a reductionist criminology which explained criminal behaviour in terms of the pathology of lower class individuals or their families was inadequate whereas differential association theory was adequate; third, that the scope of Criminology needed to be widened to take account of a wider range of conduct and the political processes that defined it as criminal or not; fourth, that one must explain, and guard against both the predatory crimes of the poor and the abuses of their power by the wealthy. That one did not do so was due to the latter's manipulation of public consciousness by the media with the collusion of the courts.

In his article, 'Who is the criminal?' Paul Tappan developed a systematic criticism of Sutherland's work. He first provided 'rigorous' definitions of crime and the criminal:

> Crime is an intentional act in violation of the criminal law (statutory and case law) committed without defense or excuse, and penalized by the state as a felony or misdemeanour. In studying the offender there can be no presumption that arrested, arraigned, indicted, or prosecuted persons are criminals unless they can also be held guilty beyond a reasonable doubt of a particular offense.
>
> (Tappan 1947, reprinted in Geis 1968: 370)

In Tappan's view, it is illegitimate of Sutherland to describe people as criminal when they have not been successfully prosecuted for a crime, and, moreover, he illegitimately extends the concept of crime to cover acts that do not violate the criminal law:

> In light of these definitions the normative issue is pointed. Who should be considered the white-collar criminal? Is it the merchant who, out of greed, business acumen, or competitive motivations, breaches a trust with his consumer by 'puffing his wares' beyond their merits, by pricing them beyond their value, or by ordinary advertising? Is it he who breaks trust with his employees in order to keep wages down, refusing to permit labor organization or to bargain collectively, and who is found guilty by a labor relations board of an unfair labor practice? May it be the white-collar worker who breaches trust with his employers by inefficient performance at work, by sympathetic strike or secondary boycott? Or is it the merchandiser who violates ethics by undercutting the prices of his fellow merchants? In general, these acts do not violate the criminal law. *All are within the framework of normal business practice.*
>
> (Tappan 1947, reprinted in Geis 1968: 369, emphasis added)

The argument that such 'regulatory offences' are inherently different from criminal offences is not, of course, restricted to Tappan. We examine such arguments in their social liberal and neo-liberal variants at length in Chapter 7. Here, however, we should emphasise that Sutherland was well aware that certain kinds of actions were viewed not as 'real crimes', but as normal business practice, and as such did not attract popular moral censure. Yet he (rightly) refused to accept that this mitigated the harm they caused:

> The law is pressing in one direction and other forces are pressing in the opposite direction. In business, the 'rules of the game' conflict with the legal rules. A businessman who wants to obey the law is driven by his competitors to adopt their methods. This is well illustrated by the persistence of commercial bribery in spite of the strenuous efforts of business organizations to eliminate it.
>
> (Sutherland, cited in Geis and Meier 1977: 48)

Nevertheless, Tappan was correct to criticise the looseness with which the category of criminal is sometimes extended to those who, if they were subject to the due process of the law, would not be found guilty of any offence. Interestingly enough, this is of contemporary importance, particularly in the area of victim studies where individual perception of criminal injury is too easily accepted as a legally adequate description of what has occurred. He is, however, only partially correct, since this criticism does not logically imply the conclusion that there are no acts which, whilst currently unknown, would not lead to a successful prosecution if the relevant facts were known. In other words, he is wrong to imply that it makes no sense to discuss undiscovered murders, or more generally, the 'dark figure of crime'.

Moreover, the law is by no means consistent about what differentiates a crime from other offences nor what constitutes due process. Sutherland had anticipated that his claim that many civil offences were really crimes would:

> be questioned on the grounds that the rules of evidence used in reaching these decisions are not the same as those used in decisions regarding other crimes, especially that some of the agencies which rendered the decisions did not require proof of criminal intent and did not presume the accused to be innocent. These rules of criminal intent and presumption of innocence, however, are not required in all prosecutions under the regular penal code and the number of exceptions is increasing. In many states a person may be committed to prison without protection of one or both of these rules on charges of statutory rape, bigamy, adultery, passing bad checks, selling mortgaged property, defrauding a hotel keeper, and other offenses ... On the one side, many of the defendants in usual criminal cases, being in relative poverty, do not get good defense and consequently secure little benefit from these rules; on the other hand, the commissions come close to observing these rules of proof and evidence although they are not required to do so.
>
> (Sutherland 1945: 358)

Thus Sutherland recognized, as Tappan did not, that there is a question as to how, and, indeed, whether, 'due process' is achieved. At the time that both were writing — prior to Gideon, Miranda, etc., — this was particularly problematic.

In Britain, there is no legal right to due process (indeed, there is now no effective 'right to silence'), in part because of the structure of the law but also because of the nature and limited availability of the legal aid system (Carlen 1976; Burton and Carlen 1979). Neither does intent always need to be demonstrated; sometimes it can be inferred. For example, under the Vagrancy Act an individual:

> may be convicted if, from circumstances of the case and from his known character, the court is of the opinion that he was intending to commit a felony.
>
> (Vagrancy Act 1824, s. 12, cited in McBarnet 1983: 32)

In the US, because of the quality, work load and *modus operandi* of public defenders, due process is still rarely realised in practice (Blumberg 1967; Feeley 1979). There, the ten year period between 1983-1993 saw the numbers of imprisoned drug offenders increase nationally by 510 per cent, from 57,000 to

353,000 (Mauer 1996: 13); and these are offences in which issues of *mens rea* rarely arise (Skolnick 1966; Manning 1980). Indeed, there is a clear racial (and class) element to this trend in incarceration for drug offences; whilst African-Americans constitute approximately 12 percent of the American population, they comprise 74 per cent of those imprisoned for drug offences (*Economist*, 8 June 1996: 23). Combining African-Americans with Hispanics raises this figure to almost 90 per cent (Mauer 1996: 13). By contrast, whether they are successful professional criminals or respectable prosperous citizens, wealthy defendants are best placed to concretely realise their formal right to due process (Chapman 1968). Indeed, Mann (1985) shows that attorneys working for white collar criminals are often able to mobilise more resources than the prosecuting agencies (see also McBarnet 1992). They frequently manage to forestall even the laying of charges, and if they do go to trial they are usually able to argue successfully for jury trial which gives their clients a much better chance of acquittal.

Sutherland also raised the crucial issue of how the relative power of different social groups affected what became criminalised and when:

> Embezzlement is usually theft from an employer by an employee, and the employee is less capable of manipulating social and legal forces in his own interest than is the employer. As might have been expected, the laws regarding embezzlement were formulated long before laws for the protection of investors and consumers.
>
> (Sutherland 1940, cited in Geis 1968: 48)

Further, he demonstrated the contingent nature of the distinction between criminal and other offences by tracing the genealogy of the laws regulating competition (antitrust), false advertising, labour relations, and infringements of patents, copyrights, and trademarks. Each:

> has a logical basis in the common law and is an adaption of common law to modern social organization. False advertising is related to common-law fraud, and infringement to larceny. The National Labor Relations Board Law, as an attempt to prevent coercion, is related to the common-law prohibition of restrictions on freedom in the form of assault, false imprisonment and extortion. For at least two centuries prior to the enactment of the modern anti-trust laws, the common law was moving against restraint of trade, monopoly and unfair competition.
>
> (Sutherland 1945, cited in Geis 1968: 354)

Thus, there are good reasons for suspecting that the differential application of law, the development of different legal categories, and distinct enforcement *modus operandi* for 'street' and corporate offenders are not rooted in any intrinsic differences in the offences *per se*. In this respect, Glasbeek and Rowland (1979) have shown that maiming and killing at work *could* easily be defined as offences under the Canadian Criminal Code. In the US, there is a longer tradition of the criminalisation of some corporate offences, albeit only the most egregious, and of attempts to apply criminal law to the corporate form. Thus, in the early 1980s Ford was prosecuted (unsuccessfully) with reckless homicide for the defective design of the gas tank of the Ford Pinto (Cullen et al. 1987). Then, in June 1985 in Illinois the Film Recovery System Corporation and its parent company Metallic Marketing Inc., were convicted of involuntary manslaughter and 14 counts of reckless conduct and fined $14,000 each after a worker died at its factory from cyanide fumes. Three of its executives were also convicted of murder and 14 counts of reckless conduct and received 26 year sentences (Coleman 1987). The judge ruled that the Film Recovery president and the managers knew that their acts would cause a strong probability of death or great bodily harm — conditions of murder in the Illinois statute.[2] In Britain, such initiatives are much less well developed. Yet as both Bergman (1991, 1994), Slapper (1993) and Wells (1993) have demonstrated, there are no insuperable problems intrinsic to law to the effective criminalisation of such offences; what is commonly lacking is political will, itself related to particular representations of 'law and order' and what constitutes real crime (Tombs 1997). These points are further developed in Chapter 7.

Crimes, then, are illegalities which are (contingently) differentiated from other illegalities by virtue of the specific administrative procedures to which they are subject. Successful criminalisation of the illegalities of the powerful would pre-empt them from arguing that their illegalities are merely 'regulatory offences', merely *mala prohibita*. To be subject to one rather than another set of procedures, of course, has important differential effects.

Further, as Blum-West and Carter argue, many illegalities can be pursued as either crimes or torts:

crimes against the person may also be dealt with as torts of assault, battery, and negligence. Property crimes, both theft and destruction of property, may be pursued in civil suits charging trespass. Libel may be both a criminal and a civil offense. Fraud and crimes of false pretense may also be remedied through the tort of deception. Even acts of embezzlement can be heard under civil suits of wrongful conversion ...

(Blum-West and Carter 1983: 550)

True, there are different legal procedures:

Torts begin with a complaint by a private citizen that results in a summons. Criminal prosecutions begin with a complaint to the police or by an arrest. The complainant in a tort case must maintain the civil suit for it to be pursued. The state, however, can pursue criminal cases regardless of the wishes of the victim, although in practice it is often difficult to do without the willing cooperation of the victim. Tort cases are decided against the defendant by a 'preponderance of evidence', while criminal cases must be decided against the defendant only by evidence of guilt 'beyond a reasonable doubt'. The result of a tort case is a 'finding' or a 'judgment', while criminal cases result in conviction or acquittal.

(Blum-West and Carter 1983: 546)

And, in addition, there are, allegedly, a number of substantive differences. First, whilst intent is required for a crime, it is not relevant for a tort. Second, crimes involve immoral conduct whereas torts involve 'social fault', deviance that happens to produce some harmful effect. Third, criminal sanctions are designed to punish while in tort they are designed to compensate. Fourth, criminal procedures are designed to protect the interests of society, torts those of individuals.

None of these distinctions hold in practice. Let us take them in turn. With 'the exception of strict and vicarious liability — which occur in both the criminal and the civil law — both criminal law and tort law require that acts be intentional before they are sanctioned' and the 'rules for determining culpability are also identical'(Blum-West and Carter 1983: 547).

Then, while distinctions are made between crimes that are *mala in se* and *mala prohibita*, at the same time, 'in the great majority of cases liability in tort rests upon some moral delinquency' (Prosser 1971: 18, cited in Blum-West and Carter 1983: 548). Further, in both crimes and torts one of the purposes of legal intervention is to discourage undesirable conduct and hence coercion and punishment are intrinsic to such sanctions. Indeed, as Celia Wells notes, offences which are *mala in se* and *mala prohibita* are *both* significant within criminal justice and *both* sit within criminal law (Wells 1990: 7). It is problematic to categorise some harms as less and more morally offensive — these are all crimes (Wells 1993: 7-8).[3]

If we examine Blum-West and Carter's discussion we see that they have gone well beyond Sutherland, for the implication of their work is that all 'illegalities' — i.e., actionable infringements on the right of others (singly or collectively) or failure to perform one's duties — could be treated as crimes. Any kind of harmful illegalities should be considered as crimes since, to use James Q. Wilson's criteria, such actions if *generalized* would undermine the well-being of individuals and 'community'.

From Criminology to a Sociology of Law

Ultimately, however, such issues cannot be resolved within criminology. We are in complete agreement with Sutherland on the direction of his general project, which amounts to a sociological critique of legal categories and processes, and a discipline which restricts itself to a focus upon these. Crucial to the dispute between Sutherland and Tappan is precisely that the former was a sociologist, the latter a legal scholar. For us, as sociologists, integral to any consideration of particular aspects of law — such as the question of what constitutes corporate crime — is the need for an understanding of the coverage and omissions of legal categories, the presences and absences within legal discourse, the social constructions of these categories and discourses, their underpinning of, treatment within and development through criminal justice systems, and the ways in which particular laws are enforced (or not enforced), interpreted, challenged, and so on.

Following Cotterell, we argue that law is best viewed as 'a body of doctrine':

> Law thus consists of social rules importing or implying certain cognitive and evaluative principles and concepts.
>
> (Cotterell 1984: 45)

Thus the focus of a sociology of law is a focus upon both those 'factors which determine how rules are interpreted in particular contexts', and 'the content of the rules themselves' (ibid.).

Further, legal doctrine is dynamic, that is, constructed in social action, or more precisely, 'in disputes; in political conflict; in the interaction between and the organisation of courts, lawyers and law enforcement agencies; in business practice; and through the actions (or inactions) of citizens' (ibid.).

Law is 'both an effect of and affects other fundamental social relations' (Pearce 1989a: 185; Woodiwiss 1987). Indeed, law requires an institutional base within the state, a body of lawyers, and a mechanism for the closure of meaning (Woodiwiss 1990a). It is a mechanism for social control, and also a resource whereby such control can be evaded (McBarnet 1992). Law defines what is lawful conduct — it prohibits behaviours, enjoins behaviours, it facilitates behaviours, it can constitute entities, such as a corporation as a legal person — it can empower. It requires a sanctioning apparatus to achieve all of these goals. Thus legal regulations can command, constitute and empower but are always backed up by sanctions.

Now, as O'Malley has noted, while Sutherland's work was responsible for generating a number of difficulties within bourgeois criminology — notably concerning the definition of crime — his work aimed at the creation of a unified theory of criminality. Thus with respect to his most troublesome work on white-collar crime, he was still concerned to integrate this into 'the same general process as other criminal behaviour, namely differential association' (O'Malley 1987: 24).

Thus, while Sutherland remained committed to criminology, there is a real sense in which a development of his arguments entails a transcendence of the boundaries of criminology (Nelken 1994a: 366). This is, after all, a discipline which, as O'Malley notes, is organised around a unifying concept, namely crime. Moreover, within legal discourse, crime bears a consistent relationship to a wide array of other theoretical concepts and assumptions — for example, that crime is a violation of rights and duties of some community, that the state acts on behalf of the interests and 'social consciousness' of this unitary community, and that the state represents an injured (collective) party in a criminal case and inflicts punishment on behalf of society. Thus, 'In this theoretical context, criminology as a unified science makes sense, ordered as it is around crime as a unified object of knowledge, and geared to a unified purpose' (O'Malley 1987: 9).

It is this particular role of the bourgeois concept of crime that leads O'Malley, like Hirst (1972) Pearce (1976) and Jones (1982), to reject a Marxist criminology as a contradictory enterprise. Now, it is certainly the case that some of the difficult definitional discussions within which radical criminologists find themselves — not least around the definition of corporate crime (Friedrichs 1992, Nelken 1994a) — relate to the peculiarity of the concept of crime highlighted by O'Malley. Indeed, the direction of his critique leads him to a rejection of any Marxism defined by this essentially bourgeois concept:

> What theoretical or political unity could be formed under the banner of 'Marxist criminology' if some criminal actions represent forms of popular struggle (e.g. illegal strike action and picketing, resisting legal prohibitions of demonstration

and on free speech), while others represent complex effects of brutalisation among the working class, which harm fellow working people ('mugging') and still others represent the less complex effects of pressures for profitability which lead corporations to endanger the lives of employees. Moreover, many such actions which are highly injurious to working people — such as the exposure of workers and their families to health-endangering pollution — may not appear as criminal at all, but are classified under some other legal category.

(O'Malley 1987: 12-13)

Such arguments are powerful and indicate the need to break from criminology towards a sociology and a political economy of law and legal regulation. This is precisely the approach adopted in this text. However, we should be clear at this point that such an enterprise generates tensions. These are partly academic tensions, but it seems to us that they are related to political tensions, perhaps analogous to that between the proposing of 'mere' reforms and 'non-reformist' reforms. We should expand upon these latter points.

Crimes Without Law?

Throughout this text we discuss *as crimes* many acts and omissions which have not been subject to any formal judicial process; thus these are phenomena which have not been interrogated as, let alone proven to be, violations of the criminal, or indeed any other form of, law. However, we seek to retain law as a reference point, and in doing so we must be clear that this law is bourgeois law. This does create a tension, then, because we are utilising categories which have developed, operated, and so on within a particular mode of production. Moreover, we are not even using these 'faithfully'.

A first rationale for this approach is to be found in our understanding of the role of law in any socialist societies. On the one hand, there seems to us to be no doubt that any modern mode of production — certainly including socialism and communism — would be organised around a legal system and the rule of law (Pearce 1989a: 179-204). As we have indicated, and as Sutherland himself is at pains to point out, existing law and legal regulation have developed from common law traditions of fraud, larceny, prohibitions of restrictions on freedom in the form of assault, false imprisonment, extortion, and so on (Sutherland 1945: 133). It is impossible to imagine a socialist society without some forms of law relating to aspects of previous traditions. On the other hand, what is clear is that the precise — and, as we have noted, non-necessary — distinctions between, and prioritisation amongst, different kinds of offences within bourgeois law need not and would not pertain within a socialist social order. Thus, for example, and as we have indicated, while there is no necessary reason that killing and injuring employees should not be treated through criminal law categories of murder and manslaughter, this is not the case within capitalist jurisdictions — but it could be. Indeed, one reason for maintaining bourgeois law as a reference point in this text, but for not being restricted to the use of the label crime relating to that currently proscribed by criminal law, is that some of the arguments we propose aim to be prefigurative.

In this respect, then, it is worth noting that we do not subscribe to any reductionist or instrumentalist view of law which sees it somehow as simply a tool of capital or some ruling class. A clear implication of the previous argument regarding the potentially prefigurative nature of legal reforms is a view of law more akin to that found in certain versions of structural Marxism, within which law is a site of, and an element within, hegemonic struggle (Jessop 1980; Palmer and Pearce 1983). Thus, while law seeks to secure closure of meaning, this is never complete, and constantly open to contest. As Moran has written of the final judgement in — or rather the collapse of — the manslaughter cases arising out of the sinking of the *Herald of Free Enterprise* (discussed below):

> writing the disaster in law is not merely a passive or inevitable process of production. It is a struggle to determine the question of a juridical capacity of the corporation set within the horizon of possibilities constituted by reference to that already said of law which may not only impose restraints but which may also provide the potential for new possibilities.
>
> (Moran 1992: 387)

Certainly, then, the nature of particular laws is never wholly pre-determined — as we noted above, Sutherland himself makes this point through reference to anti-trust laws which, although passed ostensibly to regulate corporate activity, ended up largely being utilised against trades unions (Sutherland 1945). Similarly, laws of manslaughter, developed within an individualistic tradition of law which seeks to regulate behaviours between individual human subjects, have recently been subject to contest in the UK, so that arguments around the notion of corporate manslaughter have led to the first (two) convictions for corporate manslaughter (Tombs 1995b; *The Safety and Health Practitioner*, December 1996: 3), and then to proposals for the development of new charges of corporate manslaughter (Law Commission 1996). These phenomena can only be understood within the context of a generalised struggle on the part of organised workers and various disaster action community groups which essentially became a contest over legitimacy and glaring inequality (Tombs 1995).

Second, we discuss under the rubric of crime in this text acts and omissions that have not been processed successfully through any criminal justice system; that is, where no legal verdict has been reached, let alone a guilty verdict in a criminal court. For example, we discuss Bhopal at length, despite the fact that an out-of-court settlement meant that there was never any detailed legal discussion of, let alone judgement regarding, the facts of that case (Chapter 6). Similarly, we discuss safety crimes although these form a subset of events recorded as accidents, and the vast majority of such crimes have not been subject to any legal process (Chapter 4).

However, in both instances, we organise our discussions around available empirical evidence and through theoretical and conceptual argument. Thus our discussions are based upon publicly available evidence; we examine this evidence sociologically and through reference to existent legal categories; and we attempt to do so with sufficient rigour that our judgements are open to contestation. That is, our general aim is to bring to bear sociological rigour to issues that have not been raised or settled within legal forums. To refrain from such analyses would mean that some of the most egregious corporate acts and omissions remained free of critical scrutiny through reference to the law, in many cases (as we shall see) merely because the exercise or existence of corporate power (as particular effects of class power), conflicts of interest within and between national states, or indeed technical inadequacies in state and national state legal systems had prevented the details of a case from receiving a public airing.

A third reason for maintaining reference to the law is both a methodological and political one. While there are justifications of the kind presented above for arguing that the distinctions between types of law is both non-necessary and in many ways motivated, through retaining a reference to existent legal categories we avoid the frequent charge of mere moralising, or moral entrepreneurship (Levi 1994; Nelken 1994a; Shapiro 1983). Thus it has been claimed that 'moral outrage may be good politics but bad science' (Meier 1986, cited in Friedrichs 1992: 9; see also Hirschi and Gottfredson 1987; Gottfredson and Hirschi 1990 who level this charge at sociologists in particular). Such a charge is often unjustified; as Michalowski and Kramer have rightly noted, using the law to define the boundaries of any criminological enterprise is itself 'suffused with moral choice' (Michalowski and Kramer 1987: 45). However, we intend to preempt this charge.

Let us give a concrete example here. We would not encompass within our consideration of crime the promotion and sale of tobacco products *per se*. In a different context we would argue that such products ought not to be legal, but it is hard to see how, at this time, the activities of the tobacco industry could be treated as an issue of corporate criminality — certainly unethical, or socially irresponsible, but only on occasion amounting to human rights violations or criminal conduct. We could, however, quite legitimately encompass within our definition of corporate crime some of the well-documented violations of law on the part of tobacco companies — the withholding and falsification of evidence relating to ill-health effects, the denial of knowledge of addiction, and so on. These would be included, since there is clear evidence that they represent violations of various forms of law, even though this may not be criminal law, and even though many of these violations have not been pursued through any criminal justice process.

Thus, we perceive a qualitative difference between, on the one hand, arguing about acts and omissions which existent bodies of law proscribe and/or require, albeit through different forms of law or within different national jurisdictions, and, on the other hand, simply arguing that law should encompass a whole range of acts and omissions that we wish to categorise as social harms. This is not to deride efforts of the latter kind — both moral critique and arguments with respect to human rights are crucial aspects of academic and popular critique and struggle (Schwendinger and Schwendinger 1975; Kramer 1989). But they are not an appropriate focus for a text that seeks to deal with corporate crime. Indeed, through maintaining reference to existing legal categories, this text allows us to make what ultimately is a significant political point — *that despite the fact that we are discussing bourgeois legal categories, capitalist corporations by and large do not and cannot routinely adhere to them.*

White-collar Crime as a Concept

If we return to the dispute between Sutherland and Tappan, we find that there are other aspects of this which have endured and which remain pertinent for defining and understanding white-collar crime. Tappan quite rightly criticised the term white collar crime because it refers to quite heterogeneous actions — with different kinds of offenders, offences and victims. The *victims* vary — workers, consumers, other businesses, one's own business, a business's shareholders, and so forth. The *consequences* of the illegality vary — they may be trivial or may damage life and limb. The *modus operandi* varies — an illegality may be undertaken alone, or in concert. The goal varies — it may be *primarily* for personal gain or in the interest of an organisation. Moreover, the *capacity to avoid detection and responsibility* varies as do the consequences of detection.

These aspects of the looseness of Sutherland's definition, exposed by Tappan, have led to intense debate regarding the most appropriate definition of white-collar crime. And such debate has continued through numerous attempts to delineate a clear field of inquiry, whether this has been in terms of business crime (Clarke 1990), commercial crime (Snider 1988), corporate crime (Braithwaite 1984; Clinard and Yeager 1980; Pearce and Snider 1995), crimes of the powerful (Pearce 1976), crimes at the top (Douglas and Johnson 1978), crimes of the suites (Timmer and Eitzen 1991), economic crime (Edelhertz 1970), elite deviance (Simon and Eitzen 1986), occupational crime (Green 1990), organisational deviance (Ermann and Lundman 1982; Punch 1996; Vaughan 1983) or white-collar crime (Croall 1992; Geis and Stotland 1980; Nelken 1994). It is important to be clear that these definitional disputes are not merely — or perhaps even — semantic. Essentially, such disputes can be reduced to one issue: namely, how the incidence of white-collar crime is to be explained (that is, these are disputes about causation). This fundamental question bears upon the way in which this form of crime should be measured, regulated, sanctioned, prevented, represented, and so on. Further, the disputes around this issue of causation entail disputes about values, politics, theory, epistemology and methodology, even if these issues are not made explicit.

We do not intend to join with these debates. First, they have largely been addressed within the realms of criminology, and it is our aim to transcend the boundaries of this discipline. Second, such issues have been recently treated in useful reviews by Green (1990), Croall (1992), Snider (1993a), and Nelken (1994). These latter sources either organise — or refer to — explanations of corporate crime causation at four levels — namely, at the level of individuals and/or social-psychology; with reference to occupation and industry; via various understandings of the nature of corporations or organisations; and, finally, through reference to environmental and/or structural factors. Excellent attempts at setting out the outlines of a synthesis of the key elements of these approaches have been provided by Coleman (1987, 1992), and Vaughan (1992, 1996). Yet it is of interest that each of these efforts actually ends up prioritising somewhat different aspects of those phenomena that they seek to synthesise, with Coleman emphasising *macro* and Vaughan more *micro* factors. This indicates that any effort at synthesis must ultimately give primacy to (some aspects of) one level of explanation noted above; these different levels do not, and cannot, have equivalent status, and any attempt to proceed on this basis results in a series, or list, of factors to be taken into account rather than any form of explanation.[4]

Third, such debates are of less relevance for us for a more general reason. Our starting point in this text is not with crime, which is then seen as something that requires explanation. Rather, our starting point is a particular form of organisation — the corporation — which then leads us to a consideration of how such a profit oriented organisation produces antisocial conduct, illegalities and crimes. Thus the corporation is not treated simply as a site, or location, of one phenomenon, crime, which can then be subjected to one form of theoretical explanation, as Hirschi and Gottfredson would have it (1987, 1990). Rather, it is seen as an entity which produces particular effects, some of which need to be considered in relation to law and crime.

Having set out, in the previous two chapters, the bases of the theoretical approach within which we focus upon corporate crime, an approach that is somewhat distinct from criminology, it should be clear that our emphasis is upon the activities, functions, structure, and regulation of corporations within advanced capitalist — so-called 'free market' — economies. These organisations, corporations, are dominant economic (and, to some extent, political) actors both nationally and internationally. More than 90 per cent of individuals in modern Western economies work for other people, and the bulk of these do so in relatively complex private sector organisations. In this context, it is clear one distinction which has been developed within corporate criminology that is of particular relevance here is that between occupational and organisational crimes. The former occur when individuals or groups of individuals make illegal use of their occupational position for personal advantage and victimize consumers or their own organisation, for example, either directly through theft or indirectly by damaging its reputation. *Organisational illegalities*, on the other hand, are individual or collective illegalities that help achieve the organisational goals set by the dominant coalition within an organisation. The utility of this definition — one developed by Sherman (1982), and Ellis (1988) — is that it allows one to focus on organisational features. It also allows one to differentiate between the publicly declared and even legally enjoined goals of an organisation and the goals to which it is in fact oriented.

However, the distinction between occupational and organisational crimes can be overdrawn and may take attention away from the possible relationship between occupational crime and certain organisational features. Indeed, such crime may well be tolerated by the dominant coalition that runs the organisation. A great deal of theft by employees may be accepted as a way of increasing wages in low paid industries; in the eighteenth century, theft from cargoes was an accepted 'perk' for dockworkers (Palmer 1976). In more contemporary contexts, theft may represent a relatively inexpensive wage supplement — one partly covered by insurance, tax deductions because of stock shrinkage, and involving no additional costs from social security contributions, etc. (Ditton 1977; Clark 1990). On some occasions the organisational form which leaves an individual unsupervised and, therefore, able to engage in occupational crime may also be a means of encouraging the same or other individuals to engage in organisational crime. They may be told to achieve particular profit targets which, in the circumstances, could only be achieved by breaking the law. By non-supervision, corporate executives may practise what has been labelled 'wilful blindness' or 'concerted ignorance' (Wilson 1979; Braithwaite 1984, 1989a). The tragedy of Bhopal may well be due, in part, to just such an organisational structure (Pearce and Tombs 1989, 1993; and see Chapter 6).

Inter-organisational structures may have similar effects. It has been argued that many large automakers force those who hold distribution franchises to sell cars at an uneconomic price; therefore the latter often can only make a 'normal' profit by illegally overcharging for maintenance and repairs (Farberman 1975; Leonard and Weber 1970). Similarly, individual police misconduct is likely to flourish under conditions of general corruption — or indifference to the rule of law — sanctioned by relatively superior officers (Ellis 1988; Knapp Commission 1973). In these cases one is describing *criminogenic organisations* which produce *both* occupational and organisational crime.

If we wish to question the absolute separation between occupational and organisational crime, to anticipate somewhat some alter arguments, we must also move outside of the confines of discrete organisations. We have already referred to criminogenic relations between parts of organisations and between different organisations involved in common economic projects; we must also address the issue of criminogenic market relations, and, more generally, of criminogenic environments. Barnett (1982), for example, argues that in the US each major economic sector typically engages in particular crimes; for example, hazardous products and pollution are specialties of manufacturers, and labour, trade and financial violations are more common in the distributive and service industries.

Corporate Crime

We are concerned, then, with corporate crime, as a particular form of organisational crime, rather than 'white-collar crime'. The latter term places too much emphasis upon the social characteristics of individual offenders; it leads to ultimately inadequate attempts to characterise certain forms of criminality in terms of respectability, status, trust, and so on; moreover, as we have noted (following Tappan), it subsumes within one category what is an heterogeneous group of phenomena. Indeed, despite the fact that the term white-collar crime was coined by Sutherland, and was defined explicitly in relation to people (that is, 'businessmen'), it is clear that what he actually studied empirically were corporations (Friedrichs 1992: 18-19).

Let us, therefore, explore further the question of what difference, if any, it makes in understanding organisational/business illegalities, that most contemporary businesses and hence most perpetrators of organisational business crimes are limited liability corporations.

A useful starting point for this discussion is Kramer's position on the concept of corporate crime:

> By the concept of 'corporate crime', then, we wish to focus attention on criminal acts (of omission or commission) which are the result of deliberate decision making (or culpable negligence) of those who occupy structural positions within the organization as corporate executives or managers. These decisions are organizationally based — made in accordance with the normative goals (primarily corporate profit), standard operating procedures, and cultural norms of the organization — and are intended to benefit the corporation itself.
>
> (Kramer 1984: 18)

Useful as it is, we should note that Kramer's definition is overly restrictive since many laws, enforced by administrative bodies through the civil courts, also regulate actions which cause injuries to specific individuals or which undermine social institutions. They also routinely impose punitive sanctions. Indeed, as we have seen, the content of laws and the nature of such legal distinctions as those between crimes, torts and administrative sanctions, between acts *mala in se* and *mala prohibita*, are conventional, time-bound social products without an intrinsic substantive meaning that transcends their social or historical contexts. Thus, we extend Kramer's definition: first, to encompass 'any act committed by corporations that is punished by the state, regardless of whether it is punished under administrative, civil or criminal law' (Clinard and Yeager 1980: 16; see also Box 1983); and, second, so that, in line with our earlier discussion, it includes acts that are subject to tortious litigation whatever the formal status of the litigant.

Through references to negligence and the use of the phrase 'omission or commission', Kramer's definition avoids the trap of arguing that for corporate crime to exist there must be *actus rea* and *mens rea*. Given the organisational locus or origins of corporate crime, to emphasise either an illegal *act* or an *intention* is often inappropriate. Each term is anthropomorphic and individualising, and intention in particular implies a relatively unproblematic link between an act or omission and its consequence — yet this simplistic causal sequencing leads to an obscuring of the construction and maintenance of a situation or context which, as a consequence, is fertile ground for violations. Any focus upon corporate crimes requires us to examine these in terms of their *organisational production*.

On the former point, it has been argued that 'most corporate crimes cannot be explained by the perverse personalities of their perpetrators' (Braithwaite 1984: 2), and this claim calls into question the proclivity within individualistic liberal or bourgeois cultures to locate the source of evil deeds in evil people (ibid.; see also Schrager and Short 1977: 410; Snider 1993a: 61). Corporate crime can be produced by an organisation's structure, its culture, its unquestioned assumptions, its very *modus operandi*, and so on. Thus, its understanding requires a shift from a humanist to a structural problematic.

These points concerning the organisational nature of corporate crime are not made to absolve individuals of any responsibility. They simply involve a recognition that organisations are the sites of complex relationships, invested with power and authority, between individuals and wider groups, between these groups themselves, between these groups and something called the 'organisation', and between the organisation and its various operating environments, key actors within the latter being other organisations. Some of this complexity is highlighted by Box:

> the pursuit of organisational goals is deeply implicated in the cause(s) of corporate crime. But it is important to realise that these goals are not the manifestation of personal motives cast adrift from organisational moorings, neither are they disembodied acts committed in some metaphysical sense by corporations. Rather, organisational goals are what they are perceived to be by officials who have been socialised into the organisational 'way of life' and who strive in a highly co-ordinate fashion to bring about collectively their realisation.
>
> (Box 1983: 21)

To speak of organisational goals, as does Box, or of the normative goals of an organisation, as we have done through Kramer's definition of corporate crime, should not be read as implying that there necessarily exists any simply identified set of goals within any particular organisation. Of course, to refer to organisational goals is important; such a reference begins to separate corporate crime from occupational crime. However, the reference to the furthering or pursuit of organisational goals can be problematic, since it is often read as if it conjures up images of perfect rationality on the part of corporations — that is, it implies that corporations have unequivocal sets of goals, are aware of these, that these are consistent, and that they are strategically developed and operationalised.

We address the question of corporate rationality throughout this text. Nevertheless, it is worth noting here that whether or not corporations are rational actors, they certainly *represent* themselves as such (Keane 1995) — and this representation is a key basis of calls on the part of corporations for self-regulation in various contexts (Pearce and Tombs 1993). Thus, within the chemical industry in particular, this claim is central to the technocratic paradigm, itself a means of deflecting arguments for stricter external regulation on the grounds that it is the technocrats themselves that can best manage the hazards they have created (Fischer 1990). In other words, corporate representatives represent, or construct, corporations in accordance with Kreisberg's rational-actor model (see below). Given the construction of this terrain by corporations, it is ground upon which they must be challenged in the context of corporate crime. Thus, on the one hand, if corporations *are* rational actors, as they generally claim, then they should be held strictly accountable for violations, that is, for their actions and inactions; moreover, a rational actor would be expected to respond to regulatory and sentencing policies aimed at deterrence. On the other hand, if they *are not* rational actors, that is, if they lack any 'directing mind', if they are fundamentally disorganised and are sites of competing rationalities, if they lack internal structures of accountability and responsibility, then they are surely obliged to open themselves up to increasingly interventionist forms of regulation in order for regulators to prevent corporate crimes in various contexts (for example, in relation to health, safety and environmental law). What these remarks also emphasise is the quite obvious point, namely, that to speak of corporate crime is to speak of law and regulatory strategies.

Finally, while Kramer usefully sensitises us to the importance of organisational factors in the determination of corporate conduct, what is lacking in his work, and in that of most others who discuss this issue, is a sufficiently developed analysis of the different forms of corporate organisation and the various ways in which they help generate corporate crime. Throughout this text, we seek to attend to the (varying) nature of organisational forms in the context of their articulation with different legal categories.

Corporations as Legally Privileged Criminals

To reiterate and elaborate on what was stated earlier, limited-liability corporations are legally made up of four or five elements: the corporation itself; the shareholders; its directors; its managers; and finally, there are the corporation's lower level employees.

There are many implications of this corporate form. One is that shareholders can reap large profits at relatively low risk to themselves, since they are not personally liable for any debts in excess of their stock, nor liable for any of the corporation's illegal or imprudent actions. Given the volume of corporate crime — which, as almost all commentators now recognise, vastly outweighs so-called traditional crimes in terms of economic and physical (and we would add, *contra* Wilson and others, social) costs — it is clear that shareholders routinely and massively benefit financially from such illegal activities. Directors and managers are also usually not personally liable for what the corporation does, or are insured against such liability. Routinely, when corporations are prosecuted for environmental and health and safety violations, it is only the corporation as a juristic person that is prosecuted, and given their resources, the volume of business that they engage in, and the low level of fines imposed, the latter are little more than a relatively minor tax (Etzioni 1993).

Sometimes, of course, individuals are also prosecuted for offences involving industrial accidents, but they are typically low level employees, or at most plant managers or sea captains, as in the *Herald of Free Enterprise* disaster, the Exxon Valdez spill, and the Bowbelle/Marchioness collision in the Thames. In Britain, the infamous Tesco judgment means that if illegalities occur in a branch of a business, then it is not the company directors but the manager who is personally liable (Tesco v. Nattras 1972).

Once the corporation is recognised as a legal personality there has been a tendency to view it as being like a private individual, free to engage in lawful private transactions, with its internal life and actions equally private, privileged and unregulated. In the US this has even included the right of corporations to protection under aspects of the first, fourth, fifth, sixth, seventh, and fourteenth amendments — severely limiting governmental regulation, investigation and intervention (Mayer 1990). Similar privileges have been accorded to corporations in Canada (Mandel 1989; Sargent 1990).[5] In reality the modern business corporation itself is dependent upon social engineering for its existence and continuance.

In a recent article, Weait, has pointed out that, the law, in its use of the analogy between a corporation and a person is:

both naive and sophisticated. It is naive because it does not, cannot, recognise the reality of corporate structure; it is sophisticated because its inclusive reasoning system enables it to do so with impunity ... The criminal law, rather than recognising the fact that decisions are the product of systemic processes, focuses instead on individual intentionality. Until conscious changes are made to the law through legislation (such changes are unlikely if not impossible within the law's own analogic reasoning system) this crass anthropomorphism will persist ...

(Weait 1992: 59)

An illustration of the difficulties created by this doctrine of corporate personality in the case of litigation or prosecution is provided by the failed attempt to prosecute Townsend Car Ferries Ltd. and a number of its directors for manslaughter when the *Herald of Free Enterprise* capsized. Against pressure from the coroner, the jury at the inquest returned a verdict of unlawful killing. On appeal, The Queen's Bench Divisional Court supported the coroner's view that there was insufficient evidence to prosecute Townsend Car Ferries Ltd., but accepted in principal the concept of corporate homicide provided that 'both the *mens rea* and *actus reus* of the offence could be established against those that were *identified* as the embodiment of the corporate body itself' (*Times Law Report*, 1 October 1987). After intense and continued pressure by the Herald Families' Association (Dover Port Committee 1988), the Director of Public Prosecutions (DPP) issued eight summonses for manslaughter arising out of the tragedy. P&O European Ferries (Dover) Ltd. (formerly Townsend Car Ferries Ltd.) and two of its directors, two of its captains, the Bosun, an assistant bosun and the Chief Officer were charged with manslaughter.

In the trial the argument proceeded on a charge of reckless manslaughter and turned upon an interpretation of the legal doctrine of identification. According to this, those who work for a corporation are distinguished as being either its 'hand or brain', that is, its ordinary servants and its 'directing mind and will' (Leigh 1969; Lacey et al. 1990). This latter notion informs the principle of identification, which in law requires that at least one controlling officer must be found personally guilty of manslaughter (Slapper 1993; Wells 1993). English law does not provide for the aggregation of the actions of different controlling officers (Moran 1992; Slapper 1993), even though this is possible in other jurisdictions (Slapper 1993), not least within US federal law (Wells 1993: 118-120). The presupposition in the trial was that one or more of the directors and 'directing minds' had been personally reckless as to the drownings, that is, that somebody had ignored an 'obvious and serious risk that the vessel would sail with her bow doors open, when trimmed by the head, and capsize'. The judge dismissed the case against the directors and the company, and the DPP withdrew its case against the other defendants. It was equally possible for the crown to have prosecuted on the basis of unlawful act manslaughter.

If we examine these two major kinds of manslaughter, reckless manslaughter or unlawful act manslaughter, we find that in the first it is more difficult for a prosecution to be effective. In this case the onus is on the prosecution to show that somebody was reckless about an obvious and serious risk to life caused by some action in which they engaged or for which they were responsible. In the second case it needs to be shown that, by either engaging in a specific illegal act or by failing to fulfil specific duties, somebody is responsible for the death of another. This might be the general failure of an employer to fulfil their statutory or common law duties. In the first the issue of *mens rea* by aggregation becomes a much more difficult issue than is true in the latter. If the latter doctrine had guided the prosecution's case, a conviction might well have been secured.

Although, for legal purposes, corporations may be treated as if they are persons, they only share some of the attributes of human beings, and lack many others. The contradictions that form the differences between a natural person (an individual human subject) and the naturalised legal person (an artificial, legal construct) is exemplified clearly in the issue of aggregation (Moran 1992). Thus Slapper notes that the image of individual actors is entirely inappropriate for a large corporation:

> The Bingham LJ ruling appears to make it virtually impossible for a company to be convicted of manslaughter because the way that responsibilities are distributed through a corporate body makes it extremely unlikely that the necessary fault will ever reside entirely in a single identifiable individual ... Companies gain many benefits from the principle of aggregation. With benefit comes responsibility.
>
> (Slapper 1993: 435)

Thus it is notable that while there have now been two convictions for corporate manslaughter in England and Wales, these have both proceeded against small companies where the identification of the controlling mind is straightforward. In this respect, as in so many others, larger, complexly organised corporations enjoy an unequal advantage. Cahill has argued that the public exposure of this glaring inequality is one reason behind the emergence of Law Commission proposals for an offence of corporate killing, proposals which seek to remove any requirement for *mens rea* and which rests on the common law requirement for employers to provide safe systems of work (Cahill 1997; Law Commission 1996).

It is clear that there are significant differences between corporations and individuals which should be recognised in law. Both corporations and individual human beings may engage in actions that further some or other basic overall goal but as individuals we are often also concerned with such non-teleological elements as integrity, autonomy and responsibility even when they cannot be shown to further a basic goal such as happiness. We regard them as important and valuable in themselves and not simply as means to some other more basic ends.

On the other hand, as formal organisations with particular goals such as the maximization of profits, growth, and survival, other things have ethical value for business corporations only insofar as they are instrumental in furthering their ultimate goals. Honesty and keeping one's word in one's dealings with other members of the organisation are important to the extent that without these operating principles, overall efficiency and the realization of overall goals would be severely compromised. And in dealing with those outside of the organisation they are important only if they are seen to function as operating conditions which set the upper limits to an organisation's operations, for example, the scarcity of resources, of equipment, of trained personnel, legal restrictions, and factors involving employee morale. In organisational decision-making and planning such conditions must be taken into account as *data*. In this respect information about them is on a par logically with other information utilized in planning and decision-making, e.g. cost-benefit computations. It is, therefore, pointless to expect an industrial organisation to actively avoid polluting the atmosphere on purely non-instrumental moral grounds. From the standpoint of the logic of organisational behaviour such actions would be irrational (Benjamin and Bronstein 1987: 277-282). It is equally pointless to expect those managing such an organisation for profit to be concerned with community interests out of an active communal identification with members of local communities.[6] On the other hand, it is quite possible to include in the memoranda of association of organisations, specific criteria for investments — as in 'ethical investment funds' — and for contractual relations — for example, to specify that unions must be recognised.

Now, Sutherland's comments in the 'uncut' version of *White Collar Crime*, cuts through some of the apparent complexities of the corporate form, and indicates how corporations, as large capitalist organisations, have particular key characteristics.

The corporation probably comes closer to the 'economic man' and to 'pure reason' than any person or any other organization. The executives and directors not only have explicit and consistent objectives of maximum pecuniary gain but also have research and accountancy departments by which precise determination of results is facilitated ...

The rationalistic, amoral, and nonsentimental behaviour of the corporation was aimed in earlier days at technological efficiency; in later days more than previously it has been aimed at the manipulation of people by advertising, salesmanship, propaganda and lobbies.

... [T]he corporation selects crimes which involve the smallest danger of detection and identification and against which victims are least likely to fight ... The corporation attempts to prevent the implementation of the law and to create general goodwill ...

(Sutherland 1983: 236-8)

The corporation, then, can be understood as 'an organisation for the accumulation of capital in order to maximise profits, in order to accumulate more capital, leading to more profits, etc.' (Glasbeek 1988b: 373). Thus its managers experience pressure to achieve high profits from the company's major shareholders and major creditors (above all the banks), from stock market evaluations of the corporation's performance vis-à-vis their competitors, and because their own interests are linked with the company's since significant components of their own remuneration are related to profit returns and/or are in shares in that company. They will, therefore, do everything that they can to maximise output and minimise costs and external constraints.

The relationships between corporations and profit maximization require some elaboration. First, precisely how 'profitability' should be calculated has been, and remains, subject to dispute (Cutler et al. 1977, 1978). And there is no doubt that different positions on this question have real, practical consequences. What is not in doubt is that corporate management is under pressure to maximize profitability, however that latter term is defined or calculated. Relatedly, the disciplines of business policy and business strategy reveal a range of competing arguments (in the form of techniques) as to how the aim of profit maximization might be secured (see, for example, Mintzberg and Quinn 1996); yet that this is understood to be the aim of business activity is surely not subject to question.

Second, and related to the previous point, a key variable in terms of the calculation of profitability is the time span over which profitability in general, and returns on investment in particular, is calculated. The calculative attitude which is central to corporate decision-making and behaviour can involve a commitment either to short term profits or to longer term profit and judgements regarding continuing economic viability. Thus, a central element of corporate strategy may be to assume 'the cloak of social responsibility' for actions which 'are in the long-run interest of a corporation' (Friedman 1985: 24).

Third, we should also be clear that while profit maximization is the key corporate goal, corporations do not necessarily make accurate calculations as to how this should be achieved, or manage to effect strategies and policies to this end. In other words, corporations calculate but not always accurately or successfully; they may be unsuccessful for a variety of reasons, and are sites of bounded, multiple and competing rationalities.

For all these reasons, it is perfectly possible that corporations, while striving to operate as rational actors, might not appear as such (see Pearce and Tombs 1997).

A Sociology and Politics of Corporate Organisation

This is a good point to return to the general question about the nature of the corporation because we wish to argue that realistically interpreted, the corporation is not so much a private person, as it is a political entity. But what kind of entity? Is it a shareholders' republic, as Blackstone (1966: 464) believed and Friedman (1962: 133-6) would wish? In one sense it is. Every shareholder, usually, has the vote and the capacity to withdraw from what is, after all, a voluntary association. On the other hand shareholders are many and relatively atomised compared to the top management who are few, unified, and in control of information. Do the latter, then, control the corporation? If so, are these managers socially conscious as Berle and Means (1967) believed, or, as others less sanguine argue, do they use the corporation for their own advantage rather than that of anybody else, increasing the size of the organisation to boost their salaries, for example (Marris 1964). There is an important ambiguity in the concept of a 'shareholders' republic'. Since votes are assigned per share and not per shareholder,[7] it is perfectly possible (and in practice it is common) for a minority of shareholders who own a relatively large number of shares and who are more organised than the rest to exercise control over the corporation and its assets.

There is a great deal of evidence that the management in many large corporations has significant relative autonomy from all or most shareholders. However, top managerial groups are not simply self-selecting, but require the endorsement of key sections of capital, whether stock holders, shareholders or large creditors like the banks. The phenomena of corporate raiding, shareholder revolts, massive dividend bonuses, etc., involve struggles between different groups of shareholders and between shareholders and top management. Such struggles, despite 'the rituals of a democratic contest' and 'the deployment of the symbols of democracy', are often only 'contests between adversary political machines' controlled by rival wealthy shareholders.[8] Moreover, as we indicated in Chapter 2, both shareholding and effective control remain highly concentrated in advanced capitalist economies. Yet it remains the case that the question of who is in control in particular corporations needs to be empirically established, and it is important to recognise that the exercise of control by large owners of stock is usually only partial, and won through struggle. Somewhat differently, it must also be noted that identifying those who actually own and control any particular corporation can be a complex and highly frustrating task, so much so that it lends strong support to the argument that, as a matter of course, 'the corporate veil' should be pierced (Clarke 1986: 71-74).

Thus, the corporation is some kind of aristocratic or oligopolistic republic, and one subject to bloody struggles between its elites. Like other political entities the corporation pursues its goals through a system consisting of '(1) an authoritative allocation of principal functions; (2) a symbolic system for the ratification of collective decisions; (3) an operating system of command; (4) a system of rewards and punishments; and (5) institutions for the enforcement of the common rules' (Latham 1961: 220). The corporation's goals and its 'authoritative allocation of principal functions', are specified, but only in part, by the 'constitution' provided by the corporation's 'Memorandum of Association' and its 'Articles of Association'. These are then interpreted in the interests of those who rule the organisation, either by the rulers themselves or by those who govern for them, their representatives. In either case, the controllers, as we have seen, are chosen politically.

The question then remains, how exactly does the organisation function? Kreisberg (1976) has argued that, in practice, there are three 'ideal-typical' forms of corporate organisation. One is the 'rational actor model', in which the corporation is controlled in a centralized hierarchical authoritarian way. There is an imperative specification and coordination of, at least, the key tasks of 'suitably' qualified employees. The control of the latter is facilitated by the exploitation of their 'bounded rationality' (shifting and unclear preferences, limited information, limited knowledge of cause and effect relations) and by 'premise setting' (i.e. by defining what are 'reasonable' goals and 'good' reasons for the 'normal' ways of dealing with situations, i.e. the common sense organised by and imbricated in the dominant ideology).[9] The controllers of these corporate bureaucracies however, are also subject to 'bounded rationality'. This can have positive consequences for those who control the organisation, since it can generate unexpected but constructive changes which they can capitalise upon by modifying their tactics to take advantage of these new situations (Palmer and Pearce 1983).

They may also accept the impossibility of directly controlling all of a large organisation's many activities and therefore deliberately decentralise their organisation, and let it function according to the second of Kreisberg's models, the organisational process model. In this model, while central management establishes goals and standard operating procedures, a great deal of immediate decision making takes place at the more local level.[10]

Kreisberg's third model involves 'bureaucratic politics', where the organisation's structure, its goals, its criteria for success and for the selection of top management, may be affected by internal conflict. These may be between the different professional groups within it — engineers, research scientists, lawyers, sales personnel, accountants, and so on[11] — and/or between its different component divisions, whether functional, geographical or product based. Sometimes, these conflicts may be so pervasive and unresolved that the organisation itself is characterised by a general, and potentially dangerous, disorder. A number of theoretical and empirical analyses of capitalist corporations certainly suggest that such conflicts are far from rare, (cf. Cutler et al. 1978; Thompson 1982; Burns and Stalker 1961), which, however, is not to say that they never get resolved. First, as we have seen, whilst top management may have some flexibility, there is no evidence that they ever pursue anything but some combination of profits and growth; importantly, profit and growth are predicated upon successful control within corporations. Second, a key to how disputes about leadership within organisations are resolved is provided by turning to analyses of the problems posed for organisational priorities by changes in the external environment. These may raise questions about the competences required of the top executives in order to achieve these goals of growth and profits.

Fligstein, for example, has argued that efficient corporations have successfully developed a series of different forms of organisation and market control to produce a 'relatively higher likelihood of growth and profits ... given the existing sets of social and political and economic circumstances' (Fligstein 1990: 295). Changes in their legal environment, particularly in the regulation of monopoly, have meant that in order to remain or become economically powerful, firms have needed to change their organisational form and market relations and, relatedly, the qualifications and experience of the groups from whom the top executives were recruited. There have been four distinct modes of control — the direct, manufacturing, sales and marketing, and finance modes. Currently, even with the recent changes of business organisation documented by Moss Kanter, Clegg and others (Kanter 1989; Clegg 1990; Pearce 1995), the finance mode of control remains dominant. It is of interest here that even the most sophisticated attempts to elaborate upon the variety of corporate forms, as variations upon organisation, do so through reference to metaphor (Morgan 1986; Fisse and Braithwaite 1993). For while there is no doubt that there exists 'a diversity of styles of organisational life' (Fisse and Braithwaite 1993: 122), and that these diverse styles do have real effects for the production and potential regulation of crime (ibid.), once one examines a particular organisation, the corporation, then there are equally some essential features of that organisation which a focus upon complexity and difference tends to obscure. Thus more important than organisational *forms* are organisational *modes of control*.

Fligstein overstates the extent to which these changes have occurred simply because of external legal pressure, because large corporations also significantly influence the way that the law develops. Nevertheless, his characterization of these modes of control is accurate and useful for our purposes. Moreover, his analysis reminds us again that the top managerial groups are not simply self-selecting, but require the endorsement of key sections of capital.

Currently, the major corporate actors, in the US and Britain particularly, are driven by a concern with short term gains (Fligstein 1990; Hutton 1995; Williams et al. 1990) and a continuous obsession with 'the bottom line' — tendencies that are exacerbated by the finance conception of control. Major corporations are increasingly involved in diverse markets, often with no long term commitment to staying in many of them. The top corporate executives are characteristically financial experts who can most easily compare and assess the performance and potential of their corporation's radically different kinds of businesses by closely monitoring the rate of return on the capital invested in each. This may be efficient for some purposes, as Williamson (1975) claims, but from other points of view the consequences can be inefficient or literally disastrous. It can also have negative consequences for national economies — and as we have seen it is significantly not so characteristic of Japanese and German companies (Fligstein 1990; Williams et al. 1990). For the moment, at least, the latter appear to be oriented to their countries of origin more than are American or British companies which are more nearly 'pure' multinationals (Reich 1983).

Organisational Forms and the Genesis of Corporate Crime

How, then, do these differences in organisational form affect how corporate crime occurs? If we turn first to the finance mode of control, we find that this tends to treat as homogeneous dramatically different production processes organised according to diverse time scales, and to elide the effects on profitability of the radically different and frequently changing environments within which different businesses operate. These different corporations *organise production*, in way that is in accord with Kreisberg's 'organisational process' model, but the *assessment of their performance* is primarily financial and in a mode more akin to the 'rational actor' model. And this explains why so many safety, health and environmental violations are the effects of the policies of higher management (Toffler 1991) without this necessarily being traceable to any specific decisions that they have made about product quality, health and safety, etc. This apparent organisation of production maximises the likelihood of 'wilful blindness' (Wilson 1979), since it allows them to be ignorant of what subordinates are doing and to ignore the difficulties that they face (Braithwaite 1984). As we see in Chapter Four, recent organisational changes within corporations in the British Chemical Industry indicate how systems which formally decentralize production decision making, nevertheless result in — perhaps even more urgently require — priority being given to profits rather than safety (Tombs 1992). This is why, more generally:

> the most shocking safety and environmental violations are almost exclusively the product of decisions at lower managerial levels ... The directive from the top of the organization is to increase profits by fifteen per cent but the means are left to the managerial discretion of the middle manager who is in operational control of the division ... The results of such a structure are predictable: when pressure is intensified, illegal or irresponsible means become attractive to a desperate middle manager who has no recourse against a stern but myopic notion of accountability that looks only to the bottom line of the income statement.
>
> (Coffee 1981: 389)

If a subdivision of a company is brought under rigid and effective fiscal control it may for that very reason be very much *out of control* in other ways. A recent OECD study found that the subsidiaries of large multinational corporations are allowed substantial autonomy in their decisions concerning such things as day to day production (although they were expected to follow relevant SOPs), labour relations, and marketing strategies; but they were afforded much less over their use of cash flow and their ability to borrow from banks, and had little control over the selection of their CEO, which personnel were seconded from headquarters, and the expansion of the business or the development of new product lines (OECD 1987). It is clear that strategic control tends to remain with the parent, no doubt, including the decision about acceptable profit levels. The pressure for a 'normal' return on the capital invested in an overseas subsidiary, in the context of a declining market, contributed to the cut-backs in the operating budget of the Bhopal chemical plant which were a major cause of that terrible disaster (Pearce and Tombs 1989, 1993).

Thus we should be clear that all may not be as it appears with complexly organised corporations, within which independence, autonomy, diffuse accountability and responsibility are represented as the norm. It is interesting that Braithwaite, who has focused at length upon the relationships between organisational forms and corporate crimes, has noted that:

> the presumed diffusion of accountability in a complex organisation sometimes can be a hoax that the corporation plays on the rest of the world, especially courts and sociologists ... When companies want clearly defined accountability they can generally get it. Diffused accountability is not always inherent in organisational complexity; it is in considerable measure the result of a desire to protect individuals within the organisation by presenting a confused picture to the outside world.
>
> (Braithwaite 1984: 324)

Thus, we need to be clear that the actual corporate organisation is not always accurately revealed through its formal corporate structure; we need to be clear that if companies appear to be organised in a highly complex and decentralised form, that this is itself a consequence of organisation; finally, we need to be clear that even the most decentralised, complexly organised corporations manage (internally) to distribute benefits in a clear, unambiguous (and usually hierarchical) manner — thus there are no reasons why they cannot, or do not, distribute costs, and why this should not also be identifiable from an external standpoint.

We should note, of course, as indeed Kreisberg himself emphasises, that these different forms of organisational decision-making represent ideal or pure types. Our view — for which we argue throughout this text — is that in key functions, such corporations operate, or constantly strive to operate, all too similarly to Kreisberg's rational actor model. The dominant tendency must be towards the rational actor model, given the need to achieve and maintain control as a precondition of maximising profitability. Thus Kreisberg's 'pure' rational actor mode of organisation, which we have argued, following Sutherland, is best approximated by the capitalist corporation, represents particular problems in terms of the production of crime. Within its centralized hierarchical authoritarian structure, abstract criteria are used to judge the worth of people. In order to be successful within the organisation it will be necessary for individuals to be seen to contribute to achieving high profits, and to keep out of trouble. They will thus try to control — and limit — the upward information flow, and then blame their subordinates for any problems that arise (Stone 1993). These organisational arrangements produce both 'organisational crimes' (Sherman 1982) undertaken in line with the goals of the 'organization's dominant coalition' (Ellis 1988: 86) and 'occupational crimes', where rules are bent and information is concealed to facilitate individual career goals (Coleman 1989; Green 1990). In situations characterised by bureaucratic politics with different sectors and functional groups struggling to set organisational goals, policy making, implementation and outcomes become contingent and problematic. There is a real sense in which, with the important exception of their pursuit of the bottom line, these organisations are out of control. Despite this, corporate executives justify their large salaries in terms of their managerial competence!

The danger of a micro-sociology is that, although it sensitises us to difference, and its significance, it obscures dominant forms of control within, and indeed the very rationale of, the corporation. We develop our understanding of this rationale in an empirical fashion in the following three chapters, and in a more explicitly theoretical form in Chapter 7.

Notes

1. It is clear that, in Nietzsche's words, 'whatever exists, having somehow come into being, is again and again reinterpreted to new ends, taken over, transformed, and redirected' (Nietzsche 1969: 77). This sensitises us to the fact that the historical narratives that historians create are always both partial and 'motivated' by their 'material and ideal interests', to borrow Weber's phrase (1915: 280). In this case it is worth remembering that these same American Pluralists, were also cold war liberals, some of them the less radical remnants of Roosevelt's New Deal Intellectuals.

2. Ironically, six months before the worker's death, the company had been exempted (under Reaganite regulations) from inspection by the OSHA because, according to the company's logs, it had a better than average safety record (*New York Times*, March 1988). On appeal the verdicts were set aside and a new trial ordered. Nevertheless, following the case other prosecutions followed, though many foundered upon the legal doctrine of pre-emption (Reiner and

Chatten-Brown 1989). Important developments have also emerged at state level (ibid.; Brill 1992: 67).

3. British legal textbooks are certainly equivocal about *what* constitutes a crime. According to *Harris' Criminal Law* acts are crimes if 'they are prohibited by the state and those who commit them are punished'. According to McLean and Morrish in a crime the state independently decides to prosecute and punish whatever victims say *and* whether they consent or not (Harris 1973: 3-5). Since the law usually wants to go beyond a procedural and tautological definition, the additional criterion is offered that a crime, an unlawful act or default which is 'an offense against the public', and renders the person guilty of the act liable to legal punishment. Clearly the judgement as to what is 'an offense against the public' and what is merely a private matter or what 'makes difficult or impossible the maintenance of human communities' (Wilson 1975) is arbitrary — historical and contingent. It is perhaps worth noting that a recent British legal textbook, Lacey, Wells and Meure (1990) explicitly challenges all of these assumptions.

4. Thus Punch (1996) concludes his recent text by stating:

    > In this section, I shall specify a wide range of variables that help us in explaining why companies turn to deviant solutions ... The number of factors that could be drawn on is almost limitless.
    >
    > (Punch 1996: 220).

    Despite Punch's claims, to treat variables in this way is not to provide any form of *explanation*, which requires some prioritisation, including theoretical representation of internal relationships and ordering amongst these variables.

5. For example, the Tobacco Products Control Act (1988) restricted the advertising of cigarettes and aimed for a total ban by 1993, but Judge Jean-Jube Chabot of the Quebec Superior Court, himself a heavy smoker, disallowed the Act as infringing the freedom of 'commercial speech' of corporations, claiming 'that the connection between an advertising ban and reduced cigarette consumption was 'speculation' and condemned the government's actions as 'single-minded social engineering' and 'state moralism' (Hutchinson 1991). David Goerlitz, once known as the Winston Man because he had appeared in Winston cigarette ads, asked one of a group of R.J. Reynolds Tobacco Company executives if any of them smoked, the executive shook his head. 'Are you kidding?', he asked. 'We reserve that right for the poor, the young, the black and the stupid' (Herbert 1993).

6.   For example, George Eastman subsidised health care in the city of Rochester, where he based his company, Kodak, and where he had his own home. True, this deployment of his wealth helped his pursuit of long term profit maximisation through the production of a loyal, healthy and obedient work force and increased his esteem in the eyes of local people, but it also demonstrated an empathetic concern with the well-being of the people in his community. Kodak's current directors, merely pursuing the organisational goals of profit maximisation, are not moved by such concerns, which are not part of their organisational repertoire, and they have cut back such subsidies.

7.   The self-evident rationality of such an arrangement rather than one based upon one share (rather than one-shareholder), one vote has been challenged by Ratner (1970) and Fraser (1990: 358-369).

8.   '[A]fter Robert Young's successful raid against the management of New York Central Railroad ... at their annual meeting in 1954, stockholders were persuaded to vote "to reimburse the Allegheny Corporation, of which Mr. Young was ... chairman, in the amount of $1,308,737.71, this for the necessary expenses of the campaign by which Mr. Young secured control of the road"' (Latham 1961: 225).

9.   Perrow (1986a) argues that those who control bureaucracies are not selected using bureaucratic kinds of impersonal criteria; the advancement of corporation executives to the higher levels is political. Barnard, for example, was quite clear that the 'the functions of the executive', i.e. 'maintaining communications; securing services; and formulating purpose' could only be fulfilled by an 'informal executive organization' that operated 'to select and promote executives' who fitted in (Barnard 1947).

10.   For an interesting discussion of how 'tactical responsibility' can be decentralised whilst 'strategic control' is simultaneously centralised, see Sewell and Wilkinson (1992).

11.   Top management and shareholders do not automatically have the same interests, they have to be 'brought into alignment'. That top management does not automatically internalise all the values of capital is suggested by the fact that highly skilled men and women were willing to work for the British nationalised industries, and at roughly two-thirds of the rates that they came to be paid after privatisation. (See Meacher 1991; Fine 1990a). Indeed, professionals are not inevitably motivated by narrow economic self-interest alone as so many conflict theorists argue.

PART II
CORPORATE CRIME IN THE CHEMICAL INDUSTRY

4 Understanding 'Accidents' in the Chemical Industry

Introduction

In Chapters 1 and 2, we have considered the nature of capitalist economies, the structure and functioning of the key economic actors within them, namely corporations, and the ways in which these corporations produce crime. In the following three chapters, we develop some of these general arguments through a more specific focus upon the chemicals industries. Chapters 5 and 6 provide, albeit in different ways, case studies of corporate crime, focusing upon safety and environmental crimes. In this chapter, we review empirical and theoretical arguments regarding the nature of accidents within the chemicals industries, and develop the argument that many of these accidents need to be viewed as corporate crimes (that is, safety crimes).

There is a long tradition within literature on corporate crime which focuses upon industry case studies, notably on the automobile (Leonard and Weber 1970; Needleman and Needleman 1979), electricity (Geis 1967), financial services (Clarke 1986; Shapiro 1984), offshore oil (Carson 1982, Woolfson et al. 1996), and pharmaceutical industries (Braithwaite 1984, 1993; Finlay 1996; Peppin 1995). As Braithwaite has noted, qualitative case studies are 'most likely to advance our understanding of corporate crime as a social phenomenon' (Braithwaite 1984: 7). Yet the study here is also a study of particular forms of crime, again an exercise with an established tradition; there have been studies of fraud (Levi 1987, 1993), antitrust (Bork 1978; Jamieson 1994), tax evasion (McBarnet 1992), environmental crimes (Block 1993; Edwards et al. 1996; Szasz 1984, 1986b, 1986c; Williams 1996), and safety crimes (Bergman 1991, 1994; Slapper 1993; Tombs 1992, 1997). There have been fewer attempts to focus upon particular types of crime in any specific industry, and in our view such work is especially useful in advancing an 'understanding of the contours of corporate crime and how they unfold' (Braithwaite 1984: 8). However, whilst we approach corporate crime at a high level of specificity (certainly in this and the two following chapters), on the basis of a general, and in many ways abstract, theoretical framework (Chapters 1 and 2), our aim in the course

127

of the text is to move back to a general, though empirically grounded, theoretical argument.

In this chapter, we examine what we go on to label 'first-order' causes of accidents in the chemicals industries — that is, we examine empirical evidence regarding the organisational features that produce accidents within chemicals corporations. We then go on to consider the underlying causes of these frequent empirical manifestations of organisational failure, examining second-order causes of such accidents. Finally, we argue that the language of accidents is a misleading one, and that many of the incidents framed within that general category ought to be viewed as safety crimes, as one type of the more general phenomenon of corporate crime.

The Causes of Accidents in the Chemical Industry: Some Empirical Evidence

It is easy to gain the impression, when reviewing literature upon the causes of accidents in the chemical (and, indeed, other) industries, that the key causal factor is *human error*. And for human error one should actually read *employee error*, a general category covering a variety of particular *causes* — for example, carelessness, recklessness and even, as we shall see in the Bhopal case (Chapter 6), sabotage. We do not intend to provide a critique of those claims here — suffice to say that such arguments are unsustainable, either at an empirical or a theoretical level; indeed, they have been subject to critique from a wide range of disciplines, and even by those holding conflicting positions on debates within these disciplines (see, for example, Adams 1995; Crowl 1996; Doran 1996; Quick 1991; Reasons et al. 1981; Sass and Crook 1981; Shrivastava 1994; Tombs 1991). Certainly, where any *particular* accident is subject to critical scrutiny, the results typically suggest that causation is more adequately located within management or, indeed, within organisational structures or standard operating procedures (Bergman 1994; Jasanoff, ed. 1994; Tombs 1989). Nevertheless, it remains important to enquire more generally into the nature and forms of organisational or systemic causes of accidents; such an enquiry is the aim of the rest of this chapter, and indeed will be further pursued in the following chapters which constitute Part Two of this text.

There are various empirical sources that can be consulted in order to gain an initial understanding of the causes of industrial accidents, and it is to these that we shall turn initially.

One particularly useful source is an analysis of the causes of 251 accidents in the international chemical industry undertaken by Bhola, a Principal

Surveyor in the Risk Audit and Management Group at Lloyds, who thus has a vested interest in accuracy. In the course of his argument for the significance of 'The Role of Inspection and Certification of Chemical Plant Equipment in the Control of Accident Hazards', Bhola provides data which attributes 32 per cent of the 251 accidents to causes associated with *human failure* (Bhola 1986: 261-3). Moreover, this general category includes operator error, faulty orders, faulty communication, lack of training, stress levels, untrained and unregulated behaviour (ibid.). This figure clearly undermines the claim that the majority of accidents in the chemical industry are caused by operator error; all other causes cited, save for 'external events and natural causes' (3.5 per cent of total) are in fact the responsibility of management, and certainly out of the control of operators/workers (on the various forms of *human error*, see Kletz 1990: 165-7).

On the basis of his analysis, one of the conclusions drawn by Bhola is the need for 'Regular maintenance and periodical inspection of all critical equipment, and safety controls to preplanned standards' (Bhola 1986: 256).

This emphasis on the significance of a well maintained plant clearly places the onus for improving in-plant safety upon management. Such an emphasis is further borne out by a survey of 33 Synthetic Organic Chemicals Manufacturing (SOCM) plants and 17 petroleum refineries conducted in 1980 in the US by the Environmental Protection Agency (EPA 1980). The survey's aim was to identify the most frequent sources of leaks in these plants (a leak being defined as any volatile release greater than 10,000 ppm), the rationale being that isolating specific pieces of equipment as sources of leaks will determine which equipment requires special care in terms of inspection and maintenance, and indicate what engineering controls would limit such leaks. The survey revealed that a significant number of equipment units examined in the SOCM industry are expected to leak in 'normal' operations. As Dr. Rafael Moure has said of such a finding:

> It is logical to conclude that a systematic approach to prevent and control these leaks in the identified leak-prone equipment would go a long way to prevent an uncontrolled risk situation.
>
> (cited in Morehouse and Subramaniam 1986: 164)

Of course, workers lack the authority to autonomously develop and institute any such 'systematic approach' (though they would have a crucial role to play in its implementation). They cannot, therefore, be considered responsible for the numerous accidents which occur in the absence of such an approach.

To continue with the theme of maintenance and managerial responsibility for accidents in chemical plants, it is also worth citing a Health and Safety Executive report, entitled 'Deadly Maintenance', which stated that of the 502 accidents that occurred over a four year period during maintenance work in the British chemical industry, in 75 per cent of cases, 'site management were regarded as wholly or partly responsible for failing to take all reasonably practicable precautions to prevent the accident' (HSE 1987: 2). By contrast, the report went on to state that, 'Employees were wholly or partly responsible for 10 per cent of the incidents' (ibid.: 9).

On this point, the words of David Eves, while he was Chief Inspector of Factories, are instructive, and place the findings in some kind of perspective. Stating that the chemical industry 'is no worse than any other', he went on to warn that nevertheless 'the potential for a disaster should not be underestimated', adding:

> Many chemical companies make a determined effort to manage health and safety effectively, but the study shows that without proper consideration of maintenance work, incidents can still occur at apparently well-run sites.
>
> (cited in *Chemistry & Industry*, 21 December 1987: 830)

Further, general data is available from the UK Major Hazard Incident Data Service (MHIDAS). Up to 1987, 1749 *major hazard* incidents from 95 countries had been entered in MHIDAS; classification by 'principal cause' indicates that *human factors* account for about one-fifth (20 per cent) of these accidents (Bordeau and Green 1989: 19-21); although no definition is supplied for this category, *human error* only partially constitutes *human factors* as the latter term is traditionally used within accident causation literature (ACSNI 1994). Various other reviews of accident causation have shown the general category of *human error* to be a small overall contributory factor in the causation of accidents in the chemicals industries (See, for example, Diamond 1985; Murti 1989; Vilain 1989). Indeed, what empirical work on chemical accidents demonstrates is that these can be categorised in terms of five general causal factors:

- Resourcing (personnel), Resourcing (hardware)
- Immediate Production Pressures
- Planning, Communication, Training
- Plant Design
- Plant Maintenance

The significance of such areas is further confirmed by work which makes recommendations for choosing organisational structures and designs specifically in order to prevent hazardous chemical accidents (Gephart 1987 1989).

What we actually have in the above list is a set of areas in which a lack of managerial attention/priority is crucial in causing accidents, or allowing accidents to happen in the chemical industry. Of course, these areas of inattention are not mutually exclusive categories.

Before moving on to consider the causes of such accidents at a theoretical level, it is worth briefly addressing arguments which claim that even if accidents in the chemical industry have relatively mundane causes, and are common occurrences, the frequency of such accidents is declining. While such optimism concerning a long-term improvement in the safety record of the chemical industry has been expressed by Kharbanda and Stallworthy (1991), this view is by no means shared by everyone.

For example, Shrivastava (1992) expresses concern over the increasing frequency of industrial accidents in the chemicals industries. In addition, a study by Carson and Mumford (1979) documented an increasing incidence of major accidents in the UK during the period 1954-1979. While recognizing the limited nature of their data set, the authors argue that a greater number of accidents, with multiple fatality potential, occurred in the period of study than in previous years (ibid.). The data presented by Carson and Mumford illustrates an exponential rise in the number of such incidents; they also argue that the near fatalities per year was also increasing dramatically.

Moreover, the 1980s did little to alleviate concern over major hazard risks, nor to counter such worrying trends. Bhopal (see Chapter 6) was not the only catastrophic event of this decade: the accident at Mexico City in 1984, which resulted in over 500 deaths, illustrates that the potential for such accidents persists (Chapman 1984; Pearce 1985).

Nor were Bhopal and Mexico City isolated, 'freak' incidents, at least in their causes rather than consequences. A survey commissioned by the US Environmental Protection Agency (EPA) has revealed how, between 1963-1988, there occurred seventeen potentially catastrophic releases of deadly chemicals in the US, in volumes and levels of toxicity exceeding that at Bhopal. While 'only' five people were killed in these incidents, this was on several occasions a result of *'sheer good luck'* (*New York Times*, 30 April 1989). Moreover, all but two of these incidents occurred in the 1980s — the final third of this twenty five year period. A more recent survey by the US National Environmental Law Center found almost 35,000 toxic chemical accidents between 1988 and 1992 in the US, at least one in sixteen of which caused immediate injuries, deaths or evacuations; further, these represented only *'the tip of the iceberg'*, and were concentrated in a relatively small number of densely populated US states (*Chemistry & Industry*, 3 October 1994: 796). King has recently examined accidental losses in the chemicals industries for the period 1958-1987, concluding both that the magnitude of these losses is increasing, and also that the recent record of the industry is *'truly alarming and gives no room for complacency'* (King 1990: 6). Of course, none of this necessarily demonstrates any greater risk associated with individual sites or plants. It may well be the case that such data obscures the fact that many peoples in the US and the UK, for example, are safer now than they were 100 years ago from chemical accidents — while the hazards may have increased quantitatively, and their nature altered qualitatively, improved regulation and thus management of those hazards has led to some reduction in risk. We would certainly agree that in terms of major hazards regulations such as those involving Notification of Installations Handling Hazardous Substances (NIHHS) and Control of Industrial Major Accident Hazard (CIMAH) have been progressive. Nonetheless, we cannot assume that chemical industries are now 'safe', nor can we endorse any such claims which relate to the need for a regulatory moratorium or the removal of particular 'regulatory burdens'.

The global nature of hazardous production suggests that the risks associated with it are global too. The increasing incidence of chemicals accidents and near misses is a case in point. This data can only be understood in the context of the spectacular expansion — both in terms of production and geographically — of the international chemical industries in the post Second World War period (Aftalion 1991; Vilain 1989). Bhopal itself illustrated the international dimensions of hazard generation by multinational companies, representing one instance of the *'export of hazard'* (Castleman 1979; Ives 1985; Smith and Blowers 1992). Indeed, while the international dimensions of the chemical industry means that the export of hazard has long been possible, trends towards 'liberalisation' of the international economy are likely to have increased the opportunity for, and attractiveness of, such a strategy for chemicals companies.

Thus, the evidence for a 'relatively good' record is weak. Even if we set aside the contentious issue of the chemical industry's safety record, or perhaps even accept that the industry does in fact have a relatively good record, this nevertheless does not detract from the fact that the chemicals industry is a key site of the use, production, storage, transportation and disposal of many extremely hazardous substances. Further, the kinds of processes and the inventories of substances used in the chemical industry renders the hazard potential particularly high. Indeed, it might be added that claims concerning a 'good' safety record could actually engender complacency, to such an extent that risk is increased in the industry.

The Causes of Accidents in the Chemical Industry: Towards a Theoretical Understanding

On the basis of a brief review of the empirical evidence available, we have indicated that understandings of the causes of accidents in the chemicals industries (and, we would argue, beyond) need to transcend superficial references to human error. We have further suggested that it is more useful to think in terms of general categories of accident causation, and have identified these as: resourcing (in terms of personnel and hardware; immediate production pressures; planning, communication, and training; plant design; and plant maintenance. If these are accepted as important, albeit general, empirical causes of accidents, then there is still a need to understand the persistent emergence of such factors in a theoretical sense; for example the causes of industrial accidents might be examined in a way consistent with a Realist Epistemology (Bhaskar 1978). Indeed, it is useful to make a distinction between the empirically identified causal factors of the type listed above, and more underlying causes which might help to explain the persistence and ubiquitousness of these empirical causes themselves. One way of describing this distinction is to acknowledge the importance of both *first* and *second*-order causes, where 'first-order' causes are the kinds of empirical factors listed above, and 'second-order causes' refer to the more underlying processes or factors which themselves generate the empirically identified 'first-order' causes. Such a distinction is important not least because our understanding of the causes of accidents clearly bears greatly upon any possibilities for their prevention.

While some literature exists on 'first-order' causes of industrial accidents, there has been far less work in the area of second-order causes. Nevertheless, some research approaches this issue, though not explicitly in terms of the 'first-order'/'second-order' distinction.

One commonly proposed second-order cause is the inherent drive towards maximisation of profits in a capitalist system. In other words, safety in a capitalist system is inevitably compromised when managing safely may mean managing less profitably (see, for example, Cook 1989; Grayson and Goddard 1976; Nichols and Armstrong 1973; Woolfson et al. 1996; Work Hazards Group 1988; Whyte 1996). There are a number of points worth making concerning this argument.

First, the claim that accumulation (to sustain or expand profitability) ultimately takes priority over safety — indeed, any other goal — within a corporation seems incontrovertible (Pearce and Tombs 1997: 80-86). Thus it would be ludicrous to ignore the dynamic tendency to accumulate within a capitalist system, since this provides the *raison d'être* of the private corporation. While this is an obvious point, it is an important one, and one which can become obscured (for example, in many of the exaggerated claims that safety pays or that safety is good business, or in descriptions of, and prescriptions around, the 'good' corporation).

Second, however, the primacy of accumulation does not mean that there cannot be some congruence between occupational safety and efficiency/profitability within an organisation. There is no need to accept the exaggerated claims of the 'safety pays' lobby to accept that, under certain conditions, there is some coincidence of interests between accumulation and safety, and between capital and labour; clearly, this needs to be exploited to the full. To pose a mutual exclusivity between safety and profitability leads to a misunderstanding of the causes of industrial accidents, and an under-estimation of any prospects for their prevention. Such a view would fail to account for the fact that some companies manage safety much more effectively than others, and are also in some cases among the world's most profitable corporations, and that safety measures over and above those required by the law are taken by some companies at certain times, and so on.

Third, to the extent that a strict dichotomy, or mutual exclusivity, between safety and profits is assumed, the logical extension of this becomes political passivity. If accumulation must take precedence over all other goals at all times within a corporation operating in a capitalist economy, or if a productivist logic must predominate within 'non-capitalist' economies, then reforms (rather than reformism) are rendered unlikely.

Fourth — and here we echo arguments made regarding the ways in which the amorally calculative nature of corporations may be obscured (see Chapters 7 and 9) — the safety-profits dichotomy downplays important points about the way in which profitability is calculated. For example, a corporation that engages in long-term calculations of profitability is more likely to provide safer and healthier workplaces than one driven by short-term rationalities. Equally, large organisations engaged in a range of more and less hazardous activities are able to subsidise improved safety in some aspects of their operations, and even to sustain loss-making units, for some (albeit not indefinite) period of time (Pearce and Tombs 1997).

Finally, some versions of the safety-profits dichotomy tend to pose an overly rationalistic concept of corporate managements, safety efforts, and the causes of industrial accidents. In other words, there is an implication, at least, that accidents can simply be attributed to acts or omissions based upon (financial) calculation. While this may be so in some cases, it is clearly not applicable to all industrial accidents.

For these reasons, then, while there is an ultimate and inevitable 'truth' to the argument that profit maximisation within capitalist economies is the most fundamental cause of industrial accidents — it is accurate 'in the last instance' — there is a need to move beyond this and also develop an appreciation of its articulation within a complexus of second-order causes of accidents (and indeed counter-tendencies to accidents), and thereby an understanding of whether, and how, these might be prevented.

A second candidate for a key second-order cause is technological complexity. The more simplistic (and, indeed, ideological) versions of this argument explicitly claim that a certain level of accidents is inevitable in certain contexts, due to the particularly hazardous technologies involved, or more frequently, because operations are being carried out at the 'frontiers of science'. While we should not discount the fact that unpredictability may be greater in the context of the development and use of leading edge technologies, such claims are enormously exaggerated; they conveniently ignore the fact that studies of accident causation in such contexts reveal that these are less the result of the particular technological context, and more the result of very mundane and routine managerial and organisational failures. Thus, although we do not share some of the central arguments of her text, Diane Vaughan's painstaking study of the Challenger launch decision and the subsequent loss of life demonstrates clearly that even within the one of the most 'high-tech' industrial/ organisational contexts — NASA — disaster emerges from what she refers to as the banality of organisational life (Vaughan 1996; and for excellent critical commentaries upon this ideology in the context of the North Sea offshore oil industry, see Carson 1982; Woolfson et al. 1996; and Wright 1986, 1994).

A much more sophisticated and challenging version of the technological complexity argument is that developed by Charles Perrow (1984) in his work, *Normal Accidents*. Perrow begins this text by outlining, and not entirely dismissing, 'conventional' explanations for accidents — operator error, faulty design or equipment, lack of attention to safety features, lack of operating experience, inadequately trained personnel, failure to use the most advanced technology, systems that are too big, underfinanced, or poorly run — but wants to argue that something more basic and important contributes to the failure of systems (Perrow 1984: 63). This more fundamental phenomenon is the very nature of the transformation processes upon which hazardous technologies are based.

Thus Perrow claims that chemical plants are based on complex rather than linear reactions, the former being interactions 'in which one component can interact with one or more other components outside of the normal production sequence' (Perrow 1984: 77-8). Indeed, complex systems are increasingly the norm in certain industries given their 'advantages' over linear systems:

> Complex systems are more efficient (in the narrow terms of production efficiency, which neglects accident hazards) than linear systems. There is less slack, less under-utilised space, less tolerance of low quality performance, and more multifunction components. From this point of view, for design and hardware efficiency, complexity is desirable.
>
> (Perrow 1984: 88)

Moreover, according to Perrow, some industries which are based on complex rather than linear reactions are also characterised by 'tight' rather than 'loose' coupling. Tight coupling suggests that: delays in processing are not possible; little slack is possible in supplies, equipment and personnel; there are limited possibilities of substitution of these resources; and there is an absence of designed-in buffers and redundancies (Perrow 1984: 96).

On the basis of this argument, although Perrow is far less pessimistic about the catastrophic potential of the chemical industry as compared with the nuclear industry, and less pessimistic than he would have been had he written post-Bhopal (Strauss 1985: 30), he suggests that there may be an *inevitability* in the chemical industry becoming *less* safe:

> The new processes appear to be more complex than the old (though it may always have seemed thus), the throughputs significantly higher in volume, and all but the basic feedstocks more complex and unpredictable ... Given that the very nature of the transformation system requires nonlinear interactions and even tighter coupling, the chances for systems accidents will no doubt increase.
>
> (Perrow 1984: 121)

Thus the chemical industry is characterised as a 'mature' one in which:

> It is unlikely that, reaching the point where an adequate comprehension of the possible interactions flags, the designers and the corporate officers will draw back. The culture of the industry runs counter to such restraint.
>
> (Perrow 1984: 121)

The importance of Perrow's analysis lies in his view of accidents (within high-risk technologies) as normal occurrences, his highlighting of the much greater frequency of near-misses, and his criticism of the empiricism of those who design, operate and maintain such premises and the arrogance of a technocracy which has been able to define itself as the sole source of legitimate knowledge about such technologies. However, Perrow's argument appears to border upon contradiction. His emphasis is on the inevitability of systems failures. Thus, despite this reference to culture (above), he states that the problems in the industry 'appear to lie in the nature of the highly interactive, very tightly coupled system itself, *not in any design or equipment deficiencies that humans might overcome*' (Perrow 1984: 120, emphasis added).

A similar tone is adopted in his summary of 'the major thesis' of his book (ibid.: 330).[1] Yet at the same time, he also insists that, ultimately, such systems are human constructs, which allows the possibility of improvements in their reliability, since humans can intervene in their design, maintenance, operation and so on; thus the closing paragraph to his book is an optimistic one. Perhaps this tension, and the dominance of the 'inevitability thesis' (a technological determinism), informs Perrow's view that the chemicals industry is one which should be 'tolerated but improved'. Yet he offers no indications as to how this might be achieved. For Perrow, first-order causes — or, as he terms them, 'proximate causes' — are simply too diverse and pervasive to be eradicated (Perrow 1986b), and this is due to the nature of the second-order cause upon which he has focused and which generates such first-order causes.[2]

A further reason for Perrow's 'inevitability thesis' stems from the way in which he defines 'complex' systems. Perrow argues that, among other things, such systems are characterised by: 'tight spacing of equipment ... limited substitution of supplies and materials ... [and] limited understanding of some processes' (Perrow 1984: 86). None of these particular factors are necessary or intrinsic to chemical production: for example, processes *need* not be operated if there is only a limited understanding of them. On the other hand, there are, of course, obvious reasons why chemical plants might in fact incorporate any of these features; but these reasons are intrinsic to particular types of rationale that underlie production, rather than being inherent in 'complex' or chemicals-producing plants.

Somewhat similar to Perrow's analysis is Vaughan's (1996) recent study of the loss of the NASA Space Shuttle Challenger. This 'Teacher in Space Mission' ended with the eruption of a fireball 73 seconds after launch on 28 January 1986 and resulted in the death of teacher Christa McAuliffe and six professional crew. The post-tragedy aftermath was dominated by commissions of inquiry: NASA's own, internal inquiry; the Rogers Commission, established by Reagan in early February 1986; and the 1986 inquiry of the House of Representatives Committee on Science and Technology. Design faults and flawed decision-making processes within the overall context of production pressures emerged from the latter inquiries as the dominant causal interpretation of the event. Yet Vaughan, consistent with her previous work on the complex nature of organisations (Vaughan 1983), presents a critique of these 'conventional accounts'. In the course of this critique of NASA and middle-level managers, she provides a wealth of evidence attesting that, first, NASA consistently accepted known design risks in the ten years prior to the launch of the Challenger, and, second, that the decision to proceed with the launch was taken despite some internal, expert opposition.

Vaughan argues that the decision to launch the Challenger is entirely comprehensible when restored to its real social contexts, and further that the decision to launch ought to be viewed as a normal rather than a deviant outcome — as an outcome which resulted from adherence to institutional rules and norms rather than as an aberration from them. The decision to launch was, in short, a testimony to the banality of organisational life. As in much of her other work, and in a similar fashion to Perrow, upon whose work she draws, Vaughan leaves the reader with the somewhat disturbing conclusion that there is a social inevitability to mistakes, particularly to high consequence mistakes in high risk, complex technological organisations.

Vaughan's argument is based on 'thick' ethnography, which, while impressive in its detail, is problematic. That is, she creates a bias within the text towards 'micro' rather than 'macro' description and explanation, despite her awareness of the need to treat, and connect, each of these elements (Vaughan 1996: 456-63; and passim Vaughan 1992). Thus, Vaughan's work on the Challenger leaves untouched some larger and highly pertinent issues. In our view, it is her failure to adequately address such issues which leads her to accept the social inevitability of mistakes.

First, Vaughan is only able to undermine the amoral calculator arguments regarding deviance and organisations through a stereotypical version of 'amoral calculation', thus her criticisms are rather off-target. As we have noted in Chapter 3, representations or understandings of organisations in which decision-making operates in ways consistent with Kreisberg's (1976) 'organisational processes' and 'bureaucratic politics' models are, in fact, quite consistent with amoral calculation. This can also be said, as we shall argue in Chapter 7 (and see Pearce and Tombs 1990, 1991), of Kagan and Scholz's (1984) conceptions of corporations as 'political citizens' or 'organisational incompetents'.

Secondly, Vaughan notes, but fails to adequately explore the potential of external, independent regulation of large, complex organisations. Indeed, her own text contains evidence for a much greater potential efficacy on the part of external regulation than she allows in her explicit treatment of this question

(Vaughan 1996: 264-72). Her inadequate treatment of the potential of external regulation is perhaps rooted within her *a priori* assumption that compliance strategies represent the model of best practice in terms of regulation. She writes of the three bodies designed to regulate NASA — two internal units to which, tellingly, a third was added following evidence of regulatory failure:

> *All three regulation bodies used a compliance strategy — the best strategy for accident prevention.* The goal of a compliance strategy is early detection and intervention, negotiating to correct problems before they can cause any harm. Punishments are also part of a compliance strategy but they are used as leverage in the negotiations to assure that safety standards are met. *To enforce a punishment is a sign that the regulatory system has failed.*
>
> (Vaughan 1996: 266, emphases added)

We address such *a priori* assumptions regarding the most appropriate forms of regulation in Chapter 7 (and see Pearce and Tombs 1990, 1991).

Finally, and crucially, Vaughan focuses upon the micro-processes of decision-making at the expense of larger, 'macro' questions of domestic and international political economy. Thus she notes, but fails to explore, factors such as the relationships between NASA, the Space Shuttle programme and Reagan's Strategic Defence Initiative; the power of the military-industrial complex; and the dominant cultural icon that NASA represents within the more general context of US technological, political and military hubris. These latter macro factors can help to clarify the social contexts within which the launch decision was taken, and how, within these social contexts, the decision can be seen as normal rather than deviant. That is, we need an understanding of the broader structural features within which these social contexts emerge so that we can understand that *the contexts themselves might be otherwise; they are not inevitable.*[3]

Both Perrow's and Vaughan's analyses of accidents and complex technologies can be re-theorised in a manner that liberates some of their important insights from the contradictory analyses within which they are trapped. This re-theorisation may lead us to a more adequate understanding of second-order causation.

One of the most important aspects of the work of both Perrow and Vaughan is their acknowledgement of the empiricist nature of engineering as a set of practices (see below). Given the centrality of this point to each of their respective analyses, and given our own focus upon the chemical industry, an industry to which chemical engineering appears central, and which represents itself as a key scientific-technological context, the nature of engineering and science as sets of practices within industrial contexts is worth further exploration.

One 'theme' of much research on disasters has been that although the limitations of empirical 'science' have been, and will continue to be, tragically brought home to us in the form of large-scale disasters (and, much less obviously, and, for that reason, more insidiously, via the constant stream of 'small-scale' incidents), responses to such disasters are consistently inadequate. The key factor is not the limitations of science, but the refusal to recognise or accept these limitations in a way that informs practice; there seems to be a consistent, if unsurprising, refusal (or perhaps inability) on the part of the powerful and wealthy to question the very basis of what they are doing. An analysis of the nature and effects of this hubris may lead us to a more significant second-order cause than those which have been discussed thus far.

In previous analyses, we have explored various bodies of work in order to illuminate the nature of second-order causes of industrial accidents in general, and accidents in the chemical industry in particular (Pearce 1987; Pearce and Tombs 1989, 1993; Tombs 1989, 1991). We have argued for the need to combine understandings of the nature of social relations in chemicals plants within a macro political economy. In understanding the nature of social relations within workplaces, we have drawn upon, and developed, work related to the distorted nature of communication. Of particular note here are some of the categories deployed by Turner in his analyses of the causes of disasters (Turner 1976, 1977, 1978; Pidgeon et al. 1987). Yet it is crucial to recognise that 'errors' of communication (Bellamy 1984) are rooted within the ability of corporate technocracies to define what is legitimate knowledge, what knowledge may or may not be acted upon, who do or do not constitute sources of serious statements, and so on (Pearce 1987: 120; and Pearce and Tombs 1987: 19-21). In these ways, 'errors' of communication are related to the maintenance of what Habermas has called repressive or distorted communication/speech (Habermas 1970).

A key focus for Habermas is the need for inter-subjective 'acknowledgement' as a pre-condition of 'free' speech; that is, potential participants in dialogue must acknowledge each other as legitimate potential participants in any dialogue that may occur, and thus be prepared to act upon this recognition. This is explicit in the case of discourse which Habermas defines as:

> that form of communication that is removed from contexts of experience and action and whose structure assures us: that the bracketed validity claims of assertions, recommendations, or warnings are the exclusive object of discussion;

that participants, themes, and contributions are not restricted except with reference to the goal of testing validity claims in questions; that no force except that of the better argument is exercised; and that all motives except that of the cooperative search for truth are excluded.

(Habermas 1975: 107-8)

Such an 'ideal speech situation', also implicitly underlies everyday communicative actions in which force of power should not determine which argument wins out. While ideal speech can never be fully attained in any real situation, the degree to which it can be approximated is related to the 'structures of the social system to which we belong' (Habermas 1970: 144).

Thus it is necessary to recognise those structural factors which prevent genuine dialogue and which are present within any particular 'social system'; and 'social system' is used in its broadest sense here, so that it may refer to a system of production, an industrial context, or a particular workplace. The degree of distortion in communication is related to the degree of repression within a given social system, so that distorted communication will:

increase correspondingly to the varying degrees of repression which characterise the institutional system within a given society; and that, in turn, the degree of repression depends on the developmental stage of the productive forces and on the organisation of authority, that is of the institutionalisation of political and economic power.

(Habermas 1970: 146)

Habermas's concepts of the 'ideal speech situation' and 'distorted communication' are useful. These sensitise us to the operation of power at both 'macro' and 'micro' levels and allow us to explore theoretically the concept of 'hubris'. Thus 'distorted communication', and the associated 'institutionalisation of political and economic power', limit the potential for workers and their representative organisations to participate in decision-making processes which bear crucially upon the possible prevention of industrial accidents.

How, then, can we build upon some of these insights? It is important to first distance ourselves from three aspects of Habermas's arguments. First, he tends to identify freedom with an absence of power; second, he assumes that consensus is the most worthwhile and attainable ideal; and, third he assumes that dialogue should be non-adversarial and that we can and should exclude 'all motives except that of the cooperative search for truth'. Here, we take the position that Foucault's agonistic and strategic concept of interaction is more useful. According to Foucault (1982: 225), it is our resistance to particular attempts to govern our conduct which is associated with respect for the other, and it is our subsequent inability to reduce others to mere agents of our strategies that prompts us to respect others as free subjects. Furthermore it is in struggle with others that both ourselves and our arguments are likely to develop (Simons 1995: 110-116). We need to struggle as *empowered* equals, accept difference, and, if we achieve at least some consensus, and here we agree with Habermas, it should not be through appeal to unchallengeable authority nor because of superior force.

Discursive Formations and Discursive Practices

It is useful at this point to elaborate upon some of Foucault's other arguments, notably those found in *The Archaeology of Knowledge*, as a way of theoretically informing our understanding of the nature of the chemical plant as a manufacturing enterprise. Whilst Foucault's examination of the natural sciences was somewhat limited,[4] there is no *a priori* reason why certain of his concepts cannot be used to explore such an 'applied science' as chemical engineering. To anticipate our argument, if clinical medicine (Foucault 1973) can be construed as a discursive formation, so equally can chemical engineering, and if the clinic is a site of discursive practices — a locus where different discourses intersect, and reinforce, negate or displace each other — so, too, is the chemical plant.

Now, Foucault often shows a concern with the constitutive role of discourses (Foucault 1965, 1973, 1979b) and, indeed, sometimes implies that (coherent) discourses are the bases of concepts, objects, subject positions, statements and strategic choices (Foucault 1974: 116). However, he also explicitly distanced himself from any implication that discourses alone were constitutive of the real (cf. Foucault 1971a; and his critical comments on Derrida's tendency to textualise the world, Foucault 1975; and on this debate see, generally, Boyne 1990). In our opinion, Foucault is most useful when he systematically explores, in his discussion of discursive formations, the relationship between discourses and the extra discursive:

> Whenever one can describe, between a number of statements ... a system of dispersion, whenever, between objects, types of statement, concepts or thematic choices, one can define a regularity (an order, correlations, positions and functionings, transformations), we will say, for the sake of convenience, that we are dealing with a discursive formation ... The conditions to which the elements

of this division (objects, mode of statement, concepts, thematic choices) are subjected we shall call the *rules of formation*. The rules of formation are conditions of existence (but also of co-existence, maintenance, modification and disappearance) in a given discursive division.

(Foucault 1974: 38)

Here 'rules of formation' ('règles de formation') refer to 'surfaces of emergence' (e.g. social institutions), 'authorities of delimitation' (e.g. the professions), and the relations between these, and 'grids of specification' (e.g. the body) which are most usefully thought of as ways in which the production and functioning of discursive formations comes about. Each of these elements has its own genealogy and internal logic, and while they may provide the conditions of existence of each other and the discursive formation as a whole, they may develop in a variety of different directions. The directions of development will affect, but not simply determine, the way discourses develop. Foucault's interest was in how 'statements, as events, and in their so particular specificity, can be articulated to events which are not discursive in nature, but may be of a technical, practical, economic, social, political or other variety' (Foucault 1971b: 116).

The formation of the 'objects' of nineteenth century psychopathology depended upon relations between clergy, lawyers and doctors (the Church, the Law and Medicine), which allowed issues posed by the conduct of individuals within courts, religious contexts and the family to be disputed and resolved, in part, through the tenuous demarcation of the areas of authority of the different professions. The discourses of each were defined in part in relation to each other. Furthermore *in so far as the surfaces of emergence, the authorities of delimitation and the grids of specification — here defined as the extra-discursive — are modified, so will the discursive formation also be modified, albeit in complex ways.*

The discursive formation of Chemical Engineering determines how the continuous production of chemicals takes place. This draws upon various scientific discourses but differs from them; it depends upon the existence of and relation between various certificating professions; it relies upon the relationship between different institutions such as those comprising the state and business enterprises. The nature of chemical engineering was, to some extent, explicitly recognized at the inaugural meeting of the American Institute of Chemical Engineers:

What was needed was a new breed entirely, people who combined training in chemistry and physics with training in engineering and management, who were prepared to translate their understanding of chemical processes into the efficient design and profitable management of industrial plants on a large scale. 'There must be a body of men supplied in increasing numbers', President Samuel P. Sadtler told the first AICheE convention, 'who can take the technical charge of these industries, first as aides and ultimately as managers of the several works, qualified to continue the successful administration of the same and able to push them steadily to fuller development along safe and profitable lines'.

(Noble 1977: 38)

Chemical engineers claim to be able to scientifically determine how best to organize the socio-technical system of production, and how to objectively calculate the risks thereby entailed. Thus, in addition to the general assertion of management's right to manage, chemical engineers use their scientific background as the warrant for their monopoly of organizational and practical knowledge within the chemical plant. Their arrogant presumption of competence to make 'inherently safe plants', as is not infrequently claimed (see, for example, Crowl 1996) is the basis on which the profession and the industry have always, initially at least, opposed any kind of regulation. Furthermore their own social position, the imbrication of their professional organizations with those of capitalism and the state has structured their priorities. Whilst the development of chemical production within the military industrial complex has meant that many research, development and production costs have been underwritten in a non-commercial manner, in the case of continuous volume production, commercial considerations tend to significantly limit concern with, and expenditure on, safety.[5] The case of Bhopal — to be discussed in Chapter 6 — is an excellent particular illustration of this general point.

For Foucault, discourses and discursive practices, are 'positivities', that is, sets of statements (organisational forms and actions) through which specific groups at particular times have the 'right' to understand and organize the world. This typically entails some type of apprenticeship involving academic training and certification. The nature of specialization, due to the sheer time involved and steep learning curves, ensures that only some individuals will be competent in any particular area. (Hirst 1986: 65-66). The functioning of 'statements', by their very rarity, also demonstrates how other discourses are unthought or not produced, or, how other sets of 'statements' are not taken seriously. As we have indicated in this Chapter, and discuss in greater length in Chapters 5 and 6, it is often workers themselves who first and accurately recognize the dangers associated with particular production processes only to have this recognition ignored since they are not a source of 'serious statements'.

The many recent attempts to develop 'safe systems of work' that have emerged from within chemical industries in both Britain and the US all make the *assumption* that not only are workers and capital normally in a non-antagonistic relationship, but that management's right to manage is absolute, and that workers, individually or collectively, can contribute nothing directly to either the identification of risks to health and safety, nor to the development of safer alternatives, save for their compliance with management prescriptions. These observations can be usefully connected by considering the 'contract of employment' and the central element of the capital/labour relation which:

> defines the boundaries of the discourses of production by its embodiment of the powers to hire (entry) and fire (exit) and the others signified by the term 'managerial prerogative' ... [These] decide the basic and asymmetrical configuration of the employment relation under capitalism.
>
> (Woodiwiss 1987: 312)

Trade unions have always challenged (or helped to provide a means of challenging) the exclusive authority of management and ultimately that of capital. Capital has always attempted to buttress its control by strengthening the differences between intellectual and manual labour within the workplace.

These processes are reinforced by the education system which is, of course, a major means of articulating the relationship between the social and technical division of labour, and are further consolidated by the monopoly that capital claims over patents, technical processes, and so on. At a general level, then, it is important to recognise that corporations always function through the disempowerment of the views of a range of stakeholders — be these workers, trades unions, community activists, and so on. Indeed, this is a condition of their very existence, not an epiphenomenon, even if it may be obscured by, and to some extent attenuated by, certain aspects of organisation and environment (for example, legally secured safety committees, or community rights-to-know). In the case of health and safety, the superior expertise and information acquired by capital and its agents is used to justify the exclusion of workers from any role in the decisions about this area. It is a conceit of capital and its management to believe that it has a monopoly on understanding the nature of the work process, and of how to conduct it safely.

For our purposes, we need to shift from a generalised understanding of industrial accidents, towards a more particular theorisation of their incidence within a high-technology context such as the chemical industry.

Science, Applied Science, and Chemical Engineering

Within a chemical plant, some of the discursive practices of management, their 'authoritative statements', function as both a representation of the things on which they bear and a means of attempting to organize them (Minson 1985), i.e., the raw materials (the feedstock), containers, information systems, control systems, disciplinary practices, sets of knowledges, and so on. Discursive practices produce and organise a system with significant similarities to the 'carceral system' which 'combines in a single figure discourses and architecture, coercive regulation and scientific propositions, real social effects and invincible utopias' (Foucault 1979a: 271).

Foucault quite clearly believed that 'power' has struggled to both silence the discourse of prisoners and mental patients and to force them to be subject to *its* discourses by answering *its* questions (Foucault 1979a; 1979b).

In chemical production we find the chemical engineers' 'invincible utopian' belief in their own scientificity; in their ability to maintain professional standards whilst engaging in volume production; to objectively calculate what are and are not worthwhile risks; to re-establish their authority if the overall system fails by producing expert reports. This, despite the fact that in many chemical plants production processes are inherently unpredictable, ill understood, and inadequately monitored and controlled (Pearce and Tombs 1987; Perrow 1984).[6]

The goal of laboratory based experimental chemistry is to monitor or discover entities, processes or interactions. Attempts are made to either *exclude* extraneous factors or to calculate their effects through careful monitoring and measuring. The emphasis on accurate specification means that questions of cost are of relatively little importance, and that, in general, risks of dangerous accidents *can* be reduced to an infinitesimal level. Such experimental chemistry relates to production chemistry much as the physics of gases relates to weather forecasting — there is the same unpredictability, lack of control of the process itself and an incapacity to control or monitor extraneous factors.

Indeed, in practice, engineering is an extremely *ad hoc* and empiricist activity which can rarely justify its claim to be an *applied science*.[7] The status of chemical engineering as a discursive formation and its nature as a practice is exemplified, if unwittingly, in Swift's paper (1986), entitled 'The Engineering Approach to Safer Plants'. In this he criticised earlier approaches to Emergency Relief System (ERS) design for being 'merely empirical', i.e., empiricist:

The most common empirical technique was the use of the FIA chart — now disavowed by its originators. The chart predicts vent size requirements based on vessel volume for four different classes of reaction system. *It was obtained from historical loss data of actual incidents and has no theoretical basis ...* Other empirical techniques rely on small scale simulations of the actual runaway reaction. The actual relief area on the small scale test is scaled up to full size using either area:volume, area:mass of reactant, or area:heat release ... Direct scaling in this way can result in undersized relief systems.

(Swift 1986: 213, emphasis added)[8]

We have already indicated the extent to which poor plant design (and inadequate standards of basic maintenance) play a significant role in the occurrence of accidents within the chemical industry. Our discussion of the Bhopal disaster — in Chapter 6 — reinforces the fact that the imperative to produce an economical design, subject to the need to deliver certain levels of continuous production, only too often leads to a downgrading of safety considerations. In Union Carbide's plants at both Bhopal and Institute (West Virginia), as in many others, it was accepted that there would be frequent but unpredictable leaks and discharges of dangerous gases affecting both workers and the local community. One can make the confident generalisation that whenever an industrial plant is subject to close scrutiny, it will be discovered that violations of health and safety or environmental pollution laws are extensive and routine and thus a *normal* part of production, the non-detection of which allows the firm's accountants to ignore them as mere 'externalities', and its engineers to discount them as the price of progress. Indeed, the technocrats' understanding of their production responsibilities and their managerialist understanding of the nature of the social organization of the plant leads engineers to an arrogant belief in the correctness of their own views and an indifference to the opinions (and often the welfare) of those outside of their own elite groups.

First, quantitative risk assessment techniques are of limited utility because 'sufficient data are seldom available to assign accurate probabilities of different failure events' (Swift 1986: 210), so to design a plant adequately the ERS should allow for a 'worst possible case' scenario. Yet throughout the chemical industry, a 'worst credible case' scenario is the standard reference point. Second, there is no 'objective' way of comparing and assessing the costs and benefits of hazardous production processes (Irwin et al. 1982; Griffiths 1980, 1981). Thus, in a very direct sense it is political issues which need to be addressed, e.g., how much democratic control can be exercised by those most directly involved and affected, and, what kind of information and resources they have access to.

The chemical industry may legitimate itself with reference to science, and it may make use of scientific knowledge, but chemical engineering as a discursive formation is structured by both the authorities of delimitation and its surfaces of emergence. In western societies these are capitalistic nation states, and these latter are in competition with each other.

A general goal of planning and regulation must be to create a situation where as much information as possible is made socially available and decisions must become contestable. Where costs and benefits are calculated, individuals should be able to know what these are; those who bear the costs (workers and local communities) should also receive benefits; while those receiving benefits (top management and shareholders) should also bear costs. Corporate executives of a company with its head offices in Danbury or (more usually) Delaware, or shareholders living in ecologically agreeable environments and eating high quality food are relatively safe. Really significant improvements in health and safety at work require a radical transformation of the relations of production and a net transfer of income from the salaries of executives and the profits of shareholders. This will only happen through class and popular democratic struggle and such struggle, if it is truly radical, will also have to address the issue of workers' control, access to information and *both* the social and technical division of labour. But it is also the case that the capitalist class does not 'intend' these harms, and regulation may provide it with a means of organizing collectively in order to avoid some of them.

Industrial Accidents and Political Economy

It is clear that the vast majority of accidents occur not because chemical plants are operating at the 'frontiers of science'; not because of an endless number of complex reactions that are likely to accompany particular production processes; and not because of widespread carelessness, ignorance or irresponsibility on the part of workers. Rather most accidents are of a very mundane nature (though their effects are hardly mundane) and result from particular manifestations of mismanagement. But such manifestations of mismanagement are produced *systematically*. This systematic production of mismanagement is partly rooted in the need to accumulate under capitalism. It is much less a consequence of technological complexity, although this may at times mean that the consequences of mismanagement are greater. And it is much more closely related to, or rooted in, the predominance of particular forms of communication which are both characteristic, and a consequence, of the unequal distribution of power between capital and labour.

To ground an explanation of the incidence of industrial accidents in political economy allows us to relate micro and macro levels of analysis. Such a focus can inform analyses of particular incidents (Tombs 1989), and accidents within particular economic sectors (as we have attempted in this chapter) and across societies. The significance of the latter can be illustrated by the immense deregulatory pressures during the 1980s in the UK and the US made under the administrations of Thatcher, Reagan and Bush. While the nature of these assaults upon social regulation varied — in the US they were direct and material, while in the UK they were more ideological — their effects were similar.

With the emergence of the first Thatcher government in 1979, committed to removing the 'burdens' of social regulation from business, the Health and Safety Executive (HSE) was subject to funding cuts during the first two-thirds of the 1980s, accompanied by enormous increases in its workload. The result was that there emerged a state of *de facto* deregulation in the UK. This period of regulatory weakness was accompanied by a recessionary weakening in the trade union movement, successive pieces of employment legislation, mass unemployment and governments prioritising management's 'right' to manage. In addition, many employers took the opportunity to reduce expenditure on capital investment, remove safety personnel, cut back on basic maintenance, and used the economic and new legislative climate to bypass trades unions, where these existed. These factors clearly had deleterious effects upon safety performance. The effects of these changes in the balance of power on occupational safety have been examined at the level of individual plants (Grunberg 1983, 1986), within particular industries (Walters 1987) and across manufacturing industries as a whole (Tombs 1990b).

Thus, 1980 marked a turning point in occupational injury rate trends in the UK. Although the bases of the data within the two periods differ, the change in trends is clear: between 1974 and 1980 there occurred a 20 per cent reduction in total reported accidents, while between 1981 and 1985 there was a 30 per cent increase in fatal and major injuries. Thus, there is evidence to support a deterioration in safety protection for employees in UK manufacturing industries in the first half of the 1980s (see also Barrett and James 1988; Dawson et al. 1988; James 1993).

Since the bases of data changed again in 1986/87, it is not possible to simply trace trends from 1981 to the present. It is, however, possible to examine the period from 1986 onwards, and hence to isolate the occurrences in this period, before comparing them with the trends highlighted earlier. Some conclusions, however, are unequivocal.

First, that while the increase in injuries in the early 1980s has ended, the longer term trend which this increase had interrupted — namely a longer term decline in the rates of injuries of various types of severity — has not reasserted itself.

Second, official data indicates a steady increase in injuries for non-employees in the manufacturing sector, and beyond. And non-employees are becoming more significant as many corporations undergo reorganisation along various lines (often encapsulated, somewhat misleadingly, under the umbrella term of flexibility).

Third, there is an enormous degree of non-reporting of industrial accidents and injuries. As the supplement to the 1990 Labour Force Survey indicated, less than a third of non-fatal injuries at work are actually reported. Moreover, such non-reporting is likely to be greater where workers are weaker (Nichols 1994; Wolfson et al. 1996).

If we turn to recent US data, we find that injury and illness rates show a marked increase beginning in 1982/1983 (Wokutch and McLaughlin 1992: 5). The 1980s witnessed a general increase in injury rates across manufacturing industries (ibid.), and *Newsweek* has noted that '*From 1983 onwards, a general rise in the reported injury rate began to be discernible in official Bureau of Labour Statistics, a trend that continued through the decade*' (*Newsweek*, 11 December 1989: 42).

While a vocal deregulatory movement had become discernible in the US from the early 1970s, it was only with Reagan that a crucial and antagonistic hegemonic apparatus (Mahon 1977, 1979) — the Office of Management and Budget — gained effective control over many regulatory agencies. Occupational safety and health became subject to a process of very direct deregulation. A new and unambiguously pro-business Secretary of Labor, and a pro-business OSHA director were appointed, while OSHA's budget, number of inspectors, inspections and follow up inspections were all cut, and worker's rights and inputs curtailed (Calavita 1983: 441-443; Navarro 1983: 523). Deregulation as a whole was a victory for the interests of corporate capital and its owners, and certainly helped redistribute income in their favour (Noble 1986; Edsall 1984). The Bush administration continued to pursue similar policies (Phillips 1991).

The effects of deregulatory movements are crucially linked to the political economy in which they emerge and gain momentum. While deregulation does not *cause* increases in occupational injury rates in any simplistic sense, there is no doubt that deregulatory movements are a key element of a shifting balance of power between capital, regulators and labour, and a result of this general process is greater risk, injury and death for working people.

In terms of general trends during this period, one word of caution is noted. Some have argued that OSHA initiatives to improve the reporting of occupational injuries may have created the false impression of deteriorating injury rates in the latter half of the 1970s. Wokutch and McLaughlin, for example, argue that US injury and illness rates show an increase from 3.5 injuries and illnesses per 100 full time workers in 1975, to 4.6 in 1979, followed by a decline to 3.6 in 1982 and then another increase to 4.0 in 1988. From 1975 to 1988 there was an overall 14 per cent rise in reported injury and illness rates (Wokutch and McLaughlin 1992: 5). Even if such data fail to take into account any improved reporting in the 1970s, the direction of changing incidence rates in the following decade is more marked. By contrast, data for fatalities in US manufacturing between 1977-1985 provide some indication of a continuation of a longer-term decline.

In terms of the absolute numbers of injuries and illnesses, the trend was upward from 1975 to 1979, downward from 1979 to 1982, and upward again from 1982 to 1988, with an overall increase of 63 per cent from 1975 to 1988 (Wokutch and McLaughlin 1988: 5; see also Noble 1992: 44). The mention of absolute numbers is important. While indicating trends in injury rates, it is important not to obscure the sheer scale of the carnage that is being described. For example, Tuscano and Winwow have noted that 'During 1992, slightly more than 6000 workers lost their lives because of injuries incurred on the job' (Tuscano and Winwow 1993: 39).

Moreover, as in the case of the UK, under-reporting is widespread. Slightly different to UK experience, however, is the claim that such under-reporting extends even to fatalities at work (Tuscano and Winwow 1993: 40), which in the UK are thought to be accurately recorded. Thus, while Noble is able to claim '10,000 people still die on the job each year' (Noble 1992: 44), this figure refers to fatal injuries rather than occupationally-caused fatal illness.

There remains, then, in both the US and UK, a high level and rate of occupationally induced injuries and deaths, all too many of which are avoidable. Moreover, the extent to which these injuries, illnesses and deaths are avoided can partially be explained through reference to macro political economy, and the effects that changes therein have within workplaces. That is, the crucial explanatory factors are balances of power between capital on the one hand, and workers and other pro-regulatory forces on the other.

Conclusion: Safety, Industrial Accidents, and Corporate Crime

Thus far we have sought to establish a number of important points.

First, that accidents in the chemicals industries (and in other areas of economic activity) are ubiquitous, and that this sector shows no signs of any ineluctable trend towards safer plants or production — and this reflects the more general data presented in the previous chapter on the incidence of industrial accidents and injuries.

Second, that managements, whether through the design of plants, or through acts or omissions in the running of plants, or through the maintenance and exploitation of the organisational structures within which they work, must bear responsibility for the vast majority of accidents and injuries.

Third, that a certain level of accidents cannot simply be accepted as a necessary fact of technological complexity, nor capital's 'need' to accumulate.

Fourth, that an understanding of the changing incidence of industrial accidents is intimately related to changes in the balance of power between capital and labour at national, sectoral and workplace levels. And we have characterised this balance of power in terms of the ability to communicate more or less freely or equally.

Thus, those who own and control chemicals corporations and plants structure their operations — that is, their very organisation, and the relations of production therein — in ways that produce, in a systematic (and large-scale) fashion, industrial accidents. The corollary of this is that corporations and workplace relations could be organised and managed *otherwise*, that is, in a way that would prevent or minimise industrial accidents. It is this point — that accidents are organisationally or systematically produced, and that there is no inevitability in this — that strongly suggests that accidents should not be viewed as random, discrete events, but rather should be viewed as crimes.

This does not mean, of course, that each and every industrial accident is actually the result of corporate crime; what it does mean, however, is that the strict, and highly ideological, dichotomy between real crimes and accidents needs to be broken down (see Chapter 7). In other words, some accidents are the result of corporate crimes, and unless we break down the ideological notion that accidents cannot, by definition, be the result of corporate crime, then we will never be able to reach an approximation of the extent of safety crimes, and are likely to seek inappropriate modes of enforcing occupational safety law.

Of course, one key element of breaking down this dichotomy is to shift ideological constructions of crime and the law and order problem. We need to understand the extent of corporate safety crimes, and to undermine the superfluous but ideological labelling of 'accidents' as instances of employee death, injury or work-related ill-health.

It is possible to make some estimates of the extent of industrial accidents that constitute corporate crime. While there exists a relative paucity of data on the extent of safety violations in UK industries, it is clear from such data as does exist that such violations are both commonplace and routine (Carson 1970a; *Health and Safety at Work*, April 1985; *Occupational Safety and Health*, December 1987; HSC 1992: 4). Moreover, evidence on the widespread contravention of legal duties also emerges in an oblique fashion, via data on accident causation of the kind presented above, and via case study work on the nature of safety management, such as that presented in the following chapter.

In report after report, the HSE and its Inspectorates have stated that managements bear primary responsibility for these 'accidents'. For example, as we noted above, the HSE has stated that in 75 per cent of maintenance accidents in the chemical industry, site management were found to be 'wholly or partly responsible for failing to take all reasonably practicable precautions to prevent an accident' (HSE 1987); similarly, managements have been cited as responsible for approximately two out of three deaths in general manufacturing (HSE 1983), three out of five farm deaths (HSE 1986), 78 per cent of fatal maintenance accidents in manufacturing (HSE 1985a), 70 per cent of deaths in the construction industry (HSE 1988), and so on. In other words, in the clear majority of cases examined, managements were in contravention of the general requirements (Sections 2 and 3) of the HASAWAct 1974, a criminal statute. And the force of this point is not undermined by the HSE's general refusal to prosecute under these sections, a refusal inextricably linked to its reluctance to add any greater specificity to these sections. It seems clear that the predominance of the label 'accident' to such systematic failings, and subsequent non-prosecution of corporate offenders, owes more to legal, social, political and economic modes of thought and balances of power — to a dominant ideological hegemony — than to any inherent features of the events themselves (Bergman 1991; Tombs 1989).

Further, there is no necessary reason to assume that the level of managerial responsibility varies greatly in the US. Indeed, in terms of causal responsibility for accidents, there seems to be no discernible difference across nation states — witness the data presented above on the causes of accidents. However, causal responsibility is rather different from legal responsibility — but, again, it is important to recall (from the previous chapter) that the US OSHAct, like the UK's HASAWAct, is based upon the basic general requirement of the employer, 'to furnish to each of his employees employment and a place of employment which are free from recognized hazards that are causing or are likely to cause death or serious physical harm to his employees' (Sec. 5a). One difference between the US and UK seems to be a greater propensity to use the criminal law against employers, notably at state level, although this is largely restricted to the most egregious cases of employee death (Reiner and Chatten-Brown 1989).

It is clear that for many instances of employee death, injury or ill-health arising out of work, the use of the term 'accident' is often inappropriate. Indeed, recent work indicates that the very concept of an industrial accident was 'reorganised' by official discourse through the early Factory Acts, so that these events become separated from workers' own experiences of the broader problem of their health (understood within the organisation of production), and became subject to routine interpretation (observation, recoding, codifying) by factory inspectors (Doran 1996; see also Watterson 1991). This reorganisation itself created the possibility for the emergence of the statistically recorded unavoidable accident (Doran 1996), subsequently situated within discourses of risk and insurance rather than negligence, culpability or criminality (Doran 1996; Defert 1991; Ewald 1991).

While the language of accidents suggests discrete, isolated and random events, rigorous analysis of specific incidents often casts accidents in a different light (Bergman 1991, 1994; Tombs 1989, 1991). Thus, while we cannot assume that all injuries/accidents are the result of safety crimes, there is good reason to believe that a significant number of these incidents are the consequence of criminal acts of commission or omissions. This is a particular instance, then, of the argument that we have sought to develop in this (and, indeed, the previous) chapter — namely that an understanding of the nature, structure and functioning of organisational forms is essential to understanding corporate crime. In the next chapter, we turn to examine data from a series of case studies of safety management in the UK chemical industry, as well as some evidence on environmental degradation resulting from chemical industry activities; in this chapter, we have seen further how corporate crime can be both organisationally and systematically produced, often without acts of commission by groups or individuals, without intention, without rational calculation. We thus turn our attention to a more detailed level of analysis in order to interrogate some of the conclusions reached at a sectoral or industry wide level which have been set out in this chapter.

Notes

1. Perrow sums up his central thesis thus:

    > Systems that transform potentially explosive or toxic raw materials or that exist in hostile environments appear to require designs that entail a great many interactions which are not visible and in expected production sequence. Since nothing is perfect — neither designs, equipment, operating procedures, operators, materials and supplies, nor the environment — there will be failures. If the complex interactions defeat designed-in safety devices or go around them, there will be failures that are unexpected and incomprehensible. If the system is also tightly coupled, leaving little slack in resources or fortuitous safety devices, then the failure cannot be limited to parts or units, but will bring down subsystems or systems. These accidents then are caused initially by component failures, but become accidents rather than incidents because of the nature of the system itself; they are system accidents, and are inevitable or 'normal' for these systems.
    >
    > (Perrow 1984: 330)

2. It is worth noting that there is some similarity here with the implications of inevitability that underlie what is in many respects an excellent analysis of the Risk Society, offered by Ulrich Beck (Beck 1992a), in the sense of his representation of 'techno-scientific rationality' as possessing some kind of immanent logic.

3. To reiterate. Vaughan is of course aware of this, yet her plunge into thick ethnographic detail leads her to obscure its significance.

4. See Foucault's *The Birth of the Clinic* (1973), his 'Introduction', to Georges Canguilhelm's *The Normal and the Pathological* (1989) his comments on the 'Histories of the Biological Sciences' in his response to the questions posed to him by the Cercle d'epistemologie (1968, 1971b), and the last chapter of the *Archaeology of Knowledge* (1974).

5. This overall institutional context determines what is considered to be appropriate training for the engineer. Even if moral dilemmas are acknowledged, these tend to be presented in a form which is both absolutist and at the same time assumes a complete identification of the engineer with the firm — e.g., 'should a company ... provide safe systems of working beyond those required by the Health and Safety at Work Act, 1974? ... Should it cease production of one of its products which, although not banned by law, can seriously harm the health of those who use it?' (Radford 1984: 39). In reality the major dilemma likely to confront the engineer is whether he or she should defy company policy and obey the law.

6.   The technical division of labour is strongly affected by the social division of labour in a way that reinforces the division between intellectual and manual labour. To understand chemical production processes requires a highly sophisticated grasp of chemistry and chemical engineering, the limited training and educational background of operatives reinforces the gap between them and management. Trade unions demand that they should be able to bring in their own accredited experts when they are in dispute with management over safety issues for the way an individual's technical expertise is used is structured by the interests that he or she represents. A good example of this is the debate about 'Reproductive Hazards in the Workplace' where employers, who usually try to minimise the dangers of chemicals by arguing that their effects can only be adequately assessed by (difficult, time-consuming and expensive) epidemiological studies and not by animal studies, reverse their usual stance (Bayer 1982).

7.   See Taft H. Broome Jr., 'Engineering Ethics Conjures Public Accountability Away' *International Herald Tribune*, 8 January 1987; Kharbanda 1986; and Clutterbuck, 1986: 158.

8.   The mistake which Swift has highlighted would be unlikely if one was guided by Realist Epistemology, since this sensitises one to the interrelationship between structures, mechanisms and *conditions*. (Bhaskar 1978).

5 The Corporate Production of Safety and Environmental Crimes in the Chemical Industry: The Case of Major Hazards

Introduction: Crime and Major Hazards

Taking together the arguments of the previous chapters, key issues in understanding the incidence of accidents and safety crimes become the organisational structures of corporations (in particular mechanisms of internal and external accountability) and the *modus operandi* of corporations, these existing as mediators between the organisational form and the opportunities and constraints existent in its operating environments (both actual and potential).

One key rationale for such an exercise is to establish the extent to which corporate crimes are 'exceptional' occurrences, committed by rogue companies (as could be implied from a discussion of particular events), or by contrast represent integral aspects of what are currently 'normal' structures and practices.

We have argued that crimes involving industrial accidents and injuries are often organisationally produced, in a systematic fashion. In this chapter, we present data on the management of major hazards in the chemical industry to examine these questions in greater detail. We begin by discussing the ways in which organisational structures within chemicals companies may produce safety crimes. We then turn, in the second part of the chapter, to lay on to these considerations an assessment of the management of major hazards in the chemicals industries in respect of environmental crimes.

There are two obvious ways of examining corporate crime in the particular context of the management of major hazards. One is a *post hoc* analysis of crimes, which explores the nature of the crime, pieces together its causes, and traces the latter to any relevant organisational features, acts, or omissions. Such work is growing in volume; we engage in such an exercise in Chapter 6, where we examine the circumstances surrounding the gas leak at Bhopal. Rarer, however, are attempts to examine organisational structures in the absence of any obvious crime, accident or disaster, and to assess these in terms of the production of the possible or likely occurrence of crimes. It is this form of analysis that we wish to undertake here. Such an approach is rare, though not unique — the work of Braithwaite is particularly worthy of note in this context (Braithwaite 1985; see also Dawson et al. 1988; Kasperson et al. 1988). This lack of widespread analyses of corporate organisation in the context of safety hazards and crimes is particularly strange given the plethora of calls for self-regulation in this sphere. For one might reasonably expect such calls for self-regulation to be supported by concrete evidence of effective self-regulation in practice — and effective self-regulation in practice means a functioning organisation whereby the possibilities for, and likelihood of, corporate crime are minimised if not eradicated; yet such evidence is notable by its absence. And, indeed, what follows will not provide evidence for the proponents of self-regulation — but it will form a contribution to our understanding of the ways in which safety crimes are organisationally produced, and, relatedly, of how they might be prevented.

Safety Management and the Corporate Production of Crime

The data presented in the following sections was collected between 1989-1991, as part of a broader project on the management of safety in the UK chemical industry (Tombs 1992, 1993, 1995). It is as relevant now as it was when it was originally collected, for since then, the trends in terms of organisational changes described, and highlighted as problematic, have in fact continued, perhaps accelerated (cf. McCloskey 1996; *Chemistry & Industry*, March 1996: 173; *Chemistry & Industry*, 2 December: 921).

This project involved detailed case studies of six multinational companies operating in the UK chemicals sectors. Five of the six companies owned and controlled UK sites subject to the Control of Industrial Major Accident Hazards (CIMAH) regulations, and in this sense the companies form legitimate objects of inquiry in the context of a consideration of corporate crime and major hazards. Moreover, and significantly, the cases considered here are biased towards better practice: each of the companies surveyed here are better than average safety performers (indeed five might be called 'safety leaders'); each are units of large multinational corporations, with 'household' names to protect and considerable resources at their disposal (in addition to benefitting from economies of scale in safety management); and all are listed in the top fifteen UK chemical companies by sales.[1]

In this context, it is worth noting that the UK remains one of the world's key chemicals producing nations. It has, however, slipped in its pre-eminence. Although England had established itself by the middle of the nineteenth century as home to the world's first large-scale chemical industry (Aftalion 1991), this relative advantage had been lost by the inter-war period (notably to the US, Germany, and France [Aftalion 1991; Pettigrew 1985: 67]).

Nevertheless, the UK industry has annual sales of around £33 billion or 2.2 per cent of GDP (CIA 1995). In 1994 the chemical industry employed almost 290,000 people in the UK. While this total represents 7 per cent of the manufacturing workforce (CIA 1995), it is a significant decline on a 1980 figure of over 400,000 employees (Heaton 1996: 787). The decline in employment is partly a consequence of dominant UK companies following the trend of those in other leading industrialised chemical economies in continuing to shift their operations towards speciality chemicals (intermediates and consumer-oriented products) away from bulk production (Luesby 1996: 23).

The UK chemical industry is responsible for 10 per cent of the value of output of all UK manufacturing industry; value added per employee is, and consistently has been, higher in chemicals than in almost any other sector of UK manufacturing industry (Heaton 1996). Chemicals growth rate has historically exceeded that of most other UK sectors. Between 1964 and 1974, that is, in the decade prior to the first major oil shock, the UK chemical industry grew at an average of 5.7 per cent per year, compared with Japan 11.7, Western Europe 9.7, and the United States at 8 per cent (Witcoff and Reuben 1980: 21). Moreover, between 1975 and 1985, the average rate of growth of the UK chemical and allied industries was 2.8 per cent per annum, which compares favourably with the figure for British industry as a whole (1.5 per cent per annum); indeed, during this period only one industry within the manufacturing sector had a higher growth rate than chemicals (Grant et al. 1988: 8). And from 1984-1994, that is through two major recessions, only the electrical and instrument engineering industries grew at a faster rate amongst manufacturing industries (Heaton 1996: 78).[2]

Of over 2,000 chemicals companies currently operating in the UK, rates of profitability remain highest amongst the very largest of these (Plimsoll Publishing 1996). The dominant UK company is ICI which, even after its demerger from Zeneca, remains the fifth largest chemicals company in the world. Two of the original oil giants known as the seven sisters - BP and Shell - have massive chemicals interests, and are amongst the largest chemicals companies in the world (Heaton 1996); BP is British based, whilst Shell is jointly owned between the UK and the Netherlands.

Given the well-known data on the better accident prevention records of larger companies, and given that it is often the largest, multinational companies which tend to be in the vanguard of industry claims concerning improving safety records, new levels of social responsibility, better environmental performance, and so on (see Chapters 4 and 6), we would expect the organisational arrangements for managing safety in these companies to be particularly well-developed. Moreover, in the context of economic activity as a whole, the chemical industry in general should provide one of the most advantageous contexts for effective hazard management (Tombs 1993a, 1993b). For these reasons, the cases here provide useful contexts in which to consider the ability of companies to organise production in a way that minimises accidents and adheres to external legal requirements. Put crudely, if the self-regulation of major hazard management and adherence to laws and standards designed to control hazardous production are realistic goals, then we would expect to find significant evidence of their being approximated in the companies that form these case studies.[3]

Interpreting Compliance: the principles of effective safety management

The UK Health and Safety Executive (HSE) has argued consistently that effective health and safety management consists of a number of interrelated elements (HSE 1991). According to the HSE, to manage health and safety successfully requires the development of written policies which are then put into practice through the 'creation of a positive culture' securing involvement, participation and motivation at all levels. Effective performance is sustained by effective communication, the promotion of competencies at all levels, and the 'visible and active leadership of senior managers'. Formal techniques of risk and hazard assessment should of course be used to set priorities. Performance needs to be monitored through the development of quantitative and qualitative standards, and organisations which effectively manage safety develop means of ensuring accountability for performance in relation to such standards (ibid.: 2-3, and passim).

To these requirements, which given their origin we may safely take as constituent elements of what is 'reasonably practicable' in the context of safety management, might be added the observation that these are to be even more strictly interpreted and applied in the context of the management of major hazards, where the latter are defined and covered by the CIMAH regulations.

For as the HSE commentary upon, and accompanying guidance to, the Regulations states, CIMAH 'sharpens the existing general duties on employers under Sections 2 and 3 of the HASAWAct to ensure, so far as is reasonably practicable, the health and safety of persons who might be affected by their work activities' (HSE 1985a). Indeed, Regulation 4 states that employers must be able to produce *evidence* of an identification of hazards and a *demonstration of the adequacy* of steps taken to manage these (ibid.: 68).

All the companies discussed below, and, indeed, all sites from which data was generated, possessed written safety policies; further, all used standard risk and hazard assessment techniques in their overall safety efforts. This leaves a number of factors to be examined. These are summarised under four headings, around which the remainder of this chapter is structured: corporate organisation and the organisation of safety; the monitoring of, and accountability for, safety performance; safety training for management; and employee training for, and involvement in, safety organisation.

For the purposes of this chapter, the case-study findings are presented under three headings: informal clout on the part of, and top management backing for, safety staff; the monitoring of, and accountability for, safety performance; training for compliance and the effective communication of compliance problems. The rationale for using these headings is to be found in two simple reasons. Not only are they emphasised as crucial by the Health and Safety Executive, and as such central to what is interpreted as 'reasonably practicable' in the context of the management of major hazards, but, further, the empirical work that we have cited in Chapter 4 — especially that which examines accident production in organisational settings through case studies (for example, Braithwaite 1985; Gephart 1987, 1989; Kasperson et al. 1988; Turner 1976) — attests to the significance of these aspects of the organization's production of industrial accidents.

Informal Clout and Top Management Backing

If accidents are to be prevented, and if both internal Standard Operating Procedures (SOPs) and external safety regulations are to be met, then it is to be expected that those charged with safety functions, and with ensuring compliance with corporate and legal standards, will have the necessary degree of power (or, using Braithwaite's (1985) term, 'clout',) within the corporation. Moreover, proponents of versions of self-regulation argue that private policing within organisations is likely to be more effective than external attempts to enforce regulation precisely because of various manifestations of the greater power of internal compliance and auditing staff, be these in terms of organisational expertise, access to wrongdoers, senior management, and internal records, or even moral legitimacy (Fisse and Braithwaite 1993; Punch 1996; Vaughan 1996). Further, we expect that this power can be augmented through appeals to senior management (who often promulgate their concern for safety as a priority) for support against recalcitrant individuals or groups within the corporation. This section examines the extent to which these factors are approximated in the case-study companies.

Each company consisted of independent business groups of varying degrees of autonomy, ranging from one highly devolved and decentralised corporate organisation, E, to one which was much more closely overseen from corporate headquarters in the US, D. These organisational forms were, however, relatively recent, reflecting more general shifts in organisational forms, shifts which are likely to exacerbate some of the organisational features that produce corporate crimes to be discussed in this chapter (for a discussion of these shifts, and their relationship to corporate crime, see Tombs 1995a). Thus, five of the six companies surveyed had recently undergone, or were in the process of undergoing, either radical corporate reorganisation and/or highly expensive marketing and publicity campaigns. These reorganisations and renewed marketing strategies were clearly attempts to emerge in 'better shape' from the recession of the early eighties; at the same time, they might also be partly understood as proactive initiatives in the light of the Single European Market of 1992. But within these reorganisations, safety was also given a higher priority than had been the case during the previous recession, when less attention was focused upon this issue (Hughes 1984; Freeman 1985; Stow 1983). Key factors here were: the emergence of the 'Green Issue' in the UK; the impact of a series of highly public disasters and safety scares involving the international chemical industry; and the adoption of aspirations towards 'Total Quality' (albeit in various guises) by many leading chemicals companies. As these developments — of both an internal and external nature — came together, one consequence was that all of the six companies had very recently instituted, or were about to institute, new and highly formalised safety auditing systems. In five of the six cases these had been developed by new or reconstituted central safety departments.

The above findings concerning (re)organisation reflect the 'striking result' found by Kasperson et al. relating to how *recent* hazard management activities are (Kasperson et al. 1988 : 8). They also lend support to arguments concerning the importance of the changing external environment — social, political and economic — in which companies operate for safety management practices.

While there may have been some positive aspects of the reorganisations noted above, in that these reflected a greater attention to safety management, the obvious down side of widespread moves towards smaller independent units should not be obscured: namely, that such organisational forms increase both the possibility of, and indeed incentives for, compromising safety in the interests of other business goals. The possibility is created by the very nature of autonomy itself (particularly the fact of independent cost accounting) and the degree of isolation from central corporate departments (for example, safety); incentive exists in the form of career minded individuals at the head of particular businesses. *Safety crimes are thus made more likely and more possible.* And this point is of particular significance given both prescription and description concerning the growing significance of 'new' (sometimes 'postmodern', sometimes 'postindustrial' or 'postbureaucratic') organisational forms, which consist of decentralised, autonomous units linked through strategic alliances and internal market networks rather than 'modernist'/'bureaucratic' hierarchies (Tombs 1995a); such organisational forms accentuate the organisational characteristics associated with the production of safety crimes, and overlaying these characteristics are a series of ideological prescriptions promoting 'risk-taking'.

The problems inherent within these reorganisations were made clearest in a series of discussions with members of Group Safety Services (GSS) at Company F, a company in which such reorganisation had occurred in the early-to-mid eighties. These individuals told one of us how this reorganisation had created safety problems, since at the head of each business was immediately created a small power base from which individuals would see their chance to rise through the company — 'a group of knights created but who then posed a threat to King John', as it was put by one of the interviewees; thus these 'knights' might plot their rise through crude profit maximisation.

In other words, company organisation into individual, independent accounting businesses creates a problem for managing safely. (And by logical extension, where this reorganisation is taken even further, to the extent that these organisations are described in postmodern / postbureaucratic / postindustrial terms, then these problems are greatly exacerbated). A crucial omission in the companies surveyed was the existence of any mechanism by which somebody independent of a particular site or business had the authority to intervene in the interests of safety and redress problems within that site or business.

Certainly, within Company F in particular, but more generally across the companies surveyed, this barely existed. Within the former, the Chemicals business, as a capital intensive and highly profitable part of the Group, is objectively a very powerful part of the Group. Members of the Plc board from Chemicals are thus very powerful figures; and these members are often the same people in charge of certain chemicals sites. As such, any recalcitrance on their part regarding safety improvements at particular sites may be difficult for GSS, even with the support of Plc level board members, to overcome or redress. *There existed, then, a structural problem of various power centres and conflicts of interests within the corporate organisation.*[4]

The problems of organisational autonomy and decentralisation can also be highlighted by examining the relationship between top level corporate guidelines — which give strong rhetorical support for safety and regulatory compliance — and policies at site or plant level.

As well as a general corporate level policy statement, Company F also produces a fairly detailed 'Health and Safety Manual', which details policy, including the setting of standards and general advice on means of implementation. However, it was clear from discussions that the extent to which such centrally determined objectives and procedures could or would be acted upon by Business Groups, and sites and plants within them, was problematic, given the highly devolved structure *and ethos* of the company, within which 'individual businesses tend to do very much their own thing'. In the context of this problem, it is interesting that the Main Board director, who had been nominated as 'responsible for the implementation' of safety policy (and who was also Head of the Chemicals Business Group), had recently reconstituted a Central Safety Policy Panel; this aimed to provide more workable, more practical safety policies, rather than statements of intent, in the expectation that these might be more likely to be taken up at Business Group and Site level. This panel consisted of the Director himself, Group Safety Services members, Company F's 'Divisional HSE member', and various senior managers.

At the time of conducting the case-study, it was impossible to determine any effects of this Central Safety Policy Panel. Nevertheless, its establishment does seem to be an attempt to respond to the fact that in Company F, perhaps more than in any other company studied, the safety problem created by the relative autonomy of individual businesses was highlighted. This highly devolved organisational structure created problems for the Main Board, and also, of course, for central 'Group Safety Services'.

In the context of safety and other central services, this decentralised structure had been logically extended to the formation of individual businesses as discrete 'cost centres'. This shift towards an internal market for service functions meant, for example, that individual businesses would have to contract work on quantitative risk assessment from a central research unit. The plus side of the existence of such a unit is that it develops a peculiar in-house expertise; the negative side is that its very existence relies on contracts being offered by Business Groups, and the need to pay a 'going rate' may act as a disincentive on the part of Business Groups to use the service. Indeed, a discussion document produced by GSS in 1989 urged that their work be funded centrally, and provided to Business Groups at no cost; at the time at which the research was conducted, and we believe subsequently, no action had been taken on this recommendation.

Indeed, across the companies surveyed, as typified in F, we find the existence of a devolved organisational structure, within which there stands a separate corporate 'safety services' unit. This separate organisational existence thus raises the issue of 'clout' for such a body, since, where it is lacking for central safety departments, their role is restricted to an advisory and facilitating rather than a compliance-assuring and performance-forcing one. This 'advisory' capacity summarises the role being played by such bodies in the companies studied.

This issue of clout is also crucial at the much lower level of the individual site safety officer. In each company, as has now long been established in the chemical industry, safety is seen as a line responsibility. This means that all safety personnel in the companies surveyed have an *advisory* rather than *executive* role. Importantly, the extent to which the safety adviser at this level had recourse (through a dotted line relationship) to more senior management with safety functions and responsibilities varied.

The problem of 'clout' at this lowest level was clearly illustrated to one of us in the course of a visit to a plant of Company C in Southern Scotland; this incident also vividly highlighted the reality of the potential contradiction between 'safety' on the one hand, and 'profits' on the other (Nichols and Armstrong, 1973). However, before recounting this episode, it is worth saying something of the safety officer in question. For in the very appointment of the safety officer at the largest UK production site of C, the general lack of priority attached to safety management at site level, despite fine-sounding top level rhetoric, was reflected. This safety officer had previously been a plant manager at the site, though had been forced to relinquish this position in the midst of a long absence through illness. On his return, he was appointed Safety Officer; his enthusiasm in this post was tolerated, and his encouragements / pronouncements often ignored, by superiors, colleagues, and operators on site, on the grounds that he was a 'bit of a maverick'. Moreover, he was the first to admit that he was 'a novice' in terms of safety.

In the course of a walk round a vitamin plant on the site with the Site Safety Officer, this officer entered a meeting room to tell the plant managers and the site manager that he was concerned about some work that contractors were doing. We had just passed one area of their work, where they had removed parts of flooring and were working around an unguarded gap in this flooring, above a drop of some thirty feet. The Safety Officer wanted someone with executive authority to ensure that all gaps were guarded. The site manager's reaction was hostile — he claimed this had been discussed 'yesterday' with the Safety Officer, and that it had been decided that they couldn't 'be on the backs of the contractors at all times', though they could point out to them what appeared safe/unsafe; he added that the contractors had 'their own safety guy anyway'. But the Safety Officer noted that since 'yesterday' he had heard of a fatality at one of Company B's UK plants, in precisely the same circumstances as those he was trying to prevent existing here. He was more or less told to shut up and to leave. This was surprising, given the presence of an outside researcher (who had been announced as such on entering the meeting room). Here we have a clear illustration, not only of the potential conflict between production and safety, but also the consequences of the weak position of a safety officer who has little or no clout.

This weakness in terms of formal power, individual respect and perceived capabilities can be as significant as the structural location of safety officers, having similar consequences in terms of a lack of clout. Moreover, such individual weakness is exacerbated by organisational characteristics, which deny such an individual recourse to a power base distinct from line management. Such recourse is crucial if those with safety functions at plant level are to exercise any clout. Since they lack formal executive authority in the workplace, safety being a line management function, and where they lack respect and credibility, some form of power base outside of the workplace is vital in order that their influence at plant level is not entirely dependent upon the establishment and maintenance of good working relationships with line managers.

In short, while there existed across these companies an apparently impressive top-management backing for safety, formalised in fine-sounding policy statements, there was a relative lack of clout for either plant or corporate safety staff. To put it bluntly, *safety staff were not in a position to prevent the occurrence of safety crimes, either through omission or commission, since they lacked adequate power to do so.*

Monitoring of, and Accountability for, Safety Performance

The rationale for enquiring into the ways in which safety performance is monitored, and the extent to which recalcitrant individuals are held to account for poor performance in general, or for violations of corporate SOPs or external legal standards in particular, is fairly obvious. If corporations fail to monitor such performance, or if they attempt monitoring but do this inadequately, or if they do manage to detect or record poor performance, or violations, but take no action, then any stated commitments to accident prevention, and to adherence to external safety regulations, must be treated with great scepticism.

Each company studied had a board member with safety responsibilities; but the job description for each of these was broader than simply safety, health and the environment; none of these senior executives had any specific safety expertise.

General practice was for policy *guidelines* to be set out at corporate level, the detailed development and implementation of which was determined at local level. In at least one company studied, these broad guidelines set out precisely *what* was to be achieved at local level in terms of safety performance (that is, in quantitative terms), though not *how* this was to be achieved; that is, safety policy was goal-setting rather than prescriptive. Such attempts to balance decentralisation with central oversight are of course common aspects of management in companies of such size and varied business interests.

At Company F, for example, the Company safety structure requires that all Business Groups nominate a senior executive as responsible for health, safety and the environment, and each of these must prepare reports for the Main Board. However, the extent to which the Main Board can effectively sanction Groups which are under-performing vis-à-vis safety is limited. Indeed, the Head of GSS was, during the course of the period when the case studies were being conducted, attempting to build in systems of accountability for safety at all managerial levels — yet this was proving an 'almost intractable' problem.

Of course, one of the means by which any marginalisation of safety may be overcome is through the development of mechanisms whereby safety is made to count for middle and line managers. That is, managerial performance in relation to safety, one aspect of which is compliance or otherwise with external safety legislation, is measured and appraised, just as is their performance in relations to a whole range of business functions and associated indices (for example, returns on capital investment, quarterly and annual sales, profitability, and so on). One index of safety performance is accident/near miss data, and more generally target setting for individual working groups, units, plants, or sites. Thus, we sought to examine the extent to which such target setting in particular, and calling to account over safety in general, was a tool used in the companies surveyed.

The variability in the use of target setting in order to seek to improve and to measure plant or group safety performance proved particularly interesting. Thus of the six companies, two did not set quantitative targets for safety performance: in A, accident reports were submitted for each site every month, but were not used as indices of performance or bases for action; and C had abandoned the use of safety targets and accident data as an indicator of safety performance. (While targets had been set in the past, these had not been used to appraise the performance of managers.) In the remaining four companies, accident data were used as one set of indicators of safety performance of managers, while safety performance was seen as one index among several of general managerial performance. Such companies also used qualitative indicators in order to assess managerial performance vis-à-vis safety — for example, the ways in which general safety policies had been implemented in a certain plant, the procedures developed to deal with identified accident generating contexts, and so on. But, of course, a precondition of such activity is that accident data is both collected and analysed systematically. It was staggering, then, to find that five companies had only recently established, or were even in the process of developing, the collection and use of accident and dangerous occurrence statistics in a thoroughgoing and purposeful manner; the sixth company, C, was not doing this — and indeed appeared ignorant of the means of such collation and analysis. These are striking findings: it is impossible to conceive of such a lack of availability of data, or even ignorance of how to generate such data, in the context of other business indicators, such as returns on capital investment, the state of various product markets, or general plant, site or company profitability.

These points aside, the precise nature of managerial appraisals in terms of safety performance varied in the companies surveyed. A particularly rigorous form of managerial accountability (in Company E) — recently introduced by a Board Director with a background in North American safety management — involved the introduction of the setting of (lost time accident rate) targets by Principal Executive Officers and Chief Executive Officers. Having set these targets, a Principal Executive Officer is responsible to the Main Board for meeting the targets, and every six months reports to the Board to explain safety performance in relation to these targets. This provides an incentive for that senior executive to take a keen interest in the way in which managers manage safety on a day-to-day basis. Thus, targets once set — where there are formalised systems for acting upon these as a means rather than an end — have implications all the way down the managerial hierarchy. The downside of purely numerical targets, in the form of lost time accident rates, is, of course, the incentive to massage figures for internal consumption — this is not an unknown occurrence in the industry, and is a fairly common practice when corporations produce data for external consumption (Pearce 1990: 419; Vaughan 1983: 108; see also Chapter 6 of this volume, on the falsification of accident data by Union Carbide). Company F appeared to be particularly strongly committed to the use of quantitative and qualitative safety targets, and in this commitment and its attempted practical realisation, some of the problems of such an approach are highlighted.

Each business group in Company F compiles its own Annual Safety Report; Group Safety Services uses these as one source of data to compile its own overall report. Subsidiary reports are compiled on a monthly basis, and go direct to a board member — circulation is strictly limited to the latter and to GSS. Such reports form the basis for an 'internal blacklist', consisting of sites where there are particular problems that need addressing, or which have particularly bad records; in this way, some pressure may be put on 'under performing' plants or businesses. Equally positively, both quantitative and qualitative analyses of accident data on minor incidents within Company F were used to generate programmes of work relating to improvements in safety performance and incident prevention.

More problematic is the process by which objectives are set for the company's Annual Health and Safety Report to be met by the businesses and sites over a one or two year period — and requiring that each business develops a plan to meet these objectives. These objectives fall under a number of headings: management of safety, accident prevention, occupational health, fire, environmental matters, and product safety. They are of two types — qualitative and quantitative. Yet the setting of such targets is generalised and arbitrary — as one of the senior members of GSS stated in interview, 'how these are set is a mystery to me'. This individual was particularly critical of the company's use of accident statistics. Thus, he noted that (internally) distributed targets for individual businesses were not being used to develop managerial accountability for safety, since failure of individual businesses or units to meet their respective targets 'has been accepted [by senior management] without comment'.

Further typifying the confused and arbitrary nature of target setting (and, thus, of attempts to develop accountability and performance appraisal in relation to safety) is this company's so-called 'Red Alert' list, generated by an internal working party. This lists sites which have the potential to cause considerable damage to the company as a whole as a result of causing environmental disaster and/or large loss of life. Yet once compiled, no action had been taken on the basis of the 'Red Alert' list, and, indeed, no member of

GSS was able to say with any certainty what the company actually intended to do with this list.

This more general practice of making long-term safety performance count is only one aspect of managerial accountability with respect to safety. The other aspect is much more specific accountability — that is, senior management's reaction to accidents, dangerous occurrences, environmental scares, and so on, which result from individual managerial error, an infraction of safety company practice, or, most importantly, violations of external health and safety legislation. These are themselves particular aspects of a much more general issue of accountability which, as we argued previously (Chapter 3), and will consider further in relation to Union Carbide and the Bhopal disaster (Chapter 6), is central to explaining, sanctioning, and preventing safety crimes.

While two of the companies claimed that the issue of serious managerial non-compliance was not relevant in their particular cases, the responses of the other four were particularly interesting. Company E stated that managers who had made serious errors over safety would not be sacked or demoted, but would be moved sideways to a position where safety could not be affected. This directly contradicts that company's 'Quality' statement, part of which asserts that 'a good safety performance is no different from any other business parameter in that it benefits from effective leadership and personal example'. By contrast, the reactions of Companies B, D and F are much more consistent with the principle of Total Quality: namely, that managers, in principle at least, were liable to demotion for poor safety performance since 'if they can't manage safety they can't manage much else'. However, no instances of such demotion could be recalled by interviewees.

Thus, we have a picture of largely confused, piecemeal and ineffective efforts at developing the monitoring of, and accountability for, safety performance. *The companies surveyed had developed inadequate systems whereby compliance with safety legislation could be assured through internal mechanisms. Not only did the organisational structures of these companies make safety crimes possible, but they also allowed the possibility that any crimes would remain undetected and ensured that any calling to account would be problematic.* These critical points should not obscure the fact that many of the problems had at least been recognised in these companies, and that this recognition had led to genuine attempts to remedy such problems.

Yet they are indicative of a general negligence. More cynically, and as we suggested in an earlier chapter (Chapter 3), some might suggest that such internal sloppiness allows senior management to avoid responsibility/culpability in any post-accident investigation (Wells 1993) even where it is this very sloppiness that allowed the accident, and often crime, to occur in the first place (ibid.; and see Wilson's 1979 discussion of 'The doctrine of wilful blindness').

Training for Compliance, and the Effective Communication of Compliance Problems

Any effective communication of compliance problems presupposes an understanding of what constitutes such problems, and for the latter training is required; for this reason, these two aspects of effective self-regulation are considered together. Indeed, as we shall argue in the concluding chapters of this text, adequate safety training and the ability on the part of employees to communicate warnings of compliance/safety problems *and to have these warnings taken seriously are at the heart of effective safety organisation* (Tombs 1989; 1991). Moreover, it is *unionised* workers who can exercise more clout than non-organised workers, since union organisation and rights constitute some form of power base, however much that may have been eroded in recent years (Tombs 1990a).

Within each company, safety training was considered with respect to those with managerial functions and to workers. Three companies (A, B and E) possessed what seemed to be relatively well developed training programmes for managers and, to a lesser extent, those at supervisory level. In each case, training was coordinated and generally administered by a central department (with either specific safety *or* training functions).

Training tended to be of both a proactive and reactive nature — that is, covering general areas of safety management (though such training reflected an unfortunate bias towards technical and legal matters, little attention being focused upon more strictly organisational issues), as well as responding to the identification of particular problem areas (for example, manual handling or new legislation).

One company (E) had been running what appeared to be a particularly impressive 'Management of Safety' course for a number of years, gradually involving more and more managers. However, the extent of the training task was captured by a remark that, while 168 managers could attend such courses in any one year, the courses still could not cover all new managers employed by that company annually. Even within an example of best practice, then, we perceive problems associated with safety training — here, the problem is not one of the ability to train, but a lack of willingness to devote sufficient resources to train all new managers, a lack of willingness which does not extend to many other areas of management training.

This training task was clearly causing problems for the remaining three companies in the survey (C, D and F): C had minimal 'safety management' training, restricted almost entirely to matters of law, while an individual from D told me that within the company's general training programmes, training in health and safety is the 'weakest link'. There were initial attempts to rectify this, to move beyond a situation where it was assumed that managers, all graduates, would have sufficient 'motivation and ability' regarding safety to 'pick up' the necessary knowledges 'as they go along'. Yet the development of coherent safety training programmes in this company were in their infancy. Similar problems were being encountered within Company F, where, while it was recognised that safety training for senior, middle and junior management was either absent or wholly inadequate, GSS had been unable to get the company's Board to agree to the requirement that managers above certain levels should either be required to obtain, or should no longer be appointed where they had not obtained, a minimum certificate of safety and health competence (namely, the National Examination Board in Occupational Safety and Health certificate); thus managers were simply being *encouraged* to take courses towards such minimal levels. Despite the fact that the take up of such training opportunities was hardly overwhelming, we were told, with some irony, that this 'is just as well', since GSS did not have the resources to meet widespread demand for such training.

These are appalling findings, which again indicate the relative marginalisation of safety. Safety training for managers clearly cannot be approached in any *ad hoc* way; indeed, it is clear that the increasing sophistication of safety (not to mention environmental and health) matters threatens to leave many contemporary managers behind, indicating the need for companies to prioritise safety training (Tombs 1994). This being said, clearly one of the consequences of the new and improved safety auditing systems being instituted in all the companies studied may be pedagogic, as line managers are forced to assess systematically what goes on in their plant, and how practices may be improved. Thus safety audits should be considered, among other things, as one aspect of part of an ongoing *training* process. But such an ongoing process depends upon the foundations of a good all round initial safety training having been laid.

While training for managers varied across the companies, and most generously could be described simply as adequate in just three, training for workers was much more uniform. This tended to be specifically job-oriented, with new employees undergoing a limited amount of safety training in the context of general induction, this being supplemented by on-the-job training in the course of their employment. The quality of much of this training of workers appeared dubious.

One plant manager (at C), having noted that operator training on health and safety within the company more generally tended to be 'instruction', stated, for example, that 'we've got a video on almost any safety topic you care to mention … '; emphasis in this company tended to be on safety posters, slogans and so on. Similarly, in Company A, each new employee is given a 45-60 minute 'health and safety induction course', which consists of a lecture on the company's safety policy, first aid, fire procedures, bomb threats, and general housekeeping; this is 'supplemented' by very occasional study sessions on particular problems or pieces of legislation. Even accepting these as examples of poorest practice (though within, it must be said, a survey of better safety performers), the piecemeal, specific and reactive approach to training for workers in all these companies appeared to allow limited opportunity for workers either to bring their own knowledge to bear in the training process, or to gain more holistic understandings of the processes and systems of which they are a part. Thus, even in Company E, with an impressive commitment to management safety training, such training for operators is handled entirely at works' level, is mainly the responsibility of works' safety officers (who are not trainers), is on-the-job, and is of 'varying quality'.

All these points regarding the poverty of employee training with respect to health and safety need to be viewed in the context that training in general is likely to be one of the first victims of any corporate restrictions on expenditure, such as in recession (Stow 1983). Moreover, one should also bear in mind that contemporary pressures to increase expenditure on pollution control (Ecotec 1989) may, ironically, have negative effects upon other 'soft' expenditures, safety training being a key example (Tombs 1994).

With safety training for workers so inadequate, it is perhaps not surprising that the mechanisms for employee involvement in safety management in the companies surveyed here were under-developed. Each company did have structures — in particular, joint committees — where workers' representatives formally raised safety issues. Yet the effectiveness of these bodies and the reality of the voice thus granted to workers were highly questionable in all of the companies (with a partial exception only in the case of E). Indeed, it is instructive that my raising the issue of employee involvement in the context of a discussion of the 'management' of safety was generally met with some surprise.

Related to this apparent undervaluing of a workforce contribution was the more general role of trades unions in the companies mentioned. Only one of these appeared to be dealing with a well organised workforce (E), although few of the senior executives spoken to here believed that unionisation made any difference to employee involvement in improved safety performance. In four of the other companies trades unions did exist, but were said to possess little real strength (companies A,B, C and F). In three of the cases where trades unions did exist (companies A, B and F), as in the case of the well organised workforce (E), it was pointed out to us that their power had diminished since the end of the seventies; indeed, it was noted that from the early eighties onwards safety committees in general had increasingly tended to address low-key, rather trivial issues. In the remaining company — D — recognition had recently been withdrawn from trades unions in the company's UK plants, since 'they could not move with the times'. The contribution of trades unions to effective safety organisation, clearly highlighted in the historical development of safety and health legislation and currently acknowledged by UK regulatory agencies, was being denied for the sake of flexibility and profitability.

At a different level of workforce involvement, three of the companies noted the existence of 'autonomous work groups' (Companies B, D and E). The existence of such working arrangements, whereby tasks are planned, discussed and executed, is a vital element of any Total Quality Management programme. Yet it is difficult to see how effective such groups can be in contexts where the power to make decisions rests with a limited number of individuals, namely those with formal executive authority, where trades unions are relatively marginal.

In these companies, then, training for safety is clearly a highly problematic area. Yet management training is much better developed than the training of workers. The state of the latter reflects the widespread assumption within the UK chemical industry that employees have little to contribute to the organisation of a safe workplace; and this is further reflected in the lack of mechanisms for their involvement in either proactive or reactive safety management, that is, through contributing to decision-making or monitoring compliance (Tombs 1989, 1991). *These failings ensure that there is inadequate understanding of what might constitute safety crimes, and indicate that where workers perceive either the existence or possibility of such crimes, then such information is treated less seriously than it should be due to the very source of that information.* More generally, this section has once again highlighted that the preconditions for effective self-regulation simply do not exist in the companies surveyed.

Environmental Protection and the Corporate Production of Crime

In summary, then, occupational safety has been found to be both disorganised and mismanaged within these companies, there being a number of elements to this overall assessment:

• the marginal location of safety staff and central service departments within corporate structures was a source of relative impotence;

• both formal or informal mechanisms whereby managers at various levels were called to account for safety performance were either inadequate or absent;

• the nature of management training in safety matters was varied, but generally was a source of problems for all companies; training tended to be reactive, piecemeal, with technical and legal biases to the detriment of organisational or systemic factors;

• more uniformly, employee training was highly undeveloped, being largely cursory and 'instructive';

• the degree of employee involvement in safety organisation was generally negligible and indeed diminishing — any contributions that employees might make in the context of safety management were strictly limited.

Two general conclusions suggest themselves. First, that the situation in the vast majority of companies within the sector (the 'poorer' performers) is likely to be similar or worse (and see Dawson et al. 1988; Kasperson et al. 1988). Second, that the management of safety in the chemicals industries remains located firmly within a technocratic paradigm. That is, it portrays strong biases towards technical rather than organisational solutions; it is based upon strict distinctions between 'experts' and 'non-experts'; and these distinctions reflect divisions between 'managers' and non-managers. One more general, and significant, observation can be added. Namely, that since the period in which this data was initially collected, levels of resource committed to, and the general priority for, safety management in these companies and across the UK chemicals industries has diminished. The immediate aftermath of Bhopal has passed; the increased attention to hazard management across many UK industrial sectors which followed the rash of UK disasters in the 1980s has also passed. More generally, most chemicals companies have engaged in massive restructurings in the first half of the 1990s. For all of these reasons the scenario sketched above, of poor safety management, not only holds but in fact has become exacerbated during the course of the 1990s.

Now given that this approach to safety management is one aspect of hazards management more generally, there is good reason to expect it to extend itself to the management of environmental protection. While the contemporary importance of environmentalism for industries in general can be exaggerated, there is little doubt that environmental consciousness in both the UK and the US experienced something of a 're-birth' in the latter 1980s and for what has passed of the 1990s (for a useful overview of trends in public opinion regarding the environment, see Dunlap 1991). And there are real technological and historical factors which place the chemicals industries at the centre of environmental pressures and concerns (McGrew 1993; Tombs 1993a).

From initially being attacked on environmental issues, and then claiming to develop more adequate means of responding to environmental problems, many corporate responses to environmentalism have reached a new, preemptive or proactive stage (Tombs 1993a, 1994) — that is, many large manufacturing companies have begun increasingly (and frequently) to maintain that they are leading conservationists. We have documented such responses elsewhere (Pearce and Tombs 1993), and there is no need to enter into them in any detail here, except to note a recent, particularly offensive illustration of this general phenomenon: namely, the recent revision by Royal Dutch Shell of its worldwide 'business principles' to prioritise environmental issues (and, with perhaps an even greater, and disgusting irony, human rights; *Financial Times*, 18 March 1997). Such responses to the re-emergence of environmentalism seem to be either purely rhetorical, superficial, or tactical.

Yet, at least as can be gauged through public opinion polls, such responses hardly seem to have met with any great success. The public image of the industry in many parts of the industrialised world is an increasingly tarnished one. For example, Gunningham notes that in the United States one opinion poll conducted in 1990 found that the industry's 'rating of public acceptability had dropped to 25 per cent — only the tobacco industry had a lower rating. Over 60 per cent of the public rated the industry as 'very harmful to the environment' (Gunnigham 1995: 59). Ten years after the Bhopal disaster Robert Kennedy, CEO of Union Carbide, noted how Bhopal had confirmed the direction of popular suspicion of the industry, so that 'in all the public opinion polls that we've seen, the chemical industry rates in public opinion in terms of fear pretty close to the bottom, we're above politicians and we're above the nuclear industry and we may be a notch above tobacco, but the public no longer wants to hear about the things we used to like to tell them about, the benefits of chemistry … ' (quoted in *Network First*, 1995).

Indeed, in response to low, and declining, polls of popular acceptability/favourability, the US Chemical Manufacturer's Association instituted an advertising campaign in September 1993. Following an expenditure of $40 million, this campaign was ended in December 1996. Having been targeted at two groups — 'main' and 'prime' influentials — there was a slight increase in favourable opinions towards the industry, though no discernible shift in the percentage of unfavourable opinions (*Chemistry & Industry*, 16 December 1996: 961).

Similarly, in the UK, public opinion surveys consistently indicate widespread distrust of the chemical industry, a distrust that increased significantly during the 1980s. Moreover, while this related to safety and environmental issues, measured concern for the latter began to far outstrip the former in the second half of the decade (Grant et al. 1988; Liardet 1991; Lindheim 1989; McGrew 1993).

These surveys of public opinion provide evidence for the basis of what Sutherland called 'organised public resentment' (Sutherland 1949; see also Snider 1991). Moreover, if industrial priorities in any way reflect such pressures, then one conclusion suggests itself: by the middle of the 1980s, environmental issues had assumed some degree of priority for the chemical industry over occupational safety.

It is easy to dismiss generalised, public perceptions as unfounded, ill-informed, and so on. In fact, these public perceptions are accurate, in at least two senses: first, in terms of the role of the chemicals industries in contributing to environmental degradation, and second, in the sense of comprehending the emerging significance of environmental crime as a law and order issue.

First, in the UK, the chemical industry remains the key contributor in terms of unauthorised emissions to air, land and water. Remarkably, data recorded by the UK Chemical Release Inventory — published by Her Majesty's Inspectorate of Pollution — reveals the industry as responsible for all unauthorised releases to land, and 35 per cent of unauthorised emissions to air (*Chemistry & Industry*, 18 March 1996: 199). Despite the strong likelihood that the database is incomplete, the contribution of the UK chemical industry to unauthorised emissions totals is staggering. A recent estimate calculates that 71 per cent of all toxic emissions from manufacturing are produced by just four bulk commodity industries, namely chemicals, plastics, paper and metals (Young, John 1994; cited in Smith, R. 1997).

Second, there is an increasing body of evidence which attests to the fact that environmental crimes are routine and ubiquitous. Moreover, the chemicals industries are integrally implicated in the incidence of such crimes. These typically involve the illegal dumping of hazardous wastes (Bullard 1990; Block and Scarpitti 1985; Cass 1996), crimes of environmental destruction, notably of forests and landscapes (Paehlke 1995), and crimes involving illegal emissions into land, air and waterways (Hyatt and Trexler 1996; Howarth 1991; Ross 1996). In these respects, then, public resentment relating to the scale and seriousness of environmental damage is accurate. To some extent, this resentment is slowly being reflected in official law-enforcement responses (at least the rhetorical level). Thus Cass notes that 'some officials in the United States predict that illegal dumping of hazardous materials will be the international crime of the 1990s' (Cass 1996: 99), and South refers to 'recent interviews' with officers of the FBI and the Royal Canadian Mounted Police where toxic waste dumping was identified as a 'high priority' amongst 'key turn-of-the-century crime issues' (South 1998: 18). Further, a study of local prosecutorial efforts around environmental crime by the National Institute of Justice begins by noting an opinion poll conducted for the United States Department of Justice which 'found that Americans believed environmental crime to be more serious than heroin smuggling, bank robbery and attempted murder' (NIJ 1993: xiii), noting that 'Environmental crime is a serious problem for the United States' (ibid.: xi).

For over a century, certain groups — notably organised labour — have pressured the chemical industry over its safety record.[5] Yet such pressure is typically thought of as being sectional. By contrast, environmental concerns have far greater potency in terms of popular articulation, and, from the point of view of industry, are reaching the proportions of a 'crisis' (Snider 1991). In organisational terms, it perhaps remains accurate to note that environmental pressures do not have the institutional power base which trades unions have provided for safety concerns — though as all commentators upon environmental activism note, this situation may be shifting (Hofrichter 1993; Szasz 1994). Certainly in *perceptual* terms, there are features ascribed to environmental degradation and environmental crime which might engender greater public resentment on this issue than is the case with occupational safety crimes. One important difference between safety and environmental 'crises' is that the former involve discrete, isolated incidents; their effects are temporally and spatially specific; moreover, such crises are neatly subject to enquiry, recommendation and action. Environmental crises are represented, and perceived, somewhat differently. These are both local and global; they are ubiquitous, and (represented as) non-discriminatory. Further, those voicing environmental concerns are less vulnerable to the charge of sectionalism often levelled at those who raise occupational safety issues. Moreover, despite the fact that safety incidents and environmental degradation often have similar causes, the effects of environmental hazards are less easily 'seen'; they are certainly not amenable to analysis and 'resolution' via inquiry and regulation.

These are crude distinctions which do no justice to the complex literature on risk perception. However, they are enough to highlight that there are very good reasons why chemical companies are likely to have been moved to quicker and more thoroughgoing responses to environmental pressures than to pressures around occupational safety. Further, perceptions of a crisis 'response' are reinforced by the development of (often non-governmental) international forms of oversight which are largely absent with respect to occupational safety.

Now there are, of course, a myriad of ways in which the chemicals industries have responded to environmental pressures (Tombs 1993a). Some of these responses need to be viewed, and, frankly, dismissed as public relations exercises. More importantly, these responses do not involve changes to work organisation, and are unlikely to affect the extent to which environmental crimes are committed by, or produced within, chemicals corporations. They are presentational only. Indeed, 'green marketing' is now a growth area for students and practitioners of the business function of marketing, as the torrent of books on this subject which emerged in the 1990s indicates (see, for example, Bernstein 1992; Charter 1992; Coddington 1993; Peattie 1992, 1995; Rehak 1993).

Amongst responses of companies in general, and of those within the chemicals industries in particular, the most 'adequate', though not the predominant, response has been an apparent increasing investment in new — and cleaner — process technologies, usually coupled with increasing investment in pollution abatement hardware (Tombs 1993a, 1994). As well as involving alterations to the physical nature of workplaces, this response may also entail changes to the nature of work organisation. This general response is the focus of the rest of the chapter. It is welcome in that it goes beyond rhetorical concern and represents a practical reaction to environmental concerns; yet it has possibly significant implications in terms of safety management, safety protection and the corporate production of crime. Ironically, such changes at workplace and organisational levels might actually exacerbate the tendency for crimes related to the management of major hazards.

If safety management and environmental protection — and thus compliance in each area and in the juxtaposition between the two — are to be effectively combined at operational levels, then this combination must be treated at a strategic level. In other words, dealing with these issues in a coordinated fashion at such a level is a necessary — though not sufficient — condition of effective safety management and environmental protection, while to treat either in strategic isolation will be either to 'fail' or to produce counter-productive effects. There is, at present, little empirical evidence that such strategic thinking is occurring, even in the chemical industry, a leading-edge context in many respects. Most companies continue to react to environmental threats rather than seeking out potential environmental vulnerabilities and linking these to business strategy and environmental policy (Roome 1992: 18). Most companies continue with *ad hoc* 'policies', failing to see the need for any innovative environmental strategy either now or in the foreseeable future (Schot 1992: 43). More generally, safety, health and environmental tasks remain 'managed at operations level with relatively narrow technical focus', and are 'generally ignored at the crucial strategic level of the firm' (Shrivastava 1993: 29).

It seems fruitful, then, to consider corporate performance in one sphere of activity alongside the other. We shall turn to that task shortly. We have argued that current forms of safety management and organisation create the potential for safety crimes. Thus, one way of addressing the issue of environmental crimes is to consider environmental management in precisely the same way, that is, to examine environmental management (and, indeed, compliance efforts) amongst the same, or a similar, sample of better performers. In some respects, however, this task has already been completed, in Gunningham's (1995) analysis of Responsible Care programmes.

Responsible Care is perhaps the most thoroughgoing attempt at self-regulation within the chemical, or perhaps any, industry. Thus,

> Proponents of the scheme describe it as 'the most ambitious and comprehensive environmental, safety and health improvement effort ever attempted by an industry.
>
> (Gunningham 1995: 61)

Such initiatives have been reproduced around the world, organised by chemical industry trade associations, and extended beyond the level of individual nation states — for example, the European trade body CEFIC has launched its own Responsible Care programme (Tombs 1993a). Moreover, as Gunningham notes, there are good reasons to expect the chemical industry to be in a better position to self-regulate than most other industrial contexts (Gunningham 1995: 63; see also above; and Tombs 1992). Moreover, Responsible Care seeks to address both occupational and environmental health and safety — that is, hazard management in its most holistic sense. Of further interest is the fact that the immediate catalyst for the Responsible Care initiative was the Bhopal disaster, and the regulatory and public scrutiny that followed.

Thus, Responsible Care is at once responsive (to greater external scrutiny) and also preemptive (in the context of the likelihood of more rigorous external regulation). National chemicals industries (over thirty of them) which have instituted such a programme, and the international chemical industry as a whole, have an enormous stake in the programme and its perceived efficacy.

In brief, Responsible Care is a 'chemical industry initiative whereby chemical companies commit themselves to the improvement of all aspects of their performance that relate to protection of health, safety and the environment' (Gunningham 1995: 61). As a self-regulatory scheme, it is based upon the assumption that chemicals companies themselves 'have both the motivation and the capacity to implement the changes to industry practice and culture' that are required (Gunningham 1995: 63). Thus the scheme 'promises a commitment to genuine improvement that goes "beyond compliance"' (Gunningham 1995: 63).

Gunningham's detailed assessment of Responsible Care, focusing mostly upon the US and Australia, but examining the programme in other national contexts, is a revealing one. He notes the relative inability to enforce 'compliance' on subscribing companies, and the tensions this creates amongst companies in terms of the so-called 'free-rider' problem; the problems of a system based upon self-reporting and self-evaluation, noting in passing that 'if laws about maintaining chemicals information are not complied with, arguably a voluntary code has little hope' (Gunningham 1995: 74, 101); the failure to comply with community right-to-know legislation; the lack of meaningful performance indicators; the absence of third-party oversight; and the focus within participating companies upon organising resistance to proposed government regulation.

Somewhat curiously, despite his detailed critique of the Responsible Care schemes as they currently operate, Gunningham seeks to present reforms through which they might be rescued. Ironically, he ends up arguing for external regulation, in the form of a tripartism which he terms co-regulation. Thus, 'government intervention is necessary to ensure that the industry association performs its self-regulatory tasks honestly and effectively' (Gunningham 1995: 87).

Such government intervention would be complemented by a more ongoing use of 'third-party audit, community right-to-know and other forms of community input and government oversight' (Gunningham 1995: 90). Moreover, even this system of co-regulation would, argues Gunningham, echoing Braithwaite's notion of enforced self-regulation (see Chapter 9), need to be 'complemented with an appropriate deterrence strategy' (Gunningham

1995: 90). In seeking to rescue a system of self-regulation, Gunningham ends up proposing a rather sophisticated form of external regulation!

In our view, the latter prescriptions are entirely realistic, though do not go far enough (see Chapters 7, 8 and 9). Before we move on to our remaining concerns in this chapter, it is worth noting Gunningham's words on the contexts for the emergence, and, it seems, subsequent demise of Responsible Care initiatives:

> Today, although the spectre of Bhopal still stalks the chemical industry, its impact is fading. More important, a major recession has inflicted substantial damage on the industry's profits, and environmental groups have far less influence as the economy takes center stage in national politics and policy-making. There is impressional evidence that commitment to Responsible Care is weakening, and that any aspects of the scheme that are likely to damage short-term industry profits now meet with substantial opposition, even from many major enterprises. There is also evidence of a slippage from genuine commitment toward improved environmental performance to seeking financially painless public relations benefits.
>
> (Gunningham 1995: 92-3)

We accept that such initiatives may have some positive aspects, and may contribute to the safer production, use and disposal of chemicals. But they are inherently flawed, remain highly tactical, and any real improvements are only likely to be maintained if there is sustained public pressure. Moreover, they are organised around a central assumption that the public needs to be disavowed of their unjustifiably critical attitude towards the activities of the chemical industries, and that involves corporate decisions about *which* local communities, workers and environmental groups are allowed to engage in any dialogue (Hulse 1992). Indeed, both the CMA and CIA have attempted to make a virtue of necessity, obscuring how 'responsible' practices are forced upon industry, by legislation and the fear of legislation and by their fear of 'political fallout' from disasters such as Seveso and Bhopal.

A fitting conclusion to this brief discussion of Responsible Care are the words of environmental activist Fred Millar:

> the industry has a public relations programme that says we're going to be open to the public and more forthcoming with documents, but on the other hand, in the Congress, where I think it really counts, they hammer the environmentalists just as hard as ever all the time. So my image about Responsible Care is that it's the velvet glove around the iron fist of the Chemical Manufacturers' Association.
>
> (quoted in *Network First*, 1995)

Let us now turn, in the final sections of this chapter, to a consideration of some of the potential effects of the most thorough responses to environmentalism — involving changes to plant, process and work organisation — upon compliance in general, and safety crimes in particular. That is, we need to consider the implications of some of the *ad hoc* changes introduced to meet environmental concerns on safety performance.

There exists a growing literature which focuses upon management efforts to improve standards of environmental protection in various industrial settings (McDonagh and Prothero 1996; and Smith 1993, are each illustrative collections). Much of this literature indicates both a higher priority being attached to, and some progress in managing environmental performance in industry in general, and the chemical industry in particular. However, the nature and effects of the interrelationships between these two areas of managerial effort are rarely considered. Of course, we know that some earlier practical attempts to improve industrial safety often involved a simple transfer of a hazard from the workplace to 'outside the factory fence'; this contradiction was subsequently highlighted, and is probably now an exception in advanced industrialised economies. More recently, a concern to minimise risk via the removal of hazard — for example, through the reduction of hazardous inventories or the substitution of less for more dangerous substances — has undoubtedly had mutually beneficial effects upon both environmental quality and employee safety.

However, there is no necessary reason for us to assume this happy coincidence of interests. It is at least possible that, just as some earlier efforts to improve occupational safety resulted in greater environmental degradation, then so may increased concern for, and efforts around, environmental protection result in the creation of less safe workplaces. This possibility provides the focus of this section of the chapter. Four closely related, and potentially problematic implications of this response will be noted here.

Resource Implications

The chemicals industries are highly capital-intensive, with huge start up costs, high (though varying) levels of research and development expenditures; they are relatively poor players in competitive global markets (Chenier 1986; Witcoff and Reuben 1980). Given these points, additional investment in pollution abatement equipment, new technologies in general, and new forms of work organisation adds to what are already high costs of producing and competing in the chemicals sector. Thus, a recent report on the costs of pollution abatement/control equipment found that the UK chemicals industries spent more on environmental protection than any other branch of industry in Britain. It is claimed that in 1989 the sector spent over £600 million on capital 'that can realistically be categorised as aimed at environmental improvement' (Liardet 1991: 119; see also Ecotec 1989). UK Office for National Statistics data estimated that of total industrial expenditure on air pollution control for 1994 (£2.3 billion), £503 million was spent by the chemical industry, making it by far the leading sector (Office for National Statistics 1996). Gunnigham claims that in the European Union, in the ten years up to 1995, 'the chemical industry's spending on environment has doubled' (Gunningham 1995: 97). As we might expect, levels of expenditure in the US are greater. One source calculates business expenditures on pollution abatement alone for 1992 as exceeding 55,000 million dollars (Atkinson and Hamilton 1997: 69). While no figures are provided for the chemical industry, it is reasonable to assume that this industry is the greatest contributor to this total (Gray et al. 1993). Now to the extent that such estimates rely on data provided by the industry itself, then they are likely to be over-estimates, as companies seek to exaggerate their environmental expenditures as part of their seeking to gain 'green' credentials. Nevertheless, it is clear that significant levels of resources are being expended, levels which were increasing, and increases which were forced upon companies largely through external pressures.

Moreover, expenditure at such levels has been made in the context of a sector which has been severely hit by recessions in the early and late eighties, and again at the beginning of the 1990s. Given these high and rising levels of expenditure, it is worth noting a 1991 report that while 'recession has hit the chemical industry particularly hard', leading to a general 'slashing' of investment, chemical companies are spending *an increasing proportion* of that investment on pollution control. This spending was expected to grow from a current 11 per cent of capital expenditures across the industry to almost 25 per cent in the following two years (Cowe 1991: 12). The potentially problematic juxtaposition of increasing environmentally-related expenditures in the context of harsh economic times for the international chemical industry has been illustrated graphically by ICI. At the same time as this company was claiming to be devoting 10-15 per cent of capital expenditure to 'environmentally improved processes and products' (McGavin 1991 : 19), it was also about to announce financial results (for 1992) which revealed its first loss since the recession a decade previously (*Observer*, 28 February 1993: 31). This is not to cast one phenomenon as causal of the other, but rather to provide an illustration of the economic context in which significant resources are being committed to environmental protection.

The significance of such points should be clear. There are social and political pressures to meet the environmental 'crisis', pressures particularly great in the chemical industry. Thus, chemicals companies have committed themselves to increasingly high levels of 'environmental' expenditures. Particularly in the context of recession and restructuring, it is possible that environmental expenditures will divert resources from 'safety' expenditure.

That is possible partly because both safety and environmental protection have traditionally been 'soft' business functions. It is more likely that these will be subject to budget cuts than, say, the marketing function. Moreover, each are areas that have been largely treated in corporations as relating to externalities, to the 'side-effects' of production, as secondary rather than integral matters. Thus if one of these areas becomes — through the weight of external pressures — a higher priority on corporate agendas, it is very possible that the other area will suffer.

This possibility is even more likely to be realised given the organisational structures within which environmental protection and safety management are most commonly placed. Chemicals corporations, in the UK, Western Europe and North America, generally treat these two functions within one oversight department, often located within some variation of an 'Environmental, Safety and Health' (ESH) rubric (Shrivastava 1993). This combination is reflected in the common practice of having one named director 'responsible' for environmental, safety and health matters. Relatedly, there tend to be single budgets in corporations for these three functions. Such structures facilitate the masking of any shift in expenditure from safety to environmental protection (though this is not being implied as a motive for such a structure).

Now, of course, many measures aimed at reducing environmental degradation do have beneficial effects in terms of occupational safety; but it is equally certain that some will not, and one cannot presume that spending on environmental protection benefits employees in terms of on-the-job safety. Some practical environmental improvements will *not* be compatible with occupational safety. Prioritising environmental protection can have detrimental effects upon worker safety (for some concrete examples, see Kletz 1992; Labour Research Department 1990). Further, some safety functions are distinct from measures aimed at environmental protection, and require discrete, and sustained, forms of expenditure. Increased resources being directed towards environmental protection threatens the integrity of budgets aimed strictly at worker safety.

While accidents and injuries at work cannot simplistically be attributed to inadequate resources, as we have argued above (Chapter 4), low or declining levels of investment can have an impact upon a range of key areas, for example:

the purchase or construction of safer plants; research on safer working practices; the preparation of safety assessments; routine maintenance; safety training; the employment of safety personnel. Certainly 'economies' of such kinds were common in the UK during the recession of the early eighties, and they undoubtedly combined to have detrimental effects upon safety performance in the chemicals industries (Freeman 1985; Grayham 1986; Hughes 1984; Stow 1983).

Training Implications

Within overall resource constraints, a key and specific area of likely problems is the provision of training. New processes, technologies, and working arrangements designed to improve environmental performance will require new, specific and additional forms of training for both workers and managers. This 'concomitant investment' is vital if innovations are to be successfully developed and integrated into a 'pre-existing system' (Zimmerman 1988: 250).

Although this is a commonly aired observation (Roome 1992: 22; Essery 1993: 129; McNichol 1989: 410-11; Welford 1992), training remains a highly problematic area. This is not least due to the fact recorded above, namely, that the current state of occupational safety training for managers and employees is inadequate. Thus, if training for safety is already inadequate, it is possible that the necessary additional training which should accompany any workplace changes aimed at improved environmental protection will not materialise.

The possibility of workplace changes without adequate investment in requisite training and development raises serious issues for both workers and managements. Many contemporary managers are simply not sufficiently 'capable' of managing safety. This fact, coupled with a likely inadequate provision of training in relation to responses to environmentalism, leads us to read with concern a recent claim that technological responses to environmentalism may involve 'an increasing devolution of responsibilities to more junior staff' (McGavin 1991: 16). A situation where lower-level management assume increased responsibilities yet remain lacking in ability is one fraught with danger for those employees who work with the consequences of lower-level management decisions.

Moreover, the need for employees to work with different processes or technologies, or within new forms of work organisation might, in the absence of adequate training, lead to their effective deskilling. This is so, not least because new working arrangements or conditions will erode some elements of the 'informal' skills and knowledges which employees possess, and which are often used for safety interventions. Again, workplace changes may leave employees working in less safe environments. In some industrial contexts, such changes have been introduced under the guise of 'multi-skilling', with detrimental effects upon occupational health and safety (Whyte 1996). McGavin also notes both that 'more skills might be needed by operatives' (McGavin 1991: 16) and that 'responsibilities ... will spread further throughout the workforce' (ibid.: 19). Additional responsibilities, without the concomitant training (or indeed rights) for employees will generate situations where they are viewed as the immediate cause of safety incidents.

'Top-Down' Implementation of Change

A further aspect of the introduction of new processes, technologies and working practices, relates to the *way* in which these are introduced. These changes are generally heralded by top-level statements about a company's 'concern' for the environment. As is the case in the management of safety, 'environmental' initiatives originate at the top of corporations, are announced and introduced with little or no consultation of lower-level management, let alone employees, and thus represent an imposition upon those most directly affected by them, on the 'shopfloor'. Moreover, while such prescriptive statements are often aimed at effecting cultural change, they tend to pay little or no attention to what have been labelled 'cultures in work' (Turner et al. 1989).

This approach is completely consistent with authoritarian and hierarchical forms of management which are integrally related to the production of safety crimes, as we have indicated in the previous chapter. Yet such means of introducing workplace changes have two likely and mutually reinforcing consequences. First, changes are unlikely to share the support of, and may even meet opposition from, those 'on the shopfloor' and thus may not only prove ineffective but even counter-productive (Gouldner 1954). Second, changes which are imposed are likely to be perceived as, and may actually entail, efforts to increase control over the day-to-day working lives of process workers. Management's 'right to manage' is thereby reinforced.

In contrast to such means of introducing workplace changes, management friendly theorists such as Roome have said that improved environmental performance requires senior management to 'recognise the value of building the belief and commitment of the workforce to an environmental policy' (Roome 1992: 15), so that employees can 'contribute to the central vision and codes of practice by which the company, and they, operate' (ibid.: 22; and see Shimmel 1991: 17). However, evidence from research on the management of safety does not indicate that changes around safety protection are introduced in such a fashion, and there is no reason to simply assume that this failing will be any less evident in the introduction of measures to improve environmental compliance and protection. Ironically, then, the introduction of changes in a top-down fashion is likely to reinforce that phenomenon which many 'green management' theorists argue is itself a fundamental cause of environmental degradation — namely technocracy (Fischer 1990; Smith, ed. 1993).

Implications for Technocratic Management

This leads us to a further, and perhaps more significant, observation. It should by now be clear that both the response to environmentalism and the approaches to safety management outlined previously, remain firmly rooted within a technocratic framework: the environment is yet another area to which the chemicals industries can bring the necessary technical fix. There are a number of elements to, and implications of, this approach.

First, the chemicals industries, though a key source of environmental degradation, represent themselves as best placed to redress such damage (Bruel 1990: 734). This declaration both serves as an attempt to insulate the chemicals industries from external criticism and regulatory oversight, while reinforcing the technical superiority of the polluters. Indeed, such 'framing' of the problem (and its solution) is a common tactic in crisis situations (t'Hart 1993). Ironically, through such a response the power of scientific-technical expertise is not only maintained, but strengthened.

Second, this response to environmentalism is often represented as a source of competitive advantage (Porter and van der Linde 1995). Process, technological and organisational changes — usually referred to as 'innovations' — aimed at improving environmental performance are often linked by corporate spokespeople to general 'efficiency' (Horton 1990; Woolard 1990). Such arguments have an important corollary. Within competitive markets, opportunities for some are threats for others; where there are winners, there must also be losers (Groenewegen and Vergragt 1991; McGavin 1991). For larger companies, there may well be competitive advantage to be won in delivering quick and 'effective' technical fixes to environmental issues (Leonard 1988), notwithstanding their (unevenly distributed) internal costs. However, within those companies that are competitively disadvantaged, profitability is likely to be squeezed, and soft areas of expenditure provide possible areas of resource 'saving'. Once again, employees may suffer, quite literally, for environmental 'improvements'. And these employees are likely to be those who are already the least protected and most marginalised, in smaller, poorer resourced, often non-unionised companies. This is further evidence of the exacerbation of 'structures of vulnerability' (Nichols 1986) in industrial life.

A third point follows from the above. Central to developing the technical fix, and to gaining competitive advantage, is the continued maximisation of profitability. Stated baldly, 'The ability of the industry to innovate towards a cleaner world — and it is only the industry that can do this — depends upon brute profit' (Liardet 1991: 120). Such a claim raises key contradictions within the concept of sustainable development (O'Connor 1994; Yearley 1996), and begs key questions which tend not to be asked, let alone 'answered', for example: what is the time-span over which profitability is calculated (and this is largely dependent on the workings of impersonal and abstract financial markets); how long is the 'acceptable' time-span between investments and return; precisely what is the ability of decentralised and diversified companies to carry short-term loss-making units; and are profit/loss calculations based upon private or social costs? Further, the claim raises questions concerning the varying susceptibility of, and varying abilities to respond to environmentalism on the part of different business sections of the chemicals industries, and even different 'national' or 'international' chemicals industries; at the international level, this response to environmentalism might engender a further relocation of hazard (Smith and Blowers 1992), again widening structures of vulnerability on a global scale.

Conclusion

The brief survey presented on safety management in the earlier sections of this chapter revealed a variability in means of, and abilities in, managing safety. Our overall conclusion is five of the six companies (the exception being Company C) possess *some* motivation to effectively manage safety, and to improve efforts in this sphere. However, clear examples have been revealed of a lack of motivation; and in each of the particular areas of safety management examined, all companies were experiencing difficulties in managing safety, although there were differences between them, both generally, and in respect of these particular areas. In short, while there existed some degree of motivation to improve safety management, such motivation was both highly contingent and inadequate. Moreover, even where motivation apparently was present within one part of an organisation, motivation and/or the ability of the organisation at the corporate level to secure safety improvements was often lacking. In other words, managing safety has been shown to be an enormous task that was proving extremely difficult for the companies considered here. These difficulties related to organisational features, and out of these organisational difficulties will emerge some safety crimes. *What we have identified here are organisational structures which have the potential for criminality designed into them.* That is, there exist and are maintained organisational structures and cultures within which managements will inevitably fail to meet their responsibilities under the Control of Major Accident Hazard Regulations and Sections 2 and 3 of the HASAWAct.

For those not used to treating safety violations as crimes, and who retain commonsense notions of criminality which revolve around street crimes, intention, action, and so on, such a conclusion will seem curious. Yet this possible reception does not make the conclusion false — and it is surely the task of social science to transcend commonsense (indeed, ideological) understandings of aspects of the social world.

It is important to emphasise again that the companies studied here are *all* better than average safety performers in the context of the UK chemical industry; moreover, they are more visible as companies by their size, their reputation, and their recognisable names. In the light of our conclusions, a number of points follow.

First, it is important to bear in mind that the survey here deals particularly with major hazards. Thus the survey bears out the conclusions of our discussion in the previous chapter, where we argued that, *contra* the claims of some, there is no reason at all for complacency regarding the safety performance of companies operating sites which are intrinsically hazardous and have high risk potential.

Second, one implication of this data is that if companies doing *relatively* well in managing safety, companies with considerable resources at their disposal, and considerable motivation to do so, are still not meeting some of the fundamental tasks of safety management (for example, effective top management backing for safety staff, clear lines of accountability, adequate training, employee involvement), then what of the thousands of other chemical companies in the UK? How well do *they* manage safety? What incentives are there to improve their management?[6] As we have seen (Chapter 4), where safety management is 'inadequate', it is also likely that safety crimes are being committed.

Third, although the companies discussed in this chapter are, as has been noted, all large and complexly organised across different businesses and continents, it is not our intention to imply that (safety) crimes are a 'natural accompaniment' to organisational complexity, or even a 'natural accompaniment' somehow overcome via 'self-surveillance' (Vaughan 1983:

107-112). Something which this chapter clearly illustrates is that organisational forms are potentially subject to change, and that one motivation of such change could be the desire to operate safely and within safety legislation. If companies possessed the will to manage safely, this could be achieved within complex organisational forms, just as other corporate goals are presumably achieved, or more closely approximated, within such structures.

This leads us to a further conclusion of the chapter. For the material presented here undermines claims by many commentators on hazard management that corporations should be left largely to self-regulate, whether this be on the basis of a misplaced faith in corporate rationality and an exaggerated or naive belief in the notion that effective safety and environmental management pays, or on a distrust of external regulation per se, or on a conviction that the technical expertise and the social power to ensure compliance exists only within corporations themselves. The argument of this chapter clearly warns against placing faith in self-regulation as a generalisable regulatory strategy, a point that we shall develop at much greater length in Chapters 7, 8, and 9 of this text.

None of these points are to cast those who are employed in positions of power within corporations as necessarily criminal, though of course there are many examples of corporate executives who are just that. There were certainly individuals in the companies surveyed here with a keen sense of 'social responsibility'. But to focus simply upon the level of individuals is to miss the point: we must recognise the existence of criminogenic structures, and that these can exist, and have effects, even in the absence of criminal individuals. Further, we must recognise that there are real structural constraints within capitalist corporations that militate against law-abiding activity, and that the extent and nature of compliance with external regulation is contingent upon economic, social and political factors, with improved compliance dependent upon economic, social, and political struggle and reform. We shall turn to these questions of responsibility and the role of external regulation in preventing safety crimes in later chapters (Part III).

Of most general importance is the endurance of technocratic managerial approaches to both safety management and environmental protection. Technocratic approaches to occupational safety have proven inadequate; such approaches to environmental protection will prove inadequate; and the mutual effects of these two sets of efforts within a technocratic managerial paradigm are problematic, to say the least. We now turn to a gruesome illustration of the effects of technocratic and capitalist rationality, in the form of an analysis of the Bhopal disaster.

Notes

1.   This is not, of course, to deny the importance of small businesses in corporate crime in general (Sutton and Wild 1985), nor in safety violations in particular (ILO 1985; Tombs 1988). It is merely to take the most favourable 'testing-sites' for claims concerning self-regulation.

2.   Such above average growth rates are not, of course confined to the UK. In the period between 1960 and 1985, the chemical industry 'in most developed countries' grew at 'around twice the rate of the manufacturing industry as a whole', and up to the mid-seventies average annual growth rates in the former were up to 10 per cent per annum (Pettigrew 1985: 54). The growth in the industry remains marked in relative terms, as indicated in the following table:

International Growth Rate Comparisons, 1984-1994

Average Growth % p.a.

Country	*Chemicals Industry*	*Manufacturing Industry*	*Ratio of Chemicals to all Industry*
USA	3.1	3.0	1.0
Japan	4.0	1.8	2.2
UK	**3.6**	**1.9**	**1.9**
Germany	2.1	2.0	1.1
France	3.5	1.1	3.2
Italy	2.0	1.8	1.1
Total EEC	2.9	1.7	1.7

Source: Heaton 1996: 81

3.   In conducting this research, all participating companies, sites, and individuals, were guaranteed anonymity and that is respected here. All unattributed quotes are drawn from interviews.

4. Such an organisational characteristic is a feature of those forms of organisation labelled by Kreisberg as 'organisational processes' and 'bureaucratic politics' (Kreisberg 1976); see Chapter 3 of this text; and also Pearce and Tombs (1990, 1991).

5. The General, Municipal Boilermakers and Allied Trades Union has been at the forefront of trade union struggle around occupational health and safety issues in the UK. Much of this has been specifically concerned with the chemicals industries, while other activity has had a more general focus (see, for example, GMBATU 1986, 1987; Kaufman 1985; Waterson 1988a).

6. Answers to such questions are intimated in a few texts; see for example, Dawson et al. (1988); Grayham (1986); Kasperson et al. (1988).

6 Bhopal, Union Carbide and the International Chemical Industry

Introduction

In this chapter we use the tragic gas disaster at Bhopal in December 1984 and its aftermath as a case study in corporate crime. It must be emphasised at the outset that this event represents a human tragedy on an unprecedented scale (see, for example, Cassels 1993; Chouhan et al. 1994; *Network First*, 1995) — the largest ever industrial disaster with the possible exception of the Chernobyl incident. Yet, at the same time, it stands as a case study from which we can, and indeed must, learn. As a case-study it is important and useful for a number of reasons. First, because the case poses in its starkest form many of the issues with which this text is concerned — namely, questions of corporate power, the nature of internal and external forms of accountability as these relate to corporate organisation, and the functioning of regulatory and legal systems. Second, because it raises other key issues pertinent to any consideration of corporate crime, particularly those pertaining to the advantages and disadvantages of using tort law and other existent mechanisms as a potential means of redress for victims of corporate crime. Third, because the disaster had, and continues to have, truly global ramifications in the context of environmental and occupational health and safety, particularly for the national and international chemicals industries and companies. Fourth, because many of the essential circumstances surrounding the incident are well-known, and some, at least, are (over a decade after the event) generally acknowledged. Fifth, because to understand the circumstances surrounding the disaster, and to place these circumstances in the context of the arguments presented in the previous two chapters (Chapters 4 and 5), is to be faced with a clear, if frightening, conclusion — namely, that while the Bhopal disaster was unique in its consequences, it is actually mundane in its causes. This latter point will become clear in the course of this chapter. Finally, because it allows us to examine corporate claims of social responsibility, and hence corporations' ability to self-regulate.

194

At Bhopal, Union Carbide Corporation (UCC), at the time viewed by most as a safe and responsible company, created the conditions whereby an accident was not only likely, but also that its consequences would be of far greater magnitude than need have been. Subsequently, UCC has worked hard at influencing both public opinion and the legal process through a series of spurious arguments about the accident, the nature of the Indian company, and the Bhopal plant and its employees. It was able to secure a favourable settlement, and although the settlement has been re-opened, thus exposing the company to the possibility of further legal action, it is now unlikely that much will actually change (Sarangi 1996; *Corporate Crime Reporter* 2 (26), Monday, 30 June 1997: 1).

The Emergence of a Friendlier, Law-Abiding Corporate Capitalism?

While much of the attention following Bhopal has been, quite justifiably, upon the victims of that disaster (albeit to inadequate effect), the leak of methyl iso-cyanate (MIC) from the UCC plant had wider ramifications for both the company (Lepkowski 1994) and the international chemical industry (Jasanoff ed., 1994; Smith ed., 1986). Jasanoff has written that 'the example of what had happened to Union Carbide demolished overnight a whole edifice of public confidence in the norms governing the multinational chemical industry' (Jasanoff 1994: 10).

It is not surprising, then, that in the decade following the Bhopal disaster, a whole series of phenomena appeared to converge which together created the impression of a sea change in corporate practices. Three distinct phenomena are worthy of particular note.

One phenomenon was the re-emergence of environmentalism in the 1980s and 1990s. As we have argued in the previous chapter, the general response of the chemicals industries to the re-emergence of environmentalism has been either superficial or tactical. Moreover, as we indicated therein, environmental crimes remain ubiquitous.

A second phenomenon of note has been the emergence of the academic discipline (and consultancy service) of 'crisis management' within both academic and business worlds. In its most radical variant, crisis management addresses itself to the need for capitalist corporations to revolutionise their practices and values in the interests not only of their own survival, but also more general eco-sustainability (Shrivastava 1994; Smith 1993). More usually, the conservative variant of crisis management concerns itself with the mitigation of, and responses to, potential crises for corporations. Thus, for example, a Pittsburgh-based public relations firm prepared a 'Crisis Management Plan' for the Clorox corporation, intended to greenwash its image, neutralize green 'journalists' and counter Greenpeace's campaign against the toxic effects of chlorine (Carlisle 1991: 31). Other crisis management consultants have critiqued Dow Corning's poor handling of the issue of breast implants for its similarities to Exxon's response to the Exxon Valdez oil spill, Johns Manville Corporation's treatment of its asbestos woes and A.H. Robins Co.'s debacle with its Dalkon Shield birth control device'. On the other hand, Union Carbide Corporation has been praised for its 'handling' of the Bhopal disaster (*The Globe and Mail*, 30 January 1992: B1 and *The New York Times*, 31 April 1989: B1). All too often, companies seem to be less concerned with their adequacy in alleviating the suffering of victims, and more concerned with their success or failure in handling the attendant public relations crises.

Third, the late 1970s and 1980s witnessed the re-emergence of claims around corporate social responsibility and business ethics. Whether in terms of corporate giving (philanthropy or charity), in terms of community activity, or in terms of a recognition of the need to meet and apparently exceed legal requirements placed upon them by governments, many corporations now make claims to social responsibility. Corporate social responsibility and business ethics are now established sub-discipline areas within management and business studies — tellingly, falling within the general rubric either of strategic management or business policy. And government and Quasi Non Governmental Organizations (QUANGO) activity around corporate social responsibility proliferates — the UK, for example, has recently seen the establishment of public committees on Corporate Governance (the Cadbury Committee) and Executive Pay (the Greenbury Committee). The chemical industry, on both sides of the Atlantic, has been at the forefront of claims to, and initiatives around, corporate social responsibility. This is one of the contexts in which the Responsible Care initiative, discussed in the previous chapter, needs to be understood.

Even this cursory overview of corporate claims to new and effective forms of crisis management, to being stewards of the environment, and to a new corporate social responsibility, highlights the need to look beyond the appearances that are represented by corporations to governments, publics, consumers and workers. The two previous chapters have rather undermined the significance of such claims. In this chapter, our analysis of events surrounding the Bhopal disaster seeks to problematise the claims of capital that corporations have become, through a combination of paths and for a variety of reasons, law-abiding citizens, determined to prevent crisis, protect the environment, and be socially responsible. Indeed, once the Bhopal disaster occurred, there is no evidence that UCC acted in a responsible fashion, either in its dealings with the victims of that tragedy, or in its management of other plants and relationships with regulators and local communities.

Explaining the Disaster at Bhopal

In Bhopal, India, a chemical plant, operated by Union Carbide of India Limited (UCIL), a subsidiary of Union Carbide Corporation (UCC), used the highly toxic chemicals, carbon monoxide, chlorine, phosgene ('Mustard Gas'), monomethylamine and methyl iso-cyanate (MIC) to produce carbamate pesticides. On the night of Sunday, December 2, 1984 water entered an MIC storage tank setting in process an exothermic reaction. Soon a cocktail of poisonous gases, vapours and liquids — including up to forty tons of MIC and unknown quantities of hydrogen cyanide, nitrous oxide, and carbon monoxide — was spewed into the atmosphere. Between 200,0000 and 450,000 local people were exposed to the toxic fumes, some 60,000 were seriously affected, more than 20,000 were permanently injured, and at least 1700 and as many as 10,000 people may have died as an immediate result of the tragedy.[1]

UCC immediately responded to the disaster with a series of defensive claims: that the disaster was totally unprecedented and unanticipated so it was not surprising that an 'evacuation or safety plan had never been developed'; that they had not located the MIC plant at Bhopal 'for reasons of economy or to avoid safety standards'; that they had the same safety standards in their American and overseas operations — 'in India or Brazil or someplace else ... same equipment, same design, same everything' (Everest 1986: 47-8). In short, UCC claimed that although the Bhopal plant was managed exclusively by Indian nationals, its safety standards were identical to the standards at Institute, West Virginia.

Subsequently, UCC has taken every opportunity to deny its own responsibility for the gas leak by claiming that: it had an excellent safety record, and the design of the plant's Standard Operating Procedures (SOPs) — UCC's responsibility — was basically sound; the production of MIC in India, the siting of the plant and the quality of the materials used, were all the responsibility of UCIL and the Indian State; UCIL was an independent company responsible for its own affairs; India's cultural backwardness was responsible for the poor maintenance and management, poor planning procedures and the inadequate enforcement of safety regulations; the accident was due to sabotage.

The Sabotage Theory

Let us first address the last contention — for the 'sabotage theory' plays a key role in UCC's 'definitive version' of the sequence of events that led to the leak at the plant. According to this 'theory', on the night of the accident a disgruntled employee, who was not on duty, removed a pressure gauge and then used a hose to put water into an MIC tank; his intention was to spoil a batch of chemicals rather than create a disaster. This version of events, circulated to the media and to UCC personnel, was most fully articulated when it formed the basis of a paper presented by 'independent consultant' Dr. Ashok Kalelkar at a London conference in May 1988 (Kalelkar 1988). Kalelkar had in fact been a member of the team organized by UCC in March 1985 which even then had mooted the possibility of sabotage, although a lack of evidence meant, it claimed, that 'it was unable to develop this theory further at the time' (ibid.; Pearce and Tombs 1993).

Yet, this 'definitive version' was only the last in a series of such 'theories' involving alleged saboteurs. First, it had been claimed that the disaster itself was the result of the actions of careless or malicious employees who had placed a water line where a nitrogen line should have been used. The *New York Times* on 26 March 1985 pointed out that neither an accidental nor a deliberate incorrect coupling were possible since the relevant nitrogen and water lines were of a different colour and the nozzles were of different sizes. That same day Union Carbide Chairman, Warren Anderson, had to withdraw the accusation at Congressional Hearings when he admitted that he had no evidence of sabotage. Then, between 31 July 1985 and 3 January 1986, UCC claimed that a group of Sikh extremists called the Black June Movement were responsible. But no such group was ever identified in any context other than allegedly putting up posters about Union Carbide; moreover, it was virtually impossible for anybody to actually plan a disaster of this kind. Not surprisingly, this claim was also quietly abandoned. In August 1986 a specific but unnamed employee was blamed — but it was not until May 1988 that all references to nitrogen lines were dropped and a pressure meter was mentioned.

The legal reasoning behind UCC's strategy of using the sabotage argument is clear:

> Union Carbide and UCIL are hoping, first, to avoid vicarious liability on the ground that the employee would have been acting without authority and outside

the course of his employment, and, secondly, to avoid liability under Rylands v. Fletcher, on the ground that an employee who comes onto his employers' premises without authority and causes the escape of a dangerous thing is a 'stranger' for whose acts the occupier is not responsible.

(Muchlinski 1987: 575).

What should be immediately clear is that even if we were to accept that the accident *was* caused by sabotage, then this only serves to demonstrate how unsafe the actually plant was. That is, any sabotage theory itself only serves to underline UCC's responsibility for the accident. Acceptance of such a theory raises two key questions about plant organisation. First, why was it possible to remove a pressure dial by hand when this was connected to such a toxic and volatile chemical? And, second, why was there water in the area? As a leading specialist on safety in chemical plants has written, if water is not there, 'it cannot leak in, no matter how many valves leak or how many errors are made' (Kletz 1988: 86).

Whether or not sabotage occurred, a more fundamental issue is the ease with which a disaster of almost unprecedented scale could occur. The focus on sabotage only serves to detract attention from UCC's well documented responsibility for many key factors — for example, the poor design of the Bhopal plant, its inappropriate siting, its inadequate safety systems, the lack of a proper emergency plan, and its generally run-down condition. In other words, the plant itself — the way in which it had been designed and managed — was one in which accidents and crimes were likely to be produced, and, if realised, likely to have catastrophic potential. As a crime, the Bhopal disaster was produced by a corporate structure and a corporate *modus operandi*. Let us explore these contentions in more detail.

The Context and Circumstances of the Disaster

Let us focus, in more detail, on the circumstances of the accident. At Bhopal enormous amounts of MIC were stored in three 15,000 gallon tanks. The temperatures and pressures of these were routinely too high — they should have been kept at 0-5 degrees Celsius but were in fact between 15 and 20 degrees Celsius. Furthermore, these temperatures and pressures were not rigorously logged. Because plant instrumentation was inadequate to monitor normal plant processes, leaks were detected by smell (only possible at levels 20 times higher than its Threshold Limit Value), although this was certainly not the case at the Institute, West Virginia plant which, in this and many other respects, had superior technology. On the night of 2 December, workers reported smelling MIC but could not locate its source, and so informed a supervisor of the leak, who postponed investigating its source until after a tea break. Before that was over, a tank, tank 610, was rumbling, concrete cracking, and the tank's temperature was about 200 Celsius, the pressure at over 180 psi, 140 psi in excess of the tank's rupture disk limit. Gases, vapours and liquids burst past the rupture disk, shot through the relief valve vent header, then the vent gas scrubber, and into the atmosphere. The vent gas scrubber was on standby, and although it was eventually turned on, it probably never worked. The flare tower was inoperative, and an attempt to douse the gas with water was unsuccessful because the hoses had insufficient water pressure to reach the stack from which the gas was escaping. The operators could not dilute the MIC in tank 610 since it was already overly full and the emergency dump tank had a defective gauge which indicated that it was also 22 per cent full. Although the tanks should have been refrigerated, the refrigeration unit had been turned off — to save $50 per week. There is no doubt that badly maintained equipment, lack of spare parts, inadequate SOPs and untrained staff all contributed to the accident. But equally important were *ad hoc* modifications to the plant designs, such as a jumper line that may well have been the means by which water entered the MIC tank.

There are also serious questions that need to be addressed regarding the plant design itself. Plant instrumentation was inadequate to monitor normal plant processes. Furthermore, whilst large amounts of MIC were also stored at Institute, it had larger dump tanks and an additional dedicated sump system with a capacity of 42,000 gallons. It is possible that the Bhopal storage tanks had originally been used at Institute, since they were of a type unsuitable for Indian climatic conditions. The refrigeration plant at Bhopal, *even when working*, was not powerful enough to cool all of the MIC stored there, and the vent gas scrubber and flare tower were only designed to deal with single phase (that is, gas not liquid, or gas *and* liquid) emissions. At Institute, moreover, there was an additional and more powerful emergency back-up system. *Bhopal was demonstrably inadequate and inferior to Institute*. Nevertheless, even with this inferior technology, far fewer people would have died if: the plant had not been sited near shanty towns; there had been adequate risk assessment, modelling and monitoring of discharges and emergency planning and management; the plant personnel, local medical services and the state and national government had known more about the nature and effects of the deadly gaseous emissions.

Thus it appears, *contra* the claims of Anderson and others, that the Bhopal plant was an inferior plant to the UCC plant at Institute, West Virginia. But this should not be taken as an indication that the Bhopal plant was a maverick operation of an essentially law-abiding and socially responsible corporation, nor that the Institute plant was safe. In fact, in March 1985 an acetone/mesityl oxide mixture had been accidentally released from Institute; and in August of the same year, there was a leak of aldicarb oxime, a chemical of definite but unquantified toxicity. Evidence emerged that alarm systems were either shut off or not working, staff were inadequately trained, the SOPs were imprecise and management slipshod (Jones 1988: 163-186). Subsequently, OSHA sent several teams of inspectors to conduct a 'wall-to-wall' inspection. This led to 221 charges of violations, 130 of which were 'wilful', and proposed fines totalling $1.4 million — though OSHA and UCC eventually reached a settlement of just over $4400 for five serious violations on the agreement that the others would be corrected. It is important to note that on the basis of an apparently good safety record — determined using data which UCC had itself collected and provided — UCC's Institute plant had been exempted from OSHA inspections. Of particular interest is the fact that US Labour Secretary Brock revealed that had UCC actually kept *accurate* records (that is, rather than those on the basis of which they were exempt from inspection), then their accident record would have been 'substantially higher' than the US chemical industry average (Jones 1988: 163-186; Pearce 1990). One hundred and twenty-nine of the charges originally laid by OSHA were for failings to meet legal requirements to record accidents or ill-health (Jones 1988: 176). In February 1990, there were two more leaks at the plant, one injuring seven workers, the other resulting in 15,000 people confined to their homes. In March, the Seadrift, Texas plant exploded killing one worker and injuring thirty-two others in addition to injuring another six people outside of the plant. Carbide was originally fined $2.8 million by OSHA for 115 violations, 112 of which were described as wilful (the fine was contested by Carbide).

More generally, UCC has long been a prime example of 'toxic capital' — from the Gauley Bridge disaster in West Virginia where 476 deaths from silicosis were recorded, through its role in the development and use of the carcinogen, vinyl chloride, through its nuclear weapons manufacturing plant in Oak Ridge, Tennessee, its dangerous graphite electrodes production facilities in Yabucoa, Puerto Rico (Agarwal et al. 1985: 14-23) and its plant in Alloy, West Virginia which alone puts 'out more pollution annually than the total emitted in New York City in a year' (*New York Times*, 10 September 1989). Clearly, Union Carbide's slogan of 'Safety at any Cost' portrays a corporate image that is not borne out by reality.

'Union Carbide Corporation TNC'

Whether or not Union Carbide Corporation (UCC) was legally responsible for the accident has not been resolved by the decision in the Indian courts (see below). Yet the issue of responsibility can still be explored sociologically. A useful starting point is Kelvin Jones's discussion of property relations in *Law and Economy: The Legal Regulation of Corporate Capital*. He distinguishes three distinct and necessary functions of property in the sphere of economic production: *title* 'involves the sort of calculations and conditions which govern the more general provision of finance, the socialisation of debt, the exchange of guarantees and the constitutional position of shareholders' (Jones 1982: 78); *control* 'refers to the distribution of the relevant means of production to a particular use ... to the more or less absolute power to dispose of the means of production within the relevant confines imposed by other relations of ownership' (ibid.: 77); while *possession* 'concerns the day to day relation of management' (ibid.) and the 'strategies and calculations which comprise the use or actual operation of any particular process of production irrespective of who is the agent of possession' (ibid.: 76).

In common with UCIL's other shareholders, UCC had 'title' to much of the revenue generated by UCIL. In fact, despite the rule that foreign companies should usually own no more than 40 per cent of an Indian company's stock, UCC owned 50.9 per cent; and in 1982 UCIL remitted $1.43 million in dividends to UCC (Everest 1986: 167). Such a majority ownership allowed UCC to determine, to a large extent, the decisions made about investments and dividends and the assets of the company. According to UCC's charter, the objectives of the corporation would be realised through a management system which distinguished between 'Category I policies', which provide the worldwide directives of the company, and 'Category II policies', which are operational procedures:

> Both types of policy are issued to subsidiaries (*affiliates in which Union Carbide has more than 50 per cent ownership*) for adoption and implementation. A subsidiary cannot change the substance of any policy without review by the parent.
>
> (Muchlinski 1987, emphasis added).

UCC had a significant degree of 'control' over UCIL. UCIL's production and marketing strategies were dictated by the corporate strategies of UCC (Morehouse and Subramaniam 1986: 17). Moreover, the continued existence of the Bhopal plant was UCC's decision: it had commissioned a preliminary study of the cost of dismantling the MIC unit and other pesticide production facilities at Bhopal (Dinham et al. 1986: 27). Despite such a threat to its existence, UCIL was not in a position to 'go to a competitor of Union Carbide and buy a pesticide plant' ready-made; and it would be prohibitively expensive to develop a 'pesticides plant from scratch' (Muchlinski 1987: 582).

UCC, to a large extent, 'possessed' the Bhopal plant. It had always dictated how and which chemicals were produced and stored. In the 1970s, it had 'insisted that large amounts of MIC be stored in Bhopal over UCIL's objections ... (T)he UCIL position [was] that only token storage [of the chemical at Bhopal] was necessary' (Everest 1986 :31). It monitored safety procedures and UCIL was forced to rely upon UCC for technological assistance and updates (ibid. 167-171). Indeed, at Bhopal, UCC received significant revenues from its licensing, managerial, monitoring and marketing activities, a not atypical arrangement when TNCs engage in joint ventures in less developed countries (Kolko 1988: 165). UCC had the right to intervene in day-to-day matters if safety was affected. A UCC safety team had monitored the plant in May 1982, and found 61 hazards, 30 of them considered major, of which 11 were in the phosgene/MIC unit, and areas of concern were 'procedures training and enforcement together with attention to the equipment and mechanical deficiencies' (Everest 1986: 56). Nevertheless, production was allowed and expected to continue.

Detailed reports on safety and related matters were sent to UCC every three to six months (ibid.: 171). This included decisions on plant expenditure — on investment and cutbacks, on staffing levels, on refrigeration and so on. All of these had certainly been cut back: for example, there were fewer operatives, and amongst these, fewer first class BSc graduates; theoretical and practical training had been reduced or abolished; maintenance procedures were dangerously abbreviated (Sandberg 1985: 17).

In short, then, even though it is clear that the actual social relations in the individual enterprises were 'lived' and fulfilled by specific Indian managerial personnel (and individual workers), UCC 'possessed' the enterprise.

But in many ways this was only true insofar as UCC exerted itself to ensure that UCIL would follow its SOPs. In fact it is not clear that UCC provided the resources to adequately monitor the SOPs at Bhopal or whether it took into account the social and economic environments confronting UCIL. 'Control' and 'possession' are normally only relative. They are absolute only on the occasions when drastic decisions like opening or closing a plant or hiring or firing individuals are made. Day-to-day operations are always the outcome of struggle, negotiation and compromise, albeit between unequal protagonists.

In other words there still remains the problem of identifying the nature, degree and location of 'control' and 'possession' — if indeed it exists.

If, for convenience, we treat 'control' and 'possession' as if they are both aspects of the more general issue of the control of enterprises, we find that, recently, three somewhat different schools have addressed this issue and have reached similar conclusions. First, as we have seen, Kreisberg (1976) has suggested that there are three major ways in which a corporation *can* be organized, namely the rational actor model, the 'organizational processes' model, and, finally, corporate organizations may be subject to 'bureaucratic politics' (Kreisberg 1976: 1103). It is important to note, again, however, that even if the organization *seems* to be organized in either of the latter two modes, this *may* be an ideological obfuscation. The reality may be that there is a centralised authoritarian control which is exercised informally, or that there is an implicit acceptance of illegal behaviour while executives are protected from potential legal action by a strategy of 'wilful blindness'. Kreisberg's second and third modes — if accepted literally — have strong affinities with the second perspective. This stresses the effects of different external environments on the *modus operandi* and internal structure of organisations. Thus, Box (1983, 1987) has discussed the effect of environmental factors on the criminal activities of corporations, and Meyer (1978) and Miles (1982) have asked what range of goals are feasible for organizations within their specific environments. Crucially the 'outside' of an organization is seen as (potentially) affecting both its internal organization and its goals. Finally, Jones (1984) has problematised the view that the TNC is a centred consistent social actor. Somewhat overstating the case, he argues that because there is no unitary way of assessing even such central auditing measures as profits, then corporations are necessarily 'dispersed social agencies'. There are different loci for different modes of calculation associated with differing and potentially contradictory goals.

These considerations can be made concrete. UCIL's production of the pesticides Temik and Sevin took place under commodified conditions — i.e., they were supposed to be produced and sold in such a way that subdivisions of the company showed a normal profitable return on investment. It is questionable whether it was possible for UCIL to safely make and sell these pesticides at a profit. If not, either the company could have engaged in safe but 'uneconomic' production, or it could have produced less safely and more 'economically'. It is clear that UCC's SOPs were both inadequate and (to some extent) ignored, this with the collaboration of certain of UCC's personnel. Which of these organizational models is appropriate, and how much control was — or could be — exercised by UCC must ultimately remain a moot point. *What is clear, however, is that the top management of UCC had represented itself to its shareholders as effectively controlling the different subsections of its organisation and had received the rewards and privileges commensurate with such control, and were thus responsible for, if not in fact totally in control of, the organization's actions.* UCC seems therefore to have been responsible for both the acts of commission and omission that created the Bhopal disaster. (A similar conclusion has been reached in Muchlinski's (1987) legal analysis of UCC's potential liability).

The existence of (somewhat) safer plants and production processes operated by UCC in the West (at Beziers, France, and Institute, US) shows that the relatively poor state of the Bhopal plant can be *partly* understood in terms of a racist imperialism. However, it is also necessary to raise more general issues concerning the nature of corporate activity, and the relationship between corporations and their workers, and local communities and consumers, wherever these may be. Such issues have often been addressed by the more complex Marxist analyses of the operations of TNCs. These approaches are useful in that they focus upon the class structure to be found *within* particular countries, whilst relating such an analysis to the global system in which individual states, corporations, and particular struggles are imbricated. In the case of India which is itself now a major industrial country, this means exploring the relations between the different classes involved in different modes of production and particularly in recognizing that the capitalist class — which strongly influences state activities — shares many interests with foreign corporations, benefits from their and US government initiatives such as the 'Green Revolution', and shares a similar opposition to the interests of the local working class. In raising such issues, the Union Research Group (1985a, 1985b), many of the contributors to ARENA (1985) and Everest (1986) lay some blame on those Indian interests, who through their commitment to capitalist industrialization at any cost, were responsible for the attitude of the local and national state to UCC and other transnationals. Whilst this is an advancement on the simpler anti-imperialist critiques, there remains the problematic assumption that transnational corporations normally act in concert as 'class subjects', and that they themselves understand what it is that they are doing, and thus cynically 'use' ideology to confuse their opponents.

Rhetoric, Rationalisation, and Ideology

One way of interpreting the relationship between a powerful group's public representation/misrepresentation of its actions and its true nature, is to suggest that, guided by a self-conscious awareness of their class interests and an accurate understanding of the nature of reality, such a group simply manipulates opinion.[2] This is problematic. Ideology may be a more or less adequate guide to practical action relative to interests (Marx and Engels [1845] 1976: 60-1), but since ideology is produced and developed in conflictual situations (Macdonell 1986), its content does not merely reflect an attempt at an accurate understanding but also involves an element of 'advocacy'. Positions are adopted and then different arguments are *deployed* with different audiences; different rationales inform different practices. Now, a powerful group has a (somewhat variable) capacity to *sustain* its ideology because of its relative power *vis-à-vis* other groups — a power to exclude, limit, or disregard other points of view and to avoid many, although by no means all, of the negative consequences of its misapprehensions and mistakes. What is required is an exploration of the different ways in which individuals or groups strive to articulate together what they privately say and what they publicly say and how these relate to what they do.

Let us return to the events at Bhopal. On a number of specific points, as well as on the general issue of control and in the presentation of the sabotage theory, UCC has clearly engaged in some degree of calculated and conscious misrepresentation and manipulation. For example, while UCC claimed that it would rather have imported MIC, this seems unlikely since this would make it vulnerable to transportation problems. After all, the downslide in the market 'began in 1977-78 when a consignment of MIC was delayed at sea ... In 1984 ... because of slumping demand for the pesticides ... the plant was operating at less than one third of capacity' (Sandberg 1985: 17). And this when UCIL had successfully applied for an increase in its licenced capacity — presumably to try and 'maintain a monopolistic control over prices' (APPEN 1985: 83). Elsewhere, but not at Bhopal, declining demand meant that it was willing to engage in 'facilities write-offs' of '$241 million' (Sandberg 1985: 11).

Everest reads the events at Bhopal as if the corporation's executives really understood both what occurred and what was likely to occur, and then simply disavowed responsibility by manipulating opinion — by lying and cynically producing obfuscating explanations and justifications. But Bhopal was an accident albeit an avoidable one. After all Union Carbide maintains the view that its overseas operations ultimately *benefit* Third World countries. Warren Anderson no doubt sincerely believed that 'without the technologies and the capital that multinationals help to introduce developing countries would have little hope of eradicating poverty and hunger'(cited in Everest 1986: 107).

Nevertheless, there is evidence that UCC executives used racist rationalisations to justify their carelessness and unusual level of risk taking — life is not valued in Third World countries, Indians are technologically unsophisticated, do not comprehend the purpose of safety procedures, and accidents are generally due to worker incompetence (Everest 1986: 107). Such racist beliefs pre-empted the exploration of the capacity of the people in Third World countries to be safety conscious. At a London symposium on Bhopal, the complaint of J.B. Browning, Vice President of Health Safety and Environmental Affairs at UCC, that there were poor phone links between Bhopal and the outside world was clearly intended to signify India's general backwardness (Browning 1986: 16).[3] These are examples of the rationalisation of dubious actions. This term does not simply refer to the reason that one believes has led one to act in a particular way, but rather that rationales and justifications were presented to self and others which *ignored important determinants of conduct such as unacknowledged interests and/or which allowed the actor to ignore the effects of their actions on other people.* Such rationalisations can, of course, be used to justify lies and deviance (Matza 1964; Scott and Lyman 1968). Insofar as management in the chemical industry routinely manipulates others, it itself may become somewhat confused about what is 'really' happening (Nichols and Beynon 1977: 123).

Now, despite the fact that India is sometimes represented as a less developed economy, and was certainly represented as such following the Bhopal disaster by senior Union Carbide officials, such a representation is very much a distortion. It is in many respects a major industrialised economy — certainly on the basis of common measures of economic activity, India ranks as one of the world's twenty most significant economies. This is not to obscure the fact that the majority of its population live in extreme poverty. It is unsurprising, then, that while India, as any other industrialised economy, has a significant chemical industry (Sufrin 1985: 29; Cassels 1993: 26; Shrivastava 1993: 259), the particular nature of that chemicals industry is closely related to food production (and, indeed, was developed by the state in the context of industrialisation, in general, and the so-called 'green revolution', in particular). As Cassels notes, pesticide production and use, considered essential factors in the effort to achieve self-sufficiency in agricultural production, increased dramatically during the late 1960s and early 1970s. Moreover, investment in chemical-based agriculture had been further encouraged by lending institutions, 'hoping to see rapid returns on their investments' (Cassels 1993: 39). Thus, by

1984, India was the fourth largest producer and consumer of chemical fertilisers in the world (Jalees 1985: 409).

Now, the agrochemicals industry, as a particular division of chemicals, is dominated by some of the world's largest multinational corporations. At a global level, in 1983, three companies — Bayer of West Germany, Ciba-Geigy of Switzerland and the American giant, Monsanto — controlled one-quarter of the world agrochemicals market, or 'over US $4 billion in sales' (Weir 1986: 7); about three dozen companies controlled over 90 per cent of world trade in pesticides, the top ten accounting for over 50 per cent of that total (ibid.). One of the key players in this industry at the time of the Bhopal disaster was Union Carbide (Weir 1986), which had longstanding interests in India. Indeed, it is worth noting that while IBM and Coca-Cola each refused to accept Indian Government conditions of majority state shareholding in their Indian activities, and thus disinvested, this condition was, as we have seen, waived in the case of Union Carbide.

It should also be noted that following two decades of huge growth — encouraged by government 'subsidies, tax breaks, low-cost loans and lax safety regulations' (Shrivastava 1993: 260) — the pesticides market in India had become extremely competitive by the end of the 1970s. Indeed, by the beginning of the 1980s, 'pesticide demand in India had collapsed' (ibid.: 258). This was partly structural, due to the influx of agrochemical capital. But other, contingent factors, exacerbated these new conditions of intense competition: agricultural production in India declined severely in 1980, and only recovered mildly in the next three years; and weather conditions in 1982 and 1983 caused many farmers to abandon temporarily their use of pesticides. Thus, the industry became characterised by harsher and increasing levels of competition (Shrivastava 1992: 30-5). These factors partially explain why Union Carbide had decided to 'backward integrate' and begin (in 1979) the domestic manufacture of MIC and other pesticide components at the Bhopal plant (Shrivastava 1992: 33-4). The general context of multinational-host government relations, and the particular context of the local pesticides market, are crucial contextual factors in understanding the disaster.

In respect of this latter, particular, context, then, it is clear that Union Carbide was also constrained by the circumstances in which it was operating. In 1983 UCIL, like many other affiliates of multinationals, was in the top twenty profit making Indian companies (Everest 1986: 127; Sandberg 1985: 16) and the capital/labour relationship was highly favourable to UCC. In a context of weak health and safety and pollution regulation, it was, therefore, not 'rational' for this capitalist corporation to spend money on these areas if this would not be matched by its competitors. Of course, collectively the TNCS had not pressured the Indian government to improve such regulation but rather were able, precisely because of such deficiencies, to 'export hazard'. Nevertheless, equalising costs with other corporations remains a significant consideration, and UCIL was losing money at Bhopal.

Everest, for example, overestimates both the freedom of individual enterprises and their overall unity of interest. He tends to invoke a unitary class subject variously called 'foreign capital', 'foreign investment' or 'foreign multinationals'. This unitary class subject operates within both Third World countries and within the US. Thus, Everest represents UCC's arguments that the Bhopal court case should be heard in India as an expression of the view of corporate capital (Everest 1986: 154). A more convincing interpretation is that the corporation was trying to mobilise the support of other corporate and governmental personnel. However basic the capital/labour relation, both capital and labour exist as differentiated entities — as 'many capitals' which may be organized factionally and as individual workers who may be organized in different kinds of trade unions, may work part time and so on. The capitalist class should not be assumed to be a 'class subject' with the state as its instrument, nor should it be assumed that capitalistic social formations automatically function (however complexly) to reproduce capitalistic domination. There are both conflicts that unify the capitalist class — for example, those against the working class, rival imperialistic powers, or rival social systems — and others that divide it such as competition between corporations for markets and for capital. Neither nation state, capital as a whole, nor individual capitalists and corporations are guaranteed victory. The unity of the capitalist class can be real enough but it is often fragile.

As we (and others) have shown, a major cause of the Bhopal disaster was a severe cutback in investment which resulted in an inappropriate use of technology, non-replacement of defective parts, and inadequate maintenance and monitoring of the production process. Whilst there was an overall decline in the pesticide market, there were also fluctuations in demand. The subsequent problem of supplying the market during production bottlenecks contributed to the dangerous practice of storing large quantities of MIC. Moreover, whilst such factors associated with particular 'scrimping and saving' during the plant's operation are likely to contribute to chemical disasters, so does the general need for 'economy' and the pressure of time during the design, manufacture and erection of plants.[4]

It is, thus, not surprising to find that at Bhopal on 14 May 1983 the following 'agreement' was signed by UCIL (Agricultural Products Division) and the hourly-paid plant operatives:

The selection, placement, distribution, transfer, promotion of personnel, fixing of working hours and laying down of working programmes, planning and control of factory operations, introduction of new or improved production methods, expansion of production facilities, establishment of quality standards, determination and assignment of workload, evaluation and classification of jobs and establishment of production standards, maintenance of efficiency, maintenance of discipline in the factory ... are *exclusively* rights and responsibilities of the Management.

(cited in Union Research Group 1985a: 1-2)

In Chapter 5, we noted how, for Foucault, discourses and discursive practices are 'positivities', that is, sets of statements (organisational forms and actions) through which specific groups at particular times have the 'right' to understand and organize the world. This will entail some kind of apprenticeship, with academic training and certification, and since this takes time, such specialisation means that only some individuals will be really competent in any one area (Hirst 1986: 65-6). The functioning of 'statements', by their very rarity, also demonstrates how other discourses are unthought or not produced, or, often, that other sets of 'statements' are not taken seriously. In Bhopal itself, and as we have indicated above (Chapters 4 and 5), it is often the workers who first recognize the dangers associated with particular production processes and who accurately pinpoint their nature only to be ignored since they are not a source of 'serious statements'.

Thus, there is little doubt that UCC withheld information on the dangers of the MIC production process from UCIL, and that both withheld information from the Indian State, the workers at the plant and the local community (although this was hardly for 'idiosyncratic or personal reasons'). Moreover, there is also no doubt that workers, their trade unions and local journalists all warned UCC and UCIL of the dangerous way in which MIC was being produced and yet their warnings were 'distrusted', in fact, completely ignored.

Indeed, at Bhopal, there was little attenuation of capital's ability to determine the organization of work. True, there was quite extensive factory legislation, but the regulatory agencies were under-resourced and overwhelmed by the technical expertise of UCIL (Everest 1986: 131); while there was some unionisation, overall the workers were weak and divided.

Trade unionists and journalists were not the source of 'serious statements' even when they catalogued accidents, or pointed to dangers in the production process, demanding that UCIL follow its *own* safety procedures (Union Research Group: 1985b). While there had been a series of accidents at Bhopal, including a worker dying from exposure to phosgene in 1981, nevertheless in 1982 they were still given a clean bill of health by UCC even when its own safety audit was critical of safety standards/provisions. Yet, given the hierarchical nature of corporations, and the need for managements to retain control over production processes, more is at stake here than just safety (for both the company and the union); challenges to management regarding safety can represent challenges to the exclusive authority of management and, ultimately, that of capital.[5]

The Bhopal Settlement in Perspective

It seems clear to us, on the basis of the preceding, that the contentions made by UCC concerning the Bhopal disaster in its publicity and its legal arguments do not stand up to scrutiny.

UCIL was not an independent company, nor was it Indian backwardness that was responsible for the poor state of the Bhopal plant and its unsafe manufacturing practices. The sabotage theory has been presented in a number of guises, and remains, over a decade after the event, unsubstantiated. The Bhopal plant's design and standard operating procedures were inadequate and they were the responsibility of UCC not UCIL. Bhopal was an inferior plant to that at Institute, West Virginia, but this plant was not safe either. Indeed, contrary to the version of the history of its operations presented by the Company, UCC has long been a prime example of 'toxic capital'. Yet to a large extent it was UCC's ability to make these contentions seem plausible that allowed it to achieve such a small settlement. The initial sum demanded by the Indian government had been $3.3 billion. This was anything but excessive. It included no element of punitive damages, and can be placed in perspective via Everest's comparison with the $2.5 billion received by 60,000 claimants in the Johns-Manville asbestos suit or the $2.9 billion received by 195,000 victims of A.H. Robbins' Dalkon Shield. In fact, on 14 February 1989, UCC and the Indian government, the latter acting on behalf of the victims of the Bhopal tragedy, reached an out-of-court settlement of $470 million. It was agreed that this settlement would render UCC immune from all impending litigation, including criminal charges. The money was to compensate the families of the 3,329 people officially recognized by the Indian government as having died as a result of the tragedy and the 20,000 seriously injured that it accepts as *bona fide* victims of the tragedy.

Does this mean that justice has been done and that the matter can be laid to rest? After all, the 1991 settlement in the case of the Exxon Valdez oil spill involved Exxon paying a fine of $150 million (albeit with 125 million 'forgiven' because of the company's voluntary expenditures on spill clean up),

$100 million in restitution to the Alaskan and Federal Governments immediately, and up to $900 million to them in civil suits during the next 11 years. This agreement did not even affect the settlement of the $59 billion in private law suits being brought against the oil giant (*Globe and Mail*, 1 October 1991: B8). In three senses the answer to the question of justice is no. First, the Indian government has reopened the question of the appropriateness of the settlement because 'Indian life is not so cheap'. Second, a decade after the disaster, not one single victim had received final (as opposed to interim) compensation (Cassels 1993: 289), and the nature and duration of the process whereby compensation levels were determined has been described as Bhopal's 'second tragedy' (*Network First*, 1995). Third, the settlement itself can be better understood as a somewhat sordid compromise forced upon the weak by the strong, rather than something determined according to equity and the facts of the case. Bhopal cannot be considered merely an unforeseen and unforeseeable event from which the chemical industry could learn. UCC, with the aid of the American chemical industry, the American state and the American courts has succeeded, albeit temporarily, in avoiding responsibility for the accident and in imposing an insulting and inequitable settlement.

Why did the government accept the settlement of $470 million? A large part of the reason was the successful effort by UCC to have the case tried in India rather than in the US. UCC argued that the witnesses to the disaster, the victims, the key players, the documentation and evidence were all in Bhopal, where the UCIL plant was 'managed, operated, and maintained exclusively by Indians residing in India, more than 8,000 miles away'. The Company claimed that the real reason for the attempt to have the case tried in the US was the potential for a large settlement: 'as a moth to the light, so is a litigation drawn to the United States' (cited in Baxi 1986). On the question of litigation, UCC's particular (and real) concerns have to be related to the general interests of transnational capital whose Third World operations might be threatened by any settlement with a punitive element.

Indeed, the Bhopal victims and the Indian government *had* wanted the trial in the US, providing persuasive reasons for this: that there was such a backlog of cases in India that the trial would take an inordinate amount of time; that tort law was underdeveloped and there was a lack of experienced legal experts; that there were inadequate discovery procedures in India and the laws were constructed around doctrines of negligence rather than strict liability; that this was largely due to the heritage of colonialism; that UCIL's assets in India were worth less than $100 million; and, finally, and most important of all, that UCC controlled UCIL and the relevant documents and personnel were to be found in the US and not in India:

Key management personnel of multinationals exercise a closely-held power which is neither restricted by national boundaries nor effectively controlled by international law. The complex corporate structure of the multinational, with networks of subsidiaries and subdivisions, makes it exceedingly difficult or even impossible to pinpoint responsibility for the damage caused by the enterprise to discrete corporate units or individuals. In reality there is but one entity, the monolithic multinational which is responsible for the design, development and dissemination of information and technology worldwide.

(Affidavit of the Union of India, US District Court, South District of New York, 8 April 1985, cited in Hazarika 1987: 112)

Judge Keenan, however, decided that the trial would be held in India but with three conditions: that UCC should itself consent to be tried in India; that it should accept the judgments of the courts there; that it should be willing to be subject to discovery under the model of the United States federal rules and civil procedure (Hazarika 1987: 128).

UCC accepted the first two conditions but appealed against the third. It claimed that it was unfair for the Indian government to have unrestricted access to its records when its own access to the records of the Indian government was to be more limited. Keenan himself had implicitly indicated sympathy to such a plea when he wrote in a footnote that while 'the Court feels it would be fair to bind the plaintiffs to American discovery rules, too, it has no authority to do so' (cited in Baxi 1986: 8). Not surprisingly, UCC won its appeal so that instead of using American discovery procedures which had made possible the successful actions against asbestos producers such as Johns Manville (Brodeur 1985), the inadequate Indian, or rather Anglo-Indian, discovery procedures obtained.

An apparently even-handed settlement was nothing of the sort. Essentially, the American courts had accepted UCC's presentation of the case — that the crucial evidence and events were in India — and simply ignored that of the Indian government's. Baxi summarises Keenan's reasoning on this point:

India's claim was that Union Carbide was 'the creator of the design used in the Bhopal plant, and directed UCIL's relatively minor detailing program' ... consequently only an American forum had the best access to the sources of proof. The court decides, in response, that 'most of the documentary evidence concerning design, safety, training, safety and start-ups is to be found in India'. In doing so, Judge Keenan relies on the affidavits of Messrs. Brown, Woomer and Dutta, all Union Carbide employees. The two agreements between UCIL and the Union Carbide ('Design Transfer Agreement' and 'Technical Service Agreements') were based on an arms-length corporate practice

(Baxi 1986: 23)

We have shown that to take such arms-length agreements at face value is ludicrous since it ignores the considerable evidence of the complex control exercised by UCC over its subsidiaries.

Similarly ludicrous is the fact that the American courts accepted that the interests of a sovereign (and democratic) state and a licensed (and autocratic) corporation were of an equivalent value. They did not believe that a government charged with the security of more than 650 million people had more specific and legitimate concerns with secrecy than that of a corporation. Perhaps this was related to the fact that this corporation was a large America industrial (the 35th largest in 1984), with sales of $9.5 billion and assets of $11 billion.

Union Carbide did, however, make one particularly telling series of claims, namely, that

the Indian government may have granted a licence for the Bhopal plant without adequate checks on the plant; that the relevant controlling agencies responsible for the plant were grossly understaffed, lacked powers and had little impact on conditions in the field. More particularly, the Bhopal department of labour office had only two inspectors, neither of whom had any knowledge of chemical hazards.

(Muchlinski 1987: 575)

In other words, the Indian government bore a major responsibility for the Bhopal disaster. Now, there is strong evidence that Indian regulatory agencies were indeed inadequate (Cassels 1993; Chopra 1986; Everest 1986; Hazarika 1987). But, in arguing this position Union Carbide was being disingenuous. First, because it had itself cultivated relationships with personnel at all levels of the Indian state (ARENA 1985), and seems to have itself been party to the circumvention of regulations (Granada 1986). Second, effective regulation, in what was to all intents and purposes a 'deregulated' country, would have partly curtailed UCC's ability to export hazard; and no corporation would (or could) altruistically or autonomously encourage the development of measures which would restrict its own freedom to locate production.

Conclusion

As we have seen in this chapter, in Bhopal, India, despite public commitments to health, safety and environmental protection, Union Carbide Corporation had created, or allowed to develop, the conditions whereby an accident was possible, and then had failed to take the steps necessary to mitigate the effects of any accident. Further, as our discussion of events following the gas leak has demonstrated all too clearly, Union Carbide focused their efforts upon the legal process and 'managing' public opinion through presenting a series of arguments and spurious claims; through such tactics the company secured a favourable settlement, one in which responsibility for the disaster was not determined legally. Finally, and perhaps most importantly, we have indicated why it is significant to encompass within any definition of corporate crime acts or omissions which make it legally liable, rather than simply to focus upon those which are successfully punished — there was little possibility that UCC or UCIL would have been successfully prosecuted under law, a fact related crucially to the relative powers of the actors, the desire amongst governments of developing nation states for 'First World' capital, and the nature of national (and absence of international) legal systems (Lal 1996).

In this context, it is worth noting, with no little irony, that India has in recent years (that is, since 1991) experienced a further expansion of its chemical industry, fuelled by government-defined economic and political imperative. Indeed, Asia in general has been labelled 'the centre of future growth for the chemical industry', and it is perhaps unsurprising that the continent has attracted investment and ambitions for expansion on the part of all the major chemical multinationals (Hsu 1995: 956). This expansion has not been confined to China and the Asian Tigers, although these have been key sites of chemical activity. In fact, commentators have noted that India has, since 1991, witnessed a period of dramatic expansion in chemicals production and trade (*Chemistry & Industry*, 1 April 1996: 243; Philpot 1996). While there are significant domestic producers within the Indian chemicals industry, there is no doubt that within this expansion the interests of the world's largest multinational chemicals companies are intimately imbricated. BASF, BP, Dow, Du Pont, Exxon, ICI and Shell have all developed, or are developing, significant interests in the Indian chemical industry (Marsh 1997; Nanavaty 1996; Sidhva 1995). The expansion of these interests was given particular impetus since a programme of government 'reform' was introduced in 1991, a programme which sought to liberalise trade, attract foreign direct investment and deregulate and delicense industrial production (Nanavaty 1996: 872). This influx of foreign toxic capital has occurred before any real 'lessons' from the Bhopal disaster might have been acted upon (Jasanoff ed., 1994); indeed, the desire for foreign capital may partly explain *why* any such 'lessons' have not been acted upon (Bowonder et al. 1994: 86).

We have also indicated, following the argument of the immediately preceding chapters, that UCC is not a rogue company amongst transnational corporations. In their desperate struggle for foreign investment and technology many less developed countries have offered business environments with few controls on the movement of capital, hazardous production or pollution. Sometimes, this has been the official policy of governments, as in the case of 'free production zones' (Peet 1987); on other occasions regulations exist but are simply not enforced (Cass 1996). This was not only true of India, but, to a lesser degree, also applied to the US and Britain in the 1980s (Wilson 1985). In these countries there were cutbacks in the resources and powers of those regulatory agencies concerned with occupational health and safety and environmental dangers, whilst their enforcement responsibilities were extended (Pearce 1990; Pearce and Tombs 1997; Tombs 1995b). Indeed, there is a crucial interrelationship between the possibility that capital will move to areas of weak regulation and this tendency of standards to drop in some advanced industrial countries. Yet, ironically, this is only a tendency. The political and economic fallout from Bhopal was such that in both the US and Europe as a whole, there has been a tightening of regulations (Pearce and Tombs 1994; Tombs 1995b), even if some (perhaps many) of these remain either un- or under-enforced.

More specifically, Bhopal was not one maverick plant within an otherwise safety-conscious organisation. UCC's appalling record is, therefore, even more frightening. There is something particularly distasteful, if unsurprising, in the fact that in the late 1980s Union Carbide published a whole series of pamphlets and press releases on environmental issues, including one entitled *Towards Environmental Excellence: A Progress Report* (1989), in which it lists its own achievements and gives itself good marks. Such an initiative is strictly in keeping with predominant chemical industry responses to emergent social and political pressures around clean, safe and healthy production. None of us, however, should be too ready to accept claims to corporate social responsibility.

This is not to say that improvements in the production, use, storage, transport and disposal of hazardous substances — that is, in the activities of toxic capital — cannot or do not occur. To preview the arguments that will be developed later in this text, let us be clear about the origins of such improvements. They are rarely the consequence of autonomous acts of altruism on the part of corporations. If there now exist emergency evacuation plans at some chemicals plants, these are relatively recent (and still rare) phenomena, and are subsequent to disasters, and popular and regulatory scrutiny. *If* pollution control devices are now installed, *if* some care is now taken to dispose of hazardous waste properly, it should be borne in mind that prior to the 1970s these were simply released into the atmosphere, dumped into rivers and lakes or buried. Moreover, when, in the 1970s, the disposal of solid and liquid waste became legally controlled, the chemical companies successfully lobbied for an ineffective and, indeed, 'criminogenic regulatory structure' (Szasz 1986c). Instead of the producers of hazardous wastes being 'strictly liable' for their safe and effective disposal, they were able to transfer the legal obligation by paying others to dispose of the waste. There emerged a highly competitive market which disposed of the waste cheaply, and often illegally, but nearly always with a disastrous disregard for safety. Love Canal (25th of 115 Superfund designated worst sites in the US), and the other 2,500 to 10,000 sites imminently hazardous to public health (Epstein 1982) are a consequence of the pre-1970s lack of (and then subsequently inadequate) regulation. Similarly, prior to the 1970s Clean Air Act many chemicals were simply released into the air. Furthermore, over a period of 20 years regulations were issued for only 7 of 300 chemicals that Congress determined were a health threat. For the first time, Title Three of the 1986 Superfund Amendment and Reauthorization Act has forced the chemical companies to monitor and document their emissions for at least some chemicals. Thus, the EPA has recently noted that the volume of toxic waste containing such chemicals continues to increase in the US, reaching 35 billion pounds in 1995 (a seven percent increase in 1991). (*Chemistry & Industry*, 2 June 1997: 409. And we have already provided an indication of the regularity with which major releases of chemicals occur, with acute catastrophic potential (Chapter 4).

Indeed, *although the scale of the disaster at Bhopal was a unique one, its causes were all too common.* Corporations, as organisations, can, do, and will commit health, safety and environmental crimes — workers and local communities regularly suffer death, injury and ill-health due to the actions or inactions of corporations. Understandably, they are perhaps the most sceptical audience for claims to a new corporate responsibility.

Notes

1. The analysis of Bhopal throughout this chapter draws particularly upon the discussions in Pearce (1987); Pearce and Tombs (1989, 1993); and the following, which form part of an enormous literature on the disaster: Abraham (1985); Agarwal et al. (1985); APPEN (1986); ARENA (1985); Banerjee (1986); Baxi

(1986); Bergman (1988); Cassels (1993); Chopra (1986); Dinham et al. (1986); Everest (1986); Hazarika (1987); International Coalition for Justice in Bhopal (1987); Jasanoff (1994); Jones (1988); Kalelkar (1988); Kurtzman (1987); Morehouse and Subramaniam (1986); Muchlinski (1987); *Network First* (1995); Sandberg (1985); Shrivastava (1992); Smith, ed. (1986); Union Carbide Corporation (1985, 1987); Union Research Group (1985a, 1985b); Weir (1986).

2.   This is, perhaps, exemplified in Chomsky's discussion of the tension between the overt and covert rationales for US foreign policy. He argues that in the 1940s, the US government while publicly committing itself to a postwar free world, characterised by freedom from want and fear, and by freedom of speech, worship and democracy, covertly acted to protect America's privileged position of having '50 per cent of the world's wealth but only 6.3 per cent of its population' and to combat the 'wide acceptance of the idea that the government has direct responsibility for the welfare of the people'; doing this might require 'police repression by the local government' but this was justifiable because it 'is better to have a strong regime than a liberal government if it is indulgent and relaxed and penetrated by communists' (statements by George Kennan, cited in Chomsky 1985: 48, 50, 57). While Chomsky has raised an important issue, he has underestimated the extent to which — in situations where elite groups were talking to each other about third parties — they were able to persuade each other that they still believed in democracy while advocating these measures. They were able to do so because to them socialism was self-evidently wrong and those third parties who desired it could not know their own interests. They had to be irrational and/or immature and, hence, unready for democracy. Elite groups could, therefore, sustain a public and private commitment to (a narrow and restricted conception of) democracy which would seem plausible because they invoked somewhat different (but by no means mutually exclusive) criteria as to what made individuals or societies eligible to practice democracy.

3.   At the same conference clear evidence was presented that in India a chemical company in which the Indian government holds a majority share produces fertiliser efficiently and safely (Smith 1986). Kalelkar, who had emigrated from India to the USA, whilst upholding the sabotage theory in his presentation of his (1988) paper on Bhopal, explicitly distanced himself from racist/culturalist explanations of the plant's failure.

4.   The situation at Bhopal involved a capitalist enterprise, but managers in the former Eastern bloc running local plants were controlled heteronomously by superiors committed to high levels of production at low cost, albeit for economic growth rather than profit. We are grateful to Ken Menzies of Guelph University for raising this issue.

5. This is not to deny, of course, that if trade unions seem unavoidable, every strategy will be used to co-opt them. See the discussion in Nichols and Beynon (1977) and for a radically different view Harris (1987).

PART III
HAZARDS, REGULATION
AND CLASS

7 Policing, Regulation and Ideology

Introduction

This is the first of three chapters in which we develop arguments for more appropriate and feasible regulatory strategies and mechanisms for the effective prevention and mitigation of corporate crime, focusing particularly upon safety crimes. This analysis clearly relates back to the preceding chapters of this text: thus in proposing appropriate forms of regulation we need to be able to draw upon an understanding of the genesis, nature, and consequences of corporate crimes in general, and safety crimes in particular.

In developing an argument for the principles that should inform regulation, and the practices and mechanisms that follow from these principles, we inevitably confront counter-arguments and prescription. We also need to be cognizant of the enormous economic, political and social obstacles to more effective regulation of corporate activities. In this chapter, we deal specifically with two sets of literature regarding 'social' regulation. One, which emanates from the Conservative Right, has informed much regulatory policy and practice in the US and, in a less obvious fashion, in the UK. A second, which is located within a social liberal tradition, has roots which are much stronger within the UK (and indeed have influenced policy and practice to a greater extent here), yet also resonates with some approaches to 'social' regulation taken in the US, and beyond. One point of interest is that there are clear points of complementarity between these two, apparently quite distinct, groups of arguments and theorists.

Both of these traditions — that we associate with the work of James Q. Wilson on the one hand, and social liberals whom we consider through the work of the 'Oxford School' on the other — develop their respective positions partly through reference to the policing of 'traditional' or 'street' crimes. For this reason, we too draw upon more general characterisations of crime and policing to develop our arguments. In particular, we consider the work of Left Realists on crime and policing (see Pearce 1992; Pearce and Tombs 1992, for longer treatments). While Left Realism as a criminological tradition may have

223

been relatively short-lived, its influence has been a marked one. Further, it is of interest to us because it aimed to take crime seriously, to consider crime as a social problem, and to focus upon the experiences of victims of crime. Thus 'Left Realist Criminology' emerged from an awareness that criminal and anti-social conduct disproportionately victimize the most vulnerable members of society and helps to undermine their community life. Realists have set about the task of empirically establishing the nature, distribution and severity of criminal and anti-social conduct within contemporary societies (Jones et al. 1986). By combining this information with analyses of the *modus operandi* of such agencies as the police, and, by arguing both that the latter's tasks should be more clearly specified and circumscribed, and that they should be made more accountable to the community, Realists have also tried to develop appropriate and feasible strategies to control crime and to reform the police (Kinsey et al. 1986).

For all these reasons, we might expect the Realists, more than many other criminologists, to have developed a critique of corporate crime, and to have made related proposals for the control of the crimes of the powerful. Indeed, they have recognized the abiding importance of white collar and corporate crime (Lea 1987: 362; 1992; Matthews 1987: 376; Young 1986: 23; 1987: 353, 355), and, in *What is to be Done About Law and Order*, provided a systematic examination of the relative impact of street crime and corporate crime on people's lives. In a discussion of some depth and subtlety of the similarities and differences between these two kinds of crime, Lea and Young argue that while both display 'the same ethos of individualism, competitiveness and machismo' (Lea and Young 1984: 74), the former

> is the most transparent of all injustices. It is a starting point for a double thrust against crime on all levels. If we concentrate on it alone, as the political right would wish, we are actively engaged in a diversion from the crimes of the powerful. If we concentrate solely on the latter, as many on the left would have us do, we are omitting what are real and pressing problems for working class people, and lose the ability to move from the immediate to encompass the more hidden, and thus demonstrate the intrinsic similarity of crime at all levels of our society.
>
> (Lea and Young 1984: 75)

Undoubtedly many on the left who invoke the category of corporate crime do so as an alibi for downplaying the impact of street crime. They fail to explore it in any depth; nor do they unpack it, nor isolate causal sequences, nor specify the kinds of non-reformist reforms (Gorz 1980) that could limit its occurrence now, and which may have a transformative potential.

Unfortunately, much of the treatment of, or rather also references to, corporate and white-collar crime within realism are gestural (one notable exception being Lea 1992). Matthews, for example, in his article, 'Taking Realist Criminology Seriously', may refer to white-collar crimes (1987: 376), but when he analyses the relationship between criminal offenders and the victims of crime he restricts his analysis to street crime (ibid.: 387-8). This inconsistency is not surprising because in practice realism has tended to focus on the more immediate interpersonal anti-social conduct — that is, *on crimes between subjects.*

> Crime is a social relationship. It is institutionalised; it is imbued with meaning; both offenders and victims are predictable, and above all *they relate to one another.*
>
> (Young 1987: 344, emphasis added).

As our discussion of corporate crime thus far in this text clearly indicates, Young's characterisation of the nature of crime does not adequately describe the anonymous relationship between, for example, a corporate management which illegally exposes workers, local communities or indeed consumers to a toxic substance. It does not capture the extent to which acts of omission are what cause harm in many such cases, nor that it is the failure of employers to fulfil their statutory managerial duties that lead to many workplace injuries and deaths, nor that these illegalities can be produced through organisational structures and practices without intention or knowledge. *As we have emphasised, corporate crime is poorly described or understood if we stay within a conceptual framework restricted to interpersonal relations between subjects.* Moreover, if we remain within this framework it is equally unlikely that methods will be found to control it. Thus, despite their claims to take crime seriously, Realists have failed to incorporate examinations of deaths, serious injuries and debilitating chronic illnesses caused by work and workplace exposures, while other criminologists beyond this tradition have done just this (see, for example, Boyd 1988; Box 1983; Levi 1994; Reiman 1979). Despite their claims to take crime seriously, Realists have failed to incorporate examinations of the particular forms of violence suffered by women as workers and consumers, victimised by corporate activity and omission; and this, despite the fact that some close to the Realist tradition have pointed to particular problems in the Realists' theoretical and empirical understandings of victimisation (Ruggiero 1992: 129; Walklate 1992: 114-6).

Taking corporate crime seriously requires both a broadening of the field of interest marked out by Realist criminology, and a modification of its conceptual categories. Yet we believe that we can build upon some 'Left Realist' arguments on policing to interrogate the conduct of those agencies entrusted, at least symbolically, with the regulation of business in respect of occupational and environmental health and safety. If 'Left Realist' analyses of the agencies of social control have been developed by studying the nature of and determinants of the *modus operandi* of the police and by questioning the extent to which they are responsive and democratically accountable to local communities (Kinsey et al. 1986), very similar questions can be raised about the agencies which regulate the conduct of businesses in relationship to each other, to investors, customers, employees and the local community. These agencies tend to try and achieve 'compliance' through persuasion rather than a 'policing' strategy which uses legal sanctions against businesses and executives found to be in breach of the law. For some this is far from a problematic observation; indeed, it is a necessary and desirable strategy, since corporate crimes are not really crimes and corporate criminals are not really criminals (Hawkins 1990, 1991). For many others, such as ourselves, it is a major reason why they are in practice so ineffective (Pearce and Tombs 1990, 1991).

It is true that there are fundamental problems associated with the Realists' descriptive analyses of the police, most of which have been discussed at length elsewhere (Gilroy 1987; Gilroy and Sim 1985; Ryan 1986; Sim et al. 1987; Ward and Benn 1987; Pearce and Tombs 1992), nevertheless, the aim of developing what Kinsey, Lea and Young call 'The Theory and Practice of Democratic Policing' (1986: 186-215), remains a worthwhile one. For the Realists, democratic policing is based upon two guiding principles, namely 'maximum public initiation' and 'minimum necessary coercion'. These are said to protect the rights of individuals and thus provide 'effective guarantees of an *efficient* and socially *just* system of policing' (ibid.: 193). 'Maximum public initiation' of police action is urged at both the collective and individual level. In this way, it is hoped to minimise the autonomy of police occupational culture and political attitudes in the drawing up of criteria for deciding when to intervene and when not to. 'Minimum necessary coercion' by the police requires a strict limit on police powers. The premise of policework is thus that it is for the police to cooperate with and respond to the demands of the public, rather than vice versa. The Realists then go on to set out the legislative framework of minimal policing.

Certainly the reforms proposed by the Realists are liberal rather than socialist in nature (Ryan 1986: 30). Indeed the practical effects of some of the Realist arguments are likely to be, in certain contexts, profoundly anti-democratic. Nevertheless, it is important to recognize the differential effect of implementing Realist-type reforms in the context of safety, health and environmental regulation. For such an implementation would entail empowering workers and local communities against capital, and thus these reforms may have a transformative potential, being 'non-reformist reforms' rather than 'mere' or 'liberal' reforms. The key to this potentially differential effect is to be found in the objective differences between this context, and that with which the Realists are concerned, namely street crime.

First, police officers police local communities — thus there is no *a priori* distinction between those to whom 'protection' is being offered (potential victims) and those who might be the object of police action (potential offenders). Indeed, in some of the areas focused upon in the Realists' crime surveys, the existence of very blurred boundaries between victims and offenders, particularly amongst the young, is likely. This is very different from the relationship between regulatory agencies and the groups with whom they interact. While some health, safety and environmental law obviously places duties and obligations upon workers and members of local communities, it is clear that the object of regulation is business. Moreover, it is equally clear that those in whose interests the regulations exist, and for whose protection they should be enforced, are primarily workers and local communities.

This key difference leads us onto a second, very closely related, point. Regulatory law will need to be enforced less 'minimally' than the kinds of law with which the Realists are concerned, precisely because of the immense inequalities in power between the regulated — business — and those whom the regulations primarily exist to protect — workers and local communities.[1] When the Realists discuss 'public initiation of police action', we not only endorse this with respect to worker and local community initiation of regulatory inspectorate action, but would add that the imbalance of power in this latter sphere requires the development of much more formal mechanisms to encourage, facilitate, and render effective such initiation. Just as the Realists constantly argue for more democratic means of controlling policing, this need is more urgent with respect to the activities of regulatory agencies.[2] Indeed, as we argue in a later chapter in the context of a discussion of deterrence and corporate crime, more effective policing of corporate crime serves to minimise social inequalities rather than exacerbate them, the latter often being a (legitimate) charge against calls for more effective policing of 'street' crime.

Third, while realism urges that policing become much more reactive and much less proactive, we would resist this exigence in the sphere of regulatory law. One reason for this is simply that there are some differences between the types of offence that fall within the ambit of the police on the one hand, and regulatory agencies on the other (though this should not be over-emphasised — see below). Regulatory violations are often easily observable, ongoing states of affairs in a static location, rather than discrete, often concealed, geographically dispersed acts. For these reasons, a proactive presence by the factory or pollution inspectorate can be more productive — the chances of an inspector uncovering violations on a site visit are clearly much greater than a police officer happening across an assault, burglary, car theft, and so on (although, of course, this does occur).

Two points follow from this.

One is that in the sphere of regulatory law, to the extent that workers and local communities are presented with the formal mechanisms whereby they can initiate inspectorate attention/action, to the extent that they develop trust in those inspectorates, and as far as they themselves develop confidence and expertise, the need for a proactive inspectorial commitment may decline. But this is to take a very long-term view. Moreover, the need for a proactive presence will never disappear completely — those in unorganised workplaces, for example, will continue to be particularly vulnerable, while the lack of a subjective perception of harm on the part of a local community from a local site/company may be less a consequence of the absence of objective harm, more a consequence of 'unpolitics' (Blowers 1984; Crenson 1971; Smith 1989; see also Lukes 1974).

The second point that follows is that demands for an increase in numbers of inspectors are perfectly legitimate in a way that demands for increased police resources are not. In contrast to the increase in the numbers of police officers in England and Wales which Realists document (see, for example, Kinsey et al.1986), the same period witnessed a considerable decline in the number of health and safety inspectors in both the US and the UK. At the same time the numbers of workplaces to be inspected has risen dramatically, while new legislation (in the UK emanating from the EU or as a reaction to disasters, and in the US proliferating at both state and federal levels, again as a reaction to disasters and also as a response to a more highly developed environmental consciousness), has meant a significant increase in the range (and, indeed, nature) of laws to be overseen by the Health and Safety Executive in general (Tombs 1990a; Tombs 1996). Again, this point will be developed in the context of our argument regarding deterrence, in Chapter 9.

Thus, the central thrust of the above is that while we wish to adopt the Realist argument for democratisation and maximum public initiation of action in the context of reforming the organisation and activities of regulatory agencies, the different circumstances within which these and the police operate mean that arguments for 'minimal coercion', to the extent that this implies strict limitations upon agency powers, are wholly inappropriate within the context with which we are concerned.

Before we go on to consider at length the *modus operandi* of the regulatory agencies in the sphere of health, safety and environmental laws, one further point, as yet unmentioned, needs to be emphasised from Realist writing on policework.

Realist work on the police has addressed directly the 'problem' of discretion. Many who write of policework have wrestled with the question of how to minimise the exercise of police discretion. But the Realists have adopted a slight, but significantly different position on this issue. Thus they have emphasised that *policing not only is, but must be, inherently political*. The exercise of discretion is not only inevitable but desirable, allowing the ends in the name of which the police exist to be explicitly considered. This might be one way in which Realist proposals can be developed in a socialist rather than simply liberal direction. In the context of debates on health, safety and environment, a recognition of the political nature of the questions involved is important. But so often it is precisely this fact which is at best understated, at worst denied (see, for example, Woolfson and Beck 1997). Questions of how safe is safe enough, what are acceptable costs and benefits of industrial activity, what determines 'reasonable practicability', and so on, are explicitly political issues; they are certainly not merely technical questions. A recognition of this must be progressive, and indeed is a precondition of the transcendence of a technocratic rationality which pervades much of industry and serves as a barrier to the kind of 'maximum public initiation' which was spoken about above.

Two Versions of Regulation

The first question that must be dealt with is whether regulatory violations should even be considered to be equivalent to street crimes. We have argued at length in previous chapters that many safety violations, for example, are crimes. Yet many capitalists and corporate executives, many judges and regulators, some economists and political scientists and, indeed, many legal theorists and criminologists have argued that regulatory and white collar offences are inherently different from the illegal activities of street or traditional criminals. James Q. Wilson, appropriately, has claimed

> predatory street crime is a far more serious matter than consumer fraud, anti-trust violations, [etc.] ... because predatory crime ... makes difficult or impossible the maintenance of meaningful human communities.
>
> (Wilson 1975: xx)

Further, in his book, *Crime and Human Nature*, he retained a focus on street crime because 'Robbery, stealing, incest and factory pollution were condemned by overwhelming majorities in every society' (Wilson and Herrnstein 1986: 22).

What is bizarre about this latter work is that in it, he studiously, and with no explanation, avoids any discussion of the last and ultimately potentially expansive category of 'factory pollution'. Yet the inclusion within his listing of 'real crimes', those that 'are universally abhorred', of the category 'factory pollution' rather subverts his own representation of the nature of white-collar crime. Indeed, if he had not ignored this inclusion, if he had taken it seriously, he would have then needed to explore the experiences of those whose health has been damaged by working in or living near capitalist industrial enterprises (Pearce and Tombs 1990, 1991; Reich 1991) and, even more poignantly, those who saw their whole communities destroyed in Bhopal, India (Pearce and Tombs 1989, 1993), Buffalo Creek, West Virginia or Stava, Northern Italy (Calavita, Di Mento, Geis and Forti 1991). He might also have found that those suffering from avoidable deaths, injuries and illnesses from deficient transportation systems (Brake and Hale 1992) and defective pharmaceutical products (Braithwaite 1984; Mintz 1985) and, indeed, those who know they are defrauded, have a different sense as to who are 'real' criminals and what are 'real' crimes.

Proponents of a 'compliance' (as opposed to a 'policing') regulatory strategy argue that the nature of corporate illegalities calls for different forms of regulation than is the case for other kinds of law breaking. Businesses and particularly corporations are not, as many would have it, typically 'amoral calculators', but rather 'political citizens' who may indeed sometimes err but more because of 'organizational incompetence' than deliberate wrongdoing. Although some corporations sometimes act as if they are 'amoral calculators', this is neither necessary nor typical; where regulations are violated, this is usually the result of factors other than pure economic calculation. Corporations can, and do, have a primary commitment to act in a socially responsible fashion, are not essentially criminogenic, and will not cease to commit violations because of attempts at deterrence (Kagan and Scholz 1984: 67-68; see also Hawkins 1984: 110; Hutter 1988: 45-47, 80; Richardson et al. 1983: 125-49). To accept a view of the corporation as an amoral calculator entails a corresponding view of the most appropriate regulatory response to such corporations, namely, 'strict enforcement of uniform and highly specific standards, backed by severe penalties', with regulatory officials acting quite literally as 'policemen' (Kagan and Scholz 1984: 72).

In their view, this is quite wrong, because legal infractions by business are unsuitable for criminalisation. In the case of pollution, for example, there is a need 'to preserve a fragile balance between the interests of economic activity on the one hand and the public welfare on the other' (Hawkins 1984: 9). Relatedly, it is 'the inherent nature and circumstances of factory "crime" that necessarily engender compliance response' (Jamieson 1985: i). Not only is *mens rea* inapplicable in most cases of regulatory violations, particularly since such deviance occurs within an organisational framework (Richardson et al. 1983: 56-7), but there is an inherent injustice in the use of a standard of strict liability; and anyway, many regulatory offences involve acts or omissions which are *mala prohibita* rather than *mala in se* crimes in that the former are 'morally problematic' (Hawkins 1984: 11), lack 'self-evident moral blameworthiness' (Jamieson 1985: 30) or are characterised by 'moral ambivalence' (Hutter 1988: 10-11).[3]

Thus, in his *Environment and Enforcement*, Hawkins has claimed that there are two different ways in which police work can be done, namely by 'sanctioning strategies' with a 'penal style' which is 'accusatory and adversarial', or through 'compliance strategies' with a 'conciliatory style'. The former applies a punishment for breaking a rule and doing harm but is less concerned with producing '[c]onformity with the law'. Such strategies are typically followed in situations where 'deviance has a categorical, unproblematical quality', particularly if involving 'personal harm', where 'law breaking is essentially a discrete activity' and 'unpredictable', and where 'enforcement relations tend to be compressed and abrupt'. The goal of a 'compliance strategy', on the other hand, is to 'prevent a harm rather than punish an evil', aiming thus for 'social repair and maintenance' at minimum cost. Enforcers respond to problems 'negotiating future conformity to standards which are administratively determined'. '[C]ompliance enforcement' is marked by 'an extended, incremental approach' where any ultimate prosecution is viewed by the enforcement agent as 'a sign of failure'. Enforcement tends towards compliance when victims are 'distant, diffuse and indeterminate' and where the deviance itself is a state of affairs allowing 'the development of social relationships between rule-enforcer and rule-breaker'. Hawkins refers to 'unfenced machinery, substandard housing, adulterated food, drunkenness' and 'vagrancy, prostitution or mental disturbance'. Overall, what 'prompts a sanctioning rather than a compliance response is not who does the law enforcement so much as the sort of behaviour which is subject to control'.[4]

One major problem with this ideal typical characterisation[5] is that hardly any of what police forces actually do or how they think fits within Hawkins' 'sanctioning' mode — their response to murder, some kinds of armed robbery and drunken driving leading to serious injury, perhaps, but little else. Moreover, punishing such offenders is rarely justified purely as revenge but rather is also seen as playing a role in specific deterrence (or reform), and/or general deterrence — the latter is even true for those who advocate capital punishment for murder (Van den Haag and Conrad 1983). Physical assaults tend to be prosecuted when they take place in public, but much less often when they involve wife-abuse in the home. True, this latter may be a 'state of affairs', but what seems more important is that there may be some kind of (male) police identification with the 'rights' of the abuser (Edwards 1989). Burglary and petty theft, of course, rarely involve violence. If we turn to juvenile offenders, what dictates a punitive response (and its severity) is often not the act itself (many juvenile crimes are status offences or involve generalised nuisance), nor how long the police have established a relationship with offenders, but rather *the social characteristics of the latter*. What is of particular importance is their ethnicity, demeanour and social class and the resources and power of their parents. This, of course, is what Cicourel (1967) documented so meticulously and it is a point which Hawkins himself concedes (1990: 450).

Further, to characterise the police's relationship with drunks, vagrants, the 'mentally ill', and prostitutes as one of compliance involves a sleight of hand. Such individuals are first consciously excluded from most respectable areas and then contained within specific, marginal areas. This is achieved in part through the actual or potential exercise of a very coercive and, if challenged, punitive power. The goal of policing within such areas is to keep down 'the aggregate total of troubles' (Bittner 1969: 154), not to protect the safety or rights of those who live or spend time there. Whatever relationships are created, are extremely circumscribed. It is worth noting that there may be an analogy between the latter situation and factory inspection when there are so many offences and so little possibility of effective prosecution that factory inspectors, too, may only be able to keep down the 'aggregate total of troubles'.

Interestingly, in many cases where individuals are criminally prosecuted they have been pulled from a pool of 'criminal types' (Ericson 1981) — 'rounding up the usual suspects' is not just a joke made by Claude Rains in *Casablanca*. They may also be individuals with whom the police have a symbiotic relationship (Foucault 1979a; Hobbs 1988). This raises an important question — to what extent are 'compliance' relationships tainted with corruption? An exploration of police corruption — in cases involving prostitution and illegal drug distribution, for example — could lead us to another useful analogy, this time between police/criminal relations of one kind, those involving organized crime, and what occurs within the social 'regulation of business'. In both contexts we find symbiotic relationships associated with the regulation of a social activity which employs many people and produces for the market; and in both contexts small 'fly-by-night' operations are often treated as the major social problem, willingly sacrificed by the larger operators, while their own illegalities are tolerated as long as they do not become too egregiously offensive (Marx 1981; Pearce 1976). The difference, however, is that what we find in the case of the regulation of legitimate business is more impotence than corruption. The corruption occurs at a much higher level when capital is able to dictate the political agenda. Hence, we find that we can explain differences in police strategies more usefully in terms of differences in power than in the kinds of activities that they police.

Controversies such as these are, of course, not new. As we noted in Chapter 3, Sutherland and Tappan debated the status of the concept of 'white collar crime' in the 1940s (Sutherland 1940, 1941; Tappan 1947). In our view, and as we have sought to demonstrate throughout much of this text, illegal corporate activities can be, and indeed have been, criminalised. The claims of the Oxford/compliance School seem, in this respect, simply to be wrong.

Let us then, for the moment, turn to their argument that corporations are not amoral calculators. In our view the claim that corporations cannot do anything but attempt to maximise long-term profitability is theoretically untenable. Indeed, we have argued this point at length in an earlier chapter.

Now, despite the caricatures offered by some (Hawkins 1990, 1991), to make this argument is *not* to claim that 'rational calculation' necessarily means that all regulations are ignored by corporations, nor that any particular corporation will, in practice, succeed in either a correct interpretation of what is rational, nor be able to act in accordance with that interpretation. Again as we have detailed previously in this text, corporations will clearly, at times, act less than rationally. *What the 'compliance school' calls incompetence and political citizenship are both perfectly compatible with a concept of corporations as amoral calculators.* Nor is our argument to imply that business firms or the individuals who hold positions of power and take decisions within them will all act criminally; again, this is clearly not the case. It is simply to recognise that, as Box has argued, the nature of the capitalist mode of production forces corporations to attempt to exert as much control as possible over their operating environments, which pushes them into violating those regulations that seek to prevent individual corporations from using their corporate power to exert certain forms of control over consumers, workers, governments, other corporations, and so on (Box 1983). A more plausible view, then, is that of Edwin Sutherland who, in *White Collar Crime: The Uncut Version*, argued that corporations are 'rationalistic, amoral and nonsentimental' (Sutherland 1983: 236-8).

Indeed, although recent theorists differ somewhat about the appropriate models for describing business organizations, few, if any, give any credibility to the notion of the 'soulful corporation' (Pearce and Tombs 1989, 1991). It remains the case that some social liberals (see above) wish to retain this ideological notion — albeit under the guise of 'political citizenship' and 'good appleness'; and on this basis argue that self-regulation — a concept that goes hand in hand with notions of the soulful corporation — is likely to prove an effective regulatory strategy. On this point, even economic and political neoliberals tend to part company. Thus it is interesting that in the view of the economists of the Chicago school, for example, everybody's pursuit of self interest in the free market produces an efficient allocation of resources, enhances individual self-satisfaction and promotes liberty and freedom of choice. Such self interest, they argue, is much more likely to produce a satisfactory social order than is the invocation of such vague goals as social responsibility. The latter is rejected as a conceptual nonsense, and an empirical danger to freedom. The paradigmatic statement of this position is provided by Friedman:

> If businesses do have a social responsibility other than making maximum profits for shareholders, how are they to know what it is? Can self selected private individuals decide ... how great a burden they are justified in placing on themselves or their stockholders to serve the social interest.
>
> (Friedman, M. 1962: note 26, 133-4)

Further, Friedman has written famously that the only social responsibility of corporate officials is 'to conduct the business in accordance with his [the employer's] desires, which generally means to make as much money as possible while conforming to the basic rules of society' (Friedman 1970: 33).

According to such a view, any desire to force upon managements the requirement to take socially responsible decisions is to undermine the democratic process whereby such decisions are the stuff of elected politicians, is to over-extend the capabilities of corporate executives, or at worst is to provide a justification for managements to secure (an illegitimate) autonomy from shareholders and their sovereignty. Friedman makes the point in the title of his celebrated article, 'The Social Responsibility of Business is to Make Profits' (Friedman 1970).

Although, as we will show, such economists tend to agree with the compliance school about the appropriate status of regulatory offences, their rather different approach to questions of social responsibility raises some interesting issues. As we have seen in Chapter 1, in their view in the relationship between economic activity and the state there are tremendous dangers to the working of market rationality and efficiency. Since all economic actors, including corporations and state agents, are motivated by self-interest although state activities are justified because they are alleged to correct allocative problems due to *market failure*, in fact, they primarily function to redistribute resources by interfering with the normal working of the market. The major beneficiaries are usually small groups of highly motivated and well organized economic actors — iron triangles of established companies, regulators and politicians. Control is achieved through the regulatory apparatus favouring such companies directly or by imposing prohibitive costs on potential competitors by, for example, demanding expensive safety standards. Consumers also suffer because they have to pay higher prices. In other words, they are very cynical about the autonomy of regulatory agencies and their utility for achieving any kind of social goals (see Stigler 1971; Peltzman 1976). Then, in their view, 'social regulation' is something best achieved by a combination of market forces and litigation rather than by governmental regulation. Here let us simply note that the very idea that one can distinguish between 'social regulation' and 'economic regulation' is itself ideological. For example, as Doern has observed, the

> regulation of hazardous products is the soft underbelly of economic regulation, precisely because it deals ultimately with who will bear the hidden costs of new products and production processes.
>
> (Doern 1977: 17)

James Q. Wilson is sympathetic to the arguments of these economists but he is also critical of them for certain over-simplifications. He suggests that not all regulatory agencies are captured by those that they are meant to regulate, and therefore a more complex model is required of the relationship between state agencies and the different social groups competing to influence them. First there are not one, but four political situations. He redefines as *client politics*, the situation where costs are widely distributed and benefits concentrated (e.g. state licensing laws); *majoritarian politics* occur when both costs and benefits are widespread (e.g. the Social Security and Sherman Acts); *interest group politics* exist when both costs and benefits are narrowly distributed and hence negotiation and compromise can occur (e.g. labour laws); and finally, *entrepreneurial politics* occur when benefits are widely distributed and costs are highly concentrated (e.g. environmental and auto safety regulation). Second, whilst it is true that some regulatory officials are *politicians* ambitious for higher appointive or elective office, some are *careerists* motivated by organizational bureaucratic concerns, and yet others are *professionals* responsive to the norms and interests of their wider occupational community. Third, although in economics what is relevant is not what individuals want but rather only consumer's 'revealed preferences' known through market conduct, in politics values often only emerge in the course of the political process and efforts are continuously made to change people's wants so that they are in accord with the emerging political programme.

> Both economics and politics deal with problems of scarcity and conflicting preferences. Both deal with persons who ordinarily act rationally. But politics differs from economics in that it manages conflict by forming heterogeneous coalitions out of persons with changeable and incommensurable preferences in order to make binding decisions for everyone.
>
> (Wilson 1980: 363)

This distinction had, in Wilson's view, become highly problematic in the 1970s since unqualified, irrational political actors — trade unionists and 'bureaucrats, professionals, academics, the media, those whose political position depends upon controlling resources other than [their own] wealth and whose motivations are more complex than wealth maximization' — sometimes interfered with both market forces and the internal workings of the professionally run corporation. The consequence of such a blurring is that unreasonable laws can be passed, excessive damages awarded, unworkable regulations promulgated, and product certification unfairly denied. Such individuals and attitudes — a belief in a risk free society, for example — can gain excessive influence within democratic assemblies, in the courts, amongst juries, and can capture regulatory agencies. There can emerge another iron triangle of regulatory entrepreneurs, regulatory agencies and, for example, environmentalist politicians (Wilson 1980; Weaver 1978).

Although some of the specific points made by Wilson about, for example, the different kinds of regulatory political situations are not without value, it clear that he does not attend to the wider structural context of the situations that he explores, nor does he examine long-term outcomes. Thus, for example, there is a need to examine the significance of both the Social Security Act of 1935 and the 1890 Sherman Act and ask why did the former presage such a minimal welfare state in the US (the development of which has been subject to such tremendous vagaries and extraordinary resistance (see Block et al. 1987) and why the latter, and subsequent legislation, have not stopped the economic system from becoming increasingly oligopolistic (Coleman 1989: 14; Jones 1982). Nor does he provide any explanation of why environmentalists and trade unionists advocating a healthy and safe environment within and without the workplace were successful in developing effective regulation for only three or four years in the mid-seventies. In fact, *contra* Wilson, and Vogel (1989), their short-term victory — as a result of heightened social conflict and a profound but temporary crisis in the legitimacy of the American political and economic order (Cloward and Piven 1979; Donnelly 1982) — and subsequent speedy defeat is testimony not to the plural nature of the American political system, but rather to the resources, resilience and power of business, which was able to launch the massive counter-attack associated with deregulation (Calavita 1983; Szasz 1984, 1986a, 1986b).

One can reinterpret some of the arguments of the Oxford School/compliance theorists to make this point, albeit after making some pretty fundamental criticisms. Bardach and Kagan, for example, make two objections to the 'regulator-as-policeman' strategy. First, that it engenders rigidity and/or legalism, which in turn generate 'regulatory unreasonableness' and 'unresponsiveness' (Bardach and Kagan 1982: 58). Here the regulatory inspector is represented in caricature, as something akin to an automaton, compelled towards the prosecution of each and every violation detected. Such a representation is not only stereotypical, echoing Thatcherite and Reaganite 'anti-statist' rhetoric, but is based upon a fundamental misconception of what the police actually do. As we have seen, because of the necessarily wide range of laws that they exist to enforce and for operational/practical reasons, police officers regularly and routinely exercise discretion, as an indispensable (Lustgarten 1987), and even desirable (Kinsey et al. 1986), part of their work. Their second, and more telling, objection is that this strategy stimulates 'opposition and the destruction of co-operation' (Kagan and Scholz 1984: 73). That is, business may resort to legalistic counter measures, organise politically and attack the agency at the legislative level, jeopardising 'the agency's legal mandate, its funding, and its very existence' (Kagan and Scholz 1984: 74).

On the one hand, they imply that if only regulators were more reasonable — both British and American occupational health and safety inspectors were instructed in being more polite when visiting businesses and business executives were asked to comment on their conduct to the inspectors' superiors (Wilson 1985) — then compliance would be the normal outcome. On the other hand, they argue, *and themselves find it a reasonable state of affairs*, that: regulation is viable only when it prevents the more easily *avoidable* harmful side effects of capitalist modes of wealth creation and an inspectorate's mandate would be withdrawn if it were seen to be overzealous; regulations are only passed which do not pose a fundamental challenge to an industry's economic viability and industry is powerful enough to resist the enactment or enforcement of overly-restrictive regulations. In these assertions, it becomes clear that *the legitimacy of a capitalist economic system and the illegitimacy of its being policed are in fact starting-points for the analyses of these commentators.* Yet, there is no reason for us to endorse any such view. Their own analysis suggests that there are at least two distinct, and significant inequalities of power that must enter into our considerations: those that derive from an imbalance in resources (including knowledge and expertise), and those that derive from corporate ideological hegemony. As we have shown elsewhere (Pearce and Tombs 1990, 1991), while 'compliance theorists' recognise that the enforcement realities/necessities they describe are defined and limited by the 'needs of business', they consistently fail to even attempt to transcend or subvert the limitations placed upon 'realistic' possibilities by this *de facto* dominance. Dominance, of course, implies struggle and resistance and it is important to recognize deregulation and other Reaganite policies, for example in relation to welfare, as a recuperative counterattack against some real historical gains (Block et al. 1987). Ironically, a contingent event, the Bhopal disaster, made it possible to reopen the debate about these issues. Indeed, if the workings of the capitalist system and its empowering of the major corporate actors is the omnipresent context of all political situations, this does not mean that capitalist corporations, nor capitalist states, are in total control of their own destiny. They do not automatically secure their economic, political or ideological conditions of existence.

Much of the work of the compliance school focuses upon the limitations of that which it opposes, namely 'punitive'/'sanctioning' regulatory enforcement. We have outlined our scepticism about this whole problematic (Pearce and Tombs 1990, 1991). Nevertheless, it must be said that what compliance theorists very rarely do is to detail the extent to which a compliance strategy *works* — their concern is more to highlight that 'alternatives' are unworkable. Moreover, it is important to note that Kelman and Vogel, cited by Hawkins as providing evidence of the fact that punitive strategies have similar results to, but higher costs than, compliance strategies, differ from him in important ways.

Interestingly, both Kelman (1981) and Vogel (1986) argue that the most appropriate regulatory style in the US is an adversarial one, not least because of industry's inherent opposition to implementing meaningful standards (Vogel 1986: 208). Vogel suggests that in the British context the British regulatory style worked reasonably well. Indeed, the evidence on occupational safety and health between 1974-80 seems to bear this out. However, the regulatory system put in place after the 1974 Health and Safety at Work Act differed significantly from the earlier system — there was an increase in employees covered, a reorganization of the inspectorates and a clarification and some strengthening of their powers, and, finally, the trade unions were given a greater role. Though these changes did not go far enough, they strengthened regulatory forces. Yet a situation in the late 1970s of general (if qualified) optimism about improving health and safety in Britain industry, not least because of union involvement and expertise at all levels, has been reversed since 1979, in the context of recession and anti-regulatory and anti-trade union activities of a right wing government. Indeed, the years since 1981 in Britain have highlighted inherent weaknesses within a self-regulatory system organised around 'compliance-oriented' approaches (Tombs 1990a). Given these points, for Hawkins to allege an indifference to health and safety by working people and trade unions (Hawkins 1990: 462) is a clear case of blaming the victim and, again, is not a view supported by at least one of the studies he cites (Dawson et al. 1988).[6] Dawson and her colleagues certainly note that 'union organisation alone is not, under current legislation, an adequate safeguard of worker safety. Other factors are at work, notably management provision and external enforcement' (Dawson et al. 1988: 259-60). But they also recognise the efforts of trades unions in the 1970s to raise safety as an issue and the continuing need for two 'fundamental rights' for workers' representatives (unionised and non-unionised) — namely, rights to safety information, and the legal ability to 'stop the job' (ibid.: 277); hardly the arguments of those who set little store by workers' ability and willingness to intervene in safety issues (See, more generally, Tombs 1988).

In Kelman's view, although the Swedish system for regulating health and safety is as effective as the one in the US, he valorises the latter as democratic and activist and views the former as elitist and authoritarian (Kelman 1981: ch. 4 passim and 233). Kelman, however, has a limited conception of democracy and fails to recognize how the relative strength of the Swedish trade union movement and its entrenched and active bargaining role gave the mass of the population a significant say in how industry was run and hence 'compliance' in that country involved negotiating and accepting relatively high standards (Lundqvist 1982; Albrecht 1982).[7] We find that Vogel, too, has been challenged. Hays (1987) argues that he is incorrect to suggest that the British mode of regulating air and water pollution has been effective. Our sense is that Hawkins may now agree more with Hays than Vogel. But, what this underlines again is that there is a problem with the very concept of a 'compliance strategy'. The practices of different agencies which superficially seem to be elements of similar modes of regulation may have quite different effects because of their radically different conditions of existence.

In this context it is worth referring to the work of Gabriel Kolko, since its major focus for over two decades was precisely the unpredictability and uncontrollability of the American economy (Kolko 1962, 1963, 1965, 1976). And, indeed, although he has not been concerned with the nature and function of regulatory agencies *per se*, Kolko's work is relatively compatible with a conception of regulatory bodies as more hegemonic apparatuses than captive agents, an understanding of regulatory agencies which, following Rianne Mahon, we introduced in Chapter 2. According to this conception, a stable capitalist social order depends — in both the state and civil society — upon one fraction of capital successfully claiming leadership over other fractions of capital, other privileged social groupings and also the subordinate classes. In order to do this it does all that it can to disarm these other groups whilst winning their consent through (limited) compromises with their interests. In the 'relatively autonomous' state there is established an 'unequal equilibrium of compromises' and an 'unequal structure of representation'. Regulatory agencies always involve representation of fractions of capital, of the wider state and, sometimes, of other social interests (Mahon 1979: 155).

This means that such apparatuses may give *some* privileges to businesses already operating in an area and that they may give partial recognition to the interests of subordinate groups. However, the overall control exercised over the state and civil society by the hegemonic fraction, means that such concessions are likely to be strictly circumscribed, at least in the long run. Mahon has shown how this can be achieved through the medium of the hierarchical relationship that exists between the different state apparatuses — specialist regulatory agencies can be located in relatively weak government departments and/or their activities can be subject to the review of other state agencies which more closely reflect the interests or rationales of the hegemonic fractions of capital. In the US, the Office of Management and Budget fulfilled this latter function in the 1980s (Horwitz 1989: 208-211), while the Deregulation Unit of the Department of Trade and Industry has performed a similar function in the UK in recent years (Tombs 1996). Mahon's work (1977, 1979, 1984) represents the beginnings of an alternative and more sophisticated analysis of regulatory agencies, and it is one which this text has sought to develop. Such an analysis locates each regulatory agency within a broader state apparatus, the (sometimes conflicting) functions of these, and the context of (changing) political economy. We consider further some of the details of, and questions raised by, this analysis in the next chapter.

For Wilson, however, it is bureaucratisation and inefficiency that are characteristic of state activities. Thus, the fewer the demands there are made on the state — and the less political activity there is — the better. There is little point in trying to change anything because 'the relationship between electoral needs and policy outcome is problematic' (Wilson 1980: 390). Of course he produced a similar argument, albeit with somewhat different conclusions, in the case of street crime, where he argues that nothing can be done about the social causes of crime, which anyway are unknowable, but retains deterrence very much on the policing agenda (Wilson 1975: xiv-xv; Young 1986: 9-12). Yet, whilst he usually claims that the less regulation the better, in his article 'Can the Government Regulate Itself?' he argued that regulation can in fact be very effective, but only if it is private enterprise that is being regulated and not government bureaucracies. He makes unfavourable comparisons between the effective and ineffective regulation of private and public housing, hospitals and utilities, respectively. Although there are indeed *difficulties* in regulating state activities (Hirst 1986), generally what Wilson claims are examples of the *impossibility* of such regulation are due rather to a failure to supply governmental agencies with sufficient funds, adequate guidelines, and appropriate democratic controls — for example, to maintain appropriate public housing and to both provide cheap electricity *and* to control pollution. It is conservative hostility to public enterprise that is the problem, not public enterprise itself. It is also worth noting that it is impossible to adequately regulate some markets because effective regulation makes them economically unviable for private enterprise, so that conversely they can only be viable if they are inadequately regulated. Szasz's (1986c) discussion of the regulation of hazardous waste disposal and Campbell's (1987) of the state and nuclear waste are instructive in this regard. Indeed, overall it is only too clear that,

> In the end, the politics of regulation turns less on the dynamics of coalition formation, the behaviour of regulatory officials, or the rulings of the courts, important as these are, than on the dominant vision of the larger society in which nationally organized interests, policy, entrepreneurs, bureaucrats, and courts are merely highly specialized, and unrepresentative manifestations. That vision encompasses a conception of the good society and of the place of the citizen in that society, a notion of the proper boundaries between public and private, and of the appropriate domains of community norms and individual decision. That vision, whatever its content, ultimately prescribes the tolerance within which conventional regulatory politics can be conducted.
>
> (Schuck 1981: 723)

Clearly, then, different kinds of economics and different forms of analyses are also forms of politics. Whilst these tend to claim objectivity, they are often tied to particular interests; whilst guiding and justifying actions they can also obscure what is occurring; whilst prescribing the limits of the possible and desirable, they fail to locate explicitly these definitions of possibility and desirability within social, economic, political and ideological assumptions.

This point needs equally to be made with respect to the social liberals/the compliance school as it does to the work of Wilson and others. Just as Wilson refers to deregulation as almost a natural response to (over)regulation, this inevitability sits at the heart of the compliance school's prescriptions regarding feasible regulation. Yet it is important to emphasise that recent deregulatory movements in Britain and the US have not been occasioned by a simple 'backlash' to 'regulatory unreasonableness' (Hawkins 1990: 452). Indeed, in the work of many of those cited by Hawkins to document his account of the cutbacks in OSHA — Calavita 1983; Noble 1986; Szasz 1984 — we find an explanation of the attack on OSHA and the EPA as largely a consequence of their contribution to a challenge, however brief and limited, to the long term dominance of the interests of corporate capital in US society (Woodiwiss 1990b; and on Britain see Tombs 1996). Terms like 'regulatory unreasonableness' and 'backlash' are justifications used by American right wing ideologues who have always wanted to roll back the state and whose arguments, to a limited extent, have been somewhat cynically adopted by corporate capital; their use is justified, whether consciously or unintentionally, by much of the social science of the compliance school. Capital's attack on the New Deal compromise and on the expanding role of the state began before OSHA and the EPA had much impact, and was primarily linked to internal crises of legitimacy within the US, with changes in America's relation to the global economy and with capital's desire to reassert its preeminence, particularly over the interests of organized labour (Ferguson and Rogers 1986; Edsall 1984; Bowles, Gordon and Weisskopf 1984).

Thus, in the last decades there has been a general, but by no means universal, push towards deregulatory or (ever) more conciliatory regulatory strategies and a general move to limit state control and open business opportunities (by selling off publicly owned assets though privatisation) even in countries like Britain and Canada which had histories of conciliatory 'regulatory styles'. As we argued at length in Chapter 2, international capital has been intent on creating a neoliberal economic and social international order that facilitates the growth of a transnational capitalism and imposes severe constraints on those states seeking to pursue national development, whether in a corporatist capitalist or more socialist manner (Gill and Law 1988). Further, the relations between the capitalist class and other classes and social groups in these different states vary (cf. Pearce 1976; Snider 1987: 55-9), and by no means all sections of corporate capital or all capitalist states define their interests in the same way. They do not trust the unfettered working of the market to the same degree, nor view all forms of regulation with similar distaste: economic regulation may help to provide a 'predictable and controlled business environment' but 'social regulation' interferes with 'the most minute details of production' and 'production decisions' and is thereby 'fundamentally ... antagonistic to the logic of firms within a capitalist economy' (Szasz 1984: 114).

These points, of course, raise much wider issues than we could deal with here, but one consequence of wholly ignoring them is to allow to pass unchallenged corporate definitions of 'reasonable regulation' and the invocation of vacuous notions such as regulatory backlash.[8]

That most corporations are not amoral calculators, and thus that their adherence to regulations is not conditional upon their short term or longer term self-interest, is, as we have seen, a central tenet of the arguments of those advocating compliance strategies. In *Going by the Book*, Bardach and Kagan even attempt to quantify the proportion of all corporations which are amoral calculators, or, 'bad apples'. They assume, 'for analytical purposes', that at most they 'make up about 20 per cent of the average population of regulated enterprises in most regulatory programs' (Bardach and Kagan 1982: 65). If the theoretical argument for viewing corporations as amoral calculators is unconvincing, the empirical evidence as to the spread of illegalities amongst all types of corporations seems, *contra* Bardach and Kagan, in favour of a view which sees the commitment of corporations to regulations as essentially contingent. The empirical evidence for this in relation to safety crimes and to corporate crime more generally, which we have already reviewed, suggests: that crimes against regulations are widespread, and not confined to particular sizes of firms in particular sectors; that where pressures towards compliance are reduced, illegality tends to increase; and that corporations have only contingent commitments to legality.

Thus, we have argued that the distinction between 'traditional' criminals and corporate offenders contains both real and ideological aspects. It is real in the sense that business is an activity which has certain socially-productive consequences. But it remains largely ideological in that it implies that the corporation can have a primary commitment to act in a socially responsible manner; it is ideological in that illegalities are considered to currently form a marginal element of business activity; and it is ideological in its acceptance of business's own definitions as to what constitute 'reasonable' regulations.

Once these assumptions which underpin the distinction between 'traditional' and 'regulatory' offenders, and the different regulatory responses engendered by this distinction are problematised, then both the distinction itself and the arguments against the 'policing' of industry are greatly weakened. This allows us to reopen the question of the most 'appropriate' regulatory strategy for dealing with corporate violations of health and safety laws, and to transcend at least some of the ideological 'understandings' within which both the questions we may pose and the answers we can find are presupposed. This opens up the possibilities for considering a range of regulatory mechanisms combined to form a more punitive regulatory strategy, a task upon which we will focus explicitly in the concluding chapter of this text. Thus, the transcendence of the assumption that corporations cannot be policed allows serious consideration to be given to the practicalities of such a strategy — and many of the practical problems are, indeed, attested to usefully in the work of the 'Compliance School'. Yet there is no need to conflate the immediately practicable with either the once-and-for-all possible or desirable forms of regulation. Avoiding this conflation is indeed crucial once it is recognised that what is 'feasible' is in fact a political issue, and thus subject to change.

Conclusion

In this chapter we first explored, challenged and then modified some of the arguments of Left-Realism as a prelude to exploring the phenomenon of corporate crime and to developing strategies to combat it or at least to regulate it more effectively. We were critical of the overly subject-centred nature of much Left-Realist writing and showed how this compromised their understanding of 'street crime' and inhibited their study of 'crime in the suites'. We critiqued the compliance school writing on corporate crime, particularly the view that corporations should be assisted rather than policed because corporate illegalities are not 'real crimes'. We then provided detailed examples of what this strategy could mean in practice; in doing so, we attempted to develop elements of the Realist arguments for the reform of the policing of street crime, which we had considered earlier.

Despite some of our reservations concerning the descriptive and prescriptive work of the Realists on crime and policing, the spirit underlying the argument developed here for the policing of corporations is strictly congruent with the Realist imperative that crime be taken seriously. In attempting to indicate the extent of the commonplace victimisation from corporate crimes, and to develop practical strategies for ways in which workers and local communities may be both protected and empowered to protect themselves from such illegalities, we hope that we have at least begun to stimulate Realist work in the often inadequately treated area of crime.

On the basis of the preceding, and our work presented elsewhere (particularly, Pearce and Tombs 1990, 1991), we believe that a punitive policing strategy is necessary, desirable and practicable. Such policies obviously will be resisted by capital and its allies (Snider 1989) and will only be forced upon corporations by other social groupings, such as workforces, local communities and consumers. Although the parameters of capitalist social relations place real limits on how far such reforms can proceed, that some reforms can proceed should now be clear enough. We explore some of these processes in detail in the final two chapters (8 and 9) of this text.

Notes

1. A recognition and full understanding of this imbalance of power also necessitates academic work, in terms of an adequate theorisation of the nature of the offenders under regulatory law, namely corporations.

2. This, after all, has been a central concern of the 'capture' literature of the last two decades within social science writing on regulation.

3. In Winter 1990 we published a paper in the *British Journal of Criminology* (Pearce and Tombs 1990) which developed an extended critique of the work of the Oxford School. In the same issue of that journal, there appeared a lengthy, and defensive, response by Keith Hawkins (Hawkins 1990). In a subsequent article we provided a rebuttal of many of the claims made by Hawkins (Pearce and Tombs 1991), who again was able to publish a reply in the same issue (Hawkins 1991). There seems to be no point in rehearsing our own position here, nor the main contours of the debate. These articles are, of course, in the public domain, while the exchange has generated some interest in commentaries (see, for example, Croall 1992; Hopkins 1994; Johnston 1992; Nelken 1994a; South 1998; Wells 1993).

4. All quotations are from Hawkins (1984: 1-8). On these issues, nothing new is added in Hawkins (1990).

5. Some of the other problems with the use of 'ideal types' have been explored in Hindess (1977) and Hirst (1976).

6. The other is the work of Genn (1987: 42).

7. In an article in which he documents how Swedish superiority over the US in health and safety protection is an outcome of 'different class relations in both societies' rather than of differences in political culture, Navarro criticises Kelman's work in similar terms to those we used to highlight the empiricist and ideological nature of much of the social science of the Compliance School. He

also suggests that its highly positive critical reception could not 'be attributed to its explanatory value ... (which is limited) but, rather, to its apologetic and propagandising function ... (which is large)' (Navarro 1983: 521).

8.   For a detailed discussion of the US deregulatory movement see Horwitz 1989.

8 Hegemony and Risk

Introduction

In this chapter we continue our consideration of regulation, with specific reference to developing feasible and desirable reforms which could lead to more effective regulatory strategies. In the preceding chapter, we considered some of the empirical and theoretical arguments relating to appropriate forms of regulation, drawing partly (and albeit critically) on some of the more useful academic studies of policing in order to inform that discussion. This chapter continues with a consideration of some of those themes relating to desirability and feasibility, and does so by placing regulation in an historical and longitudinal context. Further, in developing our own theoretical position, regulation is considered within: emerging and changing conceptions of risk; the wider context of governance, and differing hegemonic versions of what is meant by this; the state in its various functions and capacities, as well as relations between the state and other key sets of social actors. Thus, in the detail presented in this chapter, we examine further the constant efforts around hegemony construction and reconstruction, again highlighting the interactive nature of the process of regulatory reform, and the struggle of regulatory agencies to act as hegemonic apparatuses.

More specifically, we examine these questions within the specific industrial context of the chemicals industry. Our focus is upon changes in the regulation of chemical production in the US are related to changes in its mode of governance. Overall, we argue that there has been effected 'a passive revolution' (Gramsci 1971: 119-120; Sassoon 1987: 204-217), insofar as these changes have occurred through procedures, and through discourses, that marginally modify but crucially sustain both the overall conception of group and societal interests held by the groups comprising the power block, and, relatedly, the preexisting modes of hegemonic dominance. Yet, because of a continuous reconfiguring of social relations and social forces within the American and global context, this new 'settlement' is inevitably unstable and recuperable. To understand the nature of these changes it is necessary to articulate this Gramscian analysis with aspects of structural Marxism and some of the recent writings on governmentality, risk and insurance.

We should note here that although we draw from the governmentality / governance literature we do not accept the disdainful attitude of some of its authors towards Marxist theories (see particularly Miller and Rose 1990: 27; Rose 1993: 286). We would argue that for the concept of governmentality / governance to be useful as a means of describing (never mind explaining) concrete situations it needs to be articulated with precisely such theories. The antipathy that Foucault sometimes felt towards acknowledging situations of group conflict and social contradiction implied, however inadvertently, that modes of governance are socially consensual (albeit individualistically resisted), and meant that he often ignored the problem of exploring their conditions of existence and the extent to which these are secured as the always contingent outcome of struggle between different social groups. In undertaking these tasks one needs to include an analysis of the inequalities of power (however productive that power), and whether and how there has been a marginalisation of competing modes of governance. By articulating many of the insights of the governance literature with those derived from a consideration of hegemony (see also Said 1984; Pearce 1988) we believe that we are able to remedy some of these lacunae.

The development of the US chemical industry has undoubtedly helped increase material wealth and improved American's general standard of living (Coley 1989; Aftalion 1991). Moreover, despite a relative decline, the US chemicals industry remains the most significant chemical industry in the world (Heaton 1996). But at the same time as it has furthered 'progress', it has also helped create a society with an increased susceptibility to large scale disasters and to many chronic illnesses (Beck 1992a; 1992b). This has led to significant opposition to many of the industry's activities. In response to this, the industry has significantly modified the ways in which production takes place, and there have been crucial changes in how it is regulated. In some ways, at least within the US and in other OECD countries, production is now undertaken more safely than previously, if never as safe as government and corporate propagandists claim. In this chapter we will relate the changes in the ways in which chemical production is organised within the US to changes to what is somewhat misleadingly called 'social' regulation,[1] and to more general changes in the mode of governance (Hunt 1993) of economic relations. Overall, we want to argue that although these changes are real enough and not lacking in significance, they are by no means necessarily sustainable. After all, they have only marginally changed the relations between the bulk of the population and the hegemonic 'power block' — the relatively unified leading sectors of corporate capital, the professional and scientific/technological elite and those state functionaries that oversee national economic policy and national security

(Sklar 1988; Weinstein 1968; Lustig 1982; Woodiwiss 1993a; Wilson 1976; Greenberg 1971). Moreover, the recent move to produce more basic chemicals in less developed countries, where there is usually less regulation, both displaces risk by exporting hazard (Ives 1985), and, at the same time, may well, in the long run, contribute to a general lowering of standards in OECD countries as well (Pearce and Tombs 1994; Pearce and Snider 1995).

Finally, we should make explicit that while our focus in this chapter is the US chemical industry and US political economy, we take both the broad empirical outline, and the theoretical argument of this chapter to apply equally to the UK. To have extended our analysis to cover the UK in detail would have rendered the treatment of these issues in the context of one chapter of one text over-schematic. On the other hand, there are good reasons for believing that an extension of our empirical and theoretical argument from the US to the UK is a justifiable one.

As we have noted previously, the US and the UK have acted as hegemonic economic and political powers, albeit in different epochs and in differing ways. Nevertheless, each has played a substantial part in moulding international economic and political agendas, through attempts to establish and maintain particular versions of a world order. Each have played significant roles as ideological leaders, providing the home for ideologues and ideologies, in particular versions of neoliberalism which have re-emerged in the past two decades. Moreover, it is no coincidence that ideas of the academics of the Chicagoan law and economics group had strong resonances in the UK. And, as we have seen, there are, on both sides of the Atlantic, key representatives of what we have termed the 'compliance school' with their particular, social liberal approach to regulation.

Further, both the US and UK remain significant economic and political actors in a global context. Certainly each retains significant chemical industries important to their wider industrial performance, and are home to leading multinationals in the various businesses which constitute the sector (Heaton 1996). Each has experience of chemical-related disasters, both acute and chronic. Each has developed a great deal of legislation in the past twenty-five years which focuses directly upon hazardous production in the chemicals industry. The major piece of occupational safety and health legislation emerged in the US in 1970, and in the UK in 1974; in the context of environmental legislation, however, it has to be noted that in terms of law on the books the US has for much of the past quarter century advanced far more than the UK, and this remains the case today. Each has oppositional movements which have sought to challenge the power of capital in terms of its production of hazards and risks for human and environmental safety and health. And the balance of power between these pro-regulatory forces on the one hand, and the state and corporate capital on the other, was altered substantially by the effects of disasters both in the US and the UK in the 1980s — the UK suffered a series of disasters in the latter half of the 1980s which had profound effects (Tombs 1995b), while the US was close witness to a series of major accidents which will be noted below. Moreover, given the close interdependence of the international chemicals industries, Bhopal reverberated though both the US and UK chemical economies — many of the regulatory and industry-inspired reactions were similar (Pearce and Tombs 1994). In each context, these disasters, and the momentum that was taken from them by pro-regulatory forces, served to reign in some of the most egregious excesses of the deregulatory Governments that had taken formal political power in 1979 in the UK, and 1980 in the US (though in each country, of course, the struggle for ideological and intellectual hegemony had been fought since the 1970s by the neoliberal Right).[2]

Thus even in the US, the archetypical liberal society, the historical block has always had to deal with the threat of counter-hegemonic movements. For example, the definition of a 'risk' always involves the conceptualization of some 'object' in some way 'linked' to some 'harm' in the context of a selective representation and interpretation of what is, in fact, a complex sociotechnical network or system (Hilgartner 1992). It is and has been a site of struggle.

Hazardous Production and Modes of Governance

Structural Changes in the American Chemical Industry

The American chemical industry that emerged in the late nineteenth century was primarily involved first in the production of such industrial chemicals as alkalis, acids, dyestuffs, explosives, and metallic alloys and then, after a tremendous boost provided by the first World War, diversified into such products as paints and lacquers, man-made fibres, electro-chemicals, pesticides and pharmaceuticals (Chandler 1990: 146-188). Although organic chemicals had always played a key role in the industry, the addition of oil and natural gas feedstocks to those of wood, tar and coal happened early in the US and led to the development of polymers and plastics — some 1 billion pounds of synthetic organic chemicals were produced in 1940. The boost to this production associated with the war effort, most importantly the programmes to create synthetic rubber and high octane aviation fuel (Aftalion 1991: 214-5), helped generate major new feedstocks and a proliferation of new chemicals; by 1950,

30 billion pounds of organic chemicals were being produced, which had risen to some 300 billion pounds by 1976 (Barnett 1994: 14). The years up to 1973 were generally extremely prosperous for the chemical industry; but already there were signs of the problems that would become only too evident in the 1980s. Internationally, the chemical industry had matured, in that its markets were relatively saturated and static — major new breakthroughs were few and far between. Competition had increased — the British and French chemical industries had adjusted to the postwar status quo and were now holding their own, and the German chemical industry had risen from the ashes and Japan and other non-European industries were developing rapidly. This competition was met in all countries by an increase in investment, leading, in turn, to a crisis of overcapacity.

At the same time, and in different countries, there were somewhat uneven pressures from environmental groups to change the *modus operandi* of the industry. In the US the response of the chemical industry to this pressure was to disengage its production both upstream and downstream and to shift to specialist chemicals. It also diversified into other unrelated areas, thereby creating conglomerates, less dependent on any particular market, and into speculating in financial markets. In the 1980s, US chemical companies were pushed to a (relatively new) short term mentality by the increasing dominance of finance oriented executives (Fligstein 1990), corporate raiding, leveraged buyouts, and so on. By the end of that decade, even the largest US chemicals companies were forced into dramatic restructuring as a consequence of over-capacity, to some extent independent of the US recession (*Chemistry & Industry*, 1991: 524).

In the last thirty years, there have been changes in the ways in which companies within the American chemical industry have managed the hazards and risks associated with the use, production, distribution, and disposal of hazardous chemical substances. These practices are clearly related, in part, to the regulatory processes to which they are subject, and the past thirty years have seen the passage (sometimes tardy), implementation of, and synergy between such Federal Acts as the 1963 Food Drug and Cosmetic Act, the 1969 National Environmental Policy Act, the 1970 Clean Air Act, the 1970 Occupational Safety and Health Act, the 1972 Federal Water Pollution Act, the 1974 Safe Drinking Water Act, the 1976 Resource Conservation and Recovery Act (RCRA), the 1976 Toxic Substances Control ACT (TSCA), the 1978 Federal Insecticide, Fungicide and Rodenticide Act, the 1980 Comprehensive Environmental Response, Compensation, and Liability Act (CERCLA), the 1984 RCRA Amendment Act and the 1986 Superfund Amendment and Reauthorization Act (SARA), including, in title 7, EPCRA — Emergency

Planning and Community Right-to-Know Act. Thus, in the 1990s, many companies are now supposed to engage in more rigorous site-management, by developing inventories of hazardous substances and ensuring that they are stored in a safe manner, by developing safer production processes, by aiming at source reduction and the recovery and reuse of materials, and by on-site disposal and neutralisation of hazardous wastes. Safety and evacuation plans must be developed, and workers, local communities and government authorities informed of potential dangers, from point or moving sources, including routine discharges into the ecosphere. Land use is now more controlled, and production facilities are inspected and certified. Damage already inflicted on the ecosphere is assessed and dealt with, to some extent, according to the 'polluter pays' principle. This new regulatory regime involves regulatory agencies, some market based solutions and various uses of the legal system. Most commentators agree that chemical production in the US is now safer than in the 1950s, although many recognise that there remain important improvements that need to be effected.

Despite real improvements, it was, perhaps, inevitable that the emergent systems of regulation towards risk mitigation have failed to match the specific hopes of any group, for their programmes had first to be 'translated' into the political rationalities and programmes of government. As Miller and Rose have argued, government in its concern with 'the wealth, health and happiness of the population' must follow the procedures of consultation, encouragement, and use the carrot and stick to develop alignments that will create a new viable regime, where the 'translatability between the moralities, epistemologies and idioms of political power, and the government of a specific problem space, establishes a mutuality between what is desirable and what can be made possible through the calculated activities of political forces' (Rose and Miller 1992: 182). Now, since a key element of such regulation has been the increasingly active role of the state, it is necessary to relate the particular kinds of legislation attempted (and their relative success and failure) to the complex and often contradictory economic and political constraints within which they are developed and utilised. If there is legislation that holds corporations liable for harms to public health and the environment this imposes substantial costs on industry, the absorption of which may impair capital accumulation, the engine of growth in liberal capitalism. At the same time an absence of governmental actions that address certain harm to public health and the environment may threaten the legitimacy of the system as a whole (Barnett 1992: 105).[3]

The American Chemical Industry and Discourses of Governance

We can identify, during this century in the US, at least three discourses and technologies of governance.[4] It should be emphasised that although there is a chronological element to these, they cannot be understood in terms of a linear emergence and transcendence alone. Rather, they must also be viewed as co-existent, and as more or less dominant at particular periods; in other words, these discourses need to be understood in the context of struggles for hegemony. For this reason, while the following sections impose some chronological order upon the phenomena which we are discussing, the complexity of such phenomena renders a strictly chronological discussion both undesirable and impossible.

The 'first' discourse of governance, a corporate liberal discourse (Weinstein 1968; Lustig 1982; Sklar 1988), emerged during the first half of this century. Political authorities aimed to severely circumscribe the extent to which the state interfered with the ways in which the production and disposal of dangerous chemicals took place, delegating responsibility for its organisation to the technical expertise, self-interest, and sense of social responsibility of those operating the large chemical companies. It was believed that efficient production and social progress depended upon the activities of such large companies. They developed sophisticated and safe industrial processes that made products that were benign if used properly.

Inevitably waste products were generated, but new uses for these were continuously found (see Aftalion 1991), while any remaining excess could be disposed of into an unperturbable ecosphere. If this waste was particularly environmentally destructive, this damage would be subsequently remedied by new technologies. This discourse is essentially one of progress — of increases in scientific knowledge, leading to increasing conquest of nature and control of the world, and development of new materials all leading to continuous improvements in 'the wealth, health and happiness of the population'. Industry experts, of course, knew (and made some allowances for the fact) that they were often dealing with dangerous processes which could cause significant harm to plant workers and surrounding communities. However, within this discourse, it was damage caused by explosions and by the immediately observable effects of corrosive and poisonous chemicals that were the major concern. A certain number of disasters and accidents were the unavoidable side effects of progress, but injuries to human beings, it was believed, could be dealt with by the courts or through workers' compensation (routine accidents were easily actuariseable). Furthermore, quite extensive state intervention in the economy was accepted, for example, in the area of economic regulation and in the context of defence procurement. This discourse played a key role in creating and regulating the particular intensive (Fordist) mode of capitalist accumulation developed in the US (Aglietta 1979; Jessop 1990b: 174). However, we would stress that Fordism in the US was always an aspect of a dual economy internally, while dependent upon favourable external economic relations (Pearce and Snider 1995; and see Chapter Two) and, indeed, transnational processes also (Holman 1993). When the latter conditions of existence became problematised in the 1970s (Gill and Law 1993), there was a strong impetus to reconfigure, but not totally abandon (Woodiwiss 1993a), the corporate liberal mode of governance.

Corporate liberal arrangements, however, had already been problematised by medical professionals and trade unionists, concerned with the chronic side effects of chemical and nuclear products and production processes on the health of local residents, consumers and workers, on animals, and on the ecosystem. These issues first became 'newsworthy' at the beginning of the 1960s, with the publication of Rachel Carson's book, Silent Spring (1962); then, the radical movements associated with civil rights, nuclear war and the Vietnam War, the consumer movement with its concern with the price, quality and safety of consumer goods, and union involvement with occupational safety and health issues. These all prepared the way for debates and legislation concerning water quality, air quality, nuclear power and the production, use and disposal of toxic chemicals. In the early 1970s environmentalism *per se* became a major focus of American public consciousness.

Having 'measured the real against the ideal and found it wanting' (Rose and Miller 1992: 181), intellectuals, activist trade unionists and environmentalists developed a radical liberal discourse as a way of redescribing the real, so that programmes of action were developed which garnered enough support to influence the legislature. Those subscribing to this discourse believed that many existing Federal agencies were captured by the industries that they were meant to regulate (Fellmeth 1970; Turner 1970). On the one hand, they argued for more activist interventionist regulatory agencies. On the other hand, they argued for: independent public-interest science; greater empowerment of employees, communities and individual consumers, who were, or might well be, exposed to dangerous chemicals; and legal regimes that were conducive to the compensation of actual or potential victims. Most fundamentally their aim was to force corporate capitalism to pay for past irresponsible conduct, and to force large corporations not only to internalise externalities but also to actually take seriously the interests of other stakeholders. Aided to no small extent by a series of highly visible industrial disasters (at Flixborough, UK in 1974, Seveso, Italy in 1976, Love Canal, USA in 1978, Three Mile Island, US in 1979, Bhopal, India and San Juan Ixhuatepec, Mexico in 1984, and Chernobyl,

Ukraine and Basel, Switzerland in 1986), those subscribing to this discourse were able to play key roles in the passage of much legislation. Nevertheless, they have remained highly critical of how capitalism is regulated, how victims are compensated, how the environment is repaired, and how the costs of these are distributed (Hofrichter 1993).

There had also emerged in the 1970s and 1980s a neoliberal 'enterprise' discourse (Rose and Miller 1992; Adams and Brock 1991). This was also critical of Federal agencies (Stigler 1971; Peltzman 1976; Weaver 1978; Weidenbaum and Fina 1978), though, as we indicated in the previous chapter, this criticism was on the grounds that a deregulated economy, opened up to market forces, would not require regulators to act as 'policemen', but merely as advisors (Bardach and Kagan 1982), since regulation would be provided by the market and the legal system. General tendencies towards innovation, characteristic of high technology sectors like the chemical industry, had been further stimulated by a growing global awareness of environmental matters. Once these issues were identified industry could and did respond responsibly, for example, the US Chemical Manufacturers Association 'Responsible Care Initiative' can be seen as testimony to this. Progress had been achieved, and would continue to be achieved, when scope was given to the skills and innovatory capacity of corporate management to produce a continuous improvement in managerial skills, new technologies and new risk management techniques. Built into this perspective, however, was some kind of recognition of the limits of scientific knowledge and the need to acknowledge ignorance and uncertainty. On the other hand, there was a general belief that, overall, the wealthier the society the safer the society. The rational response to environmental problems was for the state to help industry develop new standards of conduct and for the courts to develop new — but rational — rules of liability. While some state initiatives were seen as constructive — for example, clarifying the rules for responsibility of disposing hazardous waste safely and setting up a competitive market under the RCRA in 1976 — many were deemed clearly irrational, most notably aspects of the Superfund Acts of 1980 and 1986. Over all, critics argued that greater attention should be paid to both the opportunity costs and transaction costs of policies pursued[5], and there should be a very definite refusal of their opponents' implicit utopia of a no-risk society (Aharoni 1981; Douglas and Wildavsky 1982). Indeed, this discourse stresses both the inevitability of uncertainty because of a necessary incompleteness of knowledge (Hayek 1949) and a positive conception of risk-taking as potentially productive and beneficial as well as harmful (cf. Douglas 1993). Hence, there is a negative view of risk averse behaviour and a positive evaluation of venture capital. This discourse, of course, has not been restricted to the US, but has also informed the reasoning of the IMF, World Bank and OECD (Cox 1993: 266), and thereby of many national governments.

Of interest here are the answers to such questions as: what events and processes occasioned these reactions; to what extent were these actions justified; how viable were they and what were their solutions; to what extent were these discourses adopted to guide conduct and to what extent were they used selectively and/or as a gloss for other kinds of activities? To explore these questions we need to examine the changing nature of the regulation of the American chemical industry, and of practices and discourses within the industry, with respect to various hazards associated with its production activities.

The Emergence of Risk Assessment

Insurance and Risk

While the postwar expansion in production brought immense benefit to the US chemical industry, it entailed enormous costs which were disproportionately borne by its workers and by local communities. As these, and other pro-regulatory groups, began to accumulate evidence regarding occupational ill-health, strategies of denial through a refusal to acknowledge such evidence became increasingly difficult for employers, the courts and regulatory agencies to sustain, certainly from the late 1960s. This period saw a reluctant recognition of the industrial causes of a range of diseases and a more general awareness that chemicals — in pharmaceutical products, in food, in the air, in the water, in toxic waste sites, and from chemical or nuclear disasters — negatively affect the health of people irrespective of their class, race or gender.

The long-standing efforts of the chemical industry to refuse to recognise that many chronic illnesses were induced either through occupational or more general exposure to toxic chemicals is explicable given that such illnesses and diseases, once legally acknowledged, constitute an actuarial nightmare. They involve mass victims, multiple injurers, fuzzy loss, multicollinearity (complex causal chains) and latency. They occur infrequently, they may be legally actionable under the rubric of strict liability and joint and several liability, they depend upon the vagaries of individuals deciding to make claims, and occurrences cannot be predicted but, at best, estimated using the very imprecise procedures of risk analysis (Katzman 1989: 133).

Since 1973, insurers have proved unwilling to provide Comprehensive General Liability policies to the Chemical Industry without significant exclusions, and although there was a subsequent attempt to cover these with an Environmental Impairment Policy, this did not work to the satisfaction of the insurance companies (Katzman 1989: 131-4). Indeed, much of the recent crisis in the world insurance market, most notably at Lloyds, has been associated with environmental and disaster insurance (Raphael 1994: 150-172). Insurance companies have also become increasingly concerned about the safety of chemical plants (Smith ed., 1986), while the spectacular expansion — both in the scale and geographical spread of production — of the international chemical industries in the post second World War period means that the prospect of a high consequence event has increased (King 1990).

In the context of their responsibility for first party site clean up and joint and several liability for other sites, many insurance companies are now at loggerheads with their chemical industry clients (Barnett 1994: 41), differing with the latter over what has been insured, accusing them of failing to fulfil their legally defined environmental obligations and even, on occasion, of clandestinely dumping hazardous waste (*New York Times*, 17 May 1992: F11). It is hardly surprising that insurance coverage has become increasingly difficult to secure, and is often dependent on external inspections of facilities by insurance companies. As a result, many firms and groups of firms are beginning to organise self-insurance, or at least are attempting to do so.

For Priest, recent increases in liability should be understood in terms of a new utilitarianism concerned with the most effective means of reducing both the general risk of injury and the effects of injury in society as a whole. This is achieved by using civil damage judgments as a public policy instrument 'for internalizing costs to the parties that generate them' (Priest 1993: 208), where generation means any contribution by such a party to an increase in the risk of loss faced by any other party. Here, since 'all actions can be arrayed at some point upon the risk contribution continuum, sharp moral distinctions lose moment' (ibid.: 215).[6]

Undoubtedly the greatest increase in liability, both in number of cases and in size of awards, has been for corporate, professional and governmental defendants. These increases, however, have had less to do with incentives to increase safety than with injury compensation insurance through tort law. But this is both a somewhat socially inefficient and inequitable way of providing such insurance (Galanter 1994). Because benefits and operational costs tend to be higher, and because insurers are less able to differentiate among the insured population to reduce insurance costs, the provision of insurance through an adversarial tort system is at least five to ten times as expensive as first-party insurance (Priest 1993: 225; Galanter 1994). Because all consumers end up paying the same additional amount for the cost of liability insurance, but the wealthy get larger damage settlements, this does not work to redistribute income downwards. The general historical verdict upon tort as a compensation device is that it has been, at best, 'uneven in performance'; moreover, evidence on the extent to which it has proven effective in controlling risk is highly equivocal (Galanter 1994). Furthermore, fear of liability suits may have meant that a number of useful goods and services have been withdrawn from the market and there has been a reluctance to offer new products.

On the other hand, in tort cases, where injury is caused by something of which the plaintiffs were unaware while it was affecting them, but which would be dreaded by most people, courts and juries have recently, and increasingly, tended to reject the 'minimal' accounting based upon the calculation of the probability of risks, cost/benefit analysis and risk analysis; they have instead applied a more comprehensive — and, crucially, less predictable — social concept of responsibility and reasonable risk, including a concern with human autonomy and victim compensation (Sanders 1992: 76).

More in line with Sander's view is Michael Baram's discussion of the challenges posed for the chemical industry and its insurers by what he refers to as an emerging 'moral code' established by the common law of 'toxic torts' (Baram 1987: 421). Baram charts four key adaptations within US tort law which have 'increased the economic vulnerability of industrial firms using hazardous materials' (ibid.), and he places these in the context of an increasing inability of traditional regulatory and corporate risk management methods to respond to the impression made upon 'public perceptions' and 'public consciousness' by the acute and chronic health, safety and environmental effects caused by hazardous technologies (ibid.: 416). Moreover, in introducing these adaptations he (perhaps unwittingly) summarises the nature of the challenges that these pose for the hegemony of an existent form of governance:

> The challenge for industry and its insurers is to develop the ability to overtake increasing risk and economic vulnerability, particularly for firms doing business in the USA, where vulnerability is greatest, and bring about the control and abatement of these dynamic forces.
>
> (ibid.: 417)

First, many state statutes of limitations have been revised by the 'discovery' rule, which permits the bringing of tort actions within a period of time from the discovery of the tortious act, rather than from the date of the act itself, so that the period during which tort actions can be brought is considerably extended (ibid.: 422). Second, many states have adopted the doctrine of strict liability over tests of negligence where toxic chemicals are involved (ibid.: 422-4). Third, certain states have replaced the requirement to establish whom among multiple parties caused a particular injurious effect with a 'joint and several liability' (Baram 1987: 424). Finally, Baram notes shifts in some US states towards a weakening of the burden of the proof of causation (ibid.: 425-6). Alongside this shift he notes the progressive potential of both Right-to-Know legislation and the results of biological monitoring and medical surveillance in terms of plaintiffs being able to gather the evidence necessary to show causation (ibid.). We shall consider briefly the potential significance of Rights-to-Know below. On biological monitoring and medical surveillance, it is worth noting that the optimism expressed by Baram regarding the provision of key information for oppositional groups through the use of such techniques is hardly, at present, being realised. As Draper has documented thoroughly, these techniques have been usurped by corporations themselves, and have provided a means of exclusionary and discriminatory practices in the relative distribution of what have come to be recognised as more and less healthy jobs (Draper 1991; see also Robinson 1991). The net effect of the use of such techniques in the US chemical industry has been to exacerbate 'structures of vulnerability' (Nichols 1986). As we shall note below, however, these particular consequences of the use of biological monitoring and medical surveillance reveal less about any inherent natures of these techniques, and much more about the balance of social forces within which they have been developed and deployed.

Thus, the growing awareness of the dangerous nature of modern production processes, expressed through increased litigation, environmental movements and news of dramatic disasters combined to make it impossible for the corporate executives, scientists and technologists and state administrators to retain legitimacy without making changes. Their strategy has been to claim that negative externalities are the unavoidable side effects of progress, that they were unexpected but that they can be controlled or ameliorated. They are merely a new episode in a long running saga. It is business as usual.

Risk Management via Risk Assessment?

Companies (and regulators) have made increasing use of techniques of risk analysis, safety assessment, consequence analysis, hazard operability studies, hazard analysis, and so on, which were initially developed to satisfy the demands of those insuring hazardous technologies, this remaining their primary rationale (Kletz 1990: 281). The most inclusive of these techniques is risk assessment. This generates data which is then used to define the health effects of individual or population exposures to hazardous materials and/or situations (National Research Council 1983). Risk assessment consists of four stages:

> The first step involves hazard identification or the determination that a particular chemical is linked or not linked to a particular health effect. The second stage examines the relationship between the magnitude of exposure and the probability of occurrence of the adverse health effect identified in step one. This step is often referred to as a dose-response assessment. Next is exposure assessment. In this stage the range and extent of human exposures are calculated either before or after regulatory controls are in place. The last stage is a description of the nature and magnitude of human risk as well as some measure of uncertainty for the estimate. This step is called risk characterization.
>
> (Cutter 1993: 38)

Where risk management is equated with risk assessment, then, it is reduced to a series of techniques whereby risks are represented as identifiable, quantifiable, predictable and calculable — that is as a process wholly subsumed within the discourses that claim to represent (Western) scientific rationality. Yet, each of these stages are subject to controversy. In their present form, risk assessments necessarily involve rough and ready methodologies, which means that whichever particular sets of assumptions are chosen, widely divergent results are produced. For example, if we look at hazard identification and dose response stages in assessing the risks to human health posed by particular chemicals, we find that these can be based: upon controlled tests on human volunteers; on epidemiological studies, which can be descriptive or analytic, and if the latter, either case-control studies focusing on individuals that develop particular illnesses or cohort studies that focus on the health of individuals exposed to particular chemicals; experimental studies of carcinogenic or mutagenic properties; on bioassay experiments on animals (Cutter 1993; Rodericks 1992). In each case there are merits and demerits which may be scientific, practical and ethical.

Then, in addition to specifying how dangerous particular substances are, industry also focuses on exposure assessment, which entails analysis of modes of absorption into the body, of the environmental media by which they may reach it, and the frequencies of exposure. This creates a need to monitor the nature, degree and path of emissions and also to monitor the ambient quality of the environment. It is necessary to relate such emissions to the normal workings of technology and to situations when they are not functioning as expected. These malfunctions may be a normal result of wear and tear, derived from chance events or from design flaws. In all cases even if analysis is prompted in a postfactum manner, satisfactory explanations will only be possible with different forms of modelling — for example event tree and fault tree analyses. These may make it possible to predict the likelihood of certain events occurring by specifying the probabilities of specific component failures, and, indeed, of some combination of these, and then to input these into consequence modelling. But such prediction is of limited value in many modern production processes, which characteristically contain reversible sequences, multifunctional components and subsystems, tight coupling and the geographical proximity of potentially synergistic hazards (Perrow 1984). This is particularly true when they are operated under conditions in which production predominates over safety (see Chapter 6).

Risk characterization involves a number of different numerical formulations of the nature and magnitude of human risk, including individual risk (the fraction of a particular population suffering a particular form of death per unit time); deaths suffered per unit of activity; loss of life expectancy; fatal accident frequency rate (number of fatalities suffered per 100 million person-hours of work at a given activity).

There is a significant potential for disagreement and this often functions as a resource in disputes about the degree of danger posed by chemicals. Critics of industry argue more for bioassay than epidemiological studies. The latter can only be used after people have already been harmed by the use of a substance and often rely on company data that is potentially biased or unreliable, incomplete, and difficult to analyse. The chemical industry tends to favour epidemiological studies and is much more sceptical about bioassay experiments. This is both because of the high doses often used in the latter and because of problems associated with generalising from one species to another (Sapolsky 1993: 89). Moreover, there are more specific problems with the way in which the EPA uses bioassay experiments as the basis for determining the risk of contracting cancer at particular exposure levels. That is, it tends to use the 95th percentile upper bound estimate rather than the statistically most likely relationship.[7]

> EPA's 95th percentile estimate for dioxin is reportedly as much as 5,000 times higher than the expected value estimate, while for perchlorethylene (a dry-cleaning solvent) the difference jumps to 35,000 times ... Because the levels of uncertainty vary from chemical to chemical, upper-bound estimates do not bear the same proportional relationship to expected value estimates, nor are they necessarily close ... Uniformly conservative risk assessments can produce results that would overregulate certain risks or activities and underregulate others.
>
> (Hird 1994: 43)

Contrariwise, if we turn to the question of estimating the risk to life from hazardous waste sites, we find that spokespersons for the American Chemical Manufacturers Association (CMA) consistently estimated that there were fewer sites that were seriously contaminated than did the EPA or other interested parties. Indeed, at a Congressional Hearing in 1983, Dr. Bruce Karrh, general director of medical, safety and fire protection for Du Pont, testified that a CMA study of the relationship of health problems to waste sites, found

> that claims of such relationship run counter to the experience of CMA member companies. Moreover, independent epidemiological surveys have failed to detect significant health problems ... [O]ccupational exposure and health data should provide an indication of the health effects that might be expected if similar exposure patterns were encountered by the public. Since we saw no significant increased incidence of chronic disease among employees in the chemical industry, we concluded that widespread increased incidence of chronic disease among the public is unlikely.
>
> (US Congress, House, 1983: 359, cited in Barnett 1994: 216)

Hird gives his implicit support to the industry view when he writes that in 'perhaps the most comprehensive and careful study of the relative importance of various forms of cancer, Doll and Peto estimated that environmental pollution accounts for approximately 2 per cent of all cancers, while tobacco and diet, the bulk of the problem, cause 30 and 35 percent, respectively' (Hird 1994: 63).

In fact, as Rodericks has pointed out, Doll and Peto's (1981) arguments, based primarily on epidemiological data, are not definitive, but rather are contestable and contested (Rodericks 1992: 118-9). Their figures are based largely on 'a supposedly unaccountable residue of cancers when all the causes of the major-life style cancers are added up' (Doyal et al., 1983: 4). Yet this analysis — this 'evidence' — is to a significant extent an effect of the distribution of research effort and resources, and the politics of scientific argument (Latour 1987). Moreover, their outcomes tend to place blame upon the disadvantaged. And the outcomes of such disputes are frequently explained less by scientific rationalities, more by the relationships between particular scientists and their assumptions and *modus operandi* on the one hand, and the state and corporate capital on the other. Thus lifestyle theories of cancer continue to inform much public policy towards potentially carcinogenic substances in the face of almost overwhelming contradictory evidence, so that public policy, and the analyses upon which it is based, continues to blame victims themselves, victims drawn disproportionately from the most vulnerable and disadvantaged social groups (Tombs 1991).

Research studies undertaken on the relationship between tobacco and diet have often been on a large enough scale to detect relatively small incidences of cancer, and meta-analysis has legitimated the drawing of statistical conclusions which would be illegitimate from a small number of studies. On the other hand, although a typical bioassay experiment to assess the impact of chemicals costs $400,000, this is only sufficient to examine a small number of animal subjects — 20 to 50 of each sex in each of the dose groups. These constraints have contradictory consequences. First, there is a tendency to give high doses of chemicals to produce measurable effects and then to inductively extrapolate to lower doses and lower effects, downplaying the possible existence of thresholds of toxicity. Second, there is a tendency to discount effects that are observed but not statistically significant. Thus, if we suppose that,

> unknown to the toxicologist, a certain dose of a chemical causes a serious toxic effect — damage to certain brain cells — in one out of every 50 exposed subjects. In other words, there is a 2 per cent risk of this form of toxicity occurring at our specified dose. Suppose the same dose is administered to a group of 50 rats, and the examining pathologist sees that one animal develops this particular form of brain damage. He also notes that none of the 50 untreated control animals develops the problem. Is it correct to conclude that the chemical caused this effect? ... [T]here is only a very small chance that the difference between the two groups of animals is actually due to the presence of the chemical in the diets of one of the groups, and its absence in the other. In fact, ... a difference in disease rate of at least 10% (0/50 vs. 5/50) is necessary to achieve ... a *statistically significant* effect. The difference necessary to achieve a statistical significance will be smaller if more animals are used in the test (larger denominator), and larger if fewer animals are used ...
>
> What all this means ... is that the ... 2% excess risk in our experiment — is a real risk, but remains hidden from us ... [T]he numbers of animals assigned to toxicity test groups are largely determined by practical considerations, and the interpretation of test results needs always to consider the limitations imposed by the use of relatively small numbers of animals.
>
> (Rodericks 1992: 70)

Not surprisingly, in an exchange with Peto, Samuel Epstein argued that 'it is necessary to reduce the insensitivity of carcinogenicity tests reflecting a small number of animals tested compared with large human populations at presumptive risk' (Epstein 1981 reproduced in Doyal et al. 1983: 185).[8]

Interestingly, toxicologists, including Rodericks (1992: 65), misidentify the maximum dose at which the chemical produces no observable toxicity as the 'no-observed effect level' when it is more accurately described as the 'no (statistically significant) observed effect level'.

Biases introduced into scientific research because of practical concerns are hardly surprising and not necessarily conscious. They follow from a particular technocratic paradigm, so that, as Sheila Jasanoff argues 'the principles by which we organize the "facts" of risk have to derive, at least in part, from the concerns of risk management' (1993: 37). Moreover, it is important to note that 'in an individualist culture the weak are going to be blamed for what happens to them' (Douglas 1993: 16). A focus on life style as the source of cancer fits this model only too well.

It needs to be emphasised more generally, that in addition to what appear to be essentially internal disputes regarding the range of quantitative techniques which constitute risk analysis, there are a further series of disputes over the subsequent uses to which such data are put. That is, numerical estimates do not simply translate themselves into particular kinds of policy decisions. There are various and competing strategies regarding the ways in which such a 'translation' is effected. Cost-benefit analysis, often favoured by the chemical industry, requires that experts weigh the expected benefits from a technology or activity against the expected costs. The difficulty of determining what should be included and excluded, who benefits and who loses, and, indeed, of gathering relevant data and the problems of assigning prices to often incommensurable consequences, involves:

> a weighing up of the potential costs of a product or process which may constitute a hazard against the benefit which may accrue — perhaps in terms of employment prospects for a geographical area or increased profits for a manufacturer. This 'balancing act' is by no means a simple operation when we are dealing with probabilities rather than certainties and when there is no straightforward way of playing off a possible human death against material gain or a monetary value.
>
> (Irwin et al. 1982: 258)

Indeed assigning a numerical value to the quality of life is not only inappropriate but provides an insuperable problem for such analyses. Attempts, such as those of Leonard and Zeckhauser (1986) to acknowledge that 'some social values will never fit in a cost-benefit framework and will have to be treated as "additional considerations" in coming to a final decision', are necessarily ad hoc and unpersuasive. Similar criticisms can be made against using quantitative risk assessments (favoured by the EPA). Ultimately, the only way such decisions can be made in a manner that recognises this complexity, is to recognize that they are inherently moral and political decisions, and to provide participatory mechanisms to achieve these goals (Wynne 1989). In his discussion of these issues Teuber argues that there is a need to explore how informed consent can be obtained from individuals, how their rights can be secured, including their right to act as autonomous subjects, and the exploration of what conditions must be secured, before we can argue that people are consenting to risks. Workers no more consent to expose themselves to toxic chemicals than do people walking in the park at night consent to being mugged (Teuber 1993: 264; and see below). This, again, reinforces the point that one of the rationales for the emergence of punitive penalties in tort is to suggest that certain kinds of actions and forms of calculation are simply unacceptable.[9] It need also be acknowledged, then, that if tort law is a legal technique that has historically been deployed to ensure some degree of calculability in the event that the risks associated with hazardous technologies are actually realised, then there are real signs of a shift in its more contemporary usage. Even if it may not be an effective deterrent against disregard for human and environmental health and safety, recent settlements under tort law indicate that exposure to some risks on the part of workers and the public by powerful corporate interests are beginning to be defined as socially unacceptable.

Under these circumstances, the deployment of risk analysis to develop safety strategies is necessarily limited. Indeed, the public rhetoric and the estimates presented by risk analysts are frequently pacifying, although sometimes alarmist, and based upon poorly founded claims that scientific methods are the appropriate basis to make decisions about what constitutes socially acceptable risk.

While techniques of risk assessment have been predominantly developed and deployed within the context of a technocratic scientism, these techniques have, more recently, been seized upon by deregulationists, who have urged a more effective regulatory strategy which relies upon market-based solutions and the recognition of self-interest on the part of corporations. Indeed, a critique of the burden of over-regulation was a central argument in the re-emergence of free market political forces in the US in the latter part of the 1970s. Yet as these groups manoeuvred towards formal political power, it was clear, given the nature and weight of counter-discourses around risk, that their arguments for deregulation could not simply be translated, in policy terms, into a complete withdrawal of regulatory oversight and general state abstention from any concern with the private production of hazard and risk. Risk assessment, then, provides a useful weapon for those who would otherwise pose almost moral objections to social regulation of private business by the state; moreover, and unfortunately, as regulatory capacities became undermined once these neoliberal forces assumed hegemony, social liberals also put ever greater faith into such techniques, seeing in these a better-than-nothing alternative in the face of encroaching deregulation. Thus, the use of risk assessment, and other forms of quantitative argument (such as accident and incident statistics), were central to experiments under the Reagan administrations in the removal of OSHA inspections from certain companies. Through the development of risk management programmes, based upon effective techniques of risk assessment, chemicals companies were able to 'demonstrate' — that is, on paper — that they were competent and to be trusted in effective safety and health management. Subsequently, however, a combination of events and phenomena have proven this mode of governance, within which such forms of risk assessment are central, to be an unstable one. The emergence of deregulatory arguments and a neoliberal hegemonic discourse in the US can be explored briefly in relation to one arena of sources of hazards and risk, namely workplaces.

Risk, Safety and the Workplace

Prior to the passage of the Occupational Safety and Health Act in 1970, legislation of conditions endangering the health of workers was the responsibility of individual states and relatively ineffective (Rosner and Markowitz 1989: 95). In the 1960s, Federal legislation had been initially proposed by radical discontented rank and file workers and by activist trade union leaders (Donnelly 1982: 18-19; Szasz 1984: 105), but it was Richard Nixon who eventually (and opportunistically) supported and passed a comparatively weak Occupational Safety and Health Act. The new Occupational Safety and Health Administration was under-resourced, uncritically adopted pre-existing business-generated standards (Stellman and Daum 1973: 9-11), and its inspections and enforcement activities, initially at least, were directed mainly against small businesses (Szasz 1984: 108).

Yet the Act was in many ways informed by a radical liberal discourse; the Act created a general employer duty 'to furnish to each of his employees employment and a place of employment which are free from recognized hazards that are causing or are likely to cause death or serious physical harm to his employees' (Sec. 5a). The OSHAct gave some participative rights to employees, and in legitimating occupational health and safety concerns, provided a mobilising basis for trade unions (Noble 1986). It also granted considerable powers to OSHA inspectors. These, nevertheless, usually failed to secure the imposition of maximum penalties, while many early citations were for easily observable but relatively trivial violations. Furthermore, every observed violation had to be recorded and, less happily, there was an obligation to make a formal finding of guilt. This latter provision removed from the inspector the kind of discretion, and negotiating power, that, *contra* Kagan (1984), is routine in most police work. Moreover, these practices helped provide reasons (and justifications or excuses) for the climate of opposition to OSHA which developed into the vocal deregulatory movement (see Wilson 1985).

Although the deregulationists' arguments did not, at first, affect what happened within the production process, and did not have much influence on OSHA, they were much more significant at the general political level. During the Carter administration, the President himself, Congress and the Supreme Court all acted to constrain OSHA's activities and organised labour lost political and economic power. Reasonable questions about the relative effectiveness of different regulatory strategies were subtly redefined as issues to be resolved through the application of very narrowly construed cost-benefit analyses. As we noted in Chapter 7, when Reagan came to power, the Office of Management and Budget gained effective control over many regulatory agencies. A new unambiguously pro-business Secretary of Labor and a pro-business OSHA director were appointed. The budget, number of inspectors, inspections and follow up inspections were all cut, and worker's rights and inputs curtailed (Calavita 1983: 441-3; Navarro 1983: 523).

It was argued that the OSHAct had little impact on job risk levels. The activities of OSHA were unlikely to change the behaviour of those who own and/or control businesses: first, because it was ineffective in imposing sanctions (Smith 1976: 63-4); second, because it imposed excessively high uniform standards, and demanded a re-engineering of workplaces where employers more rationally used situationally specific standards, and provided less restrictive (and cheaper) personal protection devices.

Drawing on Becker's (1975) human capital concepts, Viscusi, for example, argued that occupational safety and health was best regarded as a marketised good, bought and sold as part of the wage bargain, best regulated by labour and other markets and by the civil courts (Viscusi 1983: 35). Then, in the absence of market rigidities produced by governmental or trade union activities, the forces of supply and demand can determine the level and kinds of risk faced by individual workers, the level of investment in occupational health and safety, and the approaches taken to control hazards. Thus, while some market imperfections of course need to be remedied (Smith 1982: 330-4; Chelius 1977: 63-9), the most socially efficient health and safety standards will be realised when employers find the level of expenditure on safety which is just marginally less than the expenditure incurred by accidents. This latter consists of the cost of damage to property, of training new workers, of increased insurance premiums, of workers' compensation, of litigation and of paying workers increased wages because they know that they are engaging in relatively dangerous work. The most that regulatory agencies can realistically do is to set performance hazard standards or develop injury taxes (Oi 1977). Improving the market mechanisms thereby allows for the dismantling of OSHA and the restoration of the private system that dominated health and safety before 1970, albeit with a somewhat reformed workers' compensation program (Chelius 1977). These ideas were not merely theoretical but informed much agency practice in the 1980s when Viscusi became a consultant for OSHA. It should be clear how contemporary forms of risk assessment could thus be deployed within this general neoliberal discourse, and used to justify some degree of regulatory withdrawal. Companies were best left to determine the nature and levels of risk that they were creating, and it was in their own interests to seek effective management of these.

As has been argued at length elsewhere (Pearce 1994; Noble 1987), this representation of what determines occupational safety and health is deeply flawed. In reality for a neoliberal regulatory regime to work in a socially efficient way: insurance and workers' compensation levels must be high; injury tax tariffs must be significant; courts must be sympathetic to those who are injured, resources must be made available to equalize them and employers in the competition for legal help, and settlements must be substantial; workers need accurate information on occupational injury and illness rates; and for them to be able to demand higher wages it is essential that they have access to accurate information about company affairs. All of these require a combination of substantial legal aid, the coercive power of well funded regulatory agencies and strong trade unions (Pearce 1996) — exactly what neoliberals wish to avoid!

In oligopolistic situations firms have little incentive to worry about market pressure. They can make suppliers, competitors, customers, communities and indeed countries follow their dictates. If this is true of countries, communities and firms, it is, of course, even truer of individual workers negotiating their wages and conditions of work with employers. The market situations of employers and workers are fundamentally different. The former are merely choosing to risk (thanks to limited liability, only some of) their own or somebody else's capital, whereas workers have to routinely risk life, limb and their general health. Individuals may try to obtain adequate wages and safe conditions of work by acting individualistically, for example, by moving to areas where their skills are in short supply. A more collective response to unsafe conditions may be to demand higher wages and compensation for occupationally induced ill health. Although these activities might lead management to offer alternative working arrangements, these would still be limited by management's expertise and subordinated to the goal of maximising profits and growth. Further, these strategies would only be effective if there was realistic access to alternative employment and if there was a labour shortage in the firm's area. But, much of the time, and particularly in many hazardous jobs, there is a chronic oversupply of labor, and this is apt to shape a worker's 'preferences about the tradeoff between safety and wages, ability to choose among jobs, and ability to mount and sustain legal action' (Noble 1986: 213). Indeed, even Viscusi acknowledges that 'workers may have limited job mobility, which will impede their attempt to leave a hazardous job' (Viscusi 1983: footnote 4 for Chapter 5: 182-3). It is for this reason that it is the general standard of workplace safety that is the central issue for workers — that is, whether or not employers as a class are forced to provide safe workplaces — and not merely the safety of workplaces relative to each other (Pearce 1995).

The general level of occupational safety and health is determined by the interests of capital, by its power relative to workers, by the extent to which it dictates state policies, and by the specific ways in which the mode of regulation articulates together market relations, legal instances and regulatory agencies. For example, if we examine workers' actual exposure to toxic chemicals, we find that: information on the dangers of chemicals is rarely even generated or is inadequate; 'safe' exposure levels, if set, are often problematic, as is the monitoring of actual exposure; monitoring of workers' health is undertaken by companies who control the information that they gather. Thus, if a problem is identified, the tendency is not to develop safe working environments; rather, those individuals who are putatively most likely to suffer from exposure are excluded from these particular occupations. This has been a long-deployed strategy within the chemicals industries (Tombs 1991). There is no evidence that workers choose this solution, one based upon the freedom of employers not to contract with certain individuals, rather than keeping their options open by rendering workplaces safe for anyone to work in, the solution preferred by trade unions.

This certainly does not mean, moreover, that individuals are always excluded from occupations dangerous to their health, nor does it mean that those individuals who actually work with dangerous chemicals are not also at risk from them. Many chemicals can also affect men's reproductive capacity, and while more than 100,000 jobs are currently denied women of child bearing age because they entail using risky chemicals, there remain as many as 20 million women's jobs (that is, where industry is dependent on women workers) that equally entail toxic risks (Draper 1991: 71-3). These considerations suggest not some failure of these programmes but rather that both these concepts of marketisation and the strategies of exclusion can be made to function in relation to other strategic goals — viz. against equal rights legislation for women (and also, incidentally, for African-Americans of either gender). In fact, monitoring and screening procedures are not inherently positive or negative from the point of view of workers. Similar procedures using similar technology, when under the control of employees and their unions, can have a worker empowering and life enhancing import (Draper 1991: 138-9).

Reconstructing a Hegemonic Mode of Governance?

It is important to note that while neoliberalism began to become hegemonic through a representational and actual incorporation of a range of social forces, neoliberal forces were also quite explicit in their marginalisation and exclusion of certain social groups from this hegemony (trades unionists, welfare recipients, various ethnic minorities). There is a real sense in which neoliberal hegemony was actually only partial, to the extent that neoliberal forces actually eschewed the construction of consent in favour of dominance over some groups, even if this was often couched in terms of a 'simple' unfettering of the free market. This may well indicate an inherent fragility within this mode of governance — the neoliberal hegemonic project which has been pursued since the latter half of the 1970s in the US has been subject to strong counter-pressures.

The second half of the 1980s witnessed both heightened public opposition to the apparent hubris of science-technology, and where this conjoined with corporate capital, such opposition was being organised around a re-emergence of environmental issues. Two events in particular added a qualitatively new impetus to this opposition, and forced the chemical industry to begin to act in ways which were consistent with its own implicit questionings regarding an almost total prior faith in science-technology. It would, of course, be false to claim that the disasters to be discussed below were alone 'causal' in shifting practices and attitudes towards risk on the part of the chemical industry. Indeed, what is clear is that these need to be placed in the context of the kind of general opposition noted immediately above, so that it is recognised that disasters can potentially be used as opportunities to organise around 'resonances already present in social discourse' (Hadden 1994: 108). Crucial to the realisation of such potential is the absence or presence, and nature of the social forces that might seek to take advantage of these, such forces being most effective where they can attach themselves to existent activities, and where they have some tradition in, or experience of, political action (ibid.).

In 1984 there occurred three major chemicals disasters, at Cubatao (Brazil), Ixhuatapec (Mexico) and Bhopal. Cubatao and Ixhuatapec cannot have been without some reverberations in the US, given their relative proximity, at least in North American perceptions. But Bhopal was clearly the major disaster, not only in the obvious sense of the massive and unprecedented loss of life and chronic illness associated with that gas leak, but also because it raised fundamental questions concerning the operations of one of the largest US-based multinational companies in a host nation; and a host nation, at that, which could hardly be dismissed as backward (even if such a dismissal was precisely one of the post-disaster tactics employed by senior Carbide officials; see Chapter 6).

Following the disaster, the US chemical industry was plunged further into the insurance crisis that was noted above (Smith 1986). Indeed,

> This insurance crisis was already under way before Bhopal but was intensified by the safety crisis Bhopal produced, as well as uncertainty over the full extent of UCC's liability in Bhopal. Before Bhopal, the environmental impact liability insurance market had practically evaporated. The sudden and accidental pollution insurance market had reduced individual companies' coverage from £300 million to £50 million, with even this lower figure unavailable to large chemical companies.
>
> (Jones 1988: 198)

Moreover, the trends in the use of tort law, also referred to above, were crucial in exacerbating this crisis. As Jones again notes, the increasing number and levels of court awards won against chemicals companies is indicated somewhat by the fact that 'the number of multi-million dollar verdicts rose from one in 1961 to 251 in 1982 and 401 in 1984' (ibid.). Further compounding this sense of crisis in the US chemical industry was the near collapse of Union Carbide in the face of a hostile takeover bid following the disaster (Lepkowski 1994).

Thus, for many chemicals corporations in the US, the possibility of a Bhopal-type disaster in an industrialised economy, or in the US itself, was at once real, yet unrepresentable. In public, however, spokespeople of the industry sought to reassure workers and publics in classic technocratic fashion, claiming that 'it couldn't happen here', that US plants were technologically superior and, in frequent and often quite explicit resorts to racism, operated by well qualified Americans rather than backward Indians.

As we have seen, the Bhopal disaster was followed by a highly publicised incident at UCC's Institute plant, and Bhopal provided the context in which

Institute would be received. Yet in many respects it seems that it was the latter that provided the final impetus for many chemicals corporations to calculate that it was in their own economic interests to develop more effective systems of safety and health protection. The particular inadequacies of probabilistic techniques such as risk assessment to deal effectively with low probability/high consequence situations, such as Bhopal or Chernobyl, was implicitly accepted, as many operators of major or high hazard sites shifted their risk management strategies to encompass a recognition of worst case scenarios. Thus, in 1987 Baram could write that there were clear signs of a trend amongst the operators of hazardous facilities from what he calls a 'rudimentary' form of engineering risk analysis (Baram 1987: 427), to an approach wherein risk is viewed as 'an ongoing operational problem involving full consideration of personnel turnover, training, human factors, and other aspects of its capability for ongoing control' (ibid.: 432).

It is interesting that although these shifts have occurred in practice, they tend not to be explicitly recognised in public rhetoric on the part of the industry. The reason is clear. For these are neither formal nor procedural shifts. The increasing use of worst case scenarios is a recognition that a cataclysmic event such as Bhopal can occur, a likelihood that was effectively denied by previous forms of statistical calculations of risk which posited its probability as one in so many million years.[10] The move towards a more encompassing approach to risk management entails attention to managerial and organisational systems; and in this is the possibility of a recognition of the need to transcend technocratic forms of management and accept some participation from a range of 'outside' groups in effective risk management — namely, workers, local communities, and other potentially counter-hegemonic groups. If these changes have not been made explicit, their one most tangible effect has been the development of emergency procedures in the form of evacuation plans, ongoing 'risk education', and various other forms of contingency planning (Jones 1988). When one places these shifts in practice alongside other chemical industry initiatives during the same period, such as 'Responsible Care' and claims towards greater disclosure of information, then these changes are best viewed as both preemptive and as attempts to regain legitimacy. That is, taking these together, there is evidence here of a real threat to the chemical industry, of possibly punitive forms of 'social' regulation being forced upon local and national states, and of an attempt to reconstruct a new hegemonic discourse in the context of overwhelming threats to the previous one.

Importantly, partly through reluctant recognition of their own limitations, partly through new legal requirements regarding Rights-to-Know and Hazard Communication, and partly through the need to involve workers and local communities in emergency procedures (which has its origins in both law and the demands of insurers), this new form of governance is partially constructed in a way that is inclusive of (some) formerly 'outside' groups. Thus, crucial ground is ceded in a reluctant recognition (however implicitly) that previous reliance upon both scientific-technological capacities and rationalities was an inadequate and, to some extent, a duplicitous, one. And with this more or less public recognition, there emerges a space within which workers, local communities, and other counter-hegemonic groups can contest the ways in which risks are defined and managed. The exploitation of this space is facilitated by the techniques (such as Rights-to-Know, worker and community involvement in risk management, health monitoring and biological surveillance) which have been developed within the mode of governance itself. That is, the emerging mode of governance is one that is open to contestation and struggle, the outcomes of which are far from settled.

Conclusion

In this chapter, we have considered the management and regulation of risks and hazards associated with the US chemical industry, and have attempted to characterise these in terms of hegemonic modes of governance. Such a consideration is important since it allows an appreciation of the limits of the possible in terms of the regulation and management of such risks, both historically, and in the present. Moreover, it indicates the significance of competing and allied social groups in defining, contesting, and exploiting those limits. While arguing that there have been clear shifts in the hegemonic modes of discourse, these shifts have involved a range of social groups and forces, some of which have been counter-hegemonic, some of which have been integral to various members of the power block. Thus, industrialists, science-technologists, regulators, insurers, lawyers, workers, local communities, and various national activist groups have struggled over contested and changing ideological and material terrain, sometimes consciously but at other times not, sometimes preemptively but at other times clearly reactively, and from positions of varying strengths and weaknesses — these strengths and weaknesses determined by conditions which may or may not have been amenable to control.

For us, it is clearly the case that the contemporary regulation of major hazards associated with the production, use, storage, distribution and the disposal of the by-products of the chemical industry is infinitely better than it was thirty years ago. It is equally clear, however, that these responses to hazardous production on the part of the chemical industry have not been primarily motivated by any new humanitarianism but, rather, represent pragmatic responses to various pressures. Indeed, we have argued that recent responses by chemicals companies, and by local and national states to a combination of almost unprecedented pressures, involving a recognition of the limitations of scientific rationality, have entailed a serious challenge to neoliberal hegemony.

While the arguments of this chapter require further development, they nevertheless provide important insights into the nature of hegemony in the context of the US. Most importantly, it is clear that there are complex relationships between the hegemonic ideologies and the ways in which the power bloc actually operates. For example, whilst maintaining a representation of all citizens as of equal value, and emphasising meritocratic and individualistic factors as determinants of individual fates, marginalised groups have, and continue to be, either rendered invisible and/or subjected to disproportionate levels of risk; indeed, there is a real sense in which some social groups have never been included within any hegemonic order. However, as particular moments have revealed the extent to which large numbers of the US population find themselves included within marginalised groups, distrust in the ability or willingness of the state to attend to the social welfare (here discussed in relation to risk) of a majority of citizens has developed, so that there has developed, and is reinforced, a popular cynicism. This is clearly illustrated through even a schematic overview of popular responses and opposition to industrial activities which are recognised as entailing high levels of risk. Such cynicism makes the sustaining of hegemony highly problematic. Indeed, there must now be a real question as to whether or not there has been a shift within the US social order from hegemony, with its emphasis on an 'ethico-political' leadership and 'organised concerns' to what Gramsci called 'supremacy', where a power block rules based upon domination over a fragmented population (Gramsci 1971: 276).

Further theoretical implications follow from the analysis presented in this chapter. The recent work of Ulrich Beck, as well as that of Rose, Miller and others, while not referred to in any detail in this chapter, provide obvious theoretical backcloths against which some of our arguments might be considered.

A key virtue of Ulrich Beck's work is, as we have indicated, his highlighting of qualitative discontinuities between a modernist industrialisation and a reflexively modernist risk society, and between the ways in which these are regulated. Nonetheless, the preceding analysis also suggests that Beck has over-stated his case. New ways in which risks might be regulated are certainly essential; but to some extent, as we have indicated, these have been realised. Moreover, the struggles towards their realisation have made use of, and have been furthered by, the existence of some traditional forms of regulation. As we argue in this text, regulatory techniques based upon deterrence and punitive sanctioning strategies are crucial, so that these are necessary, though not sufficient, conditions of more effective forms of regulation of hazardous production. While we have considered shifts in regulatory strategy here, these need to be considered alongside these more traditional techniques, which in our view remain no more or less suitable than was previously the case.

Further, we argued in Chapter 3 that law, its meanings, its actual effects, are never wholly pre-determined, but are subject to contestation. More generally, then, this chapter has indicated that while particular techniques of governance — such as tort law, risk assessment, biological monitoring — may not be neutral, neither are their possibilities exhausted by their historical uses. Thus, simply because certain techniques have historically been used to distribute certain costs and benefits in particular ways does not mean that their possibilities are thereby exhausted, and that they cannot be redefined in order to redistribute such risks and benefits. Risk assessment or tort law, for example, are open to deployment for different ends. These ends are not, of course, 'open' in any infinite nor uncontested fashion. Again, as we have indicated, the historical uses of such techniques is only to be understood within the context of a more general hegemonic mode of governance, which itself is a constant site of lesser or greater struggle, resistance and counter-hegemonic pressures. In this we are perhaps closer to O'Malley (1992) than to Miller and Rose (Miller and Rose 1990; Rose and Miller 1992; Rose 1993).

We follow Beck's argument concerning the challenges that science and scientific institutions face in an age that he characterises as 'reflexive modernity'. Nonetheless, this chapter also indicates that the institutional power of science-technology grants it an enormous adaptability and durability, to the extent that it has historically reconfigured and reconstituted its internal discourses, as well as its relationships with the state and corporate capital, so that even in what Beck calls a 'Risk Society' there is no reason to underestimate its power. Where we find ourselves in opposition to Beck's thesis, is in his idealist understanding of scientific rationality (which, therefore, leads him into idealist prescriptions for effective opposition). As Rustin has observed recently, absent from Beck's analysis 'is the concept of capital itself' (Rustin 1994: 11), so that his critique becomes directed towards 'techno-scientific rationality', not to the institutional power of capital, as if he thinks that it is the mode of scientific thinking itself rather than its sponsoring corporate agencies which is the decisive agent of change.

(ibid.: 9)

More generally, if the concept of risk is to be treated not simply as one aspect of contemporary social life, but as a central or defining characteristic of a reflexively modern social order (see, for example, Beck 1992a; Beck et al. 1994), then it seems to us that this concept is treated within such literature in an overly abstracted sense. While it is important to theorise about risk, the nature of a risk society, shifts in the governance of risk, and so on, these questions/considerations need to be rooted within, and indeed developed, via a consideration of specific risks in concrete circumstances. A focus upon risks generated by or within particular workplaces is one way in which over abstraction could be avoided. A focus upon the material and concrete manifestations of risk may serve to counter an implicit idealism within such work.

Relatedly, we see that common to the work of Beck on the one hand, and theorists such as Rose and Miller on the other, is a virtual absence of any recognition of class relations in a Marxist (or, indeed, any other) sense. Even if men and women who, in the context of this chapter, are engaged in struggles against toxic capital, do not define this as a class struggle, this does not detract from the fact that such struggles are precisely that. That is, they are struggles to a large extent framed by the ownership and non-ownership of the means of (toxic) production. Further, they are struggles in which the state and law are deeply imbricated and implicated, are certainly not class-neutral arbiters, but nonetheless are also sites of struggle within which counter-hegemonic groups can win gains.

Finally, it remains for us to take issue with one popular 'truism', one which Beck himself represents, but which happens, in fact, to be only partially true. It seems to us clearly to be the case that the unifying power of issues around toxic capital, especially where these are posed in terms of environmental degradation or protection, is partly explained by the fact that the risks associated with the chemical industry constitute a threat to all, and ultimately to the eco-system upon which we all depend. Yet to accept this is not to accept that all are affected equally. The distribution of hazards and risks is not only a differential one, but it is one which is organised around traditional cleavages of class, ethnicity and gender. And that fact makes some very 'modernist' forms of analysis necessary in understanding the nature of contemporary modes of chemicals production, their regulation, how this might be improved, and how we might identify the key agents in forcing any such improvements. It is to these tasks that we now turn in our final chapter.

Notes

1. The distinction between 'social' and 'economic' regulation demonstrates a basic confusion about what is meant by 'economic' for a community. While it is often used to refer to what is profitable for a particular enterprise, this obscures the fact that economics 'is concerned with the efficient use of resources, and the criterion for whether an activity is "economic" must therefore take into account all costs and benefits whether they rise internally or externally' (Donaldson and Farquar 1988: 141).

2. None of this is to claim that the discussion of changing modes of governance in the context of the US can be simply translated into a UK context. But it is to claim that there is an empirical similarity between the two contexts, such as to make the theoretical argument developed here through reference to that empirical detail useful in considering the possibility and progress of regulatory reform in both national contexts.

3. Barnett grounds his analysis within a structural Marxism. A similar approach has been used by McNamee (1987) to discuss the relation between the American state and the chemical industry and by Horwitz (1986, 1989) to make sense of the general deregulation movement in the US.

4. These discourses are quite similar to, but were constructed quite independently from, what Dake and Wildavsky identify as the three dominant 'cultural biases' in the US, namely 'hierarchy, individualism, and egalitarianism' (Dake and Wildavsky 1993: 47). Although these authors write as if cultural and political factors are in a competitive relationship, their own data suggests that they are rather in a complementary relationship with each other.

5. With some reason. In Superfund settlements, very large industrial corporations are estimated to face transaction costs, equal to about 21 per cent of their total settlement costs and insurance companies 88 per cent (of $410 million of $470 million in 1989) (Acton and Dixon 1992).

6. This interpretation has some merit, and provides interesting independent support for Foucault's arguments concerning the growing importance of normativising disciplinary practices, and for the arguments of Castel (1991), Defert (1991), Ericson (1993), Ewald (1991) and O'Malley (1989, 1991, 1992) concerning the changing role of risk and security in contemporary societies. There is also

considerable overlap in their conception of 'legitimate' legal practices. Compare (Priest 1993: 211) and (Foucault 1979a: 17). For negative critiques see (Rose 1984; Hirst 1986), and for more appreciative critical reformulations, see (Palmer and Pearce 1983; Hunt 1993).

7. The expected value is the 50th percentile estimate of risk, where the researcher is just as likely to overstate as understate the true risks. The 95th percentile upper bound suggests that only a 5 per cent chance exists that the risk is greater than that the risk is overstated.

8. For recent assessments of these issues see Roff (1995); Proctor (1995).

9. One example is the crude calculations undertaken within Ford Motor Company during the development of the Pinto. When it was released in 1970, Ford executives knew that it was likely to explode from a rear-end collision. They calculated that appropriate safety measures would cost $135 million, but that prospective lawsuits would be unlikely to top $50 million. Five hundred to nine hundred people lost their lives and thousands of others suffered debilitating and painful burn injuries. They were never successfully prosecuted for their actions (Dowie 1979; Cullen et al. 1987).

10. We should note that when nuclear reactors were first developed the Atomic Energy Commission required substantial 'exclusion distances' around the reactors it built from which the public was banned: 'The larger the reactor, the greater the required separation between it and any neighboring populations' (Ford 1982: 43). In other words, their initial siting practices were premised on a *worst case scenario logic*. When, however, the Eisenhower administration pushed for the rapid development of atomic energy and, for ideological reasons, insisted that it should be undertaken by private companies, it allowed for significant changes in the *modus operandi* of the nuclear industry. First, to reduce the costs of electricity transmission, utilities were allowed to site plants near to population centres on the dubious and unsubstantiated assumption that there would be ongoing 'adequate technical improvements, and the accumulation of satisfactory experience' (United States Atomic Energy Commission Report on the Need for Nuclear Power, 1962, reprinted in Cantelon et al. 1991: 318). Second, after the 1957 Wash-740 study had shown that a reactor accident might cause 34 hundred deaths, 43 thousand injuries and seven billion dollars in property damage, Congress passed the 1957 Price-Anderson Act which provided a fund of $560 million, $500 million from the AEC and $60 million from private insurance companies, and which exempted the government or the nuclear industry from any further liability (Ford 1982: 45). Taken together, these changes made it possible for utilities to site their reactors near to population centres without worrying whether or not they were endangering the public and made it seem rational that

they developed various quantitative techniques of risk analysis which were then used to legitimate their practices (see generally Handford 1997).

9 Conclusion: Regulating Toxic Capitalism

Introduction

This seems an appropriate point, at the outset of our concluding chapter, to recall some of the key points of the analysis and arguments developed thus far.

In the first three chapters we examined neoliberal versions of contemporary capitalist economies, and the nature and role of corporations within these. Such versions were shown to be both conceptually incoherent and inadequate, and inaccurate as representations of society, state and economy — representations more akin to visions of, rather than any actually existing real, social order. In this latter respect, neoliberalism is to be understood in terms of a struggle for hegemony; while neoliberal descriptions and prescriptions have no doubt become somewhat hegemonic, with real, and global, effects, this hegemony is never closed, never complete, never entirely secure; it is always open to contestation. We then proceeded to examine the nature of corporate crime, through reference to the structure, functions and activities of capitalist corporations. In this way, we argued that understanding corporate crime requires a transcendence of criminology through the development of a political economy of capitalism and key social actors within capitalist economies.

In the following three chapters, we set out to examine various aspects of threats to human and environmental well-being, particularly health and safety, posed by the chemicals industries. Focusing in particular upon occupational safety, we began by engaging in an extensive critique of common representations of the causes of occupational accidents, arguing that these could not be adequately understood as the effect of operator error. In the course of this critique, we presented more accurate evidence on the nature of industrial accidents, and we have sought to more explicitly theorize their causation. Here, we introduced a distinction between first and second order causes, arguing that the corporate production of death and injury needed to be understood within a theoretical framework informed by Marxism and some of the arguments of Foucault. Further, we argued that injuries and deaths are more accurately viewed as safety crimes, rather than through the language of the 'accident', an

280

ideological and socially constructed term which has a series of significant, practical effects. The arguments regarding the corporate production of risk — and the need for much of its production to be viewed in terms of corporate crime — was further developed through a discussion of empirical material gleaned from case-studies of six large multinational chemical companies operating in the UK economy. This consisted of an examination of the organisation of these corporations, the extent to which these organisational structures might be termed criminogenic, and a consideration of whether discernible changes in organisational structures within these corporations, coupled with shifts in the nature of their operations, are more or less likely to produce corporate crimes. Finally, we interrogated the disaster at Bhopal as an instance of a series of actions/inactions on the part of a large, multinational actor in the chemical economy, and the problems that this disaster posed in both legal and sociological attempts to assess criminality and liability. We analysed the nature of possibly illegal and indeed criminal actions and inactions that led to the disaster, and addressed some of the legal complexities and, ultimately, failures of the attempt to effectively hold legally accountable, a multinational corporation operating in a less developed nation-state.

We began the final three chapters of the text by reviewing, and providing a critique of, dominant current academic and political debates concerning the most appropriate form of external regulation of corporate legal and illegal activities in order to prevent, as well as more successfully prosecute, corporate crime. Particular attention was paid to two dominant discourses in this sphere, namely, neoliberal and social liberal arguments (the latter through the work of the Compliance or Oxford School). We argued that, in different ways, these two schools of thought, and the practices which they undoubtedly inform, are ideological, and that they conflate current predominant forms of regulation with 'feasible' forms of regulation. We then turned to a more detailed examination of recent developments in the regulation of risks to human and environmental health and safety in the chemicals industries, focusing in particular on the US chemical industry. Here, we argued that various forms of regulation are best understood as techniques of governance, themselves explicable in the context of hegemonic struggle. This chapter further demonstrated the extent to which regulation needs to be viewed within a more general political economy, as a crucial aspect of state-economy-society relations; moreover, in this context, it was further argued that regulation is never simply the result of some 'programmer's dream', and that actual regulation is both an outcome of conflict and compromise, and always open to contestation.

This final chapter continues to address the nature and possibilities of regulatory reform. We note a number of trends towards the criminalisation of safety crimes in both the UK and the US, and document the crucial role in these and other trends played by a range of popular pro-regulatory forces engaged in activities of resistance, which take law as one, but not their sole, focus. We argue further that a more punitive regulatory approach must be combined with other regulatory techniques, many of which are currently in existence in various nation-states and regions, and a changed prosecutorial policy. In particular, we argue for an overall regulatory strategy which is based upon the principles of deterrence and rehabilitation, developing an understanding of regulation that is both facilitative and positive rather than merely limiting and negative, as it has historically been viewed.

Regulating Capital

In this section, we discuss the regulation of crimes against human and environmental health and safety; some of the arguments proposed here are of more general relevance for the effective regulation and sanctioning of corporate crimes in general. However, to emphasise a point we have intimated throughout: while it makes sense to delineate a form of illegality which we have referred to as corporate crime, such crime cannot always be treated usefully as if it were homogeneous in its nature and effects. This is certainly the case when considering forms of regulation (Snider 1991). Thus, some varieties of corporate crime have undoubtedly been hoisted onto social, political and legal agendas, notably 'economic' crimes such as 'insider trading' or pensions fraud. We should not be surprised that it is these kinds of corporate illegalities that have been subject to criminalisation.

Economic illegalities, certainly those within and between corporations, may be inimical to the 'effective' functioning of, and also maintenance of legitimacy for, contemporary capitalism (Pearce 1976). It is hardly a coincidence that the past decade has seen a mushrooming of both academic and governmental concern with 'economic' crimes in North America and Western Europe, in particular the UK. It was during this period when financial markets were liberalised both domestically and internationally — when it also became clear that liberalisation required new forms of regulation. Also during this period, various nation-states proceeded with programmes of privatisation and deregulation, often linked to claims regarding popular capitalism; and thus the fortunes of international financial markets were represented as of some significance for general populations (see Chapter 2). This latter fact meant that the emergence of financial crimes (albeit often represented as 'scandals') such as the Savings and Loan crimes, the collapse of BCCI, the fall of Boesky and other prominent Wall Street traders, and the subsequent exposure of illegal share dealings by senior managers at Guinness, required state responses if the probity and legitimacy of financial markets were to be protected. It is certainly no coincidence that recent years have witnessed considerable, and ongoing, upheaval in the structure and *modus operandi* of the relevant regulatory bodies on both sides of the Atlantic (Calavita and Pontell 1995; Levi 1995; *Financial Times*, 21 May 1997). More generally, then, while these responses have been represented as being designed to protect the investments of *all* sections of the population — as house or share owners, pension or insurance contributors — there is no doubt that they also helped to provide a more 'predictable and controlled business environment' for financial corporations (Szasz 1984: 114). Of further interest for us, however, is that although none of these reforms have been unequivocally successful, while some are too recent to allow us to make a judgement, the fact that they have had some impact does support the argument that more effective regulation of corporate activity, and the prevention, detection and sanctioning of corporate crime is feasible. It is no surprise that research from North America should claim that the regulation of economic crimes is likely to be more successful than the enforcement of so-called 'social' regulation (Snider 1991).

Indeed, the very distinction between economic and social regulation is an interesting ideological mechanism whereby certain forms of regulation are accorded greater legitimacy than others. Moreover, it is, of course, the case that even within social regulation, there are differences between the nature and efficacy of regulatory strategies — as we have noted (Chapter 5), environmental degradation and environmental crimes have received far greater priority in both North America and the UK in the past decade or so, although the record of regulatory enforcement hardly points towards any unequivocally positive judgement (Barnett 1995; Edwards et al. 1996; National Institute of Justice 1993). The record of protecting workers' health and safety is an even poorer one (Noble 1995; Pearce 1995; Tombs 1995a, 1995b; Tucker 1995), despite some real improvements, not least those reforms aimed at more effective regulation of chemicals industries. However, what is frequently referred to as social regulation — such as the regulation of occupational safety and environmental protection — is likely to be *relatively* ineffective since it may impinge upon 'the most minute details of production', rendering such regulation fundamentally 'antagonistic to the logic of firms within a capitalist economy' (Szasz 1984: 114; and see Snider 1991). Nevertheless, it is also undoubtedly the case that effective safety regulation *can* be functional for capital, albeit under certain conditions, for certain companies, over limited periods of time (Tombs 1989).

This latter point can be illustrated through reference to the complexities of regulating occupational safety. As we have indicated, the relationships between state regulation of human and environmental health and safety, and the interests both of capital generally and of individual corporations, are complex; such regulation may be both antithetical to capitalist logic yet also promote improved safety performance, itself potentially functional for capital. This is one reason why neither environmental and safety crimes, nor indeed accidents, can be understood simply in terms of a safety-profits dichotomy. Four points are worth making explicit here, since these bear upon these complex relationships, and remain of general relevance throughout this concluding chapter.

First, if more effective regulation of occupational safety is in the interests of some corporations, it remains the case many companies either fail to understand the costs of accidents, or do not act upon such understandings (HSE 1993). Corporations may strive towards, but do not always manage to act as, rational entities always capable of engaging in accurate forms of calculation; somewhat differently, even where they engage in accurate forms of rational calculation, they may not be able to act successfully upon such calculation. More generally, as we have noted throughout this text: corporations do not always act as unified rational entities (Pearce and Tombs 1993; Reed 1992; Silverman 1970); there exist tensions and conflicts within and between various levels of management, these conflicts both reflecting and generating tensions between organisational 'goals' (Kreisberg 1976; Mintzberg 1979; Teulings 1986); decision-making tends to be characterised by bounded rationality, whereby 'deadlines, limited participation and the number of problems under consideration' lead to decisions based upon limited information (Vaughan 1996: 37; Simon 1976); and managements fail to act strategically in a variety of business areas (Marchington and Parker 1990; Miller 1987; Purcell 1989).

Second, and relatedly, the benefits of more effective safety regulation may not be recognised by many corporations precisely because of their inability to see safety as anything other than an avoidable cost (such short-termism being particularly characteristic of British companies). That is, individual companies may not perceive longer-term economic benefits from improved levels of occupational safety, nor consider benefits for capital as a whole.

Third, and as documented by Marx in Volume I of Capital, individual employers are likely to resist the development of safety regulation on the grounds that it creates unequal conditions of competition; and it is still claimed by many larger, more visible corporations that while they are likely to have to meet such regulations, other, often smaller enterprises, are less likely to comply given their relative invisibility to regulators (National Institute of Justice

1993: 7-10). Thus, representatives of (usually larger) corporations might be seen as calling for 'equality of restraint on the exploitation of labour' (Marx [1867] 1976: 621). These claims are lent greater force where competition is truly international, with corporations subject to regulation in the 'industrialised' world able to point to weaker regulatory systems, and thus lower costs of production, in other, usually 'industrialising', economies. Consequently, where regulations are formulated and implemented, some corporations have an objective interest in their systematic and effective enforcement; for example, Carson cites petitions by employers before the 1833 Commission, the Report of which was vital to the establishment of the Factory Inspectorate, that regulations pertaining to working hours be effectively enforced (Carson 1974). Thus, what is important here is the ability of regulators to enforce in a way that any company complying has some certainty that others *not* complying will face sanctions (Levi 1987). This also suggests that effective forms of deterrence constitute a condition of existence for law-abiding behaviour on the part of corporations: that is, the existence of a likelihood of detection and credible sanctions following successful prosecution makes it possible for corporations to obey the law.

Fourth, and finally, both for individual corporations as well as for capital as a whole, more effective forms of 'social' regulation raise a real contradiction between the twin exigencies of capitalist production, namely, the need to accumulate capital and the need to manage (and thereby maintain control over) labour processes. As occupational safety has come to be recognised as less about technical and more about organisational factors, there has emerged a growing recognition amongst regulators and on the part of some corporations that safety management requires some form of ongoing role for workers, both individually and through their collective organisation. This intervention can range from the ability of individuals to raise warning signals which are taken seriously by managements, to the rights of workers' groups to negotiate changes in plant, technology or work organisation. For corporations to act upon the recognition that safety cannot effectively be managed by 'managers' alone, is in the interests of profitability if the negative economic effects of accidents and incidents are avoided; yet in this very recognition, managements also create a possible threat to their own rights to manage (Tombs 1989). This helps to explain the claim that demands for improved levels of safety are 'subversive' (Navarro 1991: 54), the logical extension of which are arguments for workplace democratisation (Tucker 1992b).

Such complexities of safety regulation for managements, and for capital in general, indicate the need to avoid any naive functionalism, and to recognise the potential significance of gains that workers and their allies might win on the basis of 'agency, struggle and resistance' (Snider 1991). There are clearly objective and subjective differences in 'interests' between corporations of different sizes, operating in different countries or markets, in different sectors, and so on. That is, we cannot consider capital or the corporate sector as simply homogeneous. This is clearly a central aspect of the argument developed in this text, namely that the state and regulatory agencies often act as hegemonic apparatuses. Finally, they sensitise us to the need to view the state's actions or inactions in this sphere in a way that transcends a narrow instrumentalism.

Nevertheless, notwithstanding these points, we also agree with Snider that it remains *generally* the case that,

> states will do as little as possible to enforce health and safety laws. They will pass them only when forced to do so by public crises or union agitation, strengthen them reluctantly, weaken them whenever possible, and enforce them in a manner calculated not to seriously impede profitability
>
> (Snider 1991: 220).

That is, all things being equal — and as the above points indicate, all things are often not equal — the preference of capital is for less rather than more regulation.

Regulating Capital: The Politics of Criminalisation

Recent experience in the UK lends weight to Snider's claims, while her own analysis is developed on the basis of recent trends in the US and Canada. Since Snider has provided an excellent analysis of these trends in the context of North America, and since we have paid some attention to these in previous chapters (particularly, in detail, in Chapter 8), we shall confine ourselves here largely to a consideration of such trends within the UK.

The UK has witnessed a series of regressive measures in relation to occupational safety regulation, yet certain factors allow some optimism. Due in no small part to 'public crises' and 'union agitation', there exist opportunities for securing improved protection from harmful corporate activities. This section examines recent and continuing developments in the regulation of occupational safety in the UK, and argues that law is an important site of struggle for safer workplaces.

Indeed 'public crises' and 'agitation' have clearly had effects in recent years in the US and the UK; that is, notwithstanding significant deregulatory pressures in these polities, there is some evidence of moves towards the criminalisation of social regulation, notably in terms of occupational safety and environmental degradation.

In the UK, for example, we have noted how the late 1980s' arguments for the prosecution of 'corporate manslaughter' began to be strongly articulated. Probably more important as a catalyst here than a half decade of rising injury rates were a series of highly publicised disasters and subsequent inquiries and reports that occurred so frequently in UK in the latter half of the 1980s (see Harrison 1992; Slapper 1993; Wells 1993). Slapper has recently provided a useful catalogue of these:

> Zeebrugge, where 193 died in March 1987 ... the Kings Cross fire, 31 deaths in November 1987; the Piper Alpha oil rig fire, 167 deaths in July 1988; the Clapham train crash, 35 deaths in December 1988; the Purley train crash, 5 deaths in March 1989; and the sinking of the Marchioness, 51 deaths in August 1989.
>
> (Slapper 1993: 424; see also Harrison 1992; Wells 1993)

In each case, evidence and official enquiries inculpated the relevant companies as significant contributors to the cause of death (Slapper 1993: 424). Importantly, most of the above events led to the loss of lives of those other than workers. They helped to 'impress' upon the public consciousness that occupational accidents did not have their effects confined within 'the factory fence'; public and worker safety became linked, and were politicised. Their cumulative effect was to raise the profile of the *public* harm that economic activities caused, often seemingly needlessly, demonstrating that corporations act irresponsibly, sometimes illegally, this at a time when environmental issues also had their highest political profile in the UK (McGrew 1993). Moreover, Conservative governments were implicated in many of the above disasters — whether generally, through attacks upon the consequences of their promotion of the enterprise culture, or specifically because some occurred in sectors which they were responsible for funding — notably public transport — or in which their interests were manifestly imbricated — for example, the extraction of North Sea oil.

It was in this context, most notably around the Zeebrugge disaster, that the charge of corporate manslaughter received its most public airing. Some of the legal complexities in pursuing the charge of corporate manslaughter have been discussed in an earlier chapter, and elsewhere (Bergman 1991; Moran 1992; Pearce 1993; Slapper 1993; Wells 1993). That this charge has now been successfully pursued (see below), must be seen as a result of struggle, rather than any simple, teleological unfolding of progressive opportunity that remained implicit within law (see Tombs 1995b).

Thus, at the end of 1994 there occurred what may prove to be a landmark event, namely, the first ever successful conviction for corporate manslaughter in English legal history, against OLL Ltd. The managing director of an activity centre was given a custodial sentence following the death of four teenagers in a canoeing accident. Certainly, the case was emotive as it involved young people away from their homes, seeking to 'have fun' in the 'charge' of others; crucially, it also involved a small company, where the identification of an individual with the controlling mind of the corporation is relatively easy; and there was also extremely clear evidence that the managing director had knowledge of the risks that led to the deaths (Slapper 1994). This combination of factors makes the case slightly unusual; it certainly has symbolic significance, though its effect upon the number of future prosecutions for corporate manslaughter 'can only be properly judged in time' (ibid.: 1735). One further successful prosecution of corporate manslaughter has followed the OLL judgement. This latter case, against Jackson Transport (Ossett) Ltd., was perhaps significant in that it followed the death of a *worker*, and centred around failings in supervision, training and protective equipment. On the other hand, it again involved a small company; Jackson Transport employs just 40 people (*The Safety and Health Practitioner*, December 1996: 3).

It is important to recognise that the revival of the issue of corporate manslaughter in the UK in recent years is largely a consequence of political action by a range of groups including trades unions, 'Hazards' groups, and victims groups (such as the Herald Families Association and Disaster Action). The disasters acted as a catalyst for new groupings and new demands, and provided a larger and perhaps more receptive political audience for more longstanding activists and activities. Many of those involved in struggles following these disasters were already active in relation to occupational safety, organising around other 'mundane' sites of employee death and injury, perhaps most notably in the construction industry. The construction industry is significant, for while organised labour has historically been in the forefront of struggles around occupational safety in the UK, this industry is one in which rates of unionisation are low, and employment is fragmented and fragile — that pressure has been applied upon employers here attests to the potential efficacy of resistance by social groupings beyond, but including, trades unions (here, mobilised through the Construction Safety Campaign). Thus, disasters need to be used as opportunities to organise around '*resonances already present in social discourse*' (Hadden 1994: 108; see also Sarangi 1996: 106-7).

The substantive outcomes of these struggles are of course important in their own right. But more generally, they also indicate that while predominant ideological representations of what constitutes 'real' crime are powerful, they can be challenged and changed (Pearce and Tombs 1990, 1991). Indeed, even the emerging use of linguistic terms such as 'safety crimes' and 'corporate manslaughter' is significant, given the social power of language (Wells 1993).[1]

Alongside the above developments, there has also emerged the language of criminalisation in relation to the sanction most commonly currently employed following prosecution of safety offences, namely, monetary fines. Now, there is no doubt that fines in both the UK and the US remain pathetically small. Even some unprecedentedly large fines remain completely unexceptional taken in the context of the annual turnover and profits of the companies involved (Bergman 1994: 96; Slapper 1993: 430). In the UK, it is interesting that in the period prior to the passage of the Criminal Justice Act 1991, it was decided by a Government committed to ostensibly neoliberal principles that the unit fine system — subsequently introduced (then quickly abandoned) for individual offenders under s. 18 of the 1991 Act — was not appropriate for informing monetary penalties levied against companies (Slapper 1992: 1038). This both reflected, yet further reinforced, the ideological distinction between 'regulatory' and 'real' crimes. Relatedly, it is of further significance that in both contexts there have been explicit calls for deterrent levels of fines, even if these have gone unheeded (HSC 1990; *Employment Gazette*, January 1991: 4; *Employment Gazette*, July 1991: 373). These latter points raise an interesting contradiction: for according to the logic of neoliberalism, within which health and safety are to be guaranteed through markets, not least a market-based legal framework, deterrent fines would be perfectly rational. Yet as Etzioni has documented, the attempts of the US Sentencing Commission on Corporate Crime to develop a scale of monetary penalties employing neoclassical economic rationale resulted in the proposing of 'astronomical' fines and the provoking of massive, and ultimately successful, opposition from the corporate sector (Etzioni 1993). In this episode, what Etzioni calls 'neo-classical fantasises' are lain bare (Etzioni 1993: 152-4). Once again, it is clear that neoliberal discourse contains contradictions, and is employed selectively by corporations and their representatives; these contradictions, and selective deployment of argument, each stand as aspects of neoliberalism to be exposed and exploited.

Other points emerged from these signs of criminalisation for corporate offenders which are of particular interest.

First, given the reluctance to link fines to 'ability to pay' (be this in terms of corporate assets, sales, turnover, or some measure of profitability), then increased levels of fines may, as in the development of charges of manslaughter in the UK, noted above, work to the relative interests of larger corporations as opposed to smaller firms. Indeed, as Geis and DiMento have noted, this is common to many forms of contemporary sanction:

> larger businesses often have viewed criminal sanctions as useful: they have the resources to meet enforcement demands and the internal strength and legal expertise to protect themselves against the consequences of failure to do so, except in egregious instances ... Criminal sanctions then will most likely fall on their smaller competitors, placating the public and advancing the interests of the industrial giants.
>
> (Geis and Di Mento 1995: 84)

Second, exceptional fines against a few individual employers constitutes no challenge to capital as a class, and again may actually strengthen its legitimacy through the symbolic effects of apparently class-neutral law and its enforcement. At the same time, however, some of these legal developments may pose a threat to capital should they become generalised or widespread. The prosecutions of OLL Ltd. and Jackson Transport in the UK, for example, may prove significant as legal precedents if they signal a new, generalised vulnerability of corporate entities to successful prosecution for manslaughter.

Third, the pronouncements of senior regulators which accompanied these changes constitute interesting endorsements of deterrence theory, indeed a discourse of deterrence which clearly links individual offenders with a potentially offending group or class of offenders.

There have been perhaps more significant shifts towards criminalisation in the US. Earlier, we noted the prosecutions of Ford Motor Company and Film Recovery Systems. The most important developments, however, have occurred at local levels. For example, while Federal OSHA recommended just 19 cases for prosecution between 1981-1988, CAL/OSHA recommended 292 during this same period, almost 40 per cent proving successful (Brill 1992: 67); moreover, these have involved large as well as small companies (Reiner and Chatten-Brown 1989). Now, Californian OSHA regulation does transcend federal legislation in certain respects, but the key difference is an approach to enforcement, particularly in the context of workplace deaths, one notable aspect being an agreement with police chiefs in LA county that requires all workplace fatalities to be investigated as potential homicides by police forces. Here, then, is a recognition that deaths at work may result from crime, rather than a simple attribution of workplace fatalities as accidents — it is in many ways a minor shift, but it is a precondition for effective regulation (Bergman 1994).

Some analogous developments can be found with respect to environmental regulation in the US. For example, while amendments to the Resource Conservation and Recovery Act (RCRA) 1976 — namely, the Hazardous and Solid Waste Amendments (HSWA) 1984 — increased criminal sanctions, its main impetus was to spur new enforcement programmes at state level (for example, in Pennsylvania, Maryland and New York). Thus, it is at local levels that attempts to more effectively criminalise and prosecute environmental offenders are developing, notwithstanding considerable obstacles (National Institute of Justice 1993).

Some 'caveats' should be entered. For example, none of the above points imply an evolution towards the criminalisation, and more effective and punitive prosecution, of safety violations. It remains important not to underestimate the individualistic nature of bourgeois law which makes it difficult to establish legal liability or responsibility of corporations (Sargent 1990), especially those which are large and complex. And this individualism inherent in legal systems is explicitly exploited by corporations:

> Corporations will fight vigorously attempts to deny them any due process protections that are available to individuals. Yet the law of individualism can never be effective against the crimes of collectivities ... Unless we can accept corporate crime as a conceptually separate problem from traditional crime, the powerful will continue to ensure that 'collectivist might' prevails in courts of law. This will be achieved by appeal to 'the very traditions of justice for which individualism stands'.
> (Braithwaite and Geis 1982: 311-14; see also Geis and DiMento 1995).

Thus, for example, the shift from the prosecution of OLL Ltd for corporate manslaughter to the successful prosecution of a large multinational would be a qualitative rather than simply quantitative one. However, lest we prove complacent concerning some ineluctable trend towards more effective legal treatment of safety crimes, we should be aware that legal developments that appear progressive can be turned on their head (see Harrison 1992; James 1993). However, to recognise that legal reforms which apparently constrain capital can be turned against labour should not be taken as an argument for refraining from struggles for such reforms. This recognition is, however, a reminder, if it is needed, that legal reform is not an end in itself; that our contemporary legal systems are not of (class-) neutral institutions; that it is vital not to underestimate the versatility of capital and its allies, not least those in the legal profession (Mann 1985); and that gains won within capitalist structures have contingent conditions of existence. It is also important not to underestimate the extent and power of more general obstacles that such attempts at criminalisation still face (see Bergman 1991, 1994). Nevertheless, the preceding observations do emphasise that relationships between criminalisation, the criminal law, and health and safety offences are far from static or immutable: this text has sought to demonstrate that while predominant ideological representations of what constitutes real crime are powerful, they can be challenged and changed. Moreover, that these changes have occurred in highly unfavourable economic and political contexts indicates that hegemony is never secure. Thus, while economic and political factors constrain, they do not determine the nature and extent of agency, struggle, and resistance (Snider 1991). If the law is an object of such struggle, it may also serve as a element within it.

Regulating Capital: The Politics of Deterrence and Rehabilitation

There are, then, in both the UK and the US some nascent signs of the criminalisation of safety offences. Criminalisation reflects, for us, one of three key principles upon which more effective regulation must be organised. Criminalisation represents punitiveness. It is significant in its own right, since a more punitive approach to corporate crime, inegalitarian in its effects, represents a shift towards greater social justice. Yet it is also of significance in a slightly different sense. For a punitive response to corporate crime helps to break down the ideological distinction between 'real' and 'regulatory' crime (a distinction upon which so much rests, as we have argued throughout). In particular, it breaks into the (powerful) tautology that real crimes are those for which there is a punitive response, so that regulatory crime is not real crime since it does not provoke a punitive response.

However, criminalisation is not an end in itself, and for us needs to be related to two further principles underlying a more effective regulatory strategy, namely, deterrence and rehabilitation. We shall approach these issues by asking how criminalisation might play a role in making workplaces and local communities safer in particular, and preventing corporate crime in general.

Let us clarify further what we mean by the term 'criminalisation' here. For us, this refers to three, intimately related, but not synonymous, phenomena. First, the adoption by regulatory agencies of a more punitive-oriented approach to enforcement, so that regulators act more like some form of 'police force' for industry (a regulatory approach discussed at length in Chapter 7). While such a shift in regulatory strategy is hardly likely in either the UK or US at present, there are pressures which might force at least a more interventionist regulatory approach; these were considered in Chapter 7, and will also be addressed below. Second, the term criminalisation here implies that sanctions, where these are invoked, involve a deterrent element. We have seen claims — perhaps symbolic — by senior regulators in the UK regarding the need for deterrent level of fines; but even these beg the question of the extent to which deterrence might actually *work*. Third, that criminal prosecution must be included in the range of sanctions. Let us take the second issue first.

It has long been accepted by most criminologists that deterrence fails when aimed at individual 'street' offenders. However, some have argued that corporate illegality offers a sphere in which deterrence is much more likely to be effective. This is clearly the implication of Sutherland's characterisation of the corporation as coming 'closer to economic man and to pure reason than any person or any other organisation' (Sutherland 1983: 236-8), a view of the corporation which, as we have argued, we find persuasive in as much as it represents that which corporations are capable of, and strive towards, even if they do not always achieve this level of rationality and calculability. It is these very features of the corporation which render it potentially liable to deterrence-based sanctions (Croall 1992: 147).

However, the applicability of deterrence theory in the context of corporate crime has been contested by others, certainly by those who do not cast the corporation as a rational, calculating entity. For example, we have noted (in Chapter 7) that some have argued that deterrence and more punitive modes of enforcement are neither desirable nor feasible. Yet, on this specific point of deterrence, even within such work there are recognitions both that most firms try to get away with violations of safety law (Hawkins 1990: 450), and that the vast majority of firms comply with regulations only if they believe that those transgressing regulations will be detected and sanctioned (Bardach and Kagan 1982: 65-6). A number of points can be made regarding these latter, much more significant concerns, vis-à-vis deterrent sanctions. Braithwaite et al. have argued that at least for certain kinds of economic actors, the use of deterrence is an effective means of achieving compliance (Braithwaite et al. 1993; Braithwaite and Makkai 1994). Indeed, Braithwaite and Geis have argued that 'the discredited doctrines of crime control by public disgrace, deterrence, incapacitation, and rehabilitation can be successfully applied to corporations' (Braithwaite and Geis 1982: 293). This general proposition is itself based upon the arguments that 'corporate crime is a conceptually different phenomenon from traditional crime' (Braithwaite and Geis 1982: 294). Thus, corporate criminals may be 'among the most deterrable types of offenders ... they do not have a commitment to crime as a way of life, and their offences are instrumental rather than expressive' (ibid.: 302-3). Indeed, in relative terms they 'usually have a good deal more than their fair share of the world's goodies, and they will be reluctant to risk losing what they have' (Geis 1996: 258).

We agree that deterrence is fundamentally flawed both as a practical strategy, and indeed at a conceptual level, when directed at 'street' or 'traditional' crime, a view commonly expressed within criminology, and which finds its most thorough and eloquent expression in the work of Mathiesen (1990). However, deterrence has a rather different potential with respect to corporate crime. There are four aspects to this rather different potential, which we present in relation to Mathiesen's cogent rejection of the principle and practice of deterrence.

First, occupational or environmental safety crimes tend not to be one-off acts of commission, but are actually ongoing states or conditions — for example, chronic exposures due to faulty plant, an absence of legally required guards or other forms of protective hardware, a failure to provide information or training, unsafe systems of work, and so on. For example, of a total of 2476 violations recorded by OSHA against US chemicals companies in 1995, the majority related to 'inadequate emergency response plans, inadequate employee training, lack of proper labelling or permits, and improper maintenance of equipment or materials' (*The Safety and Health Practitioner*, November 1996: 15). All of these are easily detectable. Moreover, once the fact of a crime has been established, then, certainly in the case of occupational safety — and to some degree in environmental and occupational health crimes — the identification of the criminal (that is, the corporation) is straightforward — not the problematic exercise as is the case with street crime. Detection and 'clearup' rates are therefore very different issues in the context of (many) corporate as opposed to street crimes. What Mathiesen (1990: 54-7) refers to as the '*low detection risk*' of crime (and see also the claim made by Braithwaite and Geis 1982: 294-6) — one of the factors which in his analysis renders general prevention (deterrence) unworkable — does not usually apply in this context.

Thus, it is important to note that we are arguing here about safety and environmental crimes, although we should also note that not all these are readily detected. Mathiesen refers to 'modern economic crime' (1990: 68, 71-2) as being difficult to detect and deter. What is also crucially pointed to here is that for those crimes which are ongoing states — the majority of safety, health and environmental crimes, certainly — then *detection is dependent upon a proactive inspectorial strategy*. Of further significance is that once a corporate crime has been detected then, rather differently to the case of many traditional crimes, 'apprehending a suspect ... is almost always easy with corporate crime' (Braithwaite and Geis 1982: 296-7).

Second, then, the requirement for a proactive inspectorial and regulatory strategy raises the issue of enforcement resources. Certainly, as in all social activities, there is a minimal level of resource required to make regulation effective, as opposed to merely gestural or symbolic (Pearce 1996). More specifically, adequate resources are required to maintain routine, or preventive, visits, and to prepare prosecutions.[2] We are thus led to a (familiar) demand for greater (here, regulatory) resources in the name of crime control. Again, however, it is worth distinguishing the contexts of corporate and street crimes. Since many corporate crimes do not pose the same problems of detection as street crimes, then greater regulatory resources *would* increase detection (Levi 1987: 281-4; Croall 1992: 154-6); this is quite distinct from the relatively marginal effect of increased resources for policing on levels of many kinds of traditional crime. In the context of safety, health and environmental crimes, significant increases in funding for relevant regulatory agencies are unlikely to emerge in any voluntary fashion upon dominant political agendas in the UK or US — yet the emergence of what Sutherland called 'organised public resentment' can have effects in this respect, even in highly unfavourable climates. Witness the increased resources for the Health and Safety Executive for the UK under the third Thatcher government (Tombs 1995b), or the renewed funding for the US Environmental Protection Agency in its Superfund enforcement under the Bush administration (Barnett 1994).

Third, a further objection raised by Mathiesen to the principle of general deterrence — namely that the 'message' of deterrence is not communicated to those who need to receive it (Mathiesen 1990: 58-69) — is also largely inapplicable in the context of safety, health and environmental crimes. Certainly, the symbolic effects of punitive sanctions against highly visible corporate offenders is one that should not be too easily dismissed. Moreover, those who own and control corporations know all too well what is required of them in law and of any likely developments in law and regulation; they strive to play formal — as well as informal and covert — roles in the development of such law, and in influencing its interpretation. And they are well aware of changes in enforcement or sanctioning practices on the part of HSE, OSHA, EPA, and so on, and of regulatory campaigns into particular sectors or types of injury, of large fines, or of trends towards custodial sentences, or other forms of sanction which are meant to include a deterrent element. Regulators — not least due to the urges of central governments — place the task of communicating with businesses high on their agendas. In these key respects, the communication mechanisms which Mathiesen argues do not work for traditional offenders are well developed in the context of relationships between corporations and regulators.

Fourth, in the context of corporate crime, deterrent forms of sentencing should not serve to exacerbate social inequality, as seems to be the case for traditional crimes (Mathiesen 1990: 72, 97, and passim). Indeed, studies of corporate crime almost routinely indicate how, and to what extent, this phenomenon results in massive economic, social and physical costs which are disproportionately borne by the weakest and most vulnerable members of society; thus any more effective regulation and prevention of such crime is likely to be more rather than less egalitarian in its consequences. Indeed, given these costs and effects, equal justice demands a punitive response to corporate crime (Geis 1996: 247 and passim).

Taken in combination, the above points indicate that deterrence as a principle informing enforcement activity and the sanctioning of corporate crime has considerable potential. Yet in contrast with the treatment of traditional crime, deterrence has rarely been used, nor its effects studied, in the context of regulating corporate crime. Notwithstanding this fact, there is evidence of its practical efficacy, not least in the context of health and safety regulation (Morgan 1983; Health and Safety Executive 1985c; Pearce and Tombs 1990, 1997; Tombs 1995b). Moreover, recent years have seen regulators themselves explicitly recognising the significance of deterrence. And of further interest is the fact that some corporations have urged the operationalisation of this principle as central to their demands for the equalisation of the conditions of competition (see National Institute of Justice 1993: 10; Tombs 1995b). Thus, contrary to the claims of neoliberals and advocates of deregulation, the opposition of corporate representatives to all kinds of regulation need not be based only upon principle, but also on perceptions of practical effects. What is important is the ability of regulators to enforce in a way that any company complying has some certainty that others *not* complying will face sanctions (Levi, Margaret 1987). This meets concerns of equity on the part of corporate representatives, but also ensures that they do not see compliance as implying a loss of competitive advantage (National Institute of Justice 1993: 7-10).[3]

What we are proposing, then, is not simply that deterrent sanctions represent a rational, just and effective response to corporate crime; but that effective forms of deterrence constitute a condition of existence for law-abiding behaviour on the part of organisations or corporations: that is, the existence of a likelihood of detection and credible sanctions following successful prosecution makes it possible for corporations to obey the law. This is consistent with our conceptualisation of corporations as amoral calculators. It is also consistent with the empirical evidence of the concerns of corporate capital over competitive advantage. Further, it is consistent with empirical work on the internal dynamics of corporate crime, which almost always identifies the existence of socially responsible individuals or groups within and around corporations, typically drawn from compliance or safety officers, engineers, middle or lower-level managers, workers, or local publics.[4] Deterrence can help to empower such individuals and groups, through creating conditions where their voices receive a hearing in the interests of the corporation as a whole. In a sense, then, deterrent law has the same characteristics that we would ascribe to law in general, namely, that it is facilitative and productive as well as being constraining and negative.

Notwithstanding these previous points, it is clear in any case that it would neither be feasible nor desirable to rely *solely* on the principle of deterrence as the basis of any sanctioning strategy. There are some contexts, for example, where deterrence would prove ineffective simply because sometimes corporations fail to act as the rational systems of control that they represent themselves to be (Tombs 1994), although this partly needs to be understood as a consequence of organisational priorities. Two points seem clear. First, that any effective regulatory strategy must include a range of regulatory tools and techniques — and there are many examples of effective regulatory mechanisms. Second, that some principle of deterrence should form part of any regulatory strategy, even if this principle is not inherent in each particular mechanism of which that strategy is comprised.

Now, it is not an aim of this chapter nor this book to consider in detail regulatory techniques *per se* (but see Pearce 1990; Pearce and Tombs 1994). Rather, we seek here to set out the principles upon which a regulatory strategy should be based. Crucial here, however, and indeed throughout this text, is that once existing constraints on forms of regulation are recognised not as necessary but as related to contingent, though obdurate, material and ideological factors, then the appropriateness of a range of regulatory techniques can then be given serious consideration.

John Braithwaite, working with various colleagues, has been particularly active in considering the range of regulatory forms, both in isolation, and as part of an overall regulatory strategy (see, particularly, Ayres and Braithwaite 1992; Fisse and Braithwaite 1993). Arguing that deterrence is not effective in all contexts, Braithwaite and colleagues have urged the use of a 'pyramid' of enforcement action and sanctions, where non-compliance results in regulators progressively shifting from one level of sanction up to a more punitive level (Ayres and Braithwaite 1992). Essentially, Braithwaite has argued that compliance is more likely where regulators have at their disposal a range of credible enforcement techniques which allow an escalation in severity of sanctions in response to uncooperativeness on the part of the regulated. There is much within Braithwaite's arguments for an enforcement pyramid with which we are in agreement. Certainly it is crucial that any sanctions that are formally at the disposal of regulators be credible ones — that is, that it should be accepted that such sanctions may be, and are, used in the face of non-compliance. Secondly, and (from the point of view of general deterrence) crucially, we concur with Braithwaite's exigence that it is important 'to transcend models of regulation as games played with single firms' (Ayres and Braithwaite 1992: 39). Third, as the argument developed in this text indicates, we also find that many corporations do make *explicit* calculations regarding the costs and benefits of compliance/non-compliance. Thus, while regulators are dealing with rational, calculating corporations, then

> the greater the heights of punitiveness to which an agency can escalate, the greater its capacity to push regulation down to the cooperative base of the pyramid.
>
> (ibid.: 40)

Thus, for these authors, and for ourselves, a deterrent, potentially punitive regulatory strategy can be cost-effective in that 'the bigger the sticks, the less they [the regulators] have to use them' (ibid: 40-41).

Thus, there are some complementarities between our general argument, and Braithwaite's claims for the efficacy of what he terms a pyramid of regulatory enforcement. However, we depart from his analysis in several respects.

One issue relates to the speed with which such escalation will or should occur. This is not a minor point, since without a commitment to a real, and rapid, escalation of enforcement tactics as part of an overall strategy, then there is a real likelihood that the regulatory pyramid will start to resemble the most lax form of compliance strategy. Indeed, we have shown previously, in the context of a debate with one of the key proponents of a compliance oriented approach, that while an argument for a punitive enforcement strategy does not entail that each and every violation is detected (a caricature often constructed of a punitive enforcement position), what is at issue is that the use of formal sanctions should begin much earlier in the regulatory process than is presently the case, and it is the present *modus operandi* of regulators that proponents of compliance strategies defend and validate. Thus, factory inspectors, for example, might begin with issuing improvement notices on the detecting of a violation, before issuing prohibition notices if the former are not met in the timescale agreed. Further, as we have argued (Pearce and Tombs 1990, 1991), a point that Hawkins seems to have missed (Hawkins 1990: 461), inspectors would exercise discretion. But this should not be discretion to revise timescales previously imposed upon recalcitrant corporations, nor to engage in protracted bargaining over compliance, whilst risks, hazards or crimes remain in place.[5]

Second, we depart significantly from Braithwaite and his colleagues in their argument that the first stage within their regulatory pyramid should be to allow corporations to self-regulate, and that only upon failing in this will escalation within the pyramid be triggered. *There is simply no evidence to support claims to the abilities or willingness of corporations to self-regulate.* As we have indicated throughout this text, and most particularly in our discussion of the organisational and structural production of safety crimes in Chapters 4 and 5, and in our discussion of the Bhopal case in Chapter 6, the vast weight of empirical and theoretical evidence points to the conclusion that lesser rather than greater external scrutiny tends to be accompanied by lesser rather than greater degrees of compliance and standards of conduct on the part of corporations (see also Pearce and Tombs 1990; Tombs 1990b, 1992).

Finally, then, we believe that arguments for self-regulation in a hostile economic and political climate are likely to be expropriated, by dominant economic and political forces, and used in ways that differ markedly from the intentions of those who had originally espoused them. Indeed, it is instructive that these arguments for an enforcement pyramid, the first stage of which is self-regulation, are predicated upon the assumption that sufficient external resources are unlikely to be devoted to corporate crime control (Braithwaite and Fisse 1987: 221). In other words, there is an implicit acceptance here that such an approach is not the best, but is pragmatically successful. This seems somewhat antithetical to some of Braithwaite's (albeit earlier) arguments for the feasibility of deterrence strategies. Most significantly, however, it offers a hostage to political fortune. For self-regulation in a hostile political climate — one where regulation itself is consistently cast as meddlesome, burdensome, bureaucratic, indeed illegitimate (Tombs 1996) — is likely to become deregulation, that is, a freedom from any form of external regulation or oversight. The evidence for this slippage is clear in the recent history of both the US and UK. Aside from this empirical evidence, a theoretical account of the nature and role of corporations points to the significance of corporate power, a power with effects in terms of influence over interpretations and actions by regulators, and a power which recent state formations in the US and the UK have done nothing to seek to counteract.

We have already accepted, however, that deterrence will not be effective in all instances. Yet even in its inefficacy in achieving its explicit goal, it still provides a challenge for corporations; it calls the corporate bluff (Pearce 1995). And to challenge or to expose corporate rhetoric in this way is a key element of hegemonic struggle, exposing contradiction within dominant representations of how corporations operate and what they are. Thus corporations frequently fail to act as successfully calculating, rational entities, certainly in particular areas of activity, notwithstanding that this very disorganisation is a product of organisation itself (Tombs 1992). But the fact that corporations do not always function as the rational systems of control that they represent themselves to be, the fact that in these instances deterrence would prove inadequate, is not a reason to abandon arguments for and strategies of deterrence: indeed it actually strengthens the potential of such argument and strategy. For at the very least deterrence poses an ideological, and subsequent material, challenge to corporations, corporate executives, and the owners of corporations. This can be posed quite simply. Corporate executives usually portray their corporations as rational systems that can be controlled effectively, and indeed this is crucial to demands by corporations that they be left to self-regulate. If such claims are to be taken at face value, deterrence should be effective, as employers would rationally respond, making utilitarian calculations regarding the certainty of detection and the likelihood and nature of punishment. On the other hand, if corporations are not the rational systems of control that their representatives would have us believe, then the failure of deterrence only further legitimates the need for intervention and the external imposition of 'rationality' — that is, organisation in a way that secures compliance, needs to be taken out of the hands of 'managers' alone. Thus insofar as they fail to respond 'rationally' to deterrent strategies, corporations prove themselves inadequately organised to maintain compliance with external regulations. This then opens up the possibilities for other regulatory strategies, including those which have been characterised previously as 'interventionist'. As Celia Wells has noted:

> Not many people argue these days that rehabilitation is an effective goal for the criminal justice system. But in dealing with corporations it may have more relevance than has proved possible for individuals.
>
> (Wells 1988)

Interventionist strategies represent, in essence, attempts to operationalise the principle of rehabilitation. That is, they are attempts to reorder, reconstruct or reconfigure a corporation's structure, functions, activities; in this respect, corporations are much more prone to rehabilitation than are individual offenders. Although the means towards, and the potential efficacy of, rehabilitation is often subject to question in the case of individual human beings, rehabilitating the corporation itself is a different matter (Braithwaite and Geis 1982: 309).

Lofquist (1993) has recently considered the innovatory potential of corporate probation, precisely as a form of 'rehabilitative and interventionist sanction' (Lofquist 1993: 161-3). Interestingly, he notes how such a sanction is particularly useful when applied to corporations which represent themselves in relation to Kreisberg's 'organisational process model':

> Organisations are viewed as complex, differentiated entities, simultaneously in pursuit of different and often conflicting goals ... In this view, supported by increasing empirical evidence, organisational crime is rooted in structural characteristics of the organisation. Crime control is most effectively exercised by altering organisational structures and procedures in a manner designed to improve internal accountability and coordination of goals and activities.
>
> (Lofquist 1993: 165)

We agree completely with Lofquist's arguments about the legitimacy of interventionist strategies. Yet such strategies do not represent any validation of the claim that corporations are not rational actors, as he argues (Lofquist 1993). Rather, we see an interventionist and rehabilitative strategy as a means of challenging corporate representations of their structure and functioning, challenging their motivated and selective claims to internal irrationality. Thus, *contra* Lofquist, the use of interventionist strategies is not an alternative to what he calls the 'punitive, adversarial approach' (Lofquist 1993: 165), but is best as an element of such an approach.

Now, if we turn to the UK, it is undoubtedly the case that the EU has become highly significant as a source of potentially progressive and protective safety, health and environmental legislation in the UK in recent years (HSC 1991: 19; McEldowney and McEldowney 1996), and that this is more interventionist and prescriptive than the legislation that has typically emerged in the UK, the latter typically being overly flexible and reflecting a more laissez-faire approach to the regulation of hazards. Thus, it is unsurprising that many British companies, with the support of the British government and regulators, have resisted the development of interventionist forms of regulation which have originated in EC directives (James 1993; Tombs 1995b, 1996). In a sense, then, the opposition of employers to the introduction of interventionist regulation is a testimony to its potential significance. It is certainly testimony to an unwillingness to open up aspects of (here, safety and health) management to detailed external oversight. In this respect, the resistance of employers to such regulation is analogous to the only aspect of the HASAWAct that UK employers keenly opposed in the mid 1970s — namely, the development of workplace rights for safety representatives to information, to inspect, to form safety committees, and so on.

This opposition emerged despite the fact that any potential efficacy of such regulation in the UK remains limited by the lack of any specific right-to-know (RTK) legislation, or any general Freedom of Information legislation. By contrast, the latter has long existed in the US, while the former, namely RTK legislation, has mushroomed following Bhopal, then Institute in the US (Lewis and Henkels 1996; Foveux 1986; McCurdy 1986). While recognising that access to information is a key to empowerment, but does not in itself constitute empowerment (and indeed can actually prove a hindrance), Hadden has described the potential of citizen participation in hazard prevention through involvement in decision-making in local plants (Hadden 1994; see also Lewis and Henkels 1996). Examples of such participation, drawn from the US, also indicate that local communities, once they have won a level of involvement in plant organisation, tend to develop more radical demands, both at local level and beyond, through alliances with other pro-regulatory forces. That is, such activity leads to demands for ever greater involvement in actual management of plants; this could extend to decisions not simply over how production occurs, under what conditions, and so on, but to what gets produced; in each of these senses, it may be transformative, prefiguring democratic forms of planning on a societal scale. As we have argued in previous chapters, capitalist corporations function on the basis of the disempowerment of the views of a range of stakeholders. And we have also argued that this disempowerment is a condition of their existence rather than an epiphenomenon. Thus, any generalised attack upon the hierarchical and exclusive nature of corporate organisation and control is an attack upon the capitalist corporate form itself.

It is also possible to see this form of activity, to the extent that it occurs on a generalised scale, as one element towards what Adaman and Devine have called 'participatory planning'. Production organised according to this principle would enable 'tacit knowledge to be articulated and economic life to be consciously controlled and coordinated in a context that dispenses with coercion, whether by state or market forces' (Adaman and Devine 1997: 75). There is no doubt that workers and communities have particular knowledges of the minutiae of production on a local scale which within contemporary, dominant forms of economic production are marginalised and excluded. This is indicative of a capacity at a social level which corporate capitalism both jealously guards for its own representatives and denies to others. Yet, as we have seen, there is an inherent irrationality in capitalist forms of decision-making, even in their own terms. Thus, the claim that 'only entrepreneurs making decisions about the use of private capital have both access to tacit

knowledge and the incentive needed for action leading to its discovery'
(Adaman and Devine 1997: 75) is undermined:

> The participatory planning approach claims that people in general have access to
> tacit knowledge and that they can discover and articulate this knowledge
> provided that they are equipped with the capacity to analyse and evaluate the
> consequences of their decision.
>
> (ibid.)[6]

This integral role for people in general might also be developed in the
context of licensing systems, a further current form of regulation which has an
interventionist element and potential. There is no doubt that at present these are
often used formalistically, but this need not always be the case, and in
potentially opening up the minutiae of compliance and more general hazard and
risk management to external bodies, they are of enormous potential
significance. Thus, thoroughgoing forms of intervention have been introduced
in some US states, in the form of licensing arrangements for hazardous facilities
(Deieso et al. 1988: 444). Moreover, the use of licensing also greatly augments
the power of formal regulatory bodies, and thus represents a regulatory tool of
more general significance. Given the plethora of licensing schemes currently in
operation, not least focused specifically at the chemicals industries, this
indicates again that the difficulty is not devising regulatory techniques through
which corporations might, in principle, be more effectively controlled, but
rather how to develop these in practice. For example, licensing becomes
feasible once it is accepted that corporations should be forced to bear costs of
production that they have historically externalised. Equally, where corporations
show themselves, despite their rhetoric, to be incapable of responding to
deterrence, then they are opened up to external intervention — this is the
rationale behind the types of schemes for corporate probation proposed by the
US Sentencing Commission on corporate crime, the actual fate of which
remains to be determined (Lofquist 1993).

Finally, in terms of developments which might legitimate interventionist
strategies, it is worth noting the emergence in both the US and the UK of
debates around corporate governance. Now, such debates are closely related to
claims around social responsibility and business ethics, claims which we have
noted are tactical at worst, or internally flawed at best. Thus, debates around
corporate governance are based upon a recognition of (some aspects) of the
socially damaging effects of unbridled corporate activities. It is worth noting,
however, that there are two extreme poles within which the debates around
corporate governance take place. At one extreme one finds a series of attempts

to urge corporations to act more ethically, more responsibly, as a more effective citizen, and so on. In short, they reflect many of the claims that capitalist corporations can and will simply decide to moderate their profit-seeking tendencies. They are based upon contradiction, and are doomed to failure. At the opposite extreme are arguments which seek to reform the structure and functioning of corporations. In this form, arguments for more effective corporate governance are arguments for greater corporate accountability and democracy, arguments based upon the classic capitalist problems of the separations of principal-agent, and of ownership and control — problems which, as we have indicated, the contemporary corporate form seeks to address but does not resolve. In fact, they are arguments for capitalist corporations to function as (neoliberal) capitalist rhetoric claims — at the behest of the wishes of shareholders. But these debates express the concern that shareholder wishes should somehow be met, and these should not be confined to those of the dominant, most powerful institutional investors.

These latter demands are those which are typically resisted most keenly by corporate representatives. They recognise that to accept certain claims for shareholder democracy and corporate accountability — to act upon their own rhetoric — is to open up the organisation and management of the corporation in ways that hierarchical, capitalist corporations must resist. Controversy surrounding Shell UK's recent Annual General Meeting illustrates what is at stake here. A resolution proposed — which included a demand for external audits of environmental and human rights performance — and supported by a small group of institutional shareholders was defeated at the AGM; this followed the opposition of the Group's chairman, who argued that such provisions would 'interfere with directors' responsibilities' (*Guardian*, 16 May 1997), a concern echoed by the Chairman of the Institute of Directors, Melville-Ross, who wondered out loud 'where such proposals', if acceded to, 'might end' (*Today*, Radio Four, 14 May 1997). Corporate representatives recognise exactly what is at stake in these latter debates; they are questions about who legitimately controls the corporation. This also indicates that even reformist aspects of proposals for greater corporate governance are likely to be opposed. Yet such reforms are now on corporate and political agendas. Of course, any reforms won through such initiatives are strictly capitalistic, are certainly precarious, and cannot be ends in themselves. Given the inherently destructive features of capitalist markets, and of the social divisions of labour upon which capitalist markets are constructed, then even radical demands around corporate governance are likely to be highly reformist. This criticism extends even to the most progressive of these arguments which advocate extensive employee share ownership, subsidised by the state, thereby extending rights of 'control' to large groups of employees (Gamble and Kelly 1996). Nevertheless, at least such arguments raise the issue of ownership alongside that of control — and it is clear that without an attack on private ownership, then gains made on the issue of control remain vulnerable to reverse (this much was, of course, illustrated in the failures of Swedish social democracy; see Chapter 2). Yet even arguments about control, framed around corporate governance, have potentially important effects. They do raise important tensions which corporate capitalism cannot resolve, so that such forms of corporate governance offer two possibly complementary possibilities. First, they expose contradictions within neoliberal rhetoric that capitalist firms can operate in the interests of the majority of shareholders. Second, they raise the issue of corporate accountability and democracy — and these are issues which cannot be resolved within capitalist forms of the corporation.

Certainly, interventionist forms of regulation have the general potential to force companies to adopt different business strategies, and the particular possibility of forcing them to internalise legitimate costs of production. In this latter respect, if this internalisation of costs is pursued, this will help to alter popular understandings of the successes of capitalism (such as those referred to in Chapter 1), by contrast raising to greater prominence the costs of such 'successes' (see Chapter 2). That is, effective forms of regulation expose some of the present contradictions within a system of production that allows enormously wealthy private actors to generate benefits while socialising much of the costs of their activity. To the extent that regulation forces the costs of production back onto corporations, then it exposes how unsustainable present modes of economic organisation are; thus, effective regulation may be prefigurative. This is clearly the case even if some aspects of the regulatory strategy do, as we have indicated, rely on private or market-based approaches. As we discussed in Chapter 8, both developments within tort law and the activity of some insurers have forced more progressive forms of regulation of chemicals companies. This is not to argue that tort and private insurance are unequivocally progressive. But as we also demonstrated in that chapter, we need to recognise that the potential in such developments is not exhausted by their design.

Regulation, Democratisation and Socialisation

These considerations on the regulatory principles of punitiveness, deterrence and rehabilitation lead us to a general, and crucial point. Effective regulation is never a question of punitive versus compliance-oriented regulatory approaches, nor based upon deterrence in any simplistic fashion, nor one which relies solely and simply on rehabilitation. Moreover, we would argue that effective regulation does not require us to think in terms of a strict dichotomy between state or market mechanisms. While we would argue that a chemical industry that was forced to internalise its full costs of production could only be possible through massive state subsidies, in effect an argument for a national or social ownership and control, it is clear that such proposals are far from the political agendas of any major political party in either the UK or US. Thus, the present conjuncture requires more effective regulatory strategies which combine state (national and local) regulatory techniques with private, or market-based, approaches (Paehlke 1995).

If more progressive regulatory reform is feasible, as we have indicated here, and argued in detail elsewhere (Pearce and Tombs 1990, 1991), it must also be clear that legal regulation can only be a means rather than an end. Yet even where regulators fail adequately to enforce, the very existence of such law can be utilised in both a material and ideological fashion since it provides both 'leverage' and a 'moral legitimacy' for pro-regulatory forces (Snider 1991: 221). Thus, the pressure upon the regulators created by the existence of regulations is real, and open to exploitation by those who would see the levels of protection for employees at work raised. Moreover, it is publicly proclaimed that safety legislation is formulated to protect workers (Brill 1992), certainly in the UK and US, and in this sense it is unequal law which formally guarantees unequal rights. Unequal law can help redress the balance of power between capital and labour; such law, if developed and enforced, helps undermine the rights of capital and is thereby radical, even prefigurative, by nature (Woodiwiss 1990a).

This is a specific instance of the potency of the discourse of collective rights, which should not be underestimated (Woodiwiss 1990a); it is quite possible to seek reforms without descending into reformism (Gorz 1980). On the other hand, it is important to guard against mere reformism. Rights politics — the right to a safe and healthy working environment, to clean air, water, land — can not be an end in themselves, since to seek such rights as ends is to leave them always precarious.

As we have argued consistently in this text, however, effective prevention and sanctioning of corporate crime, whether safety crimes or other forms of such crimes, means that we must move beyond criminology and considerations of crime and the criminal justice system. We need to consider a more general political economy of regulation.

As we have indicated here, and in previous chapters, both Snider and Mahon have highlighted the need to examine regulation, and regulatory reform, in terms of struggle, and, in particular, struggle in which a (albeit more or less) precarious hegemony is at stake. To this end, as Snider sets out, considerations of regulatory reform need to address sets of actors in at least three locations — within states (be these international, national or local), corporations (where there are clearly fissures and contradictory sets of interests), and pro-regulatory forces. Snider also argues that the most effective of the latter outside the corporate sector have been organised labour or trades unions — that is, despite their vulnerability to the charge of sectionalism, trades unions remain the key vehicle of collective resistance, with historically developed, and institutional, power bases. This is not to argue, of course, that struggles will be confined to struggles of labour; but it is to argue that class politics remains essential, and that in its absence, forms of resistance expressed through individualism, fragmentation, new social movements, identity politics, and so on, amount to little more than a 'pluralist struggle for democracy' (Fudge and Glasbeek 1992: 62). And such a form of politics, whereby a pluralist democracy — however radical — is an end rather than a means, represents no fundamental challenge to a capitalist economic and social order:

> The liberal state permits, indeed promotes, individuals and groups to assert their differences as distinct individuals or atomised segments. But the institutions in which they may do so are structured in such a way as to deny, or at the very least obfuscate, the possibility of the inter-connectedness of the sources of their various oppressions.
>
> (Fudge and Glasbeek 1992: 61)

Indeed, Gramsci himself, on whom so many theorists draw, was clear that although hegemony is both secured and fractured through inclusion of or opposition by a range of social groups, class remains central to it, and in his analysis the working class remained the key agent of transformation, rather than one amongst many social movements (Fudge and Glasbeek 1992; Morera 1990).

Interestingly in this context, trends towards the internationalisation of capitalist economic and political institutions contain fundamental contradictions which are liable to exploitation by pro-regulatory forces in general, and organised labour in particular. There are at least three inextricably linked types of internationalising trends which create both opportunities and challenges for pro-regulatory forces. And even a cursory indication of these highlights a (perhaps increasingly) complex, and contradictory, set of relationships between pro-regulatory forces, national state bodies and those institutions and practices which we might refer to as the 'international state' (Picciotto 1991).

First, we have argued that the international economy is less adequately understood in terms of a 'global economy', more accurately represented in terms of three increasingly dominant trading blocs, namely, the Americas (within which the US remains hegemonic), Western Europe (within which the Franco-German axis is crucial) and the Pacific Rim (dominated by Japan) (see Chapter 2, and Hirst and Thompson 1996: 199 and passim). If this representation of the international economy is accepted, it is likely that there will also develop bodies of law which operate on a transnational basis within each of these three trading blocs. Initially, these facilitate the very structures within which nation-states have imbricated themselves — this was the origin of the EU, of course, and we can see NAFTA as a regulatory framework for trade in the Americas. But this then creates at least two interesting and complementary possibilities. First, that the development of so-called social regulation will follow economic regulation in such blocs, signs of which are clear in the context of both the EU and NAFTA, albeit to differing extents. Second, that there may develop the coordination of actions by organised labour and allies within various social movements across nation-state boundaries. Here, the internationalisation of economic and political structures creates new objects of struggle and gives impetus to the development of forces in that struggle.[7]

Second, the emergence of more truly transnational corporations has been accompanied by a proliferation of what Picciotto has termed international economic soft law. Picciotto makes a series of important points on the emergence and nature of such law. First, he relates its emergence to the technical inefficiency — and subsequent legitimation problems — which were apparent in attempts of national state bodies to develop an international regulatory framework for international capital. Second, he notes that much of this emergent 'soft law' — certainly the Codes of Conduct for transnational corporations — was itself sponsored by international business concerns in the face of such challenges to legitimacy. Third, that even in the ineffectiveness of this latter body of 'regulation', even if it were to be dismissed as purely symbolic, there has been provided a focus of political action for 'pressure groups, trades unions and other bodies' (Picciotto 1991: 58; Sklair 1995). This political action represents a critical response to a range of issues related to the social impacts of transnational corporations, and has been:

based on notions of popular power, aiming to democratise both the political structures of the state and the international system, as well as the production dominated by the TNCs.

(Picciotto 1991: 58)

Moreover, such political action will exploit a key contradiction at the heart of corporate capitalism, even in its international forms — namely, that however 'global' capitalism becomes, it can only globalise, and maintain global activities, on the basis of regulation. The development of international regulation — whether sponsored by national state actors or new forms of international institutions — simultaneously creates new sites of potential resistance.

Third, internationally-based resistance shifts the balance of power away from particular national state bodies and 'domestic' capital. The former is much trumpeted in the more exaggerated claims of globalisation (Horsman and Marshall 1994), yet it is interesting that such arguments rarely examine the effects of any global, or even internationalising, economic order upon nationally-tied capital. Yet, it is surely the case that resistance which is organised beyond the level of any one nation-state, and operates outside the structures of international or national regulation or international 'soft law', may compromise or undermine the ability of particular states or *particular nationally-based corporations* to pursue autonomous agendas. An obvious, and recent, example was the successful opposition to Shell's plans to sink its Brent Spar installation in the North Sea. Here, we witnessed international opposition, central to which were environmental organisations, consumers, and several West European governments, to the intended activities of a multinational in a home country where it had the support of the government of that country for its intended actions.

While these trends and factors can only be indicated here, they highlight both that pro-regulatory activity *needs* to be internationalised, and that there are forces that are furthering this internationalisation. Thus Elling has observed that the internationalisation of 'the capitalist political — economic world system' may carry with it 'much of the counter culture of resistance forces from one core country to another as well as to semi-peripheral and peripheral countries' (Elling 1986, cited in Carson and Henenberg 1989: 130). Of course, there is no necessity in any emerging resistance at the level of international civil society (Hurrell and Woods 1995: 467); but resistance at this level is a possibility raised by the trajectory of capitalist 'development'.

To emphasise. Such international forms of resistance exist, even if labour has traditionally organised less effectively than capital at such a level. There is some evidence that trades unions have begun to systematise forms of international coordination around health and safety issues, through initiatives such as the European Work Hazards Network, an ICFTU coordinated information exchange between International Trade Secretariats, and international campaigns on specific issues (for example, the hazards of Free Trade Zones). We do not share the view that labour has, either inevitably or necessarily, 'failed' in its opposition to global capitalism (Sklair 1995).[8] Moreover, it is notable that recent instances of popular resistance have mostly involved issues relating to human or environmental safety. Yet reforms can be won, and neither their immediate nor longer-term significance should be underestimated. If we extend his reference to workers to include all pro-regulatory forces, the words of Eric Tucker are fitting on the significance of such activity:

> struggles for democratisation must be conducted on many issues and at a variety of levels. In the past, workers fought for rights at the enterprise level and in the nation-state. Now, the locus of such democratic struggles must change. Transnational strategies to increase democratic control by workers are needed. Health and safety may be, as it has been in the past, an area in which pioneering struggles can be successfully conducted.
>
> (Tucker 1992b: 20)

Thus, as Fudge and Glasbeek have argued, people will, indeed must, 'fight their oppressions as they experience them' (Fudge and Glasbeek 1992: 66). But this does not remove wider connections between such oppressions; it indicates the significance of the exigence to 'think globally, act locally'. Moreover, to the extent that such resistance to oppressions focuses upon capital, in national and international manifestations, then this resistance immediately takes on class dimensions. Given that it is workers and the poorest sections of any society who are likely to be those who must endure dangerous working conditions, live in close vicinity to hazardous production plants and sites of waste disposal, be denied access to clean air, water and land, then such resistance again has a class dimension, and is likely to emerge with a class-basis. The resistance of corporate capital to control of its activities in these kinds of areas is likely to be particularly trenchant. This might be contrasted, as we have noted above, to state and subsequent corporate responses where small-scale capital is involved — where the homes, pensions, and shares of the middle classes who see themselves with some financial investment in capitalism have been placed at stake, then regulation has been more likely to ensue.

The relationships between local and international responses to the Bhopal disaster provide negative and positive lessons here (Sarangi 1996). But there are many other examples of effective resistance coordinated on an international scale.[9] These demonstrate that the exigence to 'think globally, act locally' is not a mere slogan; acting locally often entails acting internationally, though in our view it cannot be a simple substitute for resistance which is explicitly international. Moreover, such examples indicate both the potential of international opposition to capital (Picciotto 1991), and the unifying power of issues that relate to human and environmental safety and health (Hofrichter 1993: 8).

Relatedly, thinking globally/acting locally requires that those who push for improved corporate performance in respect of hazardous and criminal activities must recognise that a consequence of 'successful' pressure may be displacement of such activities from one location to another; thus the prevention of the export of hazard, either intra- or inter-nationally, must be a key element of the discourses of resistance. A key element of such pressure must be an ability to call the corporate bluff in the face of constant threats to relocate economic activity, threats which are highly functional, but often exaggerated (Whyte and Tombs 1996; and see the debate in Ives, ed. 1985). Thus, those opposing the activities of capital in any locality must be clear about the precise abilities on the part of corporations to relocate, and the precise conditions under which they may actually do so. In this task, there is certainly a role for radical, committed academics (Kramer 1989; Snider 1991; and Chapter 3, above).

Further, activities of resistance must continue to focus upon (but not be restricted to) formal political groupings, namely parties, and this focus needs to be maintained at local, regional, national and international levels. Moreover, given the existence, but often marginalisation, of more socially responsible individuals and groups within corporations, pro-regulatory forces need to seek to develop alliances *within* corporations.

Real, long-term improvements in conditions for working men and women have not emerged via any evolutionary processes, nor via enlightened or socially responsible capitalism. Capitalist corporations are, as we have emphasised throughout this text, essentially amoral, calculating entities; they will only act 'responsibly' or in an enlightened fashion when the costs of, and opportunities for, doing otherwise are raised. Thus, in an assessment of the dynamics of regulatory effectiveness in general, and the prospects for improved levels of corporate performance with respect to social regulation in particular,

Snider has pointed to the significance of pro-regulatory pressures on both corporations and the state. Such pressures emanate particularly from employees and their representatives, from local communities, from various interest/pressure groups, from some formal political representatives, and even from some academics. She has described a process — albeit a slow and arduous one — of regulatory reform and improved corporate performance, one which involves:

> a gradual shift in the dominant ideology, a redefinition of 'reasonable' business behaviours. Successful ideological struggles have 'upped the ante' for the corporate sector ... they have increased the price of legitimacy for the corporation by raising the standards of corporate behaviour necessary to secure public acceptance.
>
> (Snider 1987: 57)

Such struggles are not simply confined to the legal sphere. Without returning to past debates, it is only by recognising that law is not *simply* a bourgeois tool, is not *simply* a reflection of economic relations, that its potential as an element of working class struggle vis-à-vis capital can be appreciated. Law can of course constrain, but it also creates possibilities, through creating unstable and contested spaces (Moran 1992; Pearce 1989a; Woodiwiss 1998).

Clearly there are specific legal measures which would further these processes. Some are already in place in some states, but barely used, others would require reform of existing law. For example, we would advocate the development of charges of corporate manslaughter and reckless employing; disqualification of named employers and/or directors of successfully prosecuted companies; and the development, or external imposition if necessary, of clear lines of accountability and responsibility in corporations. Further, there is a need for greater experimentation with licensing systems and other forms of interventionist regulation, accepting that the principles of public participation, access to information, and social dialogue are crucial to such forms.

Conclusion

Central to this text is a recognition of the need to reassess what we understand by the term 'regulation'. Historically this has referred to aspects of administrative, civil and criminal law and their enforcement. However, as the preceding demonstrates, regulation can only be understood as a process that involves the widest possible range of social actors and social relations. At present, corporations and their representatives themselves play dominant, often covert, roles in the development of regulations to which they are then subjected; they then play key roles in negotiating the ways in which, and the extent to which, such regulations are actually enforced. We have argued that both in the development and enforcement of regulation, there are crucial roles to be played by workers, local communities, and various activist groups. Effective regulation of criminal corporate activity, one aspect of which must be control of hazards associated with production, requires corporate and social democratisation. This is also a matter of social justice. The chemicals industries are integral to any contemporary advanced economy, and while it is perfectly possible to conceive of such economies being less dependent upon particular forms of chemicals production and use, it is inconceivable that such production and use could be entirely abandoned or even significantly marginalised. However, we must emphasise that the historical development, and continuing activity on the part of chemicals corporations is deeply implicated in, indeed dependent upon, national states. We must also emphasise that a great proportion of the real costs of chemicals production are externalised, and borne by all us; yet these costs are not distributed evenly, but are met disproportionately by the weakest social groups. Of course, the profits from chemicals production are privatised and accrue to relatively small, wealthy and powerful groups of actors. In effect then, the chemicals industries privatise most benefits and socialise most costs — they operate on the bases of massive, inequitable, and masked forms of social subsidy. On this level, also, the case for social ownership is clear.

Neither the unequal distribution of the effects of hazardous production in particular, nor the control of corporate crime in general, will be genuinely achieved without controlling corporations. And control of the corporation requires new forms of ownership, forms of ownership which must, in effect, dissolve the corporate form. This is, to say the least, a long-term project, and, as we speak, one to be conducted in a highly unfavourable economic-political conjuncture. Yet there are signs of a general popular intolerance with the criminal activities of corporations. It is clear that neoliberalism remains insecure, and that contradictions between its rhetoric and the actual practices of corporations will perhaps be exacerbated. It is clear that the science-technology paradigm is increasingly questioned. And it is clear that in internationalising economic activity, corporations also create the conditions whereby international forms of resistance are at least more likely. None of these trends are simple, and they are certainly not unilinear. But they are real, and they offer hope.

Notes

1.   Arguments around corporate manslaughter need to be viewed alongside further general signs of a criminalisation of occupational safety offences. Whilst the above discussion refers to cases brought under common law, one can also discern some moves towards using the criminal force of the HSWAct. Three cases are significant. First, in 1987, involved the first ever custodial sentence under the Act, following the contravention of a prohibition notice by a director of a small construction company. Second, June 1992 saw the first ever disqualification of a company director under s. 37 of the HSWAct, which allows a case to be taken against one or more directors of a company where an offence has been committed with their 'consent, connivance or ... attributable to any neglect on the(ir) part' (Bergman 1994: 15). Third, March 1996 saw the first custodial sentence in the UK under the Health and Safety at Work Act, again under section 37. More specifically, a freelance demolition contractor was sentenced to three months in prison for failing to prevent the spread of asbestos. The case had been brought under the Asbestos (Licensing) Regulations 1983 and the Control of Asbestos at Work Regulations 1987, regulations which are made under the Health and Safety at Work Act (*The Safety and Health Practitioner*, March 1996: 2; *Hazards* 54, Spring 1996: 3).

2.   The extent, and effect, of the inadequacy of resources is sometimes graphically illustrated. For example, the Offshore Safety Division of the UK's Health and Safety Executive, established by the Offshore Safety Act following the Piper Alpha disaster in which 167 lives were lost, is unable to visit offshore installations without giving prior notice to employers. This is due simply to the fact that the OSD does not have the resources to own a helicopter, thus requiring its inspectors to arrange to fly on helicopters owned by oil companies, thereby granting advance notice of any 'proactive' inspection.

3.   A recent text by Barnett contains an interesting illustration of such points with specific reference to the US chemical industry:

> An editorial in Chemical Week, an industry publication, stated displeasure at seeing a 'regulatory agency in turmoil'. It noted that 'in a highly competitive industry, companies cannot afford to spend their resources on environmental protection, however well conceived the rules, unless they perceive these rules to be backed up by a credible enforcement policy'. Without an effective EPA, it concluded, 'industry's contribution to pollution, which has been diminishing, is bound to grow again. In the long run, the American people will not stand for that'.
>
> (Barnett 1994: 79)

That there is a correlation between declining regulatory efficacy and increasing levels of pollution is borne out by a recent review of trends in environmental degradation in the US during the era of deregulation (Faber and O'Connor 1993).

4.   The potential significance of dissension amongst such groups within and around corporations involved in criminal activity is clearly illustrated in many of the 'classic' studies of corporate crime. On the warnings and dissension of compliance or safety officers, see Braithwaite's study of corporate crime in the pharmaceutical industry (Braithwaite 1984), or the documented histories of the design and production of the Ford Pinto (Cullen et al. 1987); the dissenting voices of groups of engineers is documented by Vaughan in the case of the Challenger launch decision (Vaughan 1996); on middle and lower-level managers, see Wells's (1993) discussion of the sinking of the *Herald of Free Enterprise*, or Vandivier's (1982) account of the Goodrich Brake Scandal; as we have noted in this text, workers and local publics had consistently raised concerns about the operation of Union Carbide's Bhopal plant (see Chapter 6; also, Chouhan 1994; and Jones 1988).

5.   In that earlier piece, we provided a highly concrete instance of how protracted this process of seeking to secure compliance can become. In 1982, a HSE Accident Investigation report detailed a series of managerial errors and omissions as the fundamental causes of a fire and explosion at 'Chemstar', which killed a driver and seriously injured an operator. Eventually, Chemstar was fined £900 for breaches of section 2 of the HASAWAct. This highlights the inadequacies of a compliance-oriented approach since the local inspectorate appears to have visited and/or inspected the site *fifteen* times between Chemstar moving onto the site in 1975 and the incident in question in 1981, both proactively as well as in response to complaints from local residents. Now, Chemstar may not have been a particularly 'bad apple', yet the Inspectorate had provided consistent advice and encouragement, and on one instance a direct threat in order to raise standards. Nevertheless, the company was clearly failing in its general duties at the time of the incident. Why, then, given the amount of regulatory attention to which the company was subject, were such failings not rectified? And, if Chemstar was not a particularly 'bad apple', how poor are standards when notices *are* issued? If there had been no explosion, at what point would the inspectorate have resorted to 'sticks' rather than 'carrots'? Similar issues, this time in the context of health and the role of the HSE/EMAS have been raised in the Ombudsman's report on blood levels at Stallite Batteries (See *Hazards*, December 1990: 1-3).

6.   The article by Adaman and Devine from which these points are taken is one devoted to a discussion of, and indeed attempt to transcend, the rather modish notion of 'market socialism'. In a sense, this debate begins at the point where the

argument in this text ends, for it is a debate regarding the feasibility and contours of a socialist economy. Moreover, it is an enormous debate, to which we could not do justice here. For the record, however, we should note that we concur with Adaman and Devine's argument that market socialism has become intellectually predominant precisely due to a combination of factors: first, the experience of Soviet-style planning; second, the recent dominance of neoclassical economics; and third, and clearly closely related to the previous points, the absence from much contemporary socialist thought of the understanding that people have the capacity to recognise that their own interests and those of others are interdependent and to be concerned not only for their own but for the general good (Adaman and Devine 1997: 79). For us, the reemergence of conceptions of human subjects as highly atomised, self-interested and indeed incompetent is one of the most destructive aspects of neoliberalism.

7.   This argument is hardly a new one, of course, having been developed in outline by Marx and Engels([1872] 1971).

8.   We are grateful to Rory O'Neill, Editor of *Hazards* and Co-Editor of *Workers' Health International Newsletter*, for these, and other, instances of international collaboration between trades unions.

9.   Numerous examples of such resistance were presented before the recent sessions of the Permanent Peoples' Tribunal on Industrial Hazards and Human Rights, at the sessions 'Beyond Bhopal: Marking the Tenth Anniversary of the Bhopal Disaster', London, England, December 1994. Another source which documents such resistance is Hofrichter (1993). One role for radical academics must be not simply to support such struggles (see text), but also to record, publicise, and assess them.

Bibliography

Abegglen, J. (1975) *Management and Worker: the Japanese Solution,* Tokyo: Sophia University Press.

Abraham, M. (1985) *The Lessons of Bhopal: a community action resource manual on hazardous technologies*, Penang: International Organization of Consumers Unions.

Abrahamson, B., and Brostom, A. (1980) *The Rights of Labor*, Beverly Hills: Sage.

Abrams, R. (1986) *Toxic Chemical Accidents in New York: the risk of another Bhopal*, New York: Environmental Protection Bureau.

Abrams, R. (1989) *New York Under a Cloud: the need to prevent toxic chemical accidents*, New York: Environmental Protection Bureau.

ACSNI (1994) *Advisory Committee on the Safety of Nuclear Installations Human Factors Study Group. Third Report: Organising for Safety*, London: HSE.

Acton, J.P and Dixon, L.S. (1992) *Superfund and Transaction Costs: The Experience of Insurers and Very Large Industrial Firms*, Santa Monica: Rand Corporation.

Adaman, F. and Devine, P. (1997) 'On the Economic Theory of Socialism', *New Left Review*, 221, January/February.

Adams, J. (1995) *Risk*, London: UCL Press.

Adams, W. and Brock, J.W. (1986) *The Bigness Complex: Industry, Labor and Government in the American Economy*, New York: Pantheon.

Adams, W. and Brock, J.W. (1987) 'Bigness and Social efficiency: A Case study of the US auto industry' in Samuels, W.J. and Miller, A.S., eds., *Corporations and Society: Power and Responsibility*, New York: Greenwood.

Adams, W. and Brock, J.W. (1989) *Dangerous Pursuits: Mergers and Acquisitions in the Age of Wall Street*, New York: Pantheon Books.

Adams, W. and Brock, J.W. (1991) *Antitrust Economics on Trial: A Dialogue on the New Laissez-Faire*, Princeton: Princeton University Press.

Aftalion, F. (1991) *A History of the International Chemical Industry*, Philadelphia: University of Pennsylvania Press.

Agarwal, A., Merrifield, J., Tandon, R. (1985) *No Place to Run: Local Realities and Global Issues of the Bhopal Disaster*, New Market Tennessee: Highlander Center and Society for Participatory Research in Asia.

Aglietta, M. (1979) *A Theory of Capitalist Regulation*, London: New Left Books.

Aharoni, Y. (1981) *The No-Risk Society*, Chatham, NJ: Chatham House.

Albrecht, S. (1982) 'Review of Kelman (1981)', *Contemporary Sociology*, Vol. 11, No. 5 (September).

Alchian, A.A. and Demsetz, H. (1972) 'Production, Information Cause, and Economic Organization', *American Economic Review* (62).

Althusser, L. and Balibar, E. (1970) *Reading Capital*, London: New Left Books.

Anderson, P. (1977) 'The Antinomies of Antonio Gramsci', *New Left Review*, 100, January/February.

Anderson, T.L. and Leal, D.R. (1991) *Free Market Economics*, Boulder: Westview Press.

APPEN (1986) *The Bhopal Tragedy - One Year Later*, Penang: Sabahat Alam Malaysia (Friends of the Earth Malaysia)

ARENA (1985) *Bhopal: Industrial Genocide?*, Hong Kong: Arena Press.

Arnold, T.W. (1937) *The Folklore of Capitalism*, New Haven: Yale University Press.

Atkinson, G. and Hamilton, K. (1997) 'Green Accounting: monitoring and policy implications', in O'Riordan, ed., *Ecotaxation*.

Atkinson, M. and Laurence, B. (1997) 'Privatisation: is it really such a good idea?' *The Observer*, 6 April 1997.

Atkinson, R. (1990) 'Government During the Thatcher Years', in S. Savage and L. Robins (eds), *Public Policy Under Thatcher*, London: Macmillan.

Atkinson, T. (1996) 'Growth and the Welfare State', *New Economy*, 3, (3), Autumn.

Ayres, I. and Braithwaite, J. (1992) *Responsive Regulation. Transcending the deregulation debate*, Oxford: Oxford University Press.

Backstrom, A. (1988) 'The Role of the Automotive Industry for the Swedish Economy and Labour Market', in Olsen, G.M., ed., *Industrial Change & Labour Adjustment in Sweden and Canada*, Toronto: Garamond Press.

Bagdakian, B.H. (1997) T*he Media Monopoly, fifth edition,* Beacon Press.

Bailey, E. (1981) 'Contestability and the Design of Regulatory and Antitrust Policy', *American Economic Review*, 71, 2, (May).

Banerjee, B.N. (1986) *Bhopal Gas Tragedy - Accident or Experiment*, Delhi: Paribus.

Baram, M. (1987) 'Chemical Industry Hazards: liability, insurance and the role of risk analysis', in Kleindorfer, P.R. and Kunreuther, H.C., eds., *Insuring and Managing Hazardous Risks: From Seveso to Bhopal and Beyond*, Springer Verlag.

Bardach, E. and Kagan, R. (1982) *Going by the Book: the problem of regulatory unreasonableness*, Philadelphia: Temple University Press.

Barnard, C.I. (1947) *The Functions of the Executive*, Cambridge, Mass.: Harvard University Press.

Barnet, R.J. and Mueller, R.E. (1974) *The Global Reach: the Power of the Multinational Corporations*, New York: Simon and Schuster.

Barnett, H. (1982) 'The Production of Corporate Crime in Corporate Capitalism', in Wickham, P. and Dailey, T., eds., *White Collar and Economic Crime*, Lexington: Lexington Books.

Barnett, H. (1992) 'Hazardous Waste, Distributional Conflict and a Trilogy of Failures', *Journal of Human Justice*, 3, (2).

Barnett, H. (1994) *Toxic Debts and the Superfund Dilemma*, Chapel Hill: The University of North Carolina Press.

Barnett, H. (1995) 'Can Confrontation, Negotiation, or Socialisation Solve the Superfund Enforcement Dilemma?', in Pearce, F. and Snider, L., eds., *Corporate Crime. Contemporary debates*.

Barnett, R.J. and Cavanagh, J. (1995) *Global Dreams: Imperial Corporations and the New World Order*, New York: Touchstone.

Barrett, B. and James, P. (1988) 'Safe Systems: Past, Present - and Future?', *Industrial Law Journal*, 17, (1).

Barrile, L. (1991) 'Corporate Crime', Paper Presented at the American Society of Criminology Annual Meetings, San Francisco, November.

Bartlett, D.L. and Steele J.B (1992) *America: What Went Wrong?*, Kansas: Andrews and MacMeel.

Bartrip, P. and Fenn, P.T. (1980) 'The Conventionalization of Factory Crime - A Re-assessment', *The International Journal of the Sociology of Law*, 8.

Barzelay, M. and Smith, R.M. (1987) 'The One Best System? A Political Analysis of Neoclassical Institutionalist Perspectives on the Modern Corporation', in Samuels, W.J. and Miller, A.S., *Corporations and Society: Power and Responsibility*, New York: Greenwood Press.

Baumol, W. (1982) 'Contestable Markets: An Uprising in the Theory of Industry Structure', *American Economic Review*, 73, 1, (March).

Baxi, U. (1986) 'Inconvenient Forum and Convenient Catastrophe: The Bhopal Case', in Baxi, U. and Paul, T., eds., *Mass Disasters and Multinational Liability*, New Delhi: Indian Law Institute.

Bayer, R. (1982) 'Reproductive Hazards in the Workplace: Bearing the Burden of Fetal Risk' *Millbank Memorial Quarterly / Health and Society*, vol. 60, 4.

Beaumont, P.B. and Leopold, J.W. (1982) 'The State of Workplace Health and Safety in Britain', in Jones, C. and Stevenson, J., eds., *The Year Book of Social Policy in Britain*, London: Routledge and Kegan Paul.

Beck, U. (1992a) *Risk Society: Towards a New Modernity*, London: Sage.

Beck, U. (1992b) 'From Industrial Society to the Risk Society: Questions of Survival, Social Structural and Ecological Enlightenment', *Theory, Culture and Society*, 9.

Beck, U., Giddens, A. and Lash, S. (1994) *Reflexive Modernisation. Politics, Tradition and Aesthetics in the Modern Social Order*, Cambridge: Polity.

Becker, G. (1958) 'Competition and Democracy', *The Journal of Law and Economics*, Volume I, October.

Becker, G. (1975) *Human Capital*, Chicago: Chicago University Press.

Bell, D. (1976) 'The End of American Exceptionalism' in Glazer, N. and Kristol, I., eds., *The American Commonwealth 1976*, New York: Basic Books.

Bellamy, L. (1984) 'Not Waving But Drowning: problems of communication in the design of safe systems', *Ergonomics Problems in Process Operations. Institution of Chemical Engineers Symposium Series No.90*, Rugby, IChemE.

Benjamin, M. and Bronstein, D.A. (1987) 'Moral and Criminal Responsibility and Corporate Persons', in Samuels, W.J. and Miller, A.S., eds., *Corporations and Society: Power and Responsibility*, New York: Greenwood Press.

Bergman, D. (1988) 'The sabotage theory and the legal strategy of Union Carbide', *New Law Journal*, 138, June 17.

Bergman, D. (1991) *Deaths at Work. Accidents or Corporate Crime*, London: The London Hazards Centre / Workers' Educational Association.

Bergman, D. (1994) *The Perfect Crime? How companies can get away with manslaughter in the Workplace*, Birmingham: West Midlands HASAC.

Berle, A. and Means, G. (1967) *The Modern Corporation and Private Property*, New York: Harcourt, Brace and World.

Berman, D.M. (1978) *Death on the Job*, New York: Monthly Review Press.

Bernstein, D. (1992) *In the Company of Green. Corporate Communications for the New Environment*, London: Incorporated Society of British Advertisers.

Bernstein, I. (1966) *The Lean Years: A History of the American Worker 1920-1933*, Baltimore: Penguin.

Bertin, G.Y. and Wyatt, S. (1988) *Multinationals and Industrial Property: the control of the world's technology*, Hemel Hempstead: Harvester Wheatsheaf.

Beynon, H. (1985) *Working for Ford, Second Edition*, Harmandsworth: Penguin Books.

Bhaskar, R. (1978) *A Realist Theory of Science*, Brighton: Harvester.

Bhola, S.M. (1986) 'The Role of Inspection and Certification of Chemical Plant Equipment in the Control of Accident Hazards', in Smith, M.A., ed., *The Chemical Industry After Bhopal*.

Bhopal Action Group (1988) *Sabotaging the Sabotage Theory: a critique of the paper by Ashok Kalelkar*, London: Transnational Information Centre.

Birkin, M. and Price, B. (1989) *C for Chemicals. Chemical hazards and how to avoid them*, London: GreenPrint.

Bishop, D.R. (1986) 'The Community's Rights and Industry's Response', in Smith, M.A., ed., *The Chemical Industry After Bhopal*.

Bishops New Criminal Law of 1892, 212 U.S. 493 1909.

Bittner, E. (1969) 'The Police on Skid-Row: A Study of Peace Keeping', in Chambliss, W., ed, *Crime and the Legal Process*, New York: McGraw-Hill.

Blackstone, Sir William (1966) *Commentaries on the Laws of England, Book 1*, New York: Oceana Publications.

Blau, J.R. and Blau, P.M. (1982), 'The Cost of Inequality: Metropolitan Structure and Violent Crime', *American Sociological Review*, 47.

Block, A. (1993) 'Defending the Mountaintop: A Campaign against Environmental Crime' in Pearce, F. and Woodiwiss, M. (eds) *Global Crime Connections*, London: Macmillan.

Block, A. and Scarpitti, F. (1985) *Poisoning for Profit*, New York: William Morrow.

Block, F. (1986) 'Political choice and the multiple "logics" of capital', *Theory and Society*, 15.

Block, F., Cloward, R.A., Ehrenreich, B., Piven, F.F. (1987) *The Mean Season*, New York: Pantheon.

Blowers, A. (1984) *Something in the Air. Corporate Power and the Environment*, London: Harper and Row.

Blum-West, S. and Carter, T.J. (1983) 'Bringing White-Collar Crime Back in: An Examination of Crimes and Torts', *Social Problems*, 30, 5.

Blumberg, A. (1967) *Criminal Justice*, Chicago: Quadrangle Books.

Bonger, W. (1905 and 1969) *Criminality and Economic Conditions*, Bloomington: Indiana University Press.

Boons, F. (1992) 'Environmental Policy and Chemical Industry in Europe: conflict, co-operation and commercialisation', *Business Strategy and the Environment*.

Bordeau, P. and Green, G. (1989) *Methods for Assessing and Reducing Injury from Chemical Accidents*, Chichester: John Wiley and Sons.

Bork, R. (1978) *The Antitrust Paradox*, New York: Basic Books.

Borkin, J. (1978) *The Crime and Punishment of IG Farben*, New York: The Free Press.

Boussemart, B. and de Brandt, J. (1988) 'The European Textile Industries: widely varying structures', in De Jong, H.W., ed. *The Structure of European Industry*, Dordrecht: Kluwer Academic.

Bowles, S. and Gintis, H. (1982) 'The Crisis of Liberal Democratic Capitalism', *Politics and Society*, 11, 1.

Bowles, S. Gordon, D. and Weisskopf T. (1984) *Beyond the Wasteland*, New York: Anchor Press, Doubleday.

Bowonder, B., Kasperson, J.X. and Kasperson, R.E. (1994) 'Industrial Risk Management in India Since Bhopal', in Jasanoff, ed., *Learning From Disaster*.

Box, S. (1983) *Power, Crime and Mystification*, London: Tavistock.

Box, S. (1987) *Recession, Crime and Punishment*, London: Tavistock.

Box, S. and Hale, C. (1986) 'Unemployment, Crime and Imprisonment', in Matthews, R. and Young, J., *Confronting Crime*, London: Sage.

Boyadjian, H.J. and Warren, J.F. (1992) *Risks: reading corporate signals*, Chichester: John Wiley.

Boyd, N. (1988) *The Last Dance: Murder in Canada*, Scarborough: Prentice-Hall Canada.

Boyne, R. (1990) *Foucault and Derrida: The other side of reason*, London: Unwin Hyman.

Braithwaite, J. (1979) *Crime, Inequality and Public Policy*

Braithwaite, J. (1984) *Corporate Crime in the Pharmaceutical Industry*, London: Routledge and Kegan Paul.

Braithwaite, J. (1985) *To Punish or Persuade: Enforcement of Coal Mine Safety*, Albany: State University of New York Press.

Braithwaite, J. (1989a) *Crime, Shame and Reintegration*, Cambridge: Cambridge University Press.

Braithwaite, J. (1989b) 'Criminological Theory and Organisational Crime', *Justice Quarterly*, 6.

Braithwaite, J. (1993) 'Transnational Regulation of the Pharmaceutical Industry', in Geis, G. and Jesilow, P. (1993) *White Collar Crime. The Annals of the American Academy of Political and Social Science Special Issue*, Newbury Park, CA: Sage.

Braithwaite, J. and Fisse, B. (1987) 'Self-Regulation and Corporate Crime' in C.D. Shearing and P.C. Stenning, eds., *Private Policing*, London: Sage.

Braithwaite, J. and Geis, G. (1982) 'On Theory and Action for Corporate Crime Control', *Crime and Delinquency*, 28.

Braithwaite, J. and Makkai, T. (1991) 'Testing an Expected Utility Model of Corporate Deterrence', *Law and Society Review*, 25.

Braithwaite, J. and Makkai, T. (1994) 'The Dialectics of Corporate Deterrence', paper presented at the Annual Meeting of the Academy of Criminal Justice Sciences, Chicago, 8-12 March.

Braithwaite, J., Makkai, T., Braithwaite, V. and Gibson, D. (1993) *Raising the Standard: resident centred nursing home regulation in Australia*, Canberra: Australian Government Publishing Service.

Brake, M. and Hale, C. (1992) *Public Order and Private Lives: The Politics of Law and Order*, London: Routledge.

Brickman, R., Jasanoff, S. and Ilgen, T. (1985) *Controlling Chemicals: the politics of regulation in Europe and the United States*, Ithaca: Cornell University Press.

Brill, H. (1992) 'Government Breaks the Law: The Sabotaging of the Occupational Safety and Health Act', *Social Justice*, Vol. 19, No. 3.

Brittan, S. (1988) *A Restatement of Economic Liberalism*, New Jersey: Humanities Press International.

Brittan, Y. (1984) *The Impact of Water Pollution Control On Industry: a case study of 50 dischargers*, Oxford: Centre for Socio-Legal Studies.

Brodeur, P. (1985) *Outrageous Misconduct: The Asbestos Industry on Trial*, New York: Pantheon.

Browning, J.P. (1986) 'After Bhopal', in Smith, M.A., ed., *The Chemical Industry After Bhopal*.

Bruel, J-M. (1990) 'Borrowing the Land of Our Children', *Chemistry & Industry*, 19 November.

Brunsson, N. (1989) *The Organisation of Hypocrisy. Talk, Decisions and Actions in Organisations*, Chichester: John Wiley & Sons.

Bullard, R. (1990) *Dumping in Dixie. Race, Class and Environmental Quality*, Boulder: Westview Press.

Burchall, G., Gordon, C., Miller, P., eds. (1991) *The Foucault Effect: Studies in Governmentality with two lectures by and an interview with Michel Foucault*, Brighton: Harvester Wheatsheaf.

Burger, E.J., ed. (1993) *Risk*, Ann Arbor: the University of Michigan Press.

Burns, T. and Stalker, G. (1961) *The Management of Innovation*, London: Tavistock.

Burton, F. and Carlen, P. (1979) *Official Discourse: on discourse analysis, government publications, ideology and the state*, London: Routledge and Kegan Paul.

Business Deregulation Task Forces (1994) *Deregulation Task Forces Proposals for Reform*, London: Department of Trade and Industry.

Cahill, S. (1997) 'Killing for Company', *Company Secretary*, March.

Cairncross, F. (1993) *Costing the Earth: The Challenge for Governments, the Opportunities for Business*, Harvard: Harvard Business School Press.

Calavita, K. (1983) 'The Demise of the Occupational Safety and Health Administration: A Case Study in Symbolic Action', *Social Problems*, 30, 4.

Calavita, K., DiMento, J., Geis, G. and Forti, G. (1991) 'Dam Disasters and Durkheim: an analysis of the theme of repressive and restitutive law', *International Journal of the Sociology of Law*, 19.

Calavita, K. and Pontell, H.N. (1995) 'Saving the Savings and Loans? US Government Response to Financial Crime', in Pearce, F. and Snider, L., eds., *Corporate Crime: contemporary debates*.

Callinicos, A. (1989) *Against Postmodernism*, Cambridge: Polity.

Campbell, J.L. (1987) 'The State and the Nuclear Waste Crisis: An Institutional Analysis of Policy Constraints', *Social Problems*, 34, 1.

Cantelon, P.L., Hewlett, R.G., and Williams, R.C. eds., (1991) *The American Atom: A Documentary History of Nuclear Policies from the Discovery of Fission to the Present* (2nd edition), Philadelphia: University of Pennsylvania Press.

Carlen, P. (1976) *Magistrates' Justice*, London: M. Robertson.

Carlisle, J. (1991) 'Targetting the Environmental Movement: bombs, lies and body wires', *Covert Action*, 38 (Fall).

Carr, A. (1985) 'Is Business Bluffing Ethical?', in desJardins, J. and McCall, J. (1985) *Contemporary Issues in Business Ethics*, Belmont, Ca: Wadsworth Publishing.

Carson, P.A. and Mumford, C. J. (1979) 'An Analysis of Incidents involving Major Hazards in the Chemical Industry', *Journal of Hazardous Materials*, 3.

Carson, R. (1962) *Silent Spring*, New York: Fawcett Crest.

Carson, W.G., (1970a) 'White-Collar Crime and the Enforcement Factory Legislation', *British Journal of Criminology*, 10.

Carson, W.G. (1970b) 'Some Sociological Aspects of Strict Liability and the Enforcement of Factory Legislation', *Modern Law Review*, 33, July.

Carson, W.G. (1974) 'Symbolic and Instrumental Dimensions of Early Factory Legislation: a case study in the social origins of criminal law', in Hood, R., ed., *Crime, Criminology and Public Policy*, London: Heinemann.

Carson, W.G. (1979) 'The Conventionalization of Early Factory Crime', *International Journal of the Sociology of Law*, 7.

Carson, W.G. (1980) 'Early Factory Inspectors and the Viable Class Society - A Rejoinder', *International Journal of the Sociology of Law*, 8.

Carson, W.G. (1982) *The Other Price of Britain's Oil*, Oxford: Martin Robertson.

Carson, W.G. and Henenberg, C. (1989) 'Social Justice at the Workplace: the political economy of health and safety laws', *Social Justice*, 16, 3.

Carson, W.G. and Johnstone, R. (1990) 'The Dupes of Hazard: Occupational Health and Safety and the Victoria Sanctions Debate' *Australian and New Zealand Journal of Sociology*, 26, 1 (March).

Carter, T.S. (1997) 'The Failure of Environmental Regulation in New York', *Crime, Law and Social Change*, 26.

Cashmore, E. (1989) *United Kingdom? Class, Race and Gender since the War*, London: Unwin Hyman.

Cass, V.J. (1996) 'Toxic Tragedy: illegal hazardous waste dumping in Mexico', in Edwards et al., eds., *Environmental Crime and Criminality. Theoretical and Practical Issues*.

Cassels, J. (1993) *The Uncertain Promise of Law*, Toronto: University of Toronto Press.

Cassidy, K. (1986) Experience with Safety Cases. Paper presented CIMAH in Action, Society of Chemical Industry, London, 30 October.

Castel, R. (1991) 'From Dangerousness to Risk', in Burchall, G., Gordon, C., Miller, P., eds. (1991) *The Foucault Effect*.

Castleman, B. (1979) 'The Export of Hazard to Developing Countries', *International Journal of Health Services*, 9, 4.

Castleman, B. (1985) 'The Double Standard in Industrial Hazards' in Ives, ed., *The Export of Hazard*.

Cerny, P.G. (1997) 'Paradoxes of the Competition State: the dynamics of political globalisation', *Government and Opposition*, 32, (1), Spring.

Chambliss, W.J. (1988) *Exploring Criminology*, New York: Macmillan.

Chandler, A.D. (1969) *Strategy and Structure*, Cambridge: Cambridge University Press.

Chandler, A.D. (1977) *The Visible Hand: The Managerial Revolution in American Business*, Cambridge, Mass.: Cambridge University Press.

Chandler, A.D. (1990) *Scale and Scope: The Dynamics of Industrial Capitalism*, The Belknap Press of Harvard University Press: Cambridge.

Chapman, D. (1968) *Sociology and the Stereotype of the Criminal*, London: Tavistock Publications.

Chapman, P. (1979) *Fuel's Paradise*, Harmandsworth: Penguin.

Chapman, P. (1984) 'Mexico's catalogue of gas disasters', *New Scientist*, 1432, 29th November.

Charter, M., ed. (1992) *Greener Marketing: a responsible approach to business*, Sheffield: Interleaf.

Chayes, A. (1961) 'The Modern Corporation and the Rule of Law' in Mason, E.S., ed., *The Corporation in Modern Society*, Cambridge, Mass.: Harvard University Press.

Chelius, J.R. (1977) *Workplace Safety and Health*, Washington DC: American Enterprise Institute.

Chemical Industries Association (1995) *UK Chemicals Industry Facts*, London: Chemicals Industries Association Ltd.

Chenier, P.J. (1986) *Survey of Industrial Chemistry*, John Wiley: New York.

Cherry, R. and D'Onofrio, C., Kurddas, C., Michl, T.R., Moseley, F., Naples, M.I. (1987) *The Imperilled Economy, Book 1. Macroeconomics from a Left Perspective*, New York: Union for Radical Political Economics.

Chomsky, N. (1985) *Turning the Tide: US Intervention in Central America and the Struggle for Peace*, London: Pluto Press.

Chopra, S.K. (1986) 'The Bhopal Disaster and the Indian Legal and Administrative System: what is wrong and what to do', a paper presented at the International Bar Association, New York, September.

Chouhan, T.R. and others (1994) *Bhopal, The Inside Story. Carbide Workers Speak Out on the World's Worst Industrial Disaster*, New York: Apex Press.

Christie, N. (1992) *Crime Control as Industry: Towards Gulags, Western Style*, London: Routledge.

Cicourel, A. (1967) *The Social Organization of Juvenile Justice*, New York: Wiley.

Clark, R.C. (1986) *Corporate Law*, Boston: Little, Brown and Company.

Clark, M. and Smith, D. (1992) 'Paradise Lost?: Issues in the disposal of waste', in Clark, M., Smith, D. and Blowers, A., eds., *Waste location: Spatial aspects of waste management, hazards and disposal*, London: Routledge.

Clarke, M. (1986) *Regulating the City. Competition, Scandal and Reform*, Open University Press: Milton Keynes.

Clarke, M. (1990) *Business Crime. Its nature and control*, Cambridge: Polity.

Clarke, S. (1988) 'Overaccumulation, Class Struggle and the Regulation Approach', *Capital and Class*, 36, Winter.

Clarke, S. (1990) 'The Crisis of Fordism or the Crisis of Social Democracy', *Telos*, 83, (Spring).

Clausen III and Mattson (1978) *Principles of Industrial Chemistry*, New York: John Wiley.

Claybrook, J. (1984) *Retreat from Safety : Reagan's Attack on America's Health*, New York: Pantheon.

Clegg, S. (1990) *Modern Organizations: Organization Studies in the Postmodern World*, London: Sage.

Clement, W. (1988) *The Challenge of Class Analysis*, Ottawa: Carleton University Press.

Clinard, M.B. and Yeager, P.C. (1980) *Corporate Crime*, New York: Free Press.

Cloward, R.A. and Piven, F.F. (1979) *Poor People's Movements*, New York: Vintage.

Clutterbuck, C. (1986) 'Death in the Plastics Industry', in Ledivow, L., ed, *Radical Science Essays*, London: Free Association Books.

Cmnd. 9571. (1985) *Lifting the Burden*, London: HMSO.

Cmnd. 9794 (1986) *Building Businesses ... not Barriers*, London: HMSO.

Coakley, J. and Harris, L. (1992) 'Financial Globalisation and Deregulation', in Michie, ed., *The Economic Legacy 1979-1992*, London: The Academic Press.

Coase, R.M. (1937) 'The Nature of the Firm', 4 *Economica* 386.

Coase, R.H. (1988) *The Firm, the Market and the Law*, Chicago: University of Chicago Press.

Coates, K. and Silburn, (1981) *Poverty: The Forgotten Englishmen*, Harmandsworth: Penguin.

Coddington, W. (1993) *Environmental Marketing. Positive strategies for reaching the Green consumer*, New York: McGraw Hill.

Coffee, J. (1981) '"No soul to damn, no body to kick": an unscandalised essay on the problem of corporate punishment', *Michigan Law Review*, 79.

Cohen, M.A. (1989) 'Corporate Crime and Punishment: A Study of Social Harm and Sentencing Practice in the Federal Courts, 1984-87', 26 *American Criminal Law Review*.

Cohen, M.A. (1992) 'Corporate Crime and Punishment: An Update on Sentencing Practices in the Federal Courts, 1988-1990', *Boston University Law Review*, 71.

Cohen, M.A., C. Ho, E. Jones III, and L. Schleich (1988) 'Organizations as Defendants in Federal Courts: A Preliminary Analysis of Prosecutions, Convictions, and Sanctions 1984-1987', *Whittier Law Review*, 10.

Coleman, J.S. (1987) 'Toward an Integrated Theory of White-Collar Crime', *American Journal of Sociology*, 93.

Coleman, J.S. (1989) *The Criminal Elite*, New York: St. Martin's Press.

Coleman, J.S. (1992) 'The Theory of White-Collar Crime: from Sutherland to the 1990s', in Schlegel, K. and Weisburd, D., eds. *White-Collar Crime Reconsidered*, Boston: Northeastern University Press.

Coley, N. (1989) 'Materials: Products of the Chemical Industry', in Chant, C., *Science, Technology and Everyday Life*, Routledge: London.

Collier, P. and Horowitz, D. (1976) *The Rockefellers: An American Dynasty*, New York: New American Library.

Comanor, W.S. (1986) 'The Political Economy of the Pharmaceutical Industry', *Journal of Economic Literature*, XXIV, September.

Cook, J. (1989) *An Accident Waiting to Happen*, London: Unwin Hyman.

Cotterell, R. (1984) *The Sociology of Law: An Introduction*, London: Butterworths.

Council of Churches for Britain and Ireland (1997) *Unemployment and the Future of Work. An Enquiry for the Churches*, London: CCBI.

Cowe, R. (1991) 'Chemical Formula for the Environment', *The Guardian*, 12th April.

Cox, R.W. (1993) 'Structural Issues of Global Governance: implications for Europe', in Gill, S., ed., *Gramsci, Historical Materialism and International Relations*, Cambridge: Cambridge University Press.

Cox, R.W. (1994) 'Global Restructuring: making sense of the changing international political economy', in Stubbs, R. and Underhill, G.R., eds., *Political Economy and the Changing Global Order*.

Cralley, L.V. and Cralley, L.W., eds. (1989) *In-Plant Practices for Job Related Health Hazards Control: Engineering Aspects (Volume 2)*, New York: John Wiley and Sons.

Cranston, R. (1979) *Regulating Business: Law and Consumer Agencies*, London: Macmillan.

Cranston, R. (1985) *Consumers and the Law*, London: Butterworth.

Crawford, A., Woodhouse, T, Young, J. (1990) *The Second Islington Crime Survey*, London: Middlesex Polytechnic.

Crenson, M. (1971) *The Un-Politics of Air Pollution: a study of non-decision making in the cities*, Baltimore: Johns Hopkins Press.

Croall, H. (1989) 'Who Is the White-Collar Criminal?', *British Journal of Criminology*, 29, (2).

Croall, H. (1992) *White Collar Crime*, Buckingham: Open University Press.

Crone, H.D. (1986) *Chemicals and Society. A guide to the new chemical age*, Cambridge: Cambridge University Press.

Crooks, H. (1993) *Giants of Garbage*, Toronto: Lorrimer.

Crow, I., Richardson, P., Riddington, C., Simon, F. (1989) *Unemployment, Crime and Young Offenders*, London: Routledge.

Crowl, D.A., ed. (1996) *Inherently Safer Chemical Processes. A Life Cycle Approach*, New York: American Institute of Chemical Engineers.

Crozier, M., Huntingdon, S.P., Wanatuki, J. (1975) *The Crisis of Democracy: report on the governability of democracies to the Trilateral Commission*, New York: New York University Press.

Cullen, F.T., Maakestad, W.J. and Cavender, G. (1987) *Corporate Crime Under Attack*, Cincinnati: Anderson.

Cunningham, F. (1995) 'Homo Democraticus: A Counter Catallactic Perspective', *Theoria*, May.

Currie, E. (1985) *Confronting Crime*, New York: Pantheon.

Currie, E. (1990) 'Heavy with Human Tears: free market policy, inequality and social provision in the United States', in Taylor, I., ed., *The Social Effects of Free Market Policies*, Hemel Hempstead: Harvester Wheatsheaf.

Currie, E. (1997) 'Market, Crime and Community: toward a mid-range theory of post-industrial violence', *Theoretical Criminology*, 1, (2), May.

Cusamo, M. (1989) *The Japanese Automobile Industry*, Cambridge: Harvard University Press.

Cutler, A., Hindess, B., Hirst, P.Q., Hussain, A. (1977) *Marx's Capital and Capitalism Today, Volume 1*, London: Routledge and Kegan Paul.

Cutler, A., Hindess, B., Hirst, P.Q., Hussain, A. (1978) *Marx's Capital and Capitalism Today: Volume 2*, London: Routledge and Kegan Paul.

Cutler, A. and James, P. (1996) 'Does Safety Pay? A critical account of the Health and Safety Executive Document: "The Costs of Accidents"', *Work, Employment & Society*, 10, (4).

Cutter, S. (1993) *Living with Risk*, London: Edwin Arnold.

Dahlman, C. J. (1979) 'The Problem of Externality', *The Journal of Law and Economics*, 22, 1 (April).

Dake, K. and Wildavsky, A. (1993) 'Theories of Risk Perception: Who Fears What and Why?', in Burger, E.J., ed., *Risk*, Ann Arbor: University of Michigan Press.

Dalton, A. (1992) 'Lessons from the United Kingdom: fightback on workplace hazards, 1979-1992', *International Journal of Health Services*, 22.

Daly, M. and McCann, A. (1992) 'How Many Small Firms?', *Employment Gazette*, February.

Davies, N.V. and Teasdale, P. (1994) *The Costs to the British Economy of Work Accidents and Work-Related Ill-Health*, London: HSE Books.

Davis, J.P. (1905 and 1971) *Corporations: A Study of the Origin and Development of Great Business Corporations and of their Relationship to the Authority of the Church*, New York: Burt Franklin.

Davis, L.N. (1984) *The Corporate Alchemists. Power and problems of the chemical industry*, London: Maurice Temple Smith.

Davis, N. and C. Stasz (1990) *Social Control for Deviance: A Critical Perspective*, New York: McGraw Hill.

Dawson, S. (1994) 'A Difficult Year: the HSC Annual Report 1992/93', *Health and Safety Information Bulletin*, 217, January.

Dawson, S., Willman, P., Bamford, M. and A. Clinton (1988) *Safety at Work: the limits of self-regulation*, Cambridge: Cambridge University Press.

de Jong, H.W. (1988) 'Market Structures in the European Economic Community', in de Jong, H.W., ed., *The Structure of European Industry*, Dordrecht: Kluwer Academic.

de Wolf, P. (1988) 'The Pharmaceutical Industry: structure, intervention and competitive strength', in de Jong, H.W., ed., *The Structure of European Industry*, Dordrecht: Kluwer Academic.

Defert, D. (1991) '"Popular Life" and Insurance Technology', in Burchall, G., Gordon, C., Miller, P., eds., *The Foucault Effect*.

Deieso, D.A., Mulvey, N.P. and Kelly, J. (1988) 'Accidental Release Prevention: a Regulator's Perspective', in *Preventing Major Chemical and Related Process Accidents. IChemE Symposium Series No. 110*, Rugby: IChemE.

Di Mento, J.F. (1986) *Environmental Law and American Business: Dilemmas of Compliance*, New York: Plenum Press.

Diamond, S. (1985) 'US Toxic Mishaps in Chemicals Put at 6,928 in Five Years', *New York Times*, October 3.

Dicken, P. (1992) *Global Shift. The internationalisation of economic activity*, London: Paul Chapman.

Dickens, W.T. (1984) 'Occupational Safety and Health Regulation and Economic Theory', in Darity Jr., W., ed., *Labor Economics* Boston: Kluwer-Nijhoff Publishing.

Dickinson, J. (1986) 'Spiking Socialist Guns: the introduction of social insurance in Germany and Britain' *Comparative Social Research*, Volume 9.

Dinham, B., Dixon, B. & Saghal, G. (1986) *The Bhopal Papers*, London: Transnationals Information Centre.

Ditton, J. (1977) *Part-Time Crime: An Ethnography of Fiddling and Pilferage,* London: Macmillan.

Dizard Jr., W. (1997) *Old Media, New Media: mass communication in the information age,* Longman: New York.

Doern, B. (1977) *Regulatory Processes and the Jurisdictional Issues in the Regulation of Hazardous Products in Canada,* Ottawa: Ministry of Supply and Services.

Doll, R. and Peto, R. (1981) *The Causes of Cancer,* Oxford: Oxford University Press.

Donaldson, P. and Farquhar, J. (1988) *Understanding the British Economy,* Harmandsworth: Penguin.

Donnelly, P. (1982) 'The Origins of the Occupational Safety and Health Act of 1970', *Social Problems,* 30, (1).

Doran, N. (1996) 'From Embodied "Health" to Official "Accidents": class, codification, and British factory legislation, 1831-1844', *Social & Legal Studies,* 5, (4), December.

Doucouliagos, C. (1990) 'Why Capitalist Firms Outnumber Labor-Managed Firms', *Review of Radical Political Economics,* 22, 4.

Douglas, J.D. and Johnson, J.M. (1978) *Crime at the Top. Deviance in Business and the Professions,* Philadelphia: J.B. Lippincott.

Douglas, M. (1993) 'Risk as a Forensic Resource', in Burger, E.J., ed., *Risk,* Ann Arbor: University of Michigan Press.

Douglas, M. and Wildavsky, A. (1982) *Risk and Culture,* Berkeley, California: University of California Press.

Dover Port Committee (1988) *Heroes Then Sacked Now. Why the sacked P&O seafarers must win,* Dover: Dover Port Committee of the National Union of Seamen.

Dowd, D.A. (1977) *The Twisted Dream,* Cambridge: Winthrop Publishers.

Downs, A. (1957a) *An Economic Theory of Democracy,* New York: Harper and Row.

Downs, A. (1957b) 'An Economic Theory of Poltical Action in Democracy', *The Journal of Poltical Economy,* LXV, February- December.

Dowie, M. (1979) 'Pinto Madness', in Skolnick, J. and Currie, E., eds, *Crisis in American Institutions, 4th edn.,* Boston: Little Brown.

Doyal, L., Green, K., Irwin, A., Russell, D., Steward, F., Williams, R., Gee, D. and Epstein, S.S. (1983) *Cancer in Britain: The Politics of Prevention,* London: Pluto Press.

Draper, E. (1991) *Risky Business. Genetic Testing and Exclusionary Practices in The Hazardous Workplace,* Cambridge: Cambridge University Press.

Dunlap, R.E. (1991) 'Trends in Public Opinion Towards Environmental Issues 1965-1990', *Society and Natural Resources,* 4, (3).

Dunning, J. (1979) 'Explaining Changing Patterns of International Production: In Defence of Eclectic Theory', *Oxford Bulletin of Economics,* No. 41, 4.

Dunning, J.H. (1988a) *Explaining International Production,* London: Unwin-Hyman.

Dunning, J.H. (1988b) *Multinationals, Technology and Competitiveness,* London: Unwin Hyman.

Dunning, J.H. (1993) *Multinational Enterprises and the Global Economy,* Wokingham: Addison-Wesley.

Durkheim, E. (1938) *The Rules of Sociological Method,* New York: Free Press.

Durkheim, E. (1984) *The Division of Labour in Society,* London: Macmillan (Halls Translation) [1983]

Ecotec (1989) *Industry Costs of Pollution Control. Final Report to the Department of Environment,* Birmingham: Ecotec Research and Publishing Ltd.

Edelhertz, H. (1970) *The Nature, Impact and Prosecution of White-Collar Crime*, National Institute for Law Enforcement and Criminal Justice, Department of Justice: Washington D.C.

Edelstein, M.R. (1989) 'Forcing a Critical Perspective on Technology: the role of community opposition to facility siting', Paper Presented at 2nd International Conference on Industrial and Organisational Crisis Management, Leonard N. Stern School of Business, New York, 3-4 December.

Edsall, T.B. (1984) *The New Politics of Inequality*, New York: Norton.

Edwards, S. (1989) *Policing Domestic Violence*, London: Sage.

Edwards, S.M., Edwards, T.D. and Fields, C.B. (1996) *Environmental Crime and Criminality. Theoretical and Practical Issues*, New York: Garland.

Elias, R. (1986) *The Politics of Victimization: Victims, Victimology and Human Rights*, New York: Oxford University Press.

Ekins, P. (1992) 'A Four Capital Model of Wealth Creation', in Ekins, P. and Max-Neef, M., *Real-Life Economics. Understanding Wealth Creation.*

Ekins, P. and Max-Neef, M. eds. (1992) *Real-Life Economics. Understanding Wealth Creation*, London: Routledge.

Elkins, C. (1989) 'Corporate Citizenship - Toxic Chemicals, the Right Response', *New York Times*, Sunday, November 13.

Ellis, D. (1988) *The Wrong Stuff*, Toronto: Macmillan.

Elling, R. (1986) *The Struggle for Workers' Health*, New York: Baywood Publishing.

Elliott, L. (1996) 'Putting Trade in its Place', *The Guardian*, 27th May.

Environmental Protection Agency (1980) *VOC Fugitive Emissions On Synthetic Organic Chemicals Manufacturing Industry*, Washington DC: Environmental Protection Agency.

Environmental Protection Agency (1990) *The Nation's Hazardous Waste Management Program at a Crossroads: the RCRA Implementation Study*, Washington, DC: Environmental Protection Agency.

Epstein, S. (1979) *The Politics of Cancer*, New York: Anchor/ Doubleday.

Epstein, S. (1981) 'Letter to Editor', Nature, Vol. 289, 15 January, reproduced in Doyal, L. et al. (1983), *Cancer in Britain.*

Epstein, S., ed. (1982) *The Disposal of Hazardous Waste*, San Francisco: The Sierra Club.

Epstein, S. and Swartz, J. (1981) 'Fallacies of Life Style Cancer Theories', Nature, 289, 15 January, reproduced in Doyal, L. et al. (1983), *Cancer in Britain.*

Ericson, R. (1981) *Making Crime: A Study of Detective Work*, Toronto: Butterworth.

Ericson, R. (1993) 'The Division of Expert Knowledge in Policing and Security' *British Journal of Sociology*, 44.

Ermann, M.D. and Lundman, R.J., eds. (1982) *Corporate and Governmental Deviance: Problems of organisational behaviour in contemporary society*, New York: Oxford University Press.

Essery, G. (1993) 'Managing Environmental Improvement within a Major Chemical Complex', in Smith, D., ed., *Business and the Environment*, London: Paul Chapman.

Etzioni, A. (1993) 'The US Sentencing Commission on Corporate Crime: a critique', in Geis, G. and Jesliow, P., eds., *White-Collar Crime.*

Evans, S., Ewing, K. and Nolan, P. (1992) 'Industrial Relations and the British Economy in the 1990s: Mrs. Thatcher's Legacy', *Journal of Management Studies*, 29, 5.

Everest, L. (1986) *Behind the Poison Cloud: Union Carbide's Bhopal Massacre*, New York: Banner Press.

Ewald, F. (1991) 'Insurance and Risk', in Burchall, G., Gordon, C., Miller, P., eds., *The Foucault Effect.*

Faber, D. and O'Connor, J. (1993) 'Capitalism and the Crisis of Environmentalism', in Hofrichter, R., ed., *Toxic Struggles. The Theory and Practice of Environmental Justice*, Philadelphia, PA: New Society Publishers.

Faberman, H.A. (1975) 'A Criminogenic Market Structure: the automobile industry', *Sociological Quarterly*, 19, Winter.

Fairman, R. (1994) 'Robens - 20 Years On', *Health and Safety Information Bulletin*, 221, May.

Fama, E.F. and Jensen, M.C. (1983) 'Agency Problems and Residual Claims', *Journal of Law and Economics*, 26, June.

Feeley, M. (1979) *The Process is the Punishment*, New York: Russell Sage Foundation.

Fellmeth, R.C. (1970) *The Interstate Commerce Commission: The Public Interests and the ICC*, New York: Grossman.

Ferguson, T. and Rogers, J. (1986) *The Decline of the Democrats and the Future of American Politics*, New York: Hill and Wang.

Field, F. (1989) *Losing Out: The Emergence of Britain's Underclass*, Oxford: Blackwell.

Fife, I. and Machin, E.A. (1982) *Redgrave's Health and Safety in Factories. Second Edition*, London: Butterworths.

Fine, B. (1990a) 'Scaling the Commanding Heights of Public Enterprise Economics', *Cambridge Journal of Economics*, 14.

Fine, B. (1990b) *The Coal Question: Political Economy and Industrial Change from the Nineteenth Century to the Present Day*, London: Routledge.

Finlay, L.M. (1996) 'The Pharmaceutical Industry and Women's Reproductive Health', in Szockyi, E. and Fox, J.G., eds., *Corporate Victimisation of Women*, Boston: Northeastern University Press.

Fischer, F. (1990) *The Politics of Technocracy*, Newbury Park, Ca.: Sage.

Fisse, B. (1981) 'Community Service as a Sanction Against Corporations', *Wisconsin Law Review*, 5.

Fisse, B. and Braithwaite, J. (1993) *Corporations, Crime and Accountability*, Cambridge: Cambridge University Press.

Fligstein, N. (1990) *The Transformation of Corporate Control*, Cambridge, MA: Harvard University Press.

Ford, D. (1982) *The Cult of the Atom: The Secret Papers of the Atomic Energy Commission*, New York: Simon and Schuster.

Foreman-Peck, J. (1989) 'The Privatization of Industry in Historical Perspective', *Journal of Law and Society*, 16, 1 (Spring).

Foucault, M. (1965) *Madness and Civilization*, New York: Random House.

Foucault, M. (1968) 'Réponse au Cercle d'épistémologie', *Cahiers pour l'Analyse, 9, Généalogie des sciences*, translated in *Theoretical Practice*, 3 & 4, (1971).

Foucault, M. (1969) *L'Archéologie du Savoir*, Paris: Editions Gallimard.

Foucault, M. (1971a) 'Orders of Discourse' *Social Sciences Information*, April.

Foucault, M. (1971b formerly 1971 in text) 'On the Archaeology of the Sciences: questions to Michel Foucault' *Theoretical Practice 3 & 4,* a translation by Athar Hussain of Foucault 1968.

Foucault, M. (1975) 'My Body, this Paper, this Fire', *Oxford Literary Review*, vol IV, no 1., Autumn.

Foucault, M. (1973) *The Birth of the Clinic: An Archaeology of Medical Perception*, London: Tavistock.

Foucault, M. (1974) *The Archaeology of Knowledge*, London: Tavistock Publications.

Foucault, M. (1977) 'Prison Talk: an Interview with Michel Foucault', *Radical Philosophy*, 16.

Foucault, M. (1978) 'About the Concept of the Dangerous Individual in the Nineteenth Century', *International Journal of Law and Psychiatry*, 1, (1).

Foucault, M. (1979b) *The History of Sexuality: Volume 1: An Introduction*, London: Allen Lane.

Foucault, M. (1979a) *Discipline and Punish*, London: Penguin Books.

Foucault, M. (1979c) 'Governmentality', *Ideology and Conscious-ness*, No. 6, (August).

Foucault, M. (1980a) 'Truth and Power', in Gordon, C., ed., *Power/Knowledge: Selected Interviews and other writings 1972-1977 Michel Foucault*, New York: Pantheon Books.

Foucault, M. (1980b) 'The Confession of the Flesh' translated by Colin Gordon, in Gordon, C., ed., *Power/Knowledge: Selected Interviews and other writings 1972-1977 Michel Foucault*, New York: Pantheon Books.

Foucault, M. (1981) 'Histories of the Biological Sciences', *Ideology and Consciousness*, 7.

Foucault, M. (1982) 'The Subject and Power', Dreyfus, H. and Rabinow, P., *Michel Foucault: Beyond Structuralism and Hermeneutics*, Chicago: University of Chicago Press.

Foucault, M. (1989) 'Introduction' to Canguilhem, G., *The Normal and the Pathological*, New York: Zone Books.

Foveaux, M. (1986) 'A Field Day for Legislators: Bhopal and its effect on the enactment of new laws in the United States', in Smith, M.A., ed., *The Chemical Industry After Bhopal*.

Fraser, A. (1983) 'The Corporation as a Body Politic', *Telos*, 57 (Fall).

Fraser, A. (1990) *The Spirit of the Laws: Republicanism and the Unfinished Project of Modernity*, Toronto: University of Toronto Press.

Freeman, S. (1985) 'Training: the decline and fall?', *The Safety Practitioner*, February.

Friedman, M. (1962) *Capitalism and Freedom*, Chicago: University of Chicago Press.

Friedman, M. (1970) 'The Social Responsibility of Business is to Make Profits', *The New York Times Magazine*, 13th September.

Friedman, M. (1985) 'The Social Responsibility of Business is to Make Profits', in desJardins, J. and McCall, J. (1985) *Contemporary Issues in Business Ethics*, Belmont, Ca: Wadsworth Publishing.

Friedrichs, D.O. (1992) 'White-Collar Crime and the Definitional Quagmire: a provisional solution', *Journal of Human Justice*, 3, (2).

Fudge, J. and Glasbeek, H. (1992) The Politics of Rights: a politics with little class', *Social & Legal Studies*, 1, (1), March.

Fuller, J. G. (1984) *The Day We Almost Lost Detroit*, New York: Berkeley Books.

Galanter, M. (1994) The Transnational Traffic in Legal Remedies", in Jasanoff, S., ed., *Learning From Disaster. Risk Management After Bhopal*, Philadelphia: University of Pennsylvania Press.

Gamble, A. (1990) *Britain in Decline: economic policy, political strategy and the British state, 3rd edition,* New York: St. Martin's Press.

Gamble, A. and Kelly, G. (1996) 'The New Politics of Ownership', *New Left Review*, 220, November/December.

Geis, G. (1967) 'White-Collar Crime: the heavy electrical equipment anti-trust cases', in Clinard, M. and Quinney, R., eds., *Criminal Behaviour Systems*, New York: Holt, Rinehart & Winston.

Geis, G. (1968) *White Collar Criminal: The Offender in Business and the Professions*, New York: Atherton Press.

Geis, G. (1975) 'Victimization Patterns in White Collar Crime', in Drapkin, I. and Viano, E., eds., *Victimology: Volume V*, Lexington: Lexington Books.

Geis, G. (1996) 'A Base on Balls for White-Collar Criminals', in Shichor, D. and Sechrest, D.K., eds., *Three Strikes and You're Out. Vengeance as Public Policy*, Thousand Oaks, CA: Sage.

Geis, G. and Dimento, J. (1995) 'Should We Prosecute Corporations and/or Individuals?', in Pearce and Snider, eds., *Corporate Crime: contemporary debates*.

Geis, G. and Jesilow, P., eds. (1993) *White-Collar Crime. Special Issue of the Annals of the American Academy of Political and Social Science*, 525, January, Newbury Park, Ca: Sage.

Geis, G. and Meier, Robert F. (1977) *White-Collar Crime: Offences in Business Politics and the Professions*, New York: Free Press.

Geis, G. and Stotland, E., eds. (1980) *White-Collar Crime: theory and research*, Beverly Hills: Sage.

GMB (1983) *Rationalisation without Recovery - the 1983 Chemical Industries Review*, Esher: General, Municipal, Boilermakers & Allied Trades Union.

Genn, H. (1987) 'Great Expectations: The Robens Legacy and Employer Self-Regulation', unpublished paper presented to the Health and Safety Executive.

Genn, H. (1988) 'Multiple Victimization', in Maguire, M. and Ponting, J., eds., *Victims of Crime: A New Deal?*, Milton Keynes: Open University Press.

Genovese, E. (1967) *The Political economy of Slavery: Studies in the Economy and Society of the Slave South*, New York: Vintage Books.

Genovese, E. (1969) 'Marxist Interpretations of the Slave South' in Bernstein, B.J. *Towards a New Past: Dissenting essays in American History*, New York: Vintage.

Genovese, E. (1971) *In Red and Black: Marxist Explorations in Southern and Afro-American History*, New York: Oxford University Press.

Gephart, R.P. (1987) 'Organisation Design for Hazardous Chemical Accidents', *Journal of World Business*, 10, Spring.

Gephart, R.P. (1989) 'Organisational Structure and the Management of Petrochemical Activity: a case comparative study', Paper Presented at 2nd International Conference on Industrial and Organisational Crisis Management, Leonard N. Stern School of Business, New York, 3-4 December.

Geuss, R. (1981) *The Idea of a Critical Theory*, Cambridge: Cambridge University Press.

Giarini, O. (1992) 'The Modern Economy as a Service Economy: the production of utilization value', in Ekins, P. and Max Neef, M., *Real-Life Economics*.

Giddens, A. (1972) *Politics and Sociology in the Thought of Max Weber*, London: Macmillan.

Gil, D. (1978) 'Violence against children' in Lee, C.M., ed., *Child Abuse: A Reader and Sourcebook*, Milton Keynes: Open University Press.

Gill, C., Morris, R., and Eaton, J. (1978) *Industrial Relations in the Chemical Industry*, Farnborough: Saxon House.

Gill, S. (1990) *American Hegemony and the Trilateral Commission*, Cambridge: Cambridge University Press.

Gill, S., ed. (1993) *Gramsci, Historical Materialism, and International Relations*, Cambridge: University of Cambridge Press.

Gill, S. (1994) 'Knowledge, Politics and Neo-Liberal Political Economy', in Stubbs, R. and Underhill, G.R.D., eds., *Political Economy and the Changing Global Order*, London: Macmillan.

Gill, S. (1995) 'Globalisation, Market Civilisation and Disciplinary Neoliberalism', *Millennium*, 24, (3).

Gill, S. and Law, D. (1988) *The Global Political Economy*, Baltimore: Johns Hopkins University Press.

Gill S. and Law, D. (1993) 'Global Hegemony and the Structural Power of Capital', in Gill, S., ed., *Gramsci, Historical Materialism and International Relations*, Cambridge: Cambridge University Press.

Gilroy, P. (1987) 'The Myth of Black Criminality', in Scraton, P., ed., *Law, Order and the Authoritarian State*, Milton Keynes: Open University Press.

Gilroy, P. and Sim, J. (1985) 'Law, Order and the State of the Left', *Capital and Class*, 25, Spring.

Glasbeek, H. (1984) 'Why Corporate Deviance is not treated as a crime - the need to make profits a dirty word', *Osgoode Hall Law Journal*, 22, (3).

Glasbeek, H. (1988a) 'A Role For Criminal Sanctions in Occupational Health and Safety', *Meredith Memorial Lectures*, Cowansville, Québec: Editions Yvon Blais.

Glasbeek, H. (1988b) 'The Corporate Social Responsibility Movement - The Latest in Maginot Lines to Save Capitalism', *Dalhousie Law Journal*, 11, (2), March.

Glasbeek, H. (1989) 'Why Corporate Deviance is not Treated as Crime. The need to make "profits" a dirty word', in Caputo, T., Kennedy, M., Reasons, C.E. and Brannigan, A., eds, *Law and Society: a critical perspective*, Toronto: Harcourt Brace Jovanovich.

Glasbeek, H. (1995) 'Preliminary Observations on Strains of, and Strains in, Corporate Law Scholarsship', in Pearce, F. and Snider, L., eds., *Corporate Crime: contemporary debates*.

Glasbeek, H. and Rowland (1979) 'Are Injuring and Killing at Work Crimes', *Osgoode Hall Law Journal*, 17.

Glazer, M.P. and Glazer, P.M. (1989) *The Whistle Blowers*, New York, Basic Books.

Glyn, A. and Miliband, D. (1994) *Paying for Inequality: The Economic Costs of Social Injustice*, London: IPRR/River Oram Press.

GMBATU (1986) *The Freedom to Kill: a response to deregulation in the workplace*, Esher: GMBATU.

GMBATU (1987) *Hazards of Work. GMB proposals for reducing risks to workers and the public*, Esher: GMBATU.

Goodman, D. and Redclift, M. (1991) *Refashioning Food: nature, ecology and culture*, London: Routledge.

Goff, C. and Reasons, C.E. (1986) 'Organizational Crimes Against Employees, Consumers and the Public', in Maclean, B., ed., *The Political Economy of Crime*, Toronto: Prentice-Hall.

Goodwyn, L. (1976) *Democratic Promise: The Populist Movement in America*, New York: Oxford University Press.

Gordon, A. and Suzuki, D. (1990) *It's A Matter of Survival*, Toronto: Stoddart.

Gordon, D. (1988) 'The Global Economy: New Edifice or Crumbling Foundations', *New Left Review*, No. 168, March/April.

Gordon, R. (1984) 'Critical Legal Histories', 36 *Stanford Law Review*, 57.

Gorz, A. (1980) *Ecology as Politics*, London: Pluto.

Gottfredson, M.R. and Hirschi, T. (1990) *A General Theory of Crime*, Stanford University Press: Stanford.

Gouldner, A.W. (1954) *Patterns of Industrial Bureaucracy*, The Free Press: New York.

Gowan, P. (1995) 'Neo-Liberal Theory and Practice for Eastern Europe', *New Left Review*, 213, September/October.

Gramsci, A. (1971) *Selections from the Prison Notebooks of Antonio Gramsci* Translated by Hoare, Q. and Nowell Smith, G. New York: International Publishers; London: Lawrence and Wisconsin.

Gramsci, A. (1975) *Quaderni del Carcere, 4 Vols*, ed. V. Gerratana, Turin: Einaudi Editore.

Granada TV (1986) *The Betrayal of Bhopal*, (Produced by Laurie Flynn).

Grant, W., Paterson, W. and Whitston, C. (1987) 'Government- Industry Relations in the Chemical Industry: an Anglo-German Comparison', in Wilks, S. and Wright, M., eds., *Comparative Government-Industry Relations*, Oxford: Clarendon.

Grant, W., Paterson, W. and Whitston, C. (1988) *Government and the Chemical Industry: a comparative study of Britain and West Germany*, Clarendon: Oxford.

Gray, R., with Bebbington, J. and Walters, D. (1993) *Accounting for the Environment*, London: Paul Chapman/The Chartered Association of Certified Accountants.

Grayham, D.A. (1986) 'The Mismanagement of Occupational Health and Safety', *The Safety Practitioner*, February.

Grayson, J. and Goddard, C. (1976) *Industrial Safety and the Trade Union Movement. Studies for Trades Unionists*, 1, (4).

Green, G.S. (1990) *Occupational Crime*, Chicago: Nelson Hall.

Green, F. and Sutcliffe, B. (1987) *The Profit System: The Economics of Capitalism*, Harmandsworth: Penguin Books.

Greenberg, D. S. (1971) *The Politics of Pure Science: an Inquiry into the relationship between Science and Government in the United States*, New York: New American Library

Greenberg, D. (1981) 'Crime and Revolution; Is Crime Progressive?', in Greenberg, D., ed, *Crime and Capitalism*, Palo Alto: Mayfield Publishing Co.

Griffiths, R. (1980) 'Acceptability and Estimation in Risk Management', *Science and Public Policy*, Vol. 7.

Griffiths, R. (1981) 'A Background of Risk', Paper Presented at Living with Uncertainty: Risks in the Energy Scene, London: Oyez IBC Ltd.

Groenewegen, P. and Vergragt, P. (1991) 'Environmental Issues as Threats and Opportunities for Technological Innovation', *Technology Analysis & Strategic Management*, 3, (1).

Grunberg, L. (1983) 'The Effects of the Social Relations of Production on Productivity and Workers' Safety: an ignored set of relationships', *International Journal of Health Services*, 13, (4).

Grunberg, L. (1986) 'Workplace Relations in the Economic Crisis: a comparison of a British and a French Automobile Plant', *Sociology*, 20, (4).

Guest, D. (1989) 'Human Resource Management: its implications for industrial relations and trade unions', in Storey, J., ed., *New Perspectives on Human Resource Management*, Routledge: London.

Gunningham, N. (1995) 'Environment, Self-Regulation and the Chemical Industry: assessing responsible care', *Law & Policy*, 17, (1), January.

Haag, E. van den and Conrad, J.P. (1983) *The Death Penalty: A Debate*, New York: Plenum Press.

Habermas, J. (1970) 'Towards a Theory of Communicative Competence', in Dreitzel, H., ed., *Recent Sociology*, New York: Macmillan.

Habermas, J. (1975) *Legitimation Crisis*, Boston: Beacon Press.

Hadden, S.G. (1994) 'Citizen Participation in Environmental Policy-making', in Jasanoff, S., ed., *Learning From Disaster. Risk Management After Bhopal*, Philadelphia: University of Pennsylvania Press.

Hadden, T. (1977) *Company Law and Capitalism*, London: Weidenfeld and Nicholson.

Hall. S. (1984) 'Authoritarian Populism, Two Nations and Thatcherism' *New Left Review*, 147.

Hampel, Sir R. (1997) 'Beyond the Millenium', *Chemistry & Industry*, 19 May.

Handford, M. (1997), *Bombs, Bulbs and Barrels - The Rise and Fall of the United States' Nuclear Complex*, M.A. Thesis, Department of Sociology, Queen's University, Kingston. (Submitted August).

Hardin, G. (1968) 'The Tragedy of the Commons', *Science*, 162, December.

Hardin, G. (1980) 'Second Thoughts on "The Tragedy of the Commons"', in Daly, H. and Townsend, K.E., *Economics, Ecology and Ethics: Essays Toward a Steady-State Economy*, Cambridge, Mass.: MIT Press.

Harding, A. (1966) *A Social History of English Law*, Harmondsworth: Penguin Books.

Harman, C. (1996) 'Globalisation: a critique of a new orthodoxy', *International Socialism*, 73, (Winter).

Harris, R. (1987) *Power and Powerlessness in Industry: An Analysis of the Social Relations of Production*, London: Tavistock.

Harris, S. F. (1973) *Harris's Criminal Law, 22nd ed., by Ian McLean and Peter Morrish*, London: Sweet and Maxwell.

Harrison, B. (1994) *Lean and Mean: The Changing Landscape of Corporate Power*, New York: Basic Books.

Harrison, K. (1992) 'Manslaughter by Breach of Employment Contract', *Industrial Law Journal*, 21, 1.

Hart, H.L.A. (1961) *The Concept of Law*, Oxford: Oxford University Press.

t'Hart, P. (1993) 'Symbols, Rituals and Power: the lost dimensions of crisis management', *Journal of Contingencies and Crisis Management*, 1, (1).

Hassard, J. and Parker, M., eds. (1993) *Postmodernism and Organisations*, London: Sage.

Hawkins, K. (1984) *Environment and Enforcement*, Oxford: Clarendon Press.

Hawkins, K. (1990) 'Compliance Strategy, Prosecution Policy and Aunt Sally: a comment on Pearce and Tombs', *British Journal of Criminology*, 30, (4), Autumn.

Hawkins, K. (1991) 'Enforcing Regulation: more of the same from Pearce and Tombs', *British Journal of Criminology*, 31, (4), Autumn.

Hawkins, K., and Thomas, J., eds. (1984) *Enforcing Regulation*, Boston: Kluwer-Hijhoff.

Hayek, F.A. (1949) *Individualism and Society*, London: Routledge and Kegan Paul.

Hayek, F.A. (1960) *The Constitution of Liberty*, Chicago: Chicago University Press.

Hayek, F.A. (1972) *The Road to Serfdom*, Chicago: Chicago University Press.

Hayes, P. (1989) *Industry and Ideology. IG Farben in the Nazi Era*, Cambridge: Cambridge University Press.

Hays, S. (1973) *The Chemicals and Allied Industries*, London: Heinemann.

Hays, S. (1987) 'Review of David Vogel's "National Styles of Regulation"', *Business History Review*, 61 (Autumn).

Hazard, G.C. (1993) 'The Role of the Legal System in Responses to Public Risk', in Burger, E.J., ed., *Risk*, Ann Arbor: University of Michigan Press.

Hazarika, S. (1987) *Bhopal: The Lessons of a Tragedy*, Delhi: Penguin Books (India) Private Ltd.

Health and Safety Commission (1990) *Annual Report 1988/89*, London: HMSO.

Health and Safety Commission (1991) *Plan of Work 1991/92 and Beyond*, London: HMSO.

Health and Safety Commission (1992) *Annual Report 1991/92*, London: HMSO.

Health and Safety Executive (1983) *Annual Report of the Chief Inspector of Factories, 1982*, London: HMSO.

Health and Safety Executive (1985a) *Deadly Maintenance. Plant and Machinery. A Study of Fatal Accidents at Work*, London: HMSO.

Health and Safety Executive (1985b) *A Guide to the Control of Industrial Major Accident Hazards Regulations 1984. HS(R) 21*, London: HMSO.

Health and Safety Executive (1985c) *Measuring the Effectiveness of HSE Field Activities. HSE Occasional Paper 11*, London: HMSO.

Health and Safety Executive (1986) *Agricultural Blackspot*, London: HMSO.
Health and Safety Executive (1987) *Dangerous Maintenance: a Study of Maintenance Accidents in the Chemical Industry and How to Prevent Them*, London: HMSO.
Health and Safety Executive (1988) *Blackspot Construction*, London: HMSO.
Health and Safety Executive (1991) *Successful Health and Safety Management*, London: HMSO.
Health and Safety Executive (1993) *The Costs of Accidents at Work*, London: HMSO.
Heaton, C.A. (1986) 'Agrochemicals', in Heaton, C.A., ed., *The Chemical Industry*, Glasgow: Blackie & Son.
Heaton, A. (1996) 'The World's Major Chemical Industries', in Heaton, A., ed., in *An Introduction to Industrial Chemistry*, London: Blackie.
Held, D. (1989) 'The Decline of the Nation State' in Hall, S. and Jacques, M., eds., *New Times*, London: Lawrence and Wishart.
Helleiner, E. (1994) *States and the Reemergence of Global Finance: From Bretton Woods to the 1990s*, Ithaca, N.Y.: Cornell University Press.
Henderson, J. (1989) *The Globalisation of High Technology Production*, London: Routledge.
Henderson, J. (1993) 'Against Economic Orthodoxy', *Economy and Society*, 22, 2, May.
Henwood, D. (1997) *Wall Street*, London: Verso.
Her Majesty's Chief Inspector of Factories (1983) *Health and Safety at Work: Report 1982-83*, London: HSE.
Herbert, B. (1993) 'Tobacco Dollars', *New York Times*, Sunday November 28.
Heyderbrand, W.V. (1989) 'New Organisational Forms', *Work and Occupations*, 16, (3), August.
Hicks, J.R. (1946) *Value and Capital, 2nd edition*, Oxford: Clarendon Press.
Hicks, J.R. (1948) 'On the Valuation of Social Income', *Economica*, August.
Hilgartner, S. (1992) 'The Social Construction of Risk Objects', in Short Jr., J. F. and Clarke, L., *Organizations, Uncertainty and Risk*, Boulder: Westview Press.
Hindess, B. (1977) *Philosophy and Methodology of the Social Sciences*, Brighton: Harvester Press.
Hindess, B. (1987) *Freedom, Equality and the Market: arguments on social policy*, London: Tavistock Publications
Hindess, B. and Hirst, P.Q. (1975) *Pre-Capitalist Modes of Production*, London: Routledge and Kegan Paul.
Hird, J.A. (1994) *Superfund: The Political Economy of Environmental Risk*, Baltimore: Johns Hopkins University Press.
Hirschi, T. and Gottfriedson, M. (1987) 'Causes of White-Collar Crime', *Criminology*, 25.
Hirst, P.Q. (1972) 'Marx and Engels on Law, Crime and Morality', *Economy and Society*, Vol. 1., 1, (February).
Hirst, P.Q. (1976) *Social Evolution and Sociological Categories*, London: George Allen and Unwin.
Hirst, P.Q. (1979) *On Law and Ideology*, London: Macmillan.
Hirst, P.Q. (1986) *Law, Socialism and Democracy*, London: Unwin-Hyman.
Hirst, P.Q. (1989) 'After Henry', in Jacques, M. and Hall, S., eds., *New Times*, London: Lawrence and Wishart.
Hirst, P.Q. (1994) *Associative Democracy: New Forms of Economic and Social Governance*, Cambridge: Polity Press.
Hirst, P.Q. and Thompson, G. (1992) 'The Problem Of Globalisation', *Economy and Society*, 21, 4, November.

Hirst, P.Q. and Thompson, G. (1996) *Globalisation in Question*, Cambridge: Polity.

Hirst, P.Q and Zeitlin, J. (1991) 'Flexible Specialization versus Post-Fordism: theory, evidence and policy implications', *Economy and Society*, Vol. 20, No. 1. February.

HMSO *Report of the Working Committee on the Costs of Crime*, London: Home Office, 1988.

Hobbes, T. (1651 and 1960) *Leviathan*, Oxford: Basil Blackwell.

Hobbs, D. (1988) *Doing the Business. Entrepreneurship, the working class, and detectives in East London*, Oxford: Oxford University Press.

Hofrichter, R., ed. (1993) *Toxic Struggles. The Theory and Practice of Environmental Justice*, Philadelphia, PA: New Society Publishers.

Hofstadter, R. (1955) *The Age of Reform*, New York: Vintage.

Hofstadter, R. (1963) *The Progressive Movement: 1900-1915*, Engelwood-Cliffs, N.J.: Prentice-Hall.

Hofstadter, R. (1967) *The American Political Tradition*, London: Jonathan Cape.

Hohfeld, W. (1913) 'Some Fundamental Legal Conceptions as Applied in Legal Reasoning', *Yale Law Journal*, 23.

Holland, S. (1975) *The Socialist Challenge*, London: Quartet Books.

Holloway, J. (1994) 'Global Capital and the Nation-State', *Capital & Class*, 52, Spring.

Holman, O. (1993) 'Internationalisation and Democratisation: Southern Europe, Latin America and the world economic order', in Gill, S., ed. (1993) *Gramsci, Historical Materialism and International Relations*.

Hopfl, H. and Jennings, M. (1993) 'Safety Culture, Corporate Culture: organisational transformations and the commitment to safety', in Vincent and Clemenson, R., eds., *Emergency Planning '93*, Lancaster: Lancaster University.

Hopkins, A. and Parnell, N. (1984) 'Why Coal-Mine Safety Regulations in Australia are not Enforced', *International Journal of the Sociology of Law*, 12.

Hopkins, A. (1994) 'Compliance with What? the fundamental regulatory question', *British Journal of Criminology*, 34, (4), Autumn.

Horsman, M. and Marshall, A. (1994) *After The Nation-State. Citizens, tribalism and the new world order*, London: Harper Collins.

Horton, R. (1990) 'Well Begun is Half Done', *Chemistry & Industry*, 19 November.

Horwitz, R.B. (1986) 'Understanding Deregulation', *Theory and Society*, Vol. 15.

Horwitz, R.B. (1989) *The Irony of Regulatory Reform*, New York: Oxford University Press.

Houck, J.W. and Williams, O.F., eds. (1996) *Is the Good Corporation Dead? Social Responsibility in a Global Economy*, Lanham, Md: Rowman & Littlefield.

Hounshell, D.A. (1984) *From the American System to Mass Production, 1800-1932*, Baltimore: Johns Hopkins University Press.

Howarth, W. (1991) 'Crimes Against the Aquatic Environment', *Journal of Law and Society*, 18, (1).

Hsu, W.K. (1995) 'Asia: the centre of future growth for the chemical industry', *Chemistry & Industry*, 4 December.

Hudson, R. and Williams, A.M. (1989) *Britain Divided*, London: Belhaven Press.

Hueting, R. (1992) 'The Economic Functions of the Environment', in Ekins, P. and Max-Neef, M., eds., *Real-Life Economics*.

Hughes, A. (1992) 'Big Business, Small Business and the "Enterprise Culture"', in Michie, ed., *The Economic Legacy 1979-1992*, London: The Academic Press.

Hughes, P.W. (1984) 'Cost Effective Health and Safety', *The Safety Practitioner*, May.

Hulse, R.J. (1992) 'Responsible Care of the Environment: a view from industry', in Drake, J., ed., *The Chemical Industry - friend to the environment?*, Cambridge: The Royal Society of Chemistry.

Hunt, A. (1993) *Explorations in Law and Society: Towards a Constitutive Theory of Law*, London: Routledge.

Hunt, B.C. (1936) *The Development of the Business Corporation in England 1800-1867*, Cambridge, Mass.: Harvard University Press.

Huntingdon, S. (1952) 'The Marasmus of the Interstate Commerce Commission', *Yale Law Review*, li (April).

Hurrell, A. and Woods, N. (1995) 'Globalisation and Inequality', *Millennium*, 24, (3).

Hutchinson, A. (1991) 'Tobacco Ruling No Triumph for Free Speech', *The Toronto Star*, Monday July 29.

Hutter, B. (1986) 'An Inspector Calls', *British Journal of Criminology*, 26, 2 (April).

Hutter, B. (1988) *The Reasonable Arm of the Law?*, Oxford: Clarendon.

Hutton, W. (1995) *The State We're In*, London: Jonathan Cape.

Hyatt, W.D. and Trexler, T.L. (1996) 'Environmental Crime and Organised Crime: what will the future hold?', in Edwards et al., eds., *Environmental Crime and Criminality. Theoretical and Practical Issues*.

International Coalition for Justice in Bhopal (1987) *We Must Not Forget - A Plea for Justice for the Bhopal Victims*, Penang: International Organization of Consumers Unions.

Ilgen, T. (1983) '"Better Living through Chemistry?": the chemical industry in the world economy', *International Organisation*, 36, Fall.

ILO (1985) *Tripartite Symposium of Specialists of Labour Inspection. Proceedings by Specialists of Seven Countries of Western Europe: Belgium, Denmark, France, Federal Republic of West Germany, Italy, Norway, United Kingdom*, Geneva: ILO.

IPMS (1993) *Health and Safety. Keep it Together. Deregulation, market testing and contracting out - the impact of Government policies on the Health and Safety Executive*, London: Institution of Professionals, Managers and Specialists.

Irwin, A., Smith, D. and Griffith, R. (1982) 'Risk Analysis and Public Policy for Major Hazards', *Physics and Technology*, Vol. 13.

Irwin, A., (1985) *Risk and the Control of Technology: public policies for road traffic safety in Britain and the United States*, Manchester: Manchester University Press.

Itoh, M. (1992) 'Japan in a new world order', in Miliband, R. and Panitch, L., eds. *The Socialist Register 1992*, London: Merlin Press.

Ives, J., ed. (1985) *The Export of Hazard. Transnational corporations and environmental control issues*, Boston: Routledge and Kegan Paul.

Jackall, R. (1988) *Moral Mazes. The World of Corporate Managers*, New York: Oxford University Press.

Jackson, P.M. and Price, C.M., eds. (1994) *Privatisation and Regulation. A Review of the Issues*, London: Longman.

Jacques, M. and Hall, S., eds. (1989) *New Times*, London: Lawrence and Wishart.

Jalees, K. (1985) 'Environmental Impacts of Fertilisers in India', *Chemistry & Industry*, 16 June.

James, P. (1989) 'Manslaughter: a new liability?', *Health and Safety Information Bulletin*, 164, 8 August.

James, P. (1993) *The European Community. A Positive Force for UK Health and Safety Law?*, Institute of Employment Rights: London.

Jamieson, K.M. (1994) *The Organisation of Corporate Crime. Dynamics of Antitrust Violation*, Thousand Oaks, Ca: Sage.

Jamieson, M. (1985) *Persuasion or Punishment: The Enforcement of Health and Safety at Work Legislation by the British Factory Inspectorate*, Oxford: Unpublished M. Phil thesis.

Jasanoff, S. (1993) 'Complete Separation of the Two Processes is a Misconception', *EPA Journal*, January/ February/ March.

Jasanoff, S. (1994) 'Introduction: learning from disaster', in Jasanoff, S., ed. (1994) *Learning From Disaster. Risk Management After Bhopal*.

Jasanoff, S., ed. (1994) *Learning From Disaster. Risk Management After Bhopal*, Philadelphia: University of Pennsylvania Press.

Jefferson, T. and Grimshaw, R. (1987) *Interpreting Policework*, London: Unwin Hyman.

Jefferey, C.R. (1957) 'The Development of Crime in Early English Society' *Journal of Criminal Law, Criminology and Police Science*.

Jenkins, C. (1959) *Power at the Top: A Critical Survey of the Nationalized Industries*, London: MacGibbon and Kee.

Jensen, M.C. and Meckling, W.H. (1976) '"Theory of the Firm": Managerial Behavior, Agency Costs, and Ownership Structure', *Journal of Financial Economics*, 3.

Jensen, M.C. and Meckling, W.H. (1979) 'Rights and Production Functions: An Application to Labor Managed Firms and Codetermination', *Journal of Business*, 52.

Jessop, B. (1980) 'On recent Marxist Theories of Law, the state, and Juridico-Political Ideology' *International Journal of the Sociology of Law*, 8.

Jessop, B. (1982) *The Capitalist State*, Oxford: Martin Robertson.

Jessop, B. (1990a) *State Theory: Putting Capitalist States in Their Place*, Cambridge: Polity Press.

Jessop, B. (1990b) 'Regulation Theories in Prospect and Retrospect', *Economy and Society*, 19, 2, May.

Jessop, B. (1993) 'Towards a Schumpeterian Welfare State? Preliminary remarks on a post-Fordist political economy', *Studies in Political Economy*, 40, Spring.

Jessop, B., Bonnett, K., Bromley, S., Ling, T. (1988), *Thatcherism: A tale of two nations*, Cambridge: Polity Press.

Johnston, L. (1992) *The Rebirth of Private Policing*, London: Routledge.

Jones, K. (1982) *Law and Economy: The Legal Regulation of Corporate Capital*, London: Academic Press.

Jones, K. (1984) 'Everywhere Abroad but Nowhere at Home: the global corporation and the international state', *International Journal of the Sociology of Law*, 12.

Jones, T., MacLean, B. and Young, J. (1986) *The Islington Crime Survey. Crime, victimisation and policing in inner-city London*, Aldershot: Gower.

Jones, T. (1988) *Corporate Killing: Bhopals Will Happen*, London: Free Association Books.

Jordan, B. (1996) *A Theory of Poverty and Social Exclusion*, Cambridge: Polity Press.

Josephson, M. (1962) *The Robber Barons*, London: Eyre and Spottiswoode.

Kagan, R. (1984) 'On Regulatory Inspectorates and Police', in Hawkins, K., and Thomas, J., eds. (1984) *Enforcing Regulation*.

Kagan, R. and Scholz, J. (1984) 'The Criminology of the Corporation and Regulatory Enforcement Strategies', in Hawkins, K. and Thomas, J., eds., *Enforcing Regulation*.

Kairys, D. (1981) *The Politics of Law: A Progressive Critique, Revised Edition*, New York: Pantheon

Kalelkar, A. (1988) 'Investigation of large magnitude incidents - Bhopal as a case study', in *Institute of Chemical Engineers Symposium Series No.110. Preventing Major Chemical and Related Process Accidents*, Rugby: IChemE.

Kanter, R.M. (1989) *When Giants Learn to Dance*, New York: Simon and Schuster.

Kanter, R.M. (1991) 'The Future of Bureaucracy and Hierarchy in Organisational Theory: A Report from the Field', in Bourdieu, P. and Coleman, J.S., eds., *Social Theory for a Changing Society*, Boulder: Westview Press / Russell Sage Foundation.

Kasperson, R.E. and Kasperson, J.X. (1987) *Nuclear Risk Analysis in Comparative Perspective*, Boston: Allen and Unwin.

Kasperson, R, Kasperson, J.X., Hohenemser, C., and Kates R.W. with Svenson, O. (1988) *Corporate Management of Health and Safety Hazards. A comparison of current practice*, Boulder, Colorado: Westview.

Katrak, H. (1983) 'Multinational Firms' Global Strategies, Host Country Indigenisation of Ownership and Welfare', *Journal of Development Economics*, 13.

Katz, J. (1988) *The Seductions of Crime*, New York: Basic Books.

Katzman, M. T. (1989) 'Pollution Liability Insurance as a Mechanism for Managing Chemical Risks', in Schnare, D. W. and Katzman, M. T. *Chemical Contamination and its Victims: Medical Remedies, Legal Redress, and Public Policy*, New York: Quorum Books.

Kaufman, C. (1985) *The Influence of Trades Unions on Health and Safety at Work*, Unpublished MPhil Thesis, University of Aston.

Kazis, R. and Grossman, R.L. (1982) *Fear at Work: Job Blackmail, Labor and the Environment*, New York: The Pilgrim Press.

Keane, C. (1995) 'Loosely Coupled Systems and Unlawful Behaviour: organisation theory and corporate crime', in Pearce, F. and Snider, L., eds., *Corporate Crime: contemporary debates*.

Kelman, M. (1987) *A Guide to Critical Legal Studies*, Cambridge: Harvard University Press.

Kelman, S. (1981) *Regulating America, Regulating Sweden*, Cambridge: The MIT Press.

Kelly, G., Kelly, D. and Gamble, A. (1997) *Stakeholder Capitalism*, London: Macmillan.

Kennedy, L. W., Silverman, R.A., Forde, D.R. (1991) 'Homicide in Urban Canada: Testing the impact of economic inequality and social disorganisation', *Canadian Journal of Sociology*, 16, 4 (Fall).

Kerr, D. (1992) 'Case Study: Water and Air Pollution Offenses (Bakelite Thermosets Ltd., Belleville, Ontario, Canada)', paper presented at Corporate Crime: ethics, law and the state, Queens University, Kingston, 12-14 November.

Keynote Report. An Industry Sector Overview: the chemical industry, 1988, London: Keynote.

Kharbanda, O.P. (1986) 'Lessons from Bhopal', in Smith, M.A., ed., *The Chemical Industry After Bhopal*.

Kharbanda, O.P and Stallworthy, E.A. (1991) 'Industrial Disasters - Will Self-Regulation Work?', *Long Range Planning*, 24, 3.

Killingsworth, M.J and Palmer, J.S. (1992) *Ecospeak: Rhetoric and Environmental Politics in America*, Carbondale and Edwardsville: Southern Illinois University Press.

King, R. (1990) *Safety in the Process Industries*, London: Butterworth-Heinemann.

Kinsey, R., Lea, J., and Young, J., (1986) *Losing the Fight Against Crime*, Oxford: Basil Blackwell.

Kletz, T. (1988) *Learning from Accidents in Industry*, London: Butterworths.

Kletz, T. (1990) *Critical Aspects of Safety and Loss Prevention*, London: Butterworths.

Kletz, T. (1992) 'Workface: Green Side-Effects', *The Chemical Engineer*, 24 September.

Kletz, T. (1993) *Lessons From Disaster*, Rugby: Institute of Chemical Engineers.

Knapp Commission (1973) *Report by the Commission to Investigate Allegations of Police Corrupiton and Anti-Corruption Procedures in New York City*, New York: George Brazilier.

Knox, P. and Agnew, J. (1989) *The Geography of the World Economy*, London: Edward Arnold.

Kolko, G. (1962) *Wealth and Power in America: An Analysis of Social Class and Income Distribution*, New York: Praeger.

Kolko, G. (1963) *The Triumph of Conservatism*, New York: Free Press.

Kolko, G. (1965) *Railroads and Regulation: 1877-1916*, Princeton: Princeton University Press.

Kolko, G. (1976) *Main Currents in Modern American History*, New York: Harper and Row.

Kolko, J. (1988) *Restructuring the World Economy*, New York: Pantheon.

Korzeniewicz, R.P. and Moran, T.P. (1997) 'World-Economic Trends in the Distribution of Income, 1965-1992', *American Journal of Sociology*, 102, 4 (January).

Kramer, R.C. (1983) 'A Prolegomenon to the Study of Corporate Violence', *Humanity and Society*, 7.

Kramer, R.C. (1984) 'Corporate Criminality: The Development of an Idea', in Hochstedler, E., ed., *Corporations as Criminals*, Beverly Hills: Sage Publications.

Kramer, R.C. (1989) 'Criminologists and the Social Movement Against Corporate Crime', *Social Justice*, 16, (2).

Kreisberg, S.M. (1976) 'Decision-Making Models and the Control of Corporate Crime', *Yale Law Journal*, 85.

Kurokawa, H. (1983) 'Recent and Future Development of the Chemical Industry in Japan', *Chemistry & Industry*, 19 December.

Kurtzman, D. (1987) *A Killing Wind: Inside Union Carbide and the Bhopal Catastrophe*, New York: McGraw Hill.

Labour Research Department (1990) *A Trade Unionists' Guide to Environmental Issues*, London: LRD.

Lacey, N., Wells, C. and Meure, D. (1990) *Reconstructing Criminal Law: Texts and Materials*, London: Weidenfeld Paperbacks.

Laclau, E. (1977) *Politics and Ideology in Marxist Theory*, London: Verso.

Laclau, E. And Mouffe, C. (1985) *Hegemony and Socialist Strategy*, Verso: London.

Lambert, B. (1990) *How Safe is Safe? Radiation Controversies Explained*, London: Unwin Paperbacks.

Lambert, J. (1991) 'Europe: the Nation-State Dies Hard', *Capital & Class*, 43, Spring.

Lampman, R. (1970) 'The Share of Top Wealth-Holders in National Wealth, 1922-1956', in Zeitlin, M., ed., *American Society Inc.*, Chicago: Markham Publishing Company.

Lang, T. and Clutterbuck, C. (1991) *P is for Pesticides*, London: Ebury.

Lappe, M. (1991) *Chemical Deception. The toxic threat to health and the environment*, San Francisco: Sierra Club Books.

Lasch, C. (1995) *The Revolt of the Elites and the Betrayal of Democracy*, New York: Norton.

Lash, S. and Urry, J. (1987) *The End of Organised Capitalism*, Cambridge: Polity.

Lal, V. (1996) 'Sovereign Immunity in an Unequal World', *Social & Legal Studies*, 5, (3).

Latham, E. (1961) 'The Body Politic of the Corporation', in Mason, E.S., ed., *The Corporation in Modern Society*, Cambridge, Mass: Harvard University Press.

Latour, B. (1987) *Science in Action*, Cambridge: Harvard University Press.

Law Commission (1996) *Legislating the Criminal Code: involuntary manslaughter*, London: HMSO.

Lawson, T. (1997) *Economics and Reality*, London: Routledge.

Lea, J. (1987) 'Left Realism: a defence', *Contemporary Crises*, 11, (4).

Lea, J., Matthews, R. and Young, J. (1987) *Law and Order. Five Years On, London: Centre for Criminology*, Middlesex: Middlesex Polytechnic.

Lea, J. (1992) 'The Analysis of Crime', in Young, J. and Matthews, R., eds. (1992) *Rethinking Criminology: the Realist Debate*, London: Sage.

Lea, J. and Young, J. (1984) *What Is to be Done about Law and Order?*, Harmandsworth: Penguin.

Leadbeater, C. (1989) 'Power to the Person', in Hall, S. and Jacques, M., eds., *New Times*, London: Lawrence and Wishart.

Legge, K. (1989) 'Human Resource Management: a critical analysis', in Storey, J., ed., *New Perspectives on Human Resource Management*, London: Routledge.

Leigh, L.H. (1969) *The Criminal Liability of Corporations in English Law*, London: Weidenfeld and Nicholson.

Leonard, H.B. and Zeckhauser, R. (1986) 'Cost-Benefit Analysis Applied to Risks: its philosophy and legitimacy', in Maclean, ed., *Values at Risk*, Totowa, NJ: Rowman and Littlefield.

Leonard, H.J. (1988) *Pollution and the Struggle for World Product: multinational corporations, environment, and international comparative advantage*, Cambridge: Cambridge University Press.

Leonard, W.N. and Weber, M.G. (1970) 'Automakers and Dealers: A Study of Criminogenic Market Forces', *Law and Society Review*, 4, February.

Lepkowski, W. (1994) 'The Restructuring of Union Carbide', in Jasanoff, S., ed., *Learning From Disaster. Risk Management After Bhopal*, Philadelphia: University of Pennsylvania Press.

Leuchtenberg, W.E. (1963) *Franklin Roosevelt and the New Deal*, New York: Harper and Row.

Lever, H.H. (1986) 'The European Chemical Industry', *Shell Petrochemicals*, 2.

Levi, M. (1987) *Regulating Fraud*, London: Tavistock.

Levi, M. (1993) 'White-Collar Crime: the British Scene', in Geis, G. and Jesilow, P., eds., *White Collar Crime*, Newbury Park, CA: Sage.

Levi, M. (1994) 'Violent Crime', in Maguire, M., Morgan, R. and Reiner, R., eds., *The Oxford Handbook of Criminology*, Oxford: Oxford University Press.

Levi, M. (1995) 'Serious Fraud in Britain: Criminal Justice versus Regulation' in Pearce, F. and Snider, L., ed. *Corporate Crime: contemporary debates*.

Levi, Margaret (1987) *Of Rule and Revenue*, Berkeley: University of California Press.

Levine, R. (1988) *Class Struggle and the New Deal: Industrial Labor, Industrial Capital and the State*, Lawrence: University Press of Kansas.

Lewis, S. and Henkels, D. (1996) 'Good Neighbour Agreements: a tool for environmental social justice', *Social Justice*, 23, (4).

Liardet, G. (1991) 'Public Opinion and the Chemical Industry', *Chemistry & Industry*, 18 February.

Lindheim, J. (1989) 'Restoring the Image of the Chemical Industry', *Chemistry & Industry*, 7 August.

Lipietz, A. (1987) *Mirages and Miracles. The Crises of Global Fordism*, London: Verso.

Lipietz, A. (1992) *Towards a New Economic Order*, New York: Oxford University Press.

Lloyd, H.D. (1894/1963) *Wealth Against Commonwealth*, Engelwood Cliffs N.J.: Prentice-Hall.

Lockwood, D. (1956) 'Some Remarks on *The Social System*', *British Journal of Sociology*, 7, (1).

Lockwood, D. (1964) 'System integration and social integration', in Zollschan, G. and Hirsch, W., eds., *Explorations in Social Change*, London: Routledge and Kegan Paul.

Lofquist, W.S. (1993) 'Organisational Probation and the US Sentencing Commission', in Geis, G. and Jesilow, P., eds., *White Collar Crime*, Newbury Park, CA: Sage.

Lone, O. (1992) 'Environmental and Resource Accounting', in Ekins, P. and Max-Neef, M., eds., *Real-Life Economics*.

Lorimer, R. (1994) *Mass Communications: a comparative approach*, Manchester: Manchester University Press.

Lowi, T.J. (1993) in Burger, E.J., ed., *Risk*, Ann Arbor: University of Michigan Press.

Luesby, J. (1996) 'New Gloss on Chemicals Giant', *Financial Times*, 1 May.

Lukes, S. (1974) *Power: a radical view*, London: Macmillan.

Lundberg, G. (1968) *The Rich and the Superrich,* New York: Bantam Books.

Lundqvist, L.L. (1982) 'Review of Kelman (1981)', *American Political Science Review*, 76, March.

Lustgarten, L. (1987) 'The Governance of the Police', paper presented at the Annual Conference of the Socio-Legal Group, Sheffield, 23-26 March.

Lustig, R.J. (1982) *Corporate Liberalism: The Origins of Modern American Political Theory, 1890-1920*, Berkeley: University of California Press.

Lyotard, J-F. (1984) *The Postmodern Condition: A Report on Knowledge*, Minneapolis: University of Minnesota Press.

Macdonell, D. (1986) *Theories of Discourse*, Oxford: Blackwell.

Macey, J.R. (1991) 'Agency Theory and the Criminal Liability of Organizations', *Boston University Law Review*, Vol. 71.

Macpherson, C.B. (1968) 'Elegant Tombstones: A Note on Friedman's Freedom', *Canadian Journal of Political Science/Revue Canadienne de Science Politique*, I, 1 (March/Mars).

Maguire, M. and Ponting, J. (1988) *Victims of Crime: A New Deal?*, Milton Keynes: Open University Press.

Magdoff, H. (1992) 'Globalization - To What End?, in Miliband, R. and Panitch L., eds., *Socialist Register 1992*, London: The Merlin Press.

Mahon, R. (1977) 'Canadian Public Policy: the unequal structure of representation', in Panitch, L., ed., *The Canadian State: Political Economy and Political Power*, Toronto: University of Toronto Press.

Mahon, R. (1979) 'Regulatory Agencies: Captive Agents or Hegemonic Apparatuses', *Studies in Political Economy*, 1, (1).

Mahon, R. (1984) *The Politics of Industrial Restructuring*, Toronto: University of Toronto Press.

Mahoney, R. (1988) 'Punitive Damages: The Costs Are Curbing Creativity', *New York Times*, December 11.

Mandel, M. (1989) *The Charter of Rights and the Legalization of Politics in Canada*, Toronto: Wall and Thompson.

Mann, K. (1985) *Defending White-Collar Crime*, New Haven: Yale University Press.

Manning, P.K. (1980) *The Narc's Game*, Cambridge, Mass.: MIT Press.

Manning, P.K. (1992) 'Managing Risk: Managing Uncertainty in the British Nuclear Installations Inspectorate', in Short Jr., J. F. and Clarke, L., *Organizations, Uncertainty and Risk*, Boulder: Westview Press.

Marchington, M. and Parker. P. (1990) *Changing Patterns of Employee Relations*, Hemel Hempstead: Harvester Wheatsheaf.

Marginson, P. (1994) 'Multinational Britain: employment and work in an internationalised economy', *Human Resource Management Journal*, 4, (4).

Marcus, A. (1980) 'Environmental Protection Agency', in Wilson, J.Q., ed., *The Politics of Regulation*.

Marris, R. (1964) *The Economic Theory of Managerial Capitalism*, London: Macmillan.

Marsh, P. (1997) 'Chemical Engineering. Globalisation: focus on Asia-Pacific', *Financial Times*, 3 April.

Marshall, T.F. (1985) *Alternatives to Criminal Courts: The Potential for Non-judicial Dispute Settlement*, Aldershot: Gower.

Martin, S. and Parker,D. (1997) *The Impact of Privatisation: Ownership and Corporate Performance in the UK*, London: Routledge.

Mauer, M. (1996) 'Shocking Disparities. Race and Sentencing', *Criminal Justice Matters*, 25, Aututmn.

Marx, G.T. (1981) 'Ironies of Social Control: Authorities as Contributors to Deviance, Through Escalation, Nonenforcement and Covert Facilitation', *Social Problems*, 28, 3 (February).

Marx, K. (1867/1976) *Capital. Volume 1*, Harmandsworth: Penguin.

Marx, K. (1867/1965) *Capital. Volume 1*, Moscow: Progress Publishers.

Marx, K. and Engels, F. (1845/1976) *The German Ideology*, London: Lawrence and Wishart.

Marx, K. and Engels, F. (1872/1971) *Manifesto of the Communist Party*, Moscow: Progress.

Mathiesen, T. (1990) *Prison On Trial*, London: Sage.

Matthews, R. and Young, J., eds. (1992) *Issues in Realist Criminology*, London: Sage.

Matthews, R. (1987) 'Taking Realist Criminology Seriously', *Contemporary Crises*, 11.

Matza, D. (1964) *Delinquency and Drift*, New York: Wiley.

Max-Neef, M. (1992) 'Development and Human Needs', in Ekins, P. and Max-Neef, M., eds., *Real-Life Economics*.

Mayer, C.J. (1990) 'Personalizing the Impersonal: Corporations and the Bill of Rights', *The Hastings Law Journal*, Volume 41, No. 3, (March).

McBarnet, D. (1992) 'Tax Evasion, Tax Avoidance, and the Boundaries of Legality', *Journal of Human Justice*, 3, (2).

McBarnet, D. (1983) *Conviction: Law, the State and the Construction of Justice*, London: Macmillan.

McChesney, R.W. (1997) *Corporate Media and the Threat to Democracy*, New York: Seven Stories Press.

McCloskey, J. (1996) 'Organisational Structures: a story of evolution', in Heaton, A., ed., *An Introduction to Industrial Chemistry*, London: Blackie.

McCurdy, P. (1986) 'The Challenge to Communications: communications in a Right-to-Know era', in Smith, M.A., ed., *The Chemical Industry After Bhopal*.

McDonagh, P. and Prothero, A., eds. (1996) *Green Management. A Reader*, London: The Dryden Press.

McEldowney, J.F. and McEldowney, S. (1996) *Environment and the Law*, Harlow: Addison Wesley Longman.

McGavin, B. (1991) 'Going Green - but what about the workers?', *Employment Gazette*, January.

McGrew, A. (1993) 'The Political Dynamics of the "New" Environmentalism', in, Smith, D., ed., *Business and the Environment*.

McGuire, M.V. and Edelhertz, H. (1980) 'Consumer Abuse of Older Americans: Victimization and Remedial Action in Two Metropolitan Areas', in Geis, G. and Stotland, E., eds., *White-Collar Crime: Theory and Research*, Lexington: Lexington Books.

McLeod, R. and Roman, A.J. (1992) 'No Hiding Behind the Corporate Veil', *The Globe and Mail*, Friday March 13.

McNamee, S.J. (1987) 'Du Pont-State Relations', *Social Problems*, 34, (1), February.

McNichol, B. (1989) 'Training. Setting Standards', *Chemistry & Industry*, 3 July.

Meacher, M. (1991) 'Executive Pay: the day of reckoning', *Observer*, Sunday 13 October.

Meidner, R. (1978) *Employee Investment Funds: An Approach to Collective Capital Formation*, London: Allen and Unwin.

Meier, R.F. (1986) 'Review Essay', *Criminology*, 24.

Meyer, M.W. (1978) *Environments and Organizations*, San Francisco: Josey Bass.

Meyer. P.B. (1986) 'The Corporate Person and Social Control: Responding to Deregulation', *Review of Radical Political Economics*, 18, 3.

Michalowski, R.J. and Kramer, R.C. (1987) 'The Space Between the Laws: the problem of corporate crime in a transnational context', *Social Problems*, 34.

Michalowski, R. (1990) 'Crime and Justice in Socialist Cuba: What can left realists learn?', a paper presented at a conference on Left Realist Criminology, May 24-25, 1990, Vancouver, British Columbia.

Miles, I. (1992) 'Social Indicators for Real-Life Economics', in Ekins, P. and Max-Neef, M., eds., *Real-Life Economics*.

Miles, R.H. (1982) *Coffin Nails and Corporate Strategies*, Engelwood Cliffs, N.J.: Prentice Hall.

Miller, D. (1987) 'Strategic Industrial Relations and Human Resource Management - distinction, definition and recognition', *Journal of Management Studies*, 24, (4), July.

Miller, P. and Rose, N. (1990) 'Governing Economic Life', *Economy and Society*, 19, 1 (February).

Minns, R. (1996) 'The Social Ownership of Capital', *New Left Review*, 219, September/October.

Minson, J. (1985) *Genealogies of Morals: Nietzsche, Foucault and Donzelot and the Eccentricity of Ethics*, London: Macmillan.

Mintz, M. (1985) *At Any Cost: corporate greed, women, and the Dalkon Shield*, New York: Panthono.

Mintzberg, H. (1979) *The Structuring of Organisations*, Prentice Hall, New Jersey.

Mintzberg, H. (1983) *Power In and Around Organisations*, Englewood Cliffs, N.J.: Prentice-Hall.

Mintzberg, H. and Quinn, J.B. (1996) *The Strategy Process. Concepts, Contexts, Cases*, Upper Saddle River, NJ: Prentice Hall International.

Mittelstaedt, M. (1992) 'New Legislation in Ontario Empowers Environmentalists', *The Globe and Mail*, Wednesday July 8.

Molle, W. (1988) 'Oil Refineries and Petrochemical Industries: Moving into Maturity', in de Jong, H.W., ed., *The Structure of European Industry*, Dordrecht: Kluwer Academic.

Moran, L.J. (1992) 'Corporate Criminal Capacity: nostalgia for representation', *Social & Legal Studies*, 1, (3).

Morehouse, W. and Subramaniam, M. A. (1986) *The Bhopal Tragedy*, New York: Council on International and Public Affairs.

Morera, E. (1990) *Gramsci's Historicism: A Realist Interpretation*, London: Routledge.

Morgan, G. (1986) *Images of Organisation*, Beverly Hills: Sage.

Morgan, P. (1983) 'The Costs and Benefits of the Power Presses Regulations', *British Journal of Industrial Relations*, (2).

Morris, A. (1935) *Criminology*, New York: Longmans, Green and Co., excerpted in Geis, ed., 1968.

Mosco, V (1989) *The Pay-Per Society: Computers and Communication in the Information Age*, Toronto: Garamond Press.

Muchlinski, P.T. (1987) 'The Bhopal Case: Controlling Ultrahazardous industrial activities undertaken by Foreign Investors', *The Modern Law Review*, 50, 5 (September).

Murti, C.R. (1989) 'Biological Effects of Chemical Disasters: human victims', in Bordeau, P. and Green, G., eds., *Methods for Assessing and Reducing Injury from Chemical Accidents*.

Mytelka, L.K. (1991) 'Global Shifts in the Textile and Clothing Industries', *Studies in Political Economy*, No. 36, Autumn.

Nanavaty, K.P. (1996) 'The Indian Petrochemical Industry', *Chemistry & Industry*, 18 November.

National Institute of Justice (1993) *Local Prosecution of Environmental Crime*, Washington, DC: US Department of Justice.

National Research Council (1983) *Risk Assessment in the Federal Government; Managing the Process*, Washington D.C.: National Academy Press.

Natural Resources Defense Council (1991) *A Who's Who of American Toxic Air Polluters: A Guide to more than 150 factories in 46 states emitting cancer causing chemicals*, Washington: Natural Resources Defense Council.

Navarro, V. (1983) 'The Determinants of Social Policy, A Case Study: Regulating Health and Safety at the Workplace in Sweden', *International Journal of Health Services*, 13.

Navarro, V. (1991) 'The Limitation of Legitimation and Fordism and the Possibility for Socialist Reform', *Rethinking Marxism*, Summer.

Neale, S. (1976) 'Propoganda' *Screen* 18, (3).

Neale, W.C. (1971) *Trade and Market in the Early Empires,* New York: The Free Press.

Needleman, M.L. and Needleman, C. (1979) 'Organisational Crime: two models of criminogenesis', *Sociology Quarterly*, 20, Autumn.

Nelken, D. (1994a) 'White-Collar Crime', in Maguire, M., Morgan, R. and Reiner, R., eds., *The Oxford Handbook of Criminology*, Oxford: Oxford University Press.

Nelken, D., ed. (1994) *White-Collar Crime,* Aldershot: Dartmouth.

Nelken, D. (1994) 'Whom Can You Trust? The future of comparative criminology', in Nelken, D., ed., *The Futures of Criminology*, London: Sage.

Nell, E. (1973) 'Economics: The Revival of Political Economy' in Blackburn, R., ed., *Ideology in Social Science: Readings in Critical Social Theory,* New York: Vintage Books/Random House.

Nelson, P.J. (1996) 'Internationalising Economic and Environmental Policy: transnational NGO networks and the World Bank's Expanding Influence', *Millennium*, 24, (3).

Network First (1995) *Bhopal: the second tragedy*, ITV, 31st January.

New York Central and Hudson River Rail Co. v. U.S., 212 U.S. 494-496 1909.

New York (City) Knapp Commission (1973) *The Knapp Commission Report on police corruption,* New York : G. Braziller.

Nichols, T. (1986) 'Industrial Injuries in British Manufacturing in the 1980s. A commentary on Wright's article', *Sociological Review*, 34, (2).

Nichols, T. (1994) 'Problems in Monitoring the Safety Performance of British Manufacturing at the end of the Twentieth Century', *Sociological Review*, 42, (1).

Nichols, T. and Armstrong, P. (1973) *Safety or Profit: Industrial Accidents and the Conventional Wisdom*, Bristol: Falling Wall Press.

Nichols, T. and Beynon H. (1977) *Living with Capitalism*, London: Routledge & Kegan Paul.

Nichols, T. (1990) 'Industrial Safety in Britain and the 1974 Health and Safety at Work Act: the case of manufacturing', *International Journal of the Sociology of Law*, 18.

Nietzsche, F. (1969) *On the genealogy of morals,* New York: Vintage Books.

Noble, C. (1986) *Liberalism at Work: The Rise and Fall of OSHA*, Philadelphia: Temple University Press.

Noble, C. (1992) 'Keeping OSHA's Feet to the Fire', *Technology Review*, V, 95, Feb/March.

Noble, C. (1995) 'Beyond OSHA: Regulatory Strategy and Institutional Structure in the Work Environment', in Pearce, F. and Snider, L., eds., *Corporate Crime: contemporary debates.*

Noble, D. (1977) *America By Design: Science, Technology and the Rise of Corporate Capitalism*, New York: Oxford.

Noble, D. (1987) *Forces of Production*, New York: Knopf.

Norris, C. (1993) 'Old Themes for New Times: Basildon revisited', in Miliband, R. and Panitch L., eds., *Socialist Register 1992*, London: The Merlin Press.

Norris, R., ed. (1982) *Pills, Pesticides and Profits*, New York: North River Press.

North, D. (1981) 'Structure and Change', *Economic History*, 7.

O'Connor, J. (1973) *The Fiscal Crisis of the State*, New York: St. Martin's Press.

O'Connor, J. (1994) 'Is Sustainable Capitalism Possible?', in McDonagh, P. and Prothero, A., eds., *Green Management. A Reader*.

O'Malley, P. (1987) 'In Place of Criminology: a Marxist Reformulation', Paper Presented to the Annual Meeting of the Canadian Sociology and Anthropology Association, Hamilton, Ontario, 2-5 June.

O'Malley, P. (1989) 'Redefining Security. Neighbourhood Watch in context', *Arena*, 86.

O'Malley, P. (1991) 'Legal Networks and Domestic Security', *Studies in Law, Politics and Society*, 11.

O'Malley, P. (1992) 'Risk, Power and Crime Prevention', *Economy and Society*, Vol.21,(3), August.

O'Malley, P. (1996) '"Indigenous" Governance', *Economy and Society*, Vol.25, (3) August.

O'Riordan, T. ed. (1997) *Ecotaxation*, London: Earthscan.

Organisation for Economic Co-operation and Development (1987) *International Investment and Multinational Enterprises: Structure and Organisation of Multinational Enterprises*, Paris: OECD.

Office for National Statistics (1996) *Pilot United Kingdom Environmental Accounts*, London: Office for National Statistics.

Ohmae, K. (1989) *The Borderless World*, London and New York: Wiley.

Oi, W. (1977) 'On Socially Acceptable Risks', in Phillipps, J., ed., *Safety At Work*, Oxford: Centre for Socio-Legal Studies and Social Science Research Council.

Olsen, G. (1991) 'The Rise and Stall of Economic Democracy in Sweden', *Studies in Political Economy*, 31.

Oppenheim, C. and Harker, L. (1996) *Poverty. The Facts*, London: Child Poverty Action Group.

Orchard, D. (1993) *The Fight for Canada: Four Centuries of Resistance to American Expansionism*, Toronto: Stoddart

Ornenstein, C. (1993), Letter to the *New York Times*, Sunday, May 16.

Pacific Asia Resource Centre (1994) *The People vs Global capital. The G-7, TNCs, SAPs and Human Rights*, ARENA: Hong Kong.

Paehlke, R. (1995) 'Environmental Harm and Corporate Crime', in Pearce, F. and Snider, L., eds., *Corporate Crime: contemporary debates*.

Palmer, J. (1976) 'Evils Merely Prohibited', *British Journal of Law and Society*, 3 (1).

Palmer, J. and Pearce, F. (1983) 'Legal Discourse and State Power: Foucault and the Juridical Relation', *International Journal of the Sociology of Law*, 11.

Parris, H., Pestieu, P., and Satnor, P. (1988) *Public Enterprise in Western Europe,* London: Croom-Helm and Acton Society Trust.

Parton, N. (1985) *The Politics of Abuse*, London: Macmillan.

Pashukhanis, E. (1978) *Law and Marxism*, London: Inklinks.

Paulus, I. (1974) *The Search for Pure Food: A Sociology of Legislation in Britain*, London: Martin Robertson.

Pauly, L.W. (1994) 'Promoting a Global Economy: the normative role of the International Monetary Fund', in Stubbs, R. and Underhill, G.R., eds., *Political Economy and the Changing Global Order.*

Pearce, F. (1976) *Crimes of the Powerful*, London: Pluto.

Pearce, F. (1985) 'Neo-Structuralist Marxism on Crime and Law in Britain', *The Insurgent Sociologist*, 13.

Pearce, F. (1987) 'Review of Matthews, R. and Young, J., 1986, Confronting Crime', in *Sociology*, 21, 3, (August).

Pearce, F. (1987) 'Corporate Crime: a review essay', *Critical Social Policy*, 19.

Pearce, F. (1988) 'The Struggle for Foucault: A Review Essay', *International Journal of the Sociology of Law*, 16, 2.

Pearce, F. (1989a) *The Radical Durkheim*, London: Unwin-Hyman.

Pearce, F. (1989b) 'Socially Responsible Corporations need Strong and Independent Regulatory Agencies', paper presented at a symposium on The Management of Safety, Society of the Chemical Industry, London, April 25.

Pearce, F. (1990) 'Responsible Corporations and Regulatory Agencies', *The Political Quarterly*, 61, (4).

Pearce, F. (1992) 'The Contribution of Left-Realism to the Study of Commerical Crime', in Maclean, B. and Lowman, J., eds., *Left Realism: An Agenda for the Nineties*, Toronto: University of Toronto Press.

Pearce, F. (1993) 'Corporate Rationality as Corporate Crime', *Studies in Political Economy*, 49, Spring.

Pearce, F. (1995) 'Accountability for Corporate Crime' in Stenning, P., ed., *Accountability for Criminal Justice*, Toronto, University of Toronto Press.

Pearce, F. (1996) 'Effective Regulation: its conditions of existence', in Mehta, M.D. (1996) *Regulatory Efficiency and the Role of Risk Assessment: Proceedings from the First Annual Policy Forum of the Eco-Research Program in Environmental Policy and the School of Policy Studies at Queen's University, October 26-27, 1995,* Ottawa, Kingston: Queen's University Environmental Policy Unit, School of Policy Studies.

Pearce, P. and Snider, L., eds., (1995) *Corporate Crime: contemporary debates*, Toronto: University of Toronto Press.

Pearce, F. and Snider, L. (1995) 'Regulating Capitalism', in *Corporate Crime: contemporary debates.*

Pearce, F. and Tombs, S. (1987) 'The Social Control of Hazardous Production', paper presented at the Annual Conference of the British Sociological Association, Leeds, 6-9 April.

Pearce, F. and Tombs, S. (1989) 'Bhopal, Union Carbide and the Hubris of a Capitalist Technocracy' *Social Justice* 16, June.

Pearce, F. and Tombs, S. (1990) 'Ideology, Hegemony and Empiricism: Compliance Theories of Regulation', *British Journal of Criminology*, 30, 4.

Pearce, F. and Tombs, S. (1991) 'Policing Corporate "Skid Rows". A reply to Keith Hawkins', *British Journal of Criminology*, 31, 4.

Pearce, F. and Tombs, S. (1992) 'Realism and Corporate Crime', in Matthews, R. and Young, J., eds., *Issues in Realist Criminology*, London: Sage.

Pearce, F. and Tombs, S. (1993) 'US Capital versus the Third World: Union Carbide and Bhopal', in Pearce, F. and Woodiwiss, M., eds., *Global Crime Connections*, London: Macmillan.

Pearce, F. and Tombs, S. (1994) 'Class, Law and Hazards', a Submission to the Permanent Peoples' Tribunal, Industrial hazards and Human Rights, 28th November-2nd December, London.

Pearce, F. and Tombs, S. (1996) 'Hegemony, Risk and Governance: "social" regulation and the US chemical industry', *Economy and Society*, 25, (3) August.

Pearce, F. and Tombs, S. (1997) 'Hazards, Law and Class: contextualising the regulation of corporate crime', *Social & Legal Studies*, 6, (1).

Pearce, Fred (1982) *Watershed,* London: Junction Books.

Pearce, Fred (1985) 'After Bhopal, who remembered Ixhuatepec?', *New Scientist*, 1465, 18th July.

Peattie, K. (1992) *Green Marketing*, London: Pitman.

Peattie, K. (1995) *Environmental Marketing Management*, London: Pitman.

Peet, R., ed. (1987) *International Capitalism and Industrial Restructuring*, London: Unwin Hyman.

Pell, E. (1990) 'Movements Buying In', *Mother Jones*, April-May, 15, (3).

Peltzman, S. (1976) 'Towards a More General Theory of Regulation' *The Journal of Law and Economics*, 19, 2.

Peppin, P. (1995) 'Science, Law and the Pharmaceutical Industry', in Pearce, F. and Snider, L., eds., *Corporate Crime: contemporary debates.*

Perrott, D. (1981) 'Changes in Attitude to Limited Liability - the European Experience', in Orhnial, T., ed., *Limited Liability and the Corporation*, London: Croom Helm.

Perrow, C. (1984) *Normal Accidents: Living with High Risk Technologies*, New York: Basic Books.

Perrow, C. (1986a) *Complex Organizations: A Critical Essay (Third Edition)*, New York: McGraw-Hill.

Perrow, C. (1986b) 'The Habit of Courting Disaster', *The Nation*, 11th October.

Perrow, C. (1991) 'A Society of Organizations', *Theory, Culture and Society*, 20, (6).

Peto, R. (1980) 'Distorting the Epidemiology of Cancer: the need for a more balanced overview', *Nature*, 284, 27 March, reproduced in Doyal, L. et al. (1983) *Cancer in Britain.*

Peto, R. and Doll, R. (1981) *The Causes of Cancer*, Oxford: Oxford University Press.

Petras, J. and Morley (1990) *US Hegemony Under Siege: Class, Politics and Development in Latin America*, London: Verso

Pettigrew, A. (1985) *The Awakening Giant. Continuity and Change in ICI*, Oxford: Basil Blackwell.

Pevsner, D.L. (1992) '.. And Mislead the Flying Public', *The New York Times Forum*, Sunday April 19.

Phillips, K. (1991) *The Politics of Rich and Poor: Wealth and the American Electorate in the Reagan Aftermath*, New York: Harper-Perrenial.

Phillips, K. (1993) *Boiling Point: Democrats, Liberals and the Decline of Middle-Class Prosperity*, New York: Harper-Perennial.

Phillips, P. (1992) 'Functional Rights: Private, Public and Collective Property' *Studies in Political Economy*, 38 (Summer).

Philpot, J. (1996) 'World Petrochemical Trade', *Chemistry & Industry*, 7 October.

Picciotto, S. (1991) 'The Internationalisation of the State', *Capital & Class*, 43, Spring.

Picciotto, S. (1997) 'Fragmented States and International Rules of Law', *Social & Legal Studies*, 6, (2).

Pidgeon, N., Turner, B. and Blockley, D. (1987) 'The Sociological Management of Safety', paper presented at the Annual Conference of the British Sociological Association, Leeds, 6-9 April.

Platt, S. (1987) 'Councils Must Sell Homes at Loss', *New Society*, 27 November.

Plimsoll Publishing (1988) *Plimsoll Portfolio Analysis: Chemicals, 2nd Edition*, Middlesbrough: Plimsoll Publishing,

Plimsoll Publishing (1996) The Plimsoll Portfolio Analysis - Chemicals, 2nd Edition 1996, Middlesborough: Plimsoll Publishing.

Polanyi, K. (1944) *The Great Transformation*, New York: Farrar and Rinehart Inc.

Pollack, N. (1962) *The Populist Response to Industrial America*, Cambridge, Mass.: Prentice-Hall.

Pontell, H.N. and Calavita, K. (1993) 'White-Collar Crime in the Savings and Loan Scandal', in Geis, G. and Jesilow, P., eds., *White Collar Crime*, Newbury Park, CA: Sage.

Pontusson, J. (1987) 'Radicalization and Retreat in Social Democracy in Sweden', *New Left Review*, 165, September/October.

Popper, K. (1961) *The Poverty of Historicism*, London: Routledge and Paul.

Porter, M. and van der Linde, C. (1995) 'Green *and* Competitive: ending the stalemate', *Harvard Business Review*, September-October.

Posner, R. (1976) *Antitrust Law*, Chicago; University of Chicago Press.

Posner, R. (1977) *Economic Analysis of Law, 2nd. Edition*, New York: Little Brown.

Posner, R. (1980) 'Optimal Sentences for White-Collar Criminals', *American Criminal Law Review*, 17.

Posner, R. (1981) *Economics of Justice*, Cambridge, Mass.: Harvard University Press.

Poulantzas, N. (1978) *State, Power and Socialism*, London: New Left Books.

Powell, W.W. (1990) 'Neither Market nor Hierarchy: Network Forms of Organization', in Staw, B.M. and Cummings, L.L., eds., *Research in Organizational Behavior Vol. 12*, Greenwich, Connecticut: JAI Press Inc.

Power, M. (1990) 'Modernism, Postmodernism and Organisation', in Hassard, J. and Pym, D., eds., *The Theory and Philosophy of Organisations. Critical Issues and New Perspectives*, London: Routledge.

Price, C.M. (1994) 'Privatisation in Less Developed Countries', in Jackson, P.M. and Price, C.M., eds., *Privatisation and Regulation. A Review of the Issues*.

Priest, G.L. (1993) 'The New Legal Structure of Risk Control', in Burger, E.J., ed., *Risk*, Ann Arbor: University of Michigan Press.

Proctor, R.N. (1995) *Cancer Wars*, New York: Basic Books.

Prosser, W. (1898 and 1971) *Handbook of the Law of Torts, 4th. ed.*, St. Paul: West Publishing Company.

Proudhon, P.-J. (1840 and 1966) *Qu'est-ce que la propriété? / ou recherches sur le principe du droit et du gouvernement, premier mémoire*, Paris: Garnier-Flammarion

Punch, M. (1996) *Dirty Business*, London: Sage.

Purcell, J. (1989) 'The Impact of Corporate Strategy on Human Resource Management', in Storey, J., ed., *New Perspectives on Human Resource Management*, London: Routledge.

Quick, A. (1991) *Unequal Risks. Accidents and Social Policy*, London: Socialist Health Association.

Quinney, R. (1974) 'The Social Reality of Crime', in Abraham S. Blumberg (ed) *Current Perspectives on Criminal Behaviour*, New York: Alfred Knopf.

Radford, J. (1984) *The Engineer and Society*.

Raphael, A. (1994) *Ultimate Risk: The Inside Story of the Lloyd's Catastrophe*, London: Bantam Press.

Ratner, D.L. (1970) 'The Government of Business Corporations: Critical Reflections on the Rule of "One Share, One Vote"', *Cornell Law Review*, 56.

Rattner, S. (1975) 'Did Industry Cry Wolf?', *New York Times*, December 28.

Reasons, C., Ross, L., and Paterson, C. (1981) *Assault on the Worker: occupational health and safety in Canada*, Toronto: Butterworths.

Reed, M. (1992) *The Sociology of Organisations*, Hemel Hempstead: Harvester Wheatsheaf.

Reed, M. and Hughes, M., eds. (1992) *Rethinking Organisation. New directions in organisation theory and analysis*, London: Sage.

Rehak, R., ed. (1993) *Green Marketing & Advertising: charting a responsible course*, Emmaus, Pa: Rodale Press.

Reich, M.R. (1991) *Toxic Politics: Responding to Chemical Disasters*, Ithaca: Cornell University Press.

Reich, M.R. (1994) 'Toxic Politics and Pollution: Victims in the Third World', in Jasanoff, S., ed., *Learning From Disaster. Risk Management After Bhopal*, Philadelphia: University of Pennsylvania Press.

Reich, M. and Frumkin, H. (1988) 'An Overview of Japanese Occupational Health', *American Journal of Public Health*, Vol. 78, No. 7, July.

Reich, R.B. (1983) *The Next American Frontier*, New York: Times Books.

Reich, R.B. (1989) 'America Pays the Price', *New York Times Magazine*, January 29.

Reiman, J. (1979) *The Rich Get Richer and the Poor Get Prison*. New York: John Wiley and Sons.

Reiner, I. and Chatten-Brown, J. (1989) 'When it is Not an Accident but a Crime: prosecutors get tough with OSHA violations', *Northern Kentucky Law Review*, 17.

Resnick, S. and Wolff, R.D. (1987) *Knowledge and Class: A Marxian Critique of Political Economy*, Chicago: University of Chicago Press.

Reuben, B.G. and Burstall, M.L. (1973) *The Chemical Economy: a guide to the technology and economics of the chemical industry*, London: Longman.

Reynolds, L.T. and Reynolds, J. (1970) *The Sociology of Sociology*, New York: McKay.

Richards, D.G. (1997) 'The Political Economy of Neo-Liberal Reform in Latin America: a critical appraisal', *Capital & Class*, 61.

Richardson, G., with Ogus, A. and Burrows, P. (1983) *Policing Pollution*, Oxford: Clarendon.

Robbins, L. (1984, 1932) *An Essay on the Nature and Significance of Economic Science*, London: Macmillan.

Robens, Lord (1972) *Safety and Health at Work. Report of the Committee 1970-72*, London: HMSO.

Roberts, J. (1989) 'Safety is Good Business', *Employment Gazette*, 97, (7).

Robinson, J.C. (1991) *Toil and Toxics. Workplace Struggles and Political Strategies for Occupational Health*, Berkeley: University of California Press.

Rodericks, J.R. (1992) *Calculated Risks: the toxicity and human health risks of chemicals in our environment*, Cambridge: Cambridge University Press.

Roff, S.R. (1995) *Hotspots: The Legacy of Hiroshima and Nagasaki*, London: Cassell.

Roome, N. (1992) 'Developing Environmental Management Systems', *Business Strategy and the Environment*, 1, (1), Spring.

Rose, G. (1984) Dialectic of Nihilism, Oxford: Basil Blackwell.

Rose, N. (1993) 'Government, Authority and Expertise in Advanced Liberalism', *Economy and Society*, 22, 3 (August).

Rose, N. and Miller. P. (1992) 'Political Power beyond the State: Problematics of Government', *British Journal of Sociology*, 43, (2).

Rosner, D. and Markowitz, G. (1989) *Dying for Work: Safety and Health in Twentieth Century America*, Bloomington: Indiana University Press.

Ross, D. (1996) 'A Review of EPA Criminal, Civil, and Administrative Enforcement Data: are the efforts measurable deterrents to environmental criminals?', in Edwards et al., eds., *Environmental Crime and Criminality. Theoretical and Practical Issues*.

Ross, E.A. (1907) 'The Criminaloid', *The Atlantic Monthly*, 99, January, reprinted in Geis, G. and Meier, R.F., eds., *White-Collar Crime: Offenses in Business, Politics, and the Professions*, New York: The Free Press.

Ross, I. (1980) 'How Lawless are Big Companies?', *Fortune*, December 1.

Rowlinson, M. (1997) *Organisations and Institutions*, London: Macmillan.

Royal Commission on Civil Liability (1978) *Statistics and Costings, Vol. 2, Cmnd. 7054*, London: HMSO.

Ruggiero, V. (1992) 'Realist Criminology: a critique', in Young, J. and Matthews, R., eds., *Rethinking Criminology: the Realist Debate*, London: Sage.

Ruggiero, V. (1996) *Organised and Corporate Crime in Europe. Offers that can't be refused*, Aldershot: Dartmouth.

Rustin, M. (1989) 'The Trouble with New Times' in Hall, S. and Jacques, M., eds., *New Times*, London: Lawrence and Wishart.

Rustin, M. (1994) 'Incomplete Modernity: Ulrich Beck's Risk Society', *Radical Philosophy*, 67, Summer.

Ryan, M. (1986) 'Law and Order: left realism against the rest', *The Abolitionist*, 22.

Sabel, C., Herrigel, G.B., Deeg, R. and Kazis, R. (1989) 'Regional Prosperities Compared: Massachusetts and Baden-Wurtemberg in the 1980s', *Economy and Society*, Vol. 18, No. 4.

Sabel, C. and Zeitlin, J. (1985) 'Historical alternatives to Mass Production: Politics, Markets and Technology in Nineteenth-Century Industrialization' *Past and Present*, 108.

Sacco, V. and Johnson (1990) *Patterns of Criminal Victimization in Canada*, Ottawa: Statistics Canada

Said, E. (1984) *The World, the Text and the Critic*, London: Faber & Faber.

Sandberg, H. (1985) *Union Carbide Corporation: A Case Study*, Geneva: International Management Institute.

Sanders, J. (1992) 'Firm Risk Management in the Face of Product Liability Rules', in Short, Jr. J. F. and Clarke, L., *Organizations, Uncertainty and Risk*, Boulder: Westview Press.

Sapolsky, H.M. (1993) 'The Politics of Risk', in Burger, E.J., ed., *Risk*, Ann Arbor: University of Michigan Press.

Sarangi, S. (1996) 'The Movement in Bhopal and its Lessons' *Social Justice*, 23, (4).

Sargent, N. (1990) 'Law, Ideology and Social Change: An Analysis of the Role of Law in the Construction of Corporate Crime', *The Journal of Human Justice*, 1, 2.

Sass, R. and Crook, G. (1981) 'Accident-Proneness: science or non-science?', *International Journal of Health Services*, 11, (2).

Sassoon, A.S. (1987) *Gramsci's Politics*, Minneapolis: University of Minnesota Press.

Saville, J. (1955) 'Sleeping Partnerships and Limited Liability, 1850-1856', *The Economic History Review (Second Series)*, 8-9 (1955-1957).

Sawyer, M. (1992) 'Industry', in Artis, M.J., ed., *Prest and Coppock's UK Economy*, London: Weidenfield and Nicolson.

Sayer, A. (1995) *Radical Political Economy. A critique*, Oxford: Blackwell.

Scheppele, (1991) 'Law Without Accidents', in Bourdieu, P. and Coleman, J.S., eds., *Social Theory for a Changing Society*, Boulder: Westview Press/Russell Sage Foundation.

Schlegel, K. (1990) *Just Desserts for Corporate Criminals*, Boston: Northeastern University Press.

Schlegel, K. and Weisburd, D., eds. (1992) *White-Collar Crime Reconsidered*, Boston, Mass.: Northeastern University Press.

Schot, J. (1992) 'Credibility and Markets as Greening Forces for the Chemical Industry', *Business Strategy and the Environment*, 1, (1), Spring.

Schrager, L.S. and Short, J.F. (1977) 'Towards a Sociology of Organisational Crime', *Social Problems*, 25.

Schuck, P. (1981) 'Review of James Q. Wilson's The Politics of Regulation', *Yale Law Journal*, 9.

Schumpeter, J.A. (1950) *Capitalism, Socialism and Democracy*, New York: Harper Torchbooks.

Schwendinger, H. and Schwendinger, J. (1975) 'Defenders of order or guardians of human rights' in Taylor, I., Walton, P. and Young, J. (1975) *Critical Criminology*, London: Routledge and Kegan Paul.

Schwendinger, H. and Schwendinger, J. (1980) *Rape and Inequality*, New York: Sage.

Scott, M.B. and Lyman, S. (1968) 'Accounts', *American Sociological Review*, 33.

Scott, J. (1979) *Corporations, Classes and Capitalism*, London: Hutchinson.

Scott, J. (1997) *Corporate Business and Capitalist Classes*, Oxford: Oxford University Press.

Scraton, P., ed., (1987) *Law, Order and the Authoritarian State*, Milton Keynes: Open University Press.

Scraton, P., Sim, J. and Skidmore, P. (1991) *Prisons Under Protest*, London: Open University Press.

Sears, A. and Mooers, C. (1994) 'The Politics of Hegemony: Democracy, Class Struggle and Social Movements', *Transformations*, I.

Selwyn, N.M. (1985) *Law of Employment*, London: Butterworths.

Sewell, G. and Wilkinson, B. (1992) '"Someone to Watch Over Me": Surveillance, Discipline and the Just-in-Time Labour Process', *Sociology*, 26, 2, (May).

Shapiro, S.P. (1983) 'The New Moral Entrepreneurs: corporate crime crusaders', *Contemporary Sociology*, 12.

Shapiro, S.P. (1984) *Wayward Capitalists. Target of the Securities and Exchange Commission*, New Haven: Yale University Press.

Shapiro, S.P. (1990) 'Collaring the Crime, Not the Criminal: reconsidering the concept of white-collar crime', *American Sociological Review*, 55.

Sherman, L. (1982) 'Deviant Organizations', in Ermann, D. and Lundman, R., eds., *Corporate and Governmental Deviance*, New York: Oxford University Press.

Shimmel P. (1991) 'Corporate Environmental Policy in Practice', *Long Range Planning*, 24, (3).

Short Jr., J.F. and Clarke, L. (1992) *Organizations, Uncertainty and Risk*, Boulder: Westview Press.

Shover, N., Clelland, D.A., Lynxwiler, J. (1986) *Enforcement or Negotiation: Constructing a Regulatory Bureaucracy*, Albany: State University of Albany Press.

Shrivastava, P. (1992) *Bhopal: Anatomy of a Crisis*, London: Paul Chapman Publishing.

Shrivastava, P. (1993) 'The Greening of Business', in Smith, D., ed., *Business and the Environment*.

Shrivastava, P. (1994) 'Societal Contradictions and Industrial Crises', in Jasanoff, S., ed., *Learning From Disaster. Risk Management After Bhopal*, Philadelphia: University of Pennsylvania Press.

Sidhva, S. (1995) 'Go Away, Says Goa', *Financial Times*, 13 May.

Silverman, D. (1970) *The Theory of Organisations*, London: Heinemann.

Sim, J. Scraton, P. and Gordon, P. (1987) 'Crime, the State and Critical Analysis', in Scraton, P., ed., *Law, Order and the Authoritarian State*, Milton Keynes: Open University Press.

Simon, D.R. and Eitzen, D.S. (1986) *Elite Deviance*, Toronto: Allyn & Bacon.

Simon, H.A. (1976) *Administrative Behaviour: a study of decision-making processes in administrative organisations*, New York: The Free Press.

Simon, W.H. (1990) 'Contract versus Politics in Corporate Doctrine', in Kairys, D., ed., *The Politics of Law: A Progressive Critique, (revised edition)*, New York: Pantheon Books.

Simons, J. (1995) *Foucault and the Political*, London: Routledge.

Sklair, L. (1995) 'Social Movements and Global Capitalism', *Sociology*, 29, (3).

Sklar, M. (1988) *The Corporate Reconstruction of American Capitalism 1890-1916*, New York: Cambridge University Press.

Skolnick, J. (1966) *Justice Without Trial*, New York: Wiley.

Slapper, G. (1992) 'Where the Buck Stops', *New Law Journal*, July 24.

Slapper, G. (1993) 'Corporate Manslaughter: an examination of the determinants of prosecutorial policy', *Social & Legal Studies*, 2.

Slapper, G. (1994a) 'Corporate Punishment', *New Law Journal*, January 7.

Slapper, G. (1994) 'A Corporate Killing', *New Law Journal*, December 16.

Smith, A. (1776 & 1937) *The Wealth of Nations*, New York: Random House.

Smith, D. (1989) 'The Un-Politics of Major Hazards', paper presented at the Second International Conference on Industrial Crisis Management, New York University, 3-4 November.

Smith, D. (1990) 'The International Trade in Hazardous Waste: a study in the geo-politics of risk', paper presented at the ECPR Workshop on Crisis Management, Bochum, 2-7 April.

Smith, D. ed. (1993) *Business and the Environment: implications of the new environmentalism*, London: Paul Chapman.

Smith, D. (1993) 'The Frankenstein Syndrome: corporate responsibility and the environment', in Smith, D., ed., *Business and the Environment*.

Smith, D. and Blowers, A. (1992) 'Here Today, There Tomorrow: the politics of transboundary hazardous waste transfers', in Clark, M., Smith, D. and Blowers, A., eds., *Waste Location. Spatial aspects of waste management, hazards and disposal*, London: Routledge.

Smith, D. and Tombs, S. (1995) 'Beyond Self-Regulation: towards a critique of self-regulation as a control strategy for hazardous activities', *Journal of Management Studies*, 32, (5).

Smith, D.L. (1964) 'The Sunshine Boys: Towards a Sociology of Happiness', *The Advocate*, (Spring), reprinted in Reynolds and Reynolds, eds. (1970), *The Sociology of Sociology*.

Smith, M.A., ed. (1986) *The Chemical Industry After Bhopal: An International symposium held in London*, London: IBC Technical Services Ltd.

Smith, P.F. (1985) *Evans: The Law of Landlord and Tenant. 2nd. edition*, London: Butterworths.

Smith, P. (1997) *Millenial Dreams. Contemporary Culture and Capital in the North*, London: Verso.

Smith, R. (1997) 'Creative Destruction: capitalist development and China's environment', *New Left Review*, 222, March/April.

Smith, R.S. (1976) *The Occupational Safety and Health Act: Its Goals and Achievements*, Washington: American Enterprise Institute.

Smith, R.S. (1979) 'The Impact of OSHA Inspections on Manufacturing Injury Rates', *The Journal of Human Resources*, 14.

Smith, R.S. (1982) 'Protecting Workers' Health and Safety', in Poole, R.W. Jr., ed., *Instead of Regulation*, Lexington, Mass. Lexington Books.

Smith, T. (1995) 'The Case Against Free Market Environmentalism', *Journal of Agricultural & Environmental Ethics*, 8, (2).

Snider, L. (1985) 'Legal Reform and Social Control: the dangers of abolishing rape', *International Journal of the Sociology of Law*, 13.

Snider, L. (1987) 'Towards a Political Economy of Reform, Regulation and Corporate Crime', *Law & Policy*, 9, (1).

Snider, L. (1988) 'Commercial Crime' in Sacco, V., ed., *Deviance, Conformity and Control in Canadian Society*, Toronto: Prentice-Hall.

Snider, L. (1989) *Models to Control Corporate Crime: Decriminalization, Recriminalization and Deterrence*, Mimeograph, Department of Sociology, Queen's University, Kingston, Ontario.

Snider, L. (1990) 'The Potential of the Criminal Justice System to Promote Feminist Concerns', *Studies in Law, Politics and Society*, 10.

Snider, L. (1991) 'The Regulatory Dance: understanding reform processes in corporate crime', *International Journal of the Sociology of Law*, 19.

Snider, L. (1992) 'Commercial Crime', in Sacco, V.,ed., *Deviance, Conformity and Control in Canadian Society*, 2nd edition, Toronto: Prentice Hall.

Snider, L. (1993a - formerly 1993) *Bad Business. Corporate Crime in Canada*, Toronto: Nelson Canada.

Snider, L. (1993b formerly 1992) 'The Politics of Corporate Crime Control', in Pearce, F. and Woodiwiss, M., eds., *Global Crime Connections*, London: Macmillan.

South, N. (1998) 'Corporate and State Crimes Against the Environment: foundations for a green perspective in European criminology', in Ruggiero, V., South, N. and Taylor, I., eds. *European Criminology*, London: Routledge (forthcoming)

Spitz, P.H. (1988) *Petrochemicals. The Rise of an Industry*, New York: John Wiley and Sons.

Stampp, K.M. (1965) *The Era of Reconstruction,* New York: Vintage Books.

Steffensmeier, D. (1989) 'On the Causes of "White-Collar" Crime. An Assessment of Hirschi and Gottfriedson's Claims', *Criminology*, 17, 2.

Stellman, J. and Daum, S. (1973) *Work Is Dangerous to Your Health*, New York: Vintage Books.

Sternberg, D. (1973) 'The New Radical-Criminal Trials: a step towards a class for itself in the American proletariat', in Quinney, R., ed., *Criminal Justice in America: A Critical Understanding*, Boston: Little, Brown.

Stevens, G. (1992) 'Workplace Injury: a view from HSE's trailer to the 1990 Labour Force Survey', *Employment Gazette*, December.

Stigler, G.J. (1952) *The Theory of Price. Revised Edition*, New York: The Macmillan Company.

Stigler, G.J. (1955) 'Mergers and Preventive Antitrust Policy', *University of Pennsylvania Law Review*, 104.

Stigler, G. J. (1971) 'The Theory of Economic Regulation', *Bell Journal of Economics and Managerial Science*, no. 2 (Spring).

Stigler, G.J. (1972) 'The Law and Economics of Public Policy: A Plea to the Scholars', *Journal of Legal Studies*, 1.

Stinchcombe, A. L. (1990) *Information and Organization*, Berkeley: University of California Press.

Stone, C.D. (1975) *Where the Law Ends: The Social Control of Corporate Behavior*, New York: Harper and Row.

Stone, C.D. (1993) *The Gnat is Older than the Man: Global Environment and Human Agenda*, Princeton: Princeton University Press.

Stopford, J.M. and Dunning, J.H. (1983) *Multinationals. Company Performance and Global Trends*, London: Macmillan.

Stover, W. (1986) 'A Field Day for the Legislators: Bhopal, and its effects on the enactment of new laws in the United States', in Smith, M.A., ed., *The Chemical Industry After Bhopal*.

Stow, D. (1983) 'Safety Officers Fight for Existence', *The Safety Practitioner*, January.

Strange, S. (1994) 'Wake Up, Krasner! The world *has* changed', *Review of International Political Economy*, 1, (2), Summer.

Strauss, K.A. (1985) 'Pulling the Plug on Nuclear Power', *Chemical and Engineering News*, 29th July.

Strauss, M. (1991) 'Lenders Leery of Hazardous Sites: Banks running tests on land before granting loans', *The Globe and Mail*, March 14.

Stubbs, R. and Underhill, G.R., eds. (1994) *Political Economy and the Changing Global Order*, London: Macmillan.

Sufrin, S.C. (1985) *Bhopal. Its setting, responsibility and challenge*, Delhi: Ajanta.

Sugarman, D. (1990) 'Introduction' in Sugarman, D. and Teubner, G. (eds.) *Regulating Corporate Groups in Europe*, Baden-Baden: Nomos Verlagsgesellschaft.

Sutherland, E.H. (1940) 'White-Collar Criminality', *American Sociological Review*, 5, (February), 1-12, reprinted in Geis, G. (1968) *White-Collar Criminal: The Offender in Business and the Professions,* New York, Atherton Press.

Sutherland, E.H. (1941) 'Crime and Business', *Annals of the American Academy of Political and Social Science*, 217, September.

Sutherland, E.H. (1945) 'Is "White-Collar Crime" Crime?', *American Sociological Review*, 10. Reprinted in Geis, G. (1968) *White Collar Criminal: The Offender in Business and the Professions*, New York: Atherton Press.

Sutherland, E.H. (1949) *White Collar Crime*, New York: Dryden Press.

Sutherland, E.H. (1983) *White Collar Crime: The Uncut Version*, New Haven: Yale University Press.

Sutton, A. and Wild, R. (1985) 'Small Businesses: white-collar villains or victims?', *International Journal of the Sociology of Law*, 13, 3.

Swift, I. (1986) 'The Engineering Approach to Safer Plants', in Smith, M.A., ed., *The Chemical Industry After Bhopal*.

Swingewood, A. (1984) *A Short History of Sociological Thought*, London: Macmillan.

Szasz, A. (1984) 'Industrial Resistance to Occupational Safety and Health Legislation 1971-1981', *Social Problems*, 32, (2).

Szasz, A. (1986a) 'The Reversal of Federal Policy Toward Worker Safety and Health: a critical examination of alternative explanations', *Science and Society*, 50.

Szasz, A. (1986b) 'The Process and Significance of Political Scandals: A Comparison of Watergate and the "Sewergate" Episode at the Environmental Protection Agency', *Social Problems*, 33, (3).

Szasz, A. (1986c) 'Corporations, Organized Crime and the Disposal of Hazardous Waste: The Making of a Criminogenic Regulatory Structure', *Criminology*, 24, (1).

Szasz, A. (1994) *Ecopopulism. Toxic waste and the movement for environmental justice*, Minneapolis: University of Minnesota Press.

Taira, K. (1970) *Economic Development and the Labor Market in Japan*, New York: Columbia University Press.

Tandy, H. (1987) *Petrochemicals in the Middle East*, London: Middle East Economic Digest.

Tappan, P. (1947) 'Who is the Criminal?', *American Sociological Review*, 12.

Taylor, I. (1997) 'Crime, Anxiety, Locality: responding to the 'condition of England' at the turn of the century', *Theoretical Criminology*, 1, (1).

Taylor, M. and Thrift, N. (1986) 'Introduction: New Theories of Multinational Corporations', in Taylor, M. and Thrift, N., eds., *Multinationals and the Restructuring of the World Economy*, London: Croom Helm.

Teuber, A. (1993) 'Justifying Risk', in Burger, E.J., ed., *Risk*, Ann Arbor: the University of Michigan Press.

Teulings, A.W.M. (1986) 'Managerial Labour Processes in Organised Capitalism; the power of corporate management and the powerlessness of the manager', in Knights, D. and Willmott, H., eds., *Managing the Labour Process*, Aldershot: Gower.

Thompson, E.P. (1980) *Whigs and Hunters*, London: Allen Lane.

Thompson, G. (1982) 'The Enterprise as a Dispersed Social Agency', *Economy and Society*, 11, (3), August.

Thompson, G. (1989) 'Flexible Specialization, Industrial Districts, Regional Economies', *Economy and Society*, 18, no. 4.

Thompson, P. and Sederblad, P. (1994) 'The Swedish Model of Work Organisation in Transition', in Elger, T. and Smith, C., eds., *Global Japanisation? The transnational transformation of the labour process*, London: Routledge.

Thornber, C.W. (1986) 'The Pharmaceutical Industry', in Heaton, C.A., ed. *The Chemical Industry*, Glasgow: Blackie & Son.

Thurow, L. (1984) *Dangerous Current: The State of Economics*, New York: Vintage Books.

Tigar, M.E. and Levy, M.R. (1977) *Law and the Rise of Capitalism*, New York: Monthly Review Press.

Timmer, D.A. and Eitzen, D.S. (1991) *Crime in the Streets and Crime in the Suites*, Toronto: Allyn & Bacon.

Tinker, T., Lehman, C., Neimark, M. (1988) 'Book-keeping for Capitalism: The Mystery of Accounting for Unequal Exchange', in Mosco, V. and Wasco, J., eds., *The Political Economy of Information*, Madison: The University of Wisconsin Press.

Toffler, B.L. (1991) 'When the Signal is "Move it or Lose It"', *The New York Times Forum*, Sunday, November 17.

Tombs, S. (1988) 'The Causes of Coal-Mine Accidents, Worker Autonomy and the Myth of the Small firm', *Industrial Relations Journal*, Autumn.

Tombs, S. (1989) 'Deviant Workplaces and Dumb Managements? Understanding and Preventing Accidents in the Chemical Industry', *Industrial Crisis Quarterly*, 3, Autumn.

Tombs, S. (1990a) 'A Case Study in Distorted Communication', in *Piper Alpha - Lessons for Life-Cycle Safety Management, Institution of Chemical Engineers Symposium Series No. 122*, Rugby: IChemE.

Tombs, S. (1990b) 'Industrial Injuries in British Manufacturing Industry', *Sociological Review*, 38, (2).

Tombs, S. (1991) 'Injury and Ill-Health in the Chemical Industry: de-centring the accident-prone victim', Industrial Crisis Quarterly, 5, January.

Tombs, S. (1992) 'Stemming the Flow of Blood? The Illusion of Self-Regulation', *Journal of Human Justice. Special Issue on Corporate Crime*, 3, (2), Spring.

Tombs, S. (1993a) 'The Chemical Industry and the Environment', in Smith, D. ed., *Business and the Environment*.

Tombs, S. (1993b) 'Corporate Crime and the "Management" of Major Hazards', *Technology Analysis and Strategic Management*, 5, (4).

Tombs, S. (1994) 'Strategic Failures? Managing environmental protection, managing safety', *Industrial & Environmental Crisis Quarterly*, 8, (3).

Tombs, S. (1995a) 'New Organisational Forms and the Further Production of Corporate Crime', in Pearce, F. and Snider, L., eds., *Corporate Crime: contemporary debates*.

Tombs, S. (1995b) 'Law, Resistance and Reform: "regulating" safety crimes in the UK', *Social & Legal Studies*, 4 (3).

Tombs, S. (1996) 'Injury, Death and the Deregulation Fetish: the politics of occupational safety regulation in UK Manufacturing', *International Journal of Health Services*, 26, (2).

Tombs, S. (1997) 'Health and Safety Crimes and the Problems of "Knowing"', paper presented at Crimes of the Powerful, University of Northumbria, 22nd March.

Tombs, S. and Smith, D. (1993) Managing Crises through Preventative Regulation. Why Self-Regulation will not Work. Paper Presented at New Avenues in Crisis and Risk Management, University of Nevada Las Vegas, 12-13 August.

Townsend, K.N. (1993) 'Steady-State Ecomomies and the Command Economy', in Daly, H. and Townsend, K.N., eds., *Valuing the Earth: Economics, Ecology, Ethics*, Cambridge: MIT Press.

Trachtenberg, A. (1982) *The Incorporation of America: Culture and Society in the Gilded Age*, New York: Hill and Wang.

Tran, M. (1996) 'UNCTAD Changes Corporate Tune', *The Guardian*, 20th May.

TUC (1994) *Better Safety Standards at Work: setting the safety agenda*, London: TUC.

Tucker, E. (1992a) 'Worker Participation in Health and Safety: Some Lessons from Sweden', *Studies in Political Economy*, 37, (Spring).

Tucker, E. (1992b) 'Worker Health and Safety Struggles: democratic possibilities and constraints', Paper presented at the International Symposium on the Social and Economic Aspects of Democratisation of Contemporary Society, Moscow, October 12-17.

Tucker, E. (1995) 'And Defeat Goes On: an assessment of "third-wave" health and safety regulation', in Pearce, F. and Snider, L., eds., *Corporate Crime: contemporary debates*.

Turner, B. (1976) 'The Development of Disasters - a sequence model for the analysis of disasters', *Sociological Review*, 24.

Turner, B. (1977) 'The Origins of Disaster', in Phillips, J., ed., *Safety at Work*, Wolfson College, Oxford: Centre for Socio-Legal Studies/Social Sciences Research Council.

Turner, B. (1978) *Man-made Disasters*, London: Wykeham.

Turner, B. (1992) *Stepping into the Same River Twice: learning to handle unique management problems. Middlesex University Inaugural Lectures, 2.* London: Middlesex University.

Turner, B. Pidgeon, N., Blockley, D. and Toft, B. (1989) 'Safety Culture: its importance in future risk management', *Position Paper for the Second World Bank Workshop on Safety Control and Risk Management*, Karlstad: Sweden.

Turner, J. (1970) *The Chemical Feast*, New York: Grossman.

Tuscano, G. and Winwow, J. (1993) 'Fatal Work Injuries: results from the 1992 national census', *Monthly Labour Review*, October.

Tushnet, M. (1981) 'The Politics of Constitutional Law', in Kairys, D., *The Politics of Law: A Progressive Critique*, Revised Edition.

U.N. Centre of Transnational Corporations (1984) The CTC Reporter, No. 17, New York: United Nations.

Union Carbide Corporation (1985) *Bhopal Methyl Isocyanate Incident Investigation Team Report, March*, Danbury, Connecticut: Union Carbide Corporation.

Union Carbide Corporation (1987) *Letter and Documents to International Coalition for Justice in Bhopal with excerpts from UCC Submission to the Indian Courts.*

Union Research Group (1985a) *The Bhopal MIC Disaster, the Beginnings of a Case for Worker's Control: a First Report*, Bombay: The Employees Union Research Group (Union Carbide India Limited).

Union Research Group (1985b) *The Role of Management Practices in the Bhopal Gas Leak Disaster: a Second Report*, Bombay: The Employees Union Research Group (Union Carbide India Limited).

United Nations (1993) *World Investment Report 1993. Transnational Corporations and Integrated International Production*, New York: United Nations.

U.S. Congress. House of Representatives (1983) *Committee on Public Works and Transportation. Subcommittee on Investigation and Oversight. Hazardous Waste Contamination of Water Resources. 98th Cong., 1st sess.*, Washington, D.C.: U.S. Government Printing Office.

United States Department of Commerce (1991) 'Gross Domestic Product as a Measure of U.S. Production', *Survey of Current Business*, Volume 71, August: 8

U.S. Department of Justice (1990) *Attacking Savings and Loan Institution Fraud. Report to the President.*

U.S. Department of Justice (1990a) *Sourcebook of Criminal Justice Statistics-1990* Washington.

Van den Haag, Ernest and Conrad, John Phillips (1983) *The Death Penalty: A Debate* New York: Plenum Press.

Vandivier, K. (1982) 'Why Should My Conscience Bother Me?', in Ermann, M.D. and Lundman, R.J., eds., *Corporate and Governmental Deviance: Problems of organisational behaviour in contemporary society*, New York: Oxford University Press.

Vanick, C. (1978) 'Corporate Tax Study 1976', in Ermann, M.D. and Lundmann, R.J. *Corporate and Organizational deviance: Problems of Organizational Behavior in Contemporary Society*, New York: Oxford University Press.

Vaughan, D. (1982) 'Transaction Systems and Unlawful Organisational Behaviour', *Social Problems*, 29, (4), April.

Vaughan, D. (1983) *Controlling Unlawful Organisational Behaviour. Social Structure and Corporate Misconduct*, Chicago: University of Chicago Press.

Vaughan, D. (1992) 'The Macro-Micro Connection in White-Collar Crime', in Schlegel, K. and Weisburd, D., eds. *White-Collar Crime Reconsidered.*

Vaughan, D. (1996) *The Challenger Launch Decision. Risky technology, culture, and deviance at NASA*, Chicago: Chicago University Press.

Vilain, J. (1989) 'The Nature of Chemical Hazards, their Accident Potential and Consequences', in Bourdeau, P. and Green, G., eds., *Methods for Assessing and Reducing Injury from Chemical Accidents*, Chichester: John Wiley.

Viscusi, W.K. (1979) *Employment Hazards: An Investigation of Market Performance*, Cambridge, Mass.: Harvard University Press.

Viscusi, W.K. (1983) *Risk by Choice: Regulating Health and Safety in the Workplace*, Cambridge, Mass.: Harvard University Press.

Vogel, D. (1986) *National Styles of Regulation: Environmental Policy in Great Britain and the United States*, Ithaca: Cornell University Press.

Vogel, D. (1989) *Fluctuating Fortunes: The Political Power of Business in America*, New York: Basic Books.

Wachtel, H.M. and Sawyers, L. (1973) 'Government Spending and the Distribution of Income', paper presented at the 13th General Conference of the International Association for Research in Income and Wealth, Balatenfured, Hungary, September.

Wade, R. (1996) 'Japan, the World Bank, and the Art of Paradigm Maintenance: the East Asian Miracle in Political Perspective', *New Left Review*, 217, May/June.

Wagstyl, S. (1996) 'A Flood Still in Full Spate. Financial Times Report. Britain' *Financial Times*, 12th June.

Wainwright, H. (1992) 'The New Left after Communism', *Studies in Political Economy*, 38, (Summer).

Walklate, S. (1989) *Victimology: The Victim and the Criminal Justice Process*, London: Unwin-Hyman.

Walklate, S. (1992) 'Appreciating the Victim: conventional, realist or critical victimology?', in Matthews, R. and Young, J., eds., *Issues in Realist Criminology*, London: Sage.

Walters, D. (1987) 'Health and Safety and Trade Union Workplace Organisation - a Study in the Printing Industry', *Industrial Relations Journal*, Spring.

Walters, D (1990) *Worker Participation in Health and Safety. A European Comparison*, London: Institute of Employment Rights.

Walters, J. (1995) 'Blunderbus' *The Observer*, Business, Sunday 19th March.

Ward, T. and Benn, M. (1987) 'Were the Police ever Innocent?', *New Society*, 19 June.

Waring, M. (1988) *If Women Counted: A New Feminist Perspective*, New York: Harper Collins.

Washington, B.T. (1967) *Up from Slavery*, New York: Airmont.

Watterson, A. (1988a) *Industrial Relations and Health and Safety at Work in Post-War Britain: a study of conflict and control in the workplace*, Unpublished PhD Thesis, University of Bristol.

Watterson, A. (1988b) *Pesticide Users' Health and Safety Handbook*, Aldershot: Gower Technical.

Watterson, A. (1991) 'Occupational Health in the UK Gas Industry: a study of employer, worker and medical knowledge and action on health hazards in the late 19th and early 20th Centuries', paper presented to the Annual Conference of the British Sociological Association, Manchester, March.

Weait, M. (1992) 'Swans Reflecting Elephants: Imagery and the Law', *Law and Critique*, (III).

Weaver, P. (1978) 'Regulation, Social Policy and Class Conflict', in Jacobs, D.P., ed., *Regulating Business: The Search for an Optimum*, San Francisco: Institute for Contemporary Studies.

Weber, M. (1915) 'The Social Psychology of World Religions', reprinted in Gerth, H. and Mills, C.W., eds. (1948) *From Max Weber*, London: Routledge and Kegan Paul.

Weber, M. (1947) *Theory of Social and Economic Organization, translated by A.M. Henderson and T. Parsons*, New York: Oxford University Press.

Weber, M. (1961) *General Economic History*, New York: Collier- Macmillan.

Weber, M. (1978) *Economy and Society*, Berkeley: University of California Press.

Weber, M. (1980 and 1895) 'National State and Economic Policy', *Economy and Society*, 9, 4. November.

Weber, M. (1978) *Economy and Society*, Berkeley: University of California Press.

Wedderburn, Lord (1990) *The Social Charter, European Company and Employment Rights. An outline agenda*, London: Institute of Employment Rights.

Wei, J., Russell, T.W.F., and Swartzlander, M.W. (1979) *The Structure of the Chemical Processing Industries*, New York: McGraw-Hill.

Weidenbaum, M. and de Fina, R. (1978) *The Costs of Federal Regulation of Economic Activity.* *AEI Reprint no. 88*, Washington, D.C.: American Enterprise Institute.

Weinstein, J. (1968) *The Corporate Ideal in the Liberal State*, Boston: Beacon Press.

Weir, D. (1986) *The Bhopal Syndrome: Pesticide Manufacturing and the Third World*, Penang: International Organization of Consumers Unions.

Welford, R. (1992) 'Linking Quality and the Environment: a strategy for the implementation of environmental management systems', *Business Strategy and the Environment*, 1, (1), Spring.

Wells, C. (1988) 'What Can We Do If the Guilty Parties are Corporations?', *The Guardian*, 26th August.

Wells, C. (1989) 'The Flaws in Corporate Liability', *The Guardian*, 21st April.

Wells, C. (1991) 'The Hydra-headed Beast', *Times Higher Education Supplement*.

Wells, C. (1993) *Corporations and Criminal Responsibility*, Oxford: Clarendon Press.

White, H. (1981) 'Where Do Markets Come From?', *American Journal of Sociology*, Vol. 87, No. 3..

Whitfield, D. (1983) *Making it Public: Evidence and Action against Privatisation*, London: Pluto Press.

Whitfield, D. (1992) *The Welfare State*, London: Pluto Press

Whyte, D. (1996) 'The Emperor's New Clothes: safety deregulation and cost-cutting in the Offshore Oil Industry', paper presented at the Annual Meeting of the British Sociological Association, 1-4 April.

Whyte, D,. and Tombs, S. (1996) 'Capital Fights Back: from Cullen to CRINE in the offshore oil industry', paper presented to the 24th Annual Conference of the European Group for the Study of Deviance and Social Control, Bangor, 12-15 September.

Willer, D. and Willer, J. (1973) *Systematic Empiricism: A Critique of Pseudo-Science*, Engelwood Cliffs, NJ: Prentice-Hall.

Williams, C., ed. (1996) *Social Justice. Special Issue: Environmental Victims*, 23, (4), Winter.

Williams, K., Cutler, T., Williams, J. and Haslam, C. (1987) 'The End of Mass Production?' *Economy and Society* 16 (3).

Williams, K., Williams, J. and Haslam, C. (1990) 'The Hollowing out of British Manufacturing and its Implications', *Economy and Society*, 19, 4, November.

Williamson, O.E. (1975) *Markets and Hierarchies: Analysis of Antitrust Implications*, New York: Free Press.

Williamson, O.E. (1983) 'Organizational Innovation: The Transaction-Cost Approach', in Ronen, J., ed., *Entrepreneurship*, Lexington, Mass: Heath Lexington.

Williamson, O.E. (1985) *The economic institutions of capitalism*, New York: Free Press.

Wilson, E. (1991) *A Very British Miracle: The Failure of Thatcherism*, London: Pluto Press.

Wilson, G.K. (1985) *The Politics of Safety and Health: Occupational Safety and Health in the United States and Britain*, Oxford: The Clarendon Press.

Wilson, H.T. (1976) *The American Ideology: Science, Technology and Organization as Modes of Rationality in Advanced Industrial Societies*, London: Routledge and Kegan Paul.

Wilson, J.Q. (1975) *Thinking About Crime*, New York: Vintage.

Wlson, J.Q. (1980) 'The Politics of Regulation' in Wilson, J.Q., ed., *The Politics of Regulation*, New York: Basic Books

Wilson, J.Q., ed. (1980) *The Politics of Regulation*, New York: Basic Books.

Wilson J.Q. and Herrnstein, R.J. (1986) *Crime and Human Nature*, New York: Touchstone, Simon & Schuster.

Wilson, J.Q. and Kelling, G. (1982) 'Broken Windows', *Atlantic Monthly*, March.

Wilson, J.Q. and Rachal, P. (1977) 'Can the Government Regulate Itself', *The Public Interest*, reprinted in Ermann, M., and Lundman, R.J. (1978) *Corporate and Governmental Deviance*, New York: Oxford University Press.

Wilson, L.C. (1979) 'The Doctrine of Willful Blindness', *University of New Brunswick Law Journal*, 28.

Wilson, W.J. (1992) 'Another look at The Truly Disadvantaged', *Political Science Quarterly*, 106.

Wilson, W.J. (1987) *The Truly Disadvantaged: The Inner City, the Underclass, and Public Policy*, Chicago: Chicago University Press.

Witcoff, H.A. and Reuben, B.G. (1980) *Industrial Organic Chemicals in Perspective, Part One: Raw Materials and Manufacture*, New York: John Wiley and Sons.

Wokutch, R.E. and McLaughlin, J.S. (1988) 'The Sociopolitical Context of Occupational Injuries', *Research in Corporate Social Performance and Policy*, 10.

Wokutch, R.E. (1990) 'Corporate Social Responsibility Japanese Style', *Academy of Management Executive*, 4, (2).

Wokutch, R.E. (1992) *Worker Protection, Japanese Style: Occupational Health and Safety in the Auto Industry*, Ithaca, New York: ILR Press.

Wokutch, R.E. and McLaughlin, J.S. (1992) 'The US and Japanese Work Injury and Illness Experience', *Monthly Labour Review*, April.

Wolf, E.R. (1982) *Europe and the People Without History*, Berkeley: University of California Press.

Wolfe, A. (1978) *The Limits of Legitimacy*, New York: Free Press.

Wood, S. and Kelly, J. (1982) 'Taylorism, Responsible Autonomy and Management Strategy', in Wood, S., ed., *The Degradation of Work*, London: Hutchinson.

Wooding, J., Levenstein, C. and Rosenberg, B. (1997) 'The Oil, Chemical and Atomic Workers International Union: refining strategies for labor', *International Journal of Health Services*, 27, (1).

Woodiwiss, A. (1987) 'The Discourses of Production (1)', *Economy and Society*, Vol. 16., No. 3.

Woodiwiss, A. (1990a) *Social Theory after Postmodernism*, London: Pluto Press.

Woodiwiss, A. (1990b) *Rights v. Conspiracy: A Sociological Essay on the History of Labour Law in the United States*, Berg: New York.

Woodiwiss, A. (1992) *Law, Labour and Society in Japan: From Repression to Reluctant Recognition*, London: Routledge.

Woodiwiss, A. (1993a) *Postmodernity USA*, London: Sage.

Woodiwiss, A. (1993b) *Human Rights, Labour Law and Transnational Sociality around the Pacific Rim*, mimeo, University of Essex.

Woodiwiss, A. (1995) *Governance: Transnational Sociality, and Paciifc Capitalism: The Possibility of a New Familialism?*, mimeo, University of Essex.

Woodiwiss, A. (1998) *Globalisation, Human Rights and Labour Law in Pacific Asia*, Cambridge: Cambridge University Press.

Woodward, C. Vann (1938) *Tom Watson, Agrarian Rebel*, New York: Rinehart and Co.

Woodward, C. Vann (1960) *The Burden of Southern History*, New York: Vintage Books.

Woodward, C. Vann (1966a) *Reunion and Reaction: The Compromise of 1877 and the End of Reconstruction*, Boston: Little Brown.

Woodward, C. Vann (1966b) *The Strange Career of Jim Crow*, New York: Oxford University Press.

Woolard, E.S. (1990) 'A Sustainable World', *Chemistry & Industry*, 19 November.

Woolf, A. (1973) 'Robens - the Wrong Approach', *Industrial Law Journal*.

Woolfson, C. and Beck, M. (1997) *From Self-Regulation to Deregulation: the politics of health and safety in Britain*, Mimeo, Universities of Glasgow and St. Andrews.

Woolfson, C., Foster, J. and Beck, M. (1996) *Paying for the Piper? Capital and labour in the offshore oil industry*, Aldershot: Mansell.

Work Hazards Group (1987) *Death at Work*, London: WEA.

World Bank (1989) *Sub-Saharan Africa from Crisis to Sustainable Growth*, Washington D.C.: World Bank.

World Bank (1994) *Averting the Age Old Crisis. Policies to Protect the Old and Promote Growth*, Oxford: Oxford University Press.

Wright, C. (1986) 'Routine Deaths: fatal accidents in the oil industry', *Sociological Review*, 34, (2).

Wright, C. (1994) 'A Fallible Safety System: institutionalised irrationality in the offshore oil and gas industry', *Sociological Review*, 42, (1).

Wynne, B. (1989) 'Frameworks of Rationality in Risk Management: towards the testing of naive sociology', in Brown, J. ed., *Environmental Threats: perception, analysis and management*, London: Belhaven/ESRC.

Yeager, P. (1991) *The Limits of the Law: The Public Regulation of Private Pollution*, Cambridge: Cambridge University Press.

Yearley, S. (1996) *Sociology, Environmentalism, Globalisation*, London: Sage.

Young, J. (1986) 'The Failure of Criminology: the need for a Radical Realism', in Matthews, R. and Young, J., eds., *Confronting Crime*, London: Sage.

Young, J. (1987) 'The Tasks Facing a Realist Criminology', *Contemporary Crises*, 11.

Young, J. (1994) 'Incessant Chatter: recent paradigms in criminology', in Maguire, M., Morgan, R. and Reiner, R., eds., *The Oxford Handbook of Criminology*, Clarendon: Oxford.

Young, J. and Matthews, R., eds. (1992) *Rethinking Criminology: the Realist Debate*, London: Sage.

Young, John (1994) 'The New Materialism: a matter of policy', *World Watch*, September-October.

Young, T. (1995) '"A Project to be Realised": global liberalism and contemporary Africa', *Millennium*, 24, (3).

Zeitlin, M. (1989) *The Large Corporation and Contemporary Classes* New Brunswick, New Jersey: Rutgers University Press.

Zimmerman, R. (1988) 'Understanding Industrial Accidents associated with New Technologies: a human resources management approach', *Industrial Crisis Quarterly*, 2.

Zinn, H. (1980) *A People's History of the United States*, New York: Harper and Row.

Index